Praise for
The Elephant in the Brain

"Many of the details of Hanson and Simler's thesis are persuasive, and the idea of an 'introspective taboo' that prevents us from telling the truth to ourselves about our motives is worth contemplating. (That taboo is the *Elephant [in the Brain]*)."
—*The New Yorker*

"This book will make you see the world in a whole new light."
—Tyler Cowen, Bloomberg columnist;
author of *The Great Stagnation*

"*The Elephant in the Brain* is a masterpiece."
—Scott Aaronson, Director, Quantum Information Center,
University of Texas, Austin

"In this ingenious and persuasive book, Simler and Hanson mischievously reveal that much of our behavior is for social consumption: we make decisions that make us look good, rather than good decisions."
—Hugo Mercier, Research Scientist,
French Institute for Cognitive Sciences

"A thoughtful examination of the human condition."
—David Biello, Science Curator at TED;
author of *The Unnatural World*

"Simler and Hanson have done it again—a big new idea, well told."
—Gregory Benford, Professor of Physics,
University of California, Irvine; two-time Nebula
Award Winner; author of *The Berlin Project*

"Deeply important, wide-ranging, beautifully written, and fundamentally right."
—Bryan Caplan, Professor of Economics, George Mason University;
author of *The Case Against Education*

"This is the most unconventional and uncomfortable self-help book you will ever read. But probably also the most important."
—Andrew McAfee,
Principal Research Scientist at MIT;
coauthor of *Machine*

"Thorough, insightful, fun to read, with the slight negative that everything is now ruined forever."
—Zach Weinersmith,
author of *Saturday Morning Breakfast Cereal*

"This book will change how you see the world."
—Allan Dafoe, Professor of Political Science,
Yale University

"A captivating book about the things your brain does not want you to know."
—Jaan Tallinn, Founder of Skype,
Centre for the Study of Existential Risk, and Future of Life Institute

"It's hard to overstate how impactful this book is."
—Tucker Max, author of *I Hope They Serve Beer in Hell*

"An eye-opening look at how we deceive ourselves in order to deceive others."
—Ramez Naam, author of *Nexus*

"A provocative and compellingly readable account of how and why we lie to our rivals, our friends, and ourselves."
—Steven Landsburg, Professor of Economics,
University of Rochester

"Simler and Hanson reveal what's beneath our wise veneer—a maelstrom of bias and rationalization that we all must—for survival's sake—help each other overcome."
—David Brin, two-time Hugo Award Winner;
author of *Existence*

"A thoughtful and provocative book."

—**Andrew Gelman, Professor of Statistics, Columbia University**

"Simler and Hanson uncover the hidden and darker forces that shape much of what we say and do."

—**William MacAskill, Professor of Philosophy, Oxford University; author of _Doing Good Better_**

"There are only a few people alive today worth listening to. Robin Hanson is one of them."

—**Ralph Merkle, co-inventor of public key cryptography**

"Brilliantly written and entertaining on every page."

—**Alex Tabarrok, author of _Modern Principles of Economics_**

"A disturbing and important book."

—**Arnold Kling, author of _The Three Languages of Politics_**

"Coauthors Simler, a software engineer, and Hanson (_The Age of Em_), an economics professor, bring a light touch in this thought-provoking exploration of how little understanding people have of their own motivations...This is a fascinating and accessible introduction to an important subject. "

—**_Publisher's Weekly_**

"An entertaining and insightful book that sheds light on a diverse collection of perplexing human behaviors from laughter to religion to the origin of language."

—**_Quillette_**

"The argument that Simler and Hanson make is rather comprehensive, and compelling. They bring together research on various topics of limited reach that, when combined, speak to the outrageous gall of the mind in recreating reality to its own liking, and then covering its tracks."

—**Katherine Oktober Matthews, _Riding the Dragon_**

"Charles Darwin, Dan Kahneman and Malcolm Gladwell walk into a bar. . . It's no joke! Reading *The Elephant in the Brain* is like eavesdropping on a fascinating conversation among a group of well-read and clever iconoclasts as they speculate on why we vote against our economic interests, spend too much on health care, give to the wrong charities and pray to gods we aren't sure really exist."

—**Steven Pearlstein, Columnist at The Washington Post;**
Pulitzer Prize Winner

"Drawing upon evolutionary psychology, the authors tackle the basic capacity of humans for self-deception, not merely at the level of the Freudian intrapsychic but collectively as well. Self-deception, they argue, allows people to better manipulate others. In exposing the darker side of human nature, the authors take readers on a fascinating journey into hidden motivations in such diverse realms as education, religion, and politics." —*CHOICE*

"If you want to know what makes people tick, read *The Elephant in the Brain*. Simler and Hanson have created the most comprehensive, powerful, unified explanation of human nature and behavior to date."

—**Jason Brennan, Professor of Business,**
Georgetown University

The Elephant in the Brain

Hidden Motives in Everyday Life

KEVIN SIMLER AND ROBIN HANSON

Oxford University Press is a department of the University of Oxford. It furthers
the University's objective of excellence in research, scholarship, and education
by publishing worldwide. Oxford is a registered trade mark of Oxford University
Press in the UK and certain other countries.

Published in the United States of America by Oxford University Press
198 Madison Avenue, New York, NY 10016, United States of America.

First issued as an Oxford University Press paperback, 2020

Library of Congress Cataloging-in-Publication Data
Names: Simler, Kevin, 1982– author. | Hanson, Robin, 1959– author.
Title: The elephant in the brain : hidden motives in everyday life / Kevin
Simler, Robin Hanson.
Description: 1 Edition. | New York : Oxford University Press, 2018.
Identifiers: LCCN 2017004296| ISBN 9780190495992 (hardback) |
ISBN 9780197551950 (paperback) | ISBN 9780190496012 (epub)
Subjects: LCSH: Self-deception. | Subconsciousness. | Cognitive psychology. |
BISAC: PSYCHOLOGY / Cognitive Psychology.
Classification: LCC BF697.5.S426 S56 2017 | DDC 153.8—dc23
LC record available at https://lccn.loc.gov/2017004296

9 8 7 6 5 4 3 2

Printed by Sheridan Books, Inc., United States of America

For Lee Corbin,
who kindled my intellectual life
and taught me how to think.
—Kevin

To the little guys, often grumbling in a corner,
who've said this sort of thing for ages:
you were right more than you knew.
—Robin

CONTENTS

Although Robin has blogged on related topics for over a decade, the book in your hands—or on your screen—would not have happened but for Kevin's initiative. In 2013, Kevin considered taking his second stab at a PhD, but instead approached Robin with a suggestion that they forego the academic formalities and simply talk and work together, informally, as student and advisor. This is the fruit of our collaboration: a doctoral thesis of sorts. And we suppose that makes you, dear reader, one of our thesis committee.

Unlike a conventional dissertation, however, this work makes less of a claim to originality. Our basic thesis—that we are strategically blind to key aspects of our motives—has been around in some form or another for millennia. It's been put forward not only by poets, playwrights, and philosophers, but also by countless wise old souls, at least when you catch them in private and in the right sort of mood. And yet the thesis still seems to us neglected in scholarly writings; you can read a mountain of books and still miss it. For Robin, it's the view he would have been most eager to hear early in his research career, to help him avoid blind alleys. So we hope future scholars can now find at least one book in their library that clearly articulates the thesis.

As we put our final touches on this book, we find that our thoughts are now mostly elsewhere. This is, in part, because other tasks and projects clamor for our attention, but also because it's just really hard to look long and intently at our selfish motives, at what we've called "the elephant in the brain." Even we, the authors of a book on the subject, are relieved for the chance to look away, to let our minds wander to safer, more comfortable topics.

We're quite curious to see how the world reacts to our book. Early reviews were almost unanimously positive, and we expect the typical reader to accept roughly two-thirds of our claims about human motives and institutions. Yet, we find it hard to imagine the book's central thesis becoming widely accepted among any large population, even of scholars. As better minds than ours have long advanced similar ideas, but to little apparent effect, we suspect that human minds and cultures must contain sufficient antibodies to keep such concepts at bay.

Of course, no work like this comes together without a community of support. We're grateful for the advice, feedback, and encouragement of a wide network of colleagues, friends, and family:

- Our book agent, Teresa Hartnett, and our editors, Lynnee Argabright and Joan Bossert.
- For feedback on early drafts: Scott Aaronson, Shanu Athiparambath, Mills Baker, Stefano Bertolo, Romina Boccia, Joel Borgen, Bryan Caplan, David Chapman, Tyler Cowen, Jean-Louis Dessalles, Jay Dixit, Kyle Erickson, Matthew Fallshaw, Charles Feng, Joshua Fox, Eivind Kjørstad, Anna Krupitsky, Brian Leddin, Jeff Lonsdale, William MacAskill, Dave McDougall, Geoffrey Miller, Luke Muehlhauser, Patrick O'Shaughnessy, Laure Parsons, Adam Safron, Carl Shulman, Mayeesha Tahsin, Toby Unwin, and Zach Weinersmith.
- Robin received no financial assistance for this book and its related research, other than the freedom that academic tenure gives. For that unusual privilege, Robin deeply thanks his colleagues at George Mason University.
- For additional support, encouragement, ideas, and inspiration, Kevin would like to thank Nick Barr, Emilio Cecconi, Ian Cheng, Adam D'Angelo, Joseph Jordania, Dikran Karagueuzian, Jenny Lee, Justin Mares, Robin Newton, Ian Padgham, Sarah Perry, Venkat Rao, Naval Ravikant, Darcey Riley, Nakul Santpurkar, Joe Shermetaro, Prasanna Srikhanta, Alex Vartan, and Francelle Wax, with a special shout-out to Charles Feng for the suggestion to think of the book as a dissertation, and to Jonathan Lonsdale for the suggestion to look for a "PhD advisor." Kevin is also particularly grateful for the support of his parents, Steve and Valerie, and his wife Diana.
- Finally, Kevin would like to thank Lee Corbin, his mentor and friend of 25 years. This project would not have been possible without Lee's influence.

The Elephant in the Brain

Introduction

> *elephant in the **room***, n. An important issue that people are reluctant to acknowledge or address; a social taboo.
>
> *elephant in the **brain***, n. An important but unacknowledged feature of how our minds work; an introspective taboo.

Robin caught his first glimpse of the elephant in 1998.

He had recently finished his doctoral work at Caltech, studying abstract economic theory, and was beginning a two-year postdoc focused on healthcare policy. At first he concentrated on the standard questions: Which medical treatments are effective? Why do hospitals and insurance companies operate the way they do? And how can the whole system be made more efficient?

As he immersed himself in the literature, however, he started noticing data that didn't add up, and soon he began to question even the most basic, bedrock assumptions. Why do patients spend so much on medical care? To get healthier: That's their one and only goal, right?

Maybe not. Consider some of the puzzling data points that Robin discovered. To start with, people in developed countries consume way too much medicine—doctor visits, drugs, diagnostic tests, and so forth—well beyond what's useful for staying healthy. Large randomized studies, for example, find that people given free healthcare consume a lot more medicine (relative to an unsubsidized control group), yet don't end up noticeably healthier. Meanwhile, *non-medical* interventions—such as efforts to alleviate stress or improve diet, exercise, sleep, or air quality—have a much bigger apparent effect on health, and yet patients and policymakers are far less eager to pursue them. Patients are also easily satisfied with the *appearance* of good medical care, and show shockingly little interest in digging beneath the surface—for example, by getting second opinions or asking for outcome statistics from their doctors or hospitals. (One astonishing study found that only 8 percent of patients about to undergo a dangerous heart surgery were willing to pay $50 to learn the different death rates for that very surgery at nearby hospitals.) Finally, people spend exorbitantly on heroic end-of-life care even though cheap, palliative care is usually just as effective at prolonging life and even better at preserving quality of life. Altogether, these puzzles cast considerable doubt on the simple idea that medicine is strictly about health.

To explain these and other puzzles, Robin took an approach unusual among health policy experts. He suggested that people might have *other motives* for buying medicine—motives beyond simply getting healthy—and that these motives are largely unconscious. On introspection, we see only the health motive, but when we step back and triangulate our motives from the outside, reverse-engineering them from our behaviors, a more interesting picture begins to develop.

When a toddler stumbles and scrapes his knee, his mom bends down to give it a kiss. No actual healing takes place, and yet both parties appreciate the ritual. The toddler finds comfort in knowing his mom is there to help him, especially if something more serious were to happen. And the mother, for her part, is eager to show that she's worthy of her son's trust. This small, simple example shows how we might be programmed both to seek and give healthcare even when it isn't medically useful.

Robin's hypothesis is that a similar transaction lurks within our modern medical system, except we don't notice it because it's masked by all the genuine healing that takes place. In other words, expensive medical care *does* heal us, but it's simultaneously an elaborate adult version of "kiss the boo-boo." In this transaction, the patient is assured of social support, while those who provide such support are hoping to buy a little slice of loyalty from the patient. And it's not just doctors who are on the "kissing" or supportive side of the transaction, but everyone who helps the patient along the way: the spouse who insists on the doctor's visit, the friend who watches the kids, the boss who's lenient about work deadlines, and even the institutions, like employers and national governments, that sponsored the patient's health insurance in the first place. Each of these parties is hoping for a bit of loyalty in exchange for their support. But the net result is that patients end up getting more medicine than they need strictly for their health.

The conclusion is that medicine isn't just about health—it's also an exercise in *conspicuous caring*.

Now, we don't expect our readers to believe this explanation just yet. We'll examine it in more detail in Chapter 14. What's important is getting a feel for the *kind* of explanation we're proposing. First, we're suggesting that key human behaviors are often driven by multiple motives—even behaviors that seem pretty single-minded, like giving and receiving medical care. This shouldn't be too surprising; humans are complex creatures, after all. But second, and more importantly, we're suggesting that some of these motives are unconscious; we're less than fully aware of them. And they aren't mere mouse-sized motives, scurrying around discreetly in the back recesses of our minds. These are elephant-sized motives large enough to leave footprints in national economic data.

Thus medicine was Robin's first glimpse of the elephant in the brain. Kevin, meanwhile, caught his first glimpse while working at a software startup in Silicon Valley.

Initially, Kevin took the startup scene for a straightforward exercise in company-building: gather some people together; give them time to think, talk, and write code; and eventually, like Legos clicking into place, out pops useful software. Then he read *Hierarchy in the Forest* by anthropologist Christopher Boehm, a book that analyzes human societies with the same concepts used to analyze chimpanzee communities. After reading Boehm's book, Kevin began to see his environment very differently. An office full of software engineers soon morphed, under the flickering fluorescent lights, into a tribe of chattering primates. All-hands meetings, shared meals, and team outings became elaborate social grooming sessions. Interviews began to look like thinly veiled initiation rituals. The company logo took on the character of a tribal totem or religious symbol.

But the biggest revelation from Boehm's book concerned social status. Of course office workers, being primates, are constantly jockeying to keep or improve their position in the hierarchy, whether by dominance displays, squabbles over territory, or active confrontations. None of these behaviors is surprising to find in a species as social and political as ours. What's interesting is how people obfuscate all this social competition by dressing it up in clinical business jargon. Richard doesn't complain about Karen by saying, "She gets in my way"; he accuses her of "not caring enough about the customer." Taboo topics like social status aren't discussed openly, but are instead swaddled in euphemisms like "experience" or "seniority."

The point is, people don't typically think or talk in terms of maximizing social status—or, in the case of medicine, showing conspicuous care. And yet we all instinctively act this way. In fact, we're able to act quite skillfully and strategically, pursuing our self-interest without explicitly acknowledging it, even to ourselves.

But this is odd. Why should we be less than fully conscious of such important motives? Biology teaches us that we're competitive social animals, with all the instincts you'd expect from such creatures. And consciousness is useful—that's why it evolved. So shouldn't it stand to reason that we'd be *hyper-conscious* of our deepest biological incentives? And yet, most of the time, we seem almost willfully unaware of them.

It's not that we're literally incapable of perceiving these motives within our psyches. We all know they're there. And yet they make us uncomfortable, so we mentally flinch away.

THE CORE IDEA

"We are social creatures to the inmost centre of our being."—Karl Popper[1]

"Every man alone is sincere. At the entrance of a second person, hypocrisy begins."—Ralph Waldo Emerson[2]

Here is the thesis we'll be exploring in this book: We, human beings, are a species that's not only capable of acting on hidden motives—we're designed to do it. Our brains are built to act in our self-interest while at the same time trying hard not to appear selfish in front of other people. And in order to throw them off the trail, our brains often keep "us," our conscious minds, in the dark. The less we know of our own ugly motives, the easier it is to hide them from others.

Self-deception is therefore *strategic*, a ploy our brains use to look good while behaving badly. Understandably, few people are eager to confess to this kind of duplicity. But as long as we continue to tiptoe around it, we'll be unable to think clearly about human behavior. We'll be forced to distort or deny any explanation that harks back to our hidden motives. Key facts will remain taboo, and we'll forever be mystified by our own thoughts and actions. It's only by confronting the elephant, then, that we can begin to see what's really going on.

Again, it's not that we're completely unaware of our unsavory motives—far from it. Many are readily apparent to anyone who chooses to look. For each "hidden" motive that we discuss in the book, some readers will be acutely aware of it, some dimly aware, and others entirely oblivious. This is why we've chosen the elephant as our metaphor (see Box 1). The elephant—whether in a room or in our brains—simply stands there, out in the open, and can easily be seen if only we steel ourselves to look in its direction (see Figure 1). But generally, we prefer to ignore the elephant, and as a result, we systematically give short shrift to explanations of our behavior that call attention to it.

Box 1: "The Elephant"

So what, exactly, is the elephant in the brain, this thing we're reluctant to talk and think about? In a word, it's selfishness—the selfish parts of our psyches.

But it's actually broader than that. Selfishness is just the heart, if you will, and an elephant has many other parts, all interconnected. So throughout the book, we'll be using "the elephant" to refer not just to human selfishness, but to a whole cluster of related concepts: the fact that we're competitive social animals fighting for power, status, and sex; the fact that we're sometimes willing to lie and cheat to get ahead;

the fact that we hide some of our motives—and that we do so in order to mislead others. We'll also occasionally use "the elephant" to refer to our hidden motives themselves. To acknowledge any of these concepts is to hint at the rest of them. They're all part of the same package, subject to the same taboo.

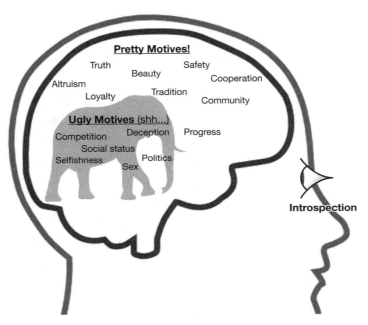

Figure 1. The Elephant in the Brain.

Human behavior is rarely what it seems—that's the main lesson here. Of course, we're hardly the first people to make this point. Thinkers across the ages have delighted in identifying many ways, large and small, that our actions don't seem to align with our supposed reasons. "We should often blush at our noblest deeds," wrote François de La Rochefoucauld in the 17th century, "if the world were to see all their underlying motives."[3]

Sigmund Freud, of course, was a major champion of hidden motives. He posited a whole suite of them, along with various mechanisms for keeping them unconscious. But although the explanations in this book may seem Freudian at times, we follow mainstream cognitive psychology in rejecting most of Freud's methods and many of his conclusions.[4] Repressed thoughts and conflict within the psyche? Sure, those are at the heart of our thesis. But the Oedipus complex? Dreams as a reliable source of evidence? Memories from the womb uncovered during psychoanalysis? None of these will play a role in our story.

Instead, we start closer to evolutionary psychology, drawing from scholars like Robert Trivers and Robert Kurzban, along with Robert Wright—yes, they're all Roberts—who have written clearly and extensively about self-deception from a Darwinian perspective. The human brain, according to this view, was *designed* to deceive itself—in Trivers' words, "the better to deceive others."

We start with evolutionary psychology, but we don't end there. We continue to seek hidden motives at larger social levels, taking inspiration from Thorstein Veblen, an economist and sociologist writing roughly a century ago. Veblen famously coined the term "conspicuous consumption" to explain the demand for luxury goods. When consumers are asked why they bought an expensive watch or high-end handbag, they often cite material factors like comfort, aesthetics, and functionality. But Veblen argued that, in fact, the demand for luxury goods is driven largely by a *social* motive: flaunting one's wealth. More recently, the psychologist Geoffrey Miller has made similar arguments from an evolutionary perspective, and we draw heavily from his work as well.

Our aim in this book, therefore, is not just to catalog the many ways humans behave unwittingly, but also to suggest that many of our most venerated institutions—charities, corporations, hospitals, universities—serve covert agendas alongside their official ones. Because of this, we *must* take covert agendas into account when thinking about these institutions, or risk radically misunderstanding them.

What will emerge from this investigation is a portrait of the human species as strategically self-deceived, not only as individuals but also as a society. Our brains are experts at flirting, negotiating social status, and playing politics, while "we"—the self-conscious parts of the brain—manage to keep our thoughts pure and chaste. "We" don't always know what our brains are up to, but we often pretend to know, and therein lies the trouble.

THE BASIC ARGUMENT

At least four strands of research all lead to the same conclusion—that we are, as the psychologist Timothy Wilson puts it, "strangers to ourselves":

1. *Microsociology.* When we study how people interact with each other on the small scale—in real time and face to face—we quickly learn to appreciate the depth and complexity of our social behaviors and how little we're consciously aware of what's going on. These behaviors include laughter, blushing, tears, eye contact, and body language. In fact, we have such little introspective access into these behaviors, or voluntary control over them, that it's fair to say "we" aren't really in charge. Our brains choreograph these interactions on our behalves, and with surprising skill. While "we" anguish over what to say next, our brains manage to laugh at just the right moments, flash the right facial expressions, hold or break eye contact as appropriate, nego-tiate territory and social status with our posture, and interpret and react to all these behaviors in our interaction partners.

2. *Cognitive and social psychology.* The study of cognitive biases and self-deception has matured considerably in recent years. We now realize that our brains aren't just hapless and quirky—they're *devi-ous.* They intentionally hide information from us, helping us fab-ricate plausible prosocial motives to act as cover stories for our less savory agendas. As Trivers puts it: "At every single stage [of processing information]—from its biased arrival, to its biased encoding, to organizing it around false logic, to misremembering and then misrepresenting it to others—the mind continually acts to distort information flow in favor of the usual goal of appearing better than one really is."[5] Emily Pronin calls it the *introspection illusion,* the fact that we don't know our own minds nearly as well as we pretend to. For the price of a little self-deception, we get to

have our cake and eat it too: act in our own best interests without having to reveal ourselves as the self-interested schemers we often are.

3. *Primatology.* Humans are primates, specifically apes. Human nature is therefore a modified form of ape nature. And when we study primate groups, we notice a lot of Machiavellian behavior—sexual displays, dominance and submission, fitness displays (showing off), and political maneuvering. But when asked to describe our *own* behavior—why we bought that new car, say, or why we broke off a relationship—we mostly portray our motives as cooperative and prosocial. We don't admit to nearly as much showing off and political jockeying as we'd expect from a competitive social animal. Something just doesn't add up.

4. *Economic puzzles.* When we study specific social institutions—medicine, education, politics, charity, religion, news, and so forth—we notice that they frequently fall short of their stated goals. In many cases, this is due to simple execution failures. But in other cases, the institutions behave as though they were designed to achieve other, unacknowledged goals. Take school, for instance. We say that the function of school is to teach valuable skills and knowledge. Yet students don't remember most of what they're taught, and most of what they do remember isn't very useful. Furthermore, our best research says that schools are structured in ways that actively interfere with the learning process, such as early wake-up times and frequent testing. (These and many other puzzles will be discussed in Chapter 13.) Again, something doesn't add up.

This focus on large-scale social issues is, in fact, what most distinguishes our book. Plenty of other thinkers have examined self-deception in the context of our personal lives and individual behaviors. But few have taken the logical next step of using those insights to study our institutions.

The point is, we act on hidden motives together, in public, just as often as we do by ourselves, in private. And when enough of our hidden motives harmonize, we end up constructing stable, long-lived institutions—like schools, hospitals, churches, and democracies—that are designed, at least partially, to accommodate such motives. This was Robin's conclusion about medicine, and similar reasoning applies to many other areas of life.

Here's another way to look at it. The world is full of people acting on motives they'd rather not acknowledge. But most of the time, opposing interest groups are eager to call them out for it. For example, when U.S. bankers angled for a bailout during the 2008 financial crisis, they argued that it would benefit the entire economy, conveniently neglecting to mention that it would line their own pockets. Thankfully, many others stood ready to accuse them of profiteering. Similarly, during the Bush administration, U.S. antiwar protestors—most of whom were liberal—justified their efforts in terms of the harms of war. And yet when Obama took over as president, they drastically reduced their protests, even though the wars in Iraq and Afghanistan continued unabated.[6] All this suggested an agenda that was more partisan than pacifist, and conservative critics were happy to point out the disconnect.[7]

But what happens when our hidden motives don't line up with a tribal or partisan agenda? In areas of life in which we're *all* similarly complicit in hiding our motives, who will call attention to them?

This book attempts to shine light on just those dark, unexamined facets of public life: venerated social institutions in which almost all participants are strategically self-deceived, markets in which both buyers and sellers pretend to transact one thing while covertly transacting another. The art scene, for example, isn't just about "appreciating beauty"; it also functions as an excuse to affiliate with impressive people and as a sexual display (a way to hobnob and get laid). Education isn't just about learning; it's largely about getting graded, ranked, and credentialed, stamped for the approval of employers. Religion isn't just about private belief in God or the afterlife, but about conspicuous public *professions* of belief that help bind groups together. In each of these areas, our hidden agendas explain a surprising amount of our behavior—often a majority. When push comes to shove, we often make choices that prioritize our hidden agendas over the official ones.

This line of thinking suggests that many of our institutions are prodigiously wasteful. Under the feel-good veneer of win-win cooperation— teaching kids, healing the sick, celebrating creativity—our institutions harbor giant, silent furnaces of intra-group competitive signaling, where trillions of dollars of wealth, resources, and human effort are being shoveled in and burned to ash every year, largely for the purpose of showing off. Now, our institutions *do* end up achieving many of their official, stated goals, but they're often rather inefficient because they're simultaneously serving purposes no one is eager to acknowledge.

This may sound like pessimism, but it's actually great news. However flawed our institutions may be, we're already living with them—and life, for most of us, is pretty good. So if we can accurately diagnose what's holding back our institutions, we may finally succeed in reforming them, thereby making our lives even better.

Of course, not everyone cares about the design of large-scale social institutions. A more practical use for our book is to help readers develop better *situational awareness* (to borrow a term from the military). Whether in meetings, at church, or while watching politicians jabber on TV, we all want deeper insight into what's happening and why. Human social behavior is complex and often nearly inscrutable, but this book provides a framework for helping readers make sense of it, especially the parts that are otherwise counterintuitive. *Why do people laugh? Who's the most important person in the room (and how can I tell)? Why are artists sexy? Why do so many people brag about travel? Does anyone really, truly believe in creationism?* If we listen to what people *say* about themselves, we'll often be led astray, because people strategically misconstrue their motives. It's only by cross-examining these motives, using data about how people *behave*, that we're able to learn what's really driving human behavior (see Box 2).

Box 2: Our Thesis in Plain English

1. People are judging us all the time. They want to know whether we'll make good friends, allies, lovers, or leaders. And one of the important things they're judging is our *motives*. Why do we behave the way we do? Do we have others' best interests at heart, or are we entirely selfish?

2. Because others are judging us, we're eager to look good. So we emphasize our pretty motives and downplay our ugly ones. It's not *lying*, exactly, but neither is it perfectly honest.

3. This applies not just to our words, but also to our thoughts, which might seem odd. Why can't we be honest with ourselves? The answer is that our thoughts aren't as private as we imagine. In many ways, conscious thought is a rehearsal of what we're ready to say to others. As Trivers puts it, "We deceive ourselves the better to deceive others."[8]

4. In some areas of life, especially polarized ones like politics, we're quick to point out when others' motives are more selfish than they claim. But in other areas, like medicine, we prefer to believe that almost all of us have pretty motives. In such cases, we can all be quite wrong, together, about what drives our behavior.

TRAJECTORY OF THE BOOK

The book is divided into two parts.

Part I, "Why We Hide Our Motives," explores how the incentives of social life distort our minds, inducing awkward contortions of self-deception. Matthew 7:3 asks, "Why worry about a speck in your friend's eye when you have a log in your own?" In our metaphor, we might just as well ask, "Why worry about a mouse in your friend's mind when you have an elephant in your own?" In Part I, our goal is to confront the elephant as directly as possible—to stare it down, without blinking or flinching away.

Part II, "Hidden Motives in Everyday Life," uses our new understanding of the elephant to deconstruct a wide range of human behaviors, both at the small, personal scale and in the context of our broadest institutions. What we'll find is that things are often not what they seem on the surface.

A WORD OF WARNING

For those of us who want to understand the world, it's unsettling to think our brains might be deceiving us. Reality is bewildering enough without an elephant clouding our vision. But the ideas in this book have an even more serious handicap, which is that they're difficult to celebrate publicly.

Consider how some ideas are more naturally viral than others. When a theory emphasizes altruism, cooperation, and other feel-good motives, for example, people naturally want to share it, perhaps even shout it from the rooftops: "By working together, we can achieve great things!" It reflects well on both speakers and listeners to be associated with something so inspirational. This is the recipe for ideas that draw large audiences and receive standing ovations, the time-honored premise of sermons, TED talks, commencement speeches, and presidential inaugurations.

Many other ideas, however, face an uphill battle and may never achieve widespread acceptance. When an idea emphasizes competition and other ugly motives, people are understandably averse to sharing it. It sucks the energy out of the room. As your two coauthors have learned firsthand, it can be a real buzzkill at dinner parties.

In light of this, it's important to emphasize where we're coming from. The line between cynicism and misanthropy—between thinking ill of human *motives* and thinking ill of *humans*—is often blurry. So we want readers to understand that although we may be skeptical of human motives, we love human beings. (Indeed, many of our best friends are human!) We aren't trying to put our species down or rub people's noses in their own short-comings. We're just taking some time to dwell on the parts of human nature that don't get quite as much screen time. All in all, we doubt an honest exploration will detract much from our affection for these fine creatures.

If we're being honest with ourselves—and true to the book's thesis—then we must admit there is a risk to confronting our hidden motives. Human beings are self-deceived because self-deception is useful. It allows us to reap the benefits of selfish behavior while posing as unselfish in front of others; it helps us look better than we really are. Confronting our delusions must therefore (at least in part) undermine their very reason for existing. There's a very real sense in which we might be better off not knowing what we're up to.

But we see this choice—of whether to look inward and confront the elephant or continue to avert our gaze—as similar to the choice Morpheus offers Neo in *The Matrix*. "After this," Morpheus warns, holding out a blue pill in one hand and a red pill in the other, "there is no turning back. You take the blue pill—the story ends, you wake up in your bed and believe whatever you want to believe. You take the red pill—you stay in Wonderland, and I show you how deep the rabbit hole goes."[9]

If curiosity killed the cat, then Kevin and Robin would be dead cats. We just can't resist an offer like this. We choose the red pill, and hope that you, dear reader, feel likewise.

PART I

Why We Hide
Our Motives

Animal Behavior

Before we get mired in the complexities of *human* social life, let's start at a simpler beginning. Because humans are an animal species, we can learn a lot about ourselves by studying other animals (and even plants, as we'll see in the next chapter). In fact, it can be especially useful to study other species because we have fewer preconceptions about them. Think of it as a "training wheels" exercise, if you will.

In this chapter, we're going to take a quick look at two animal behaviors that are hard to decipher. In each case, the animals appear to be doing something simple and straightforward, but as we dig below the surface—the same way we'll approach our own behavior in later chapters—we'll find extra layers of complexity.

Note, however, that these nonhuman animals don't necessarily *hide* their motives like we do, psychologically; if their motives seem cryptic, it's not because they're playing mind games. We'll discuss this in more detail at the end of the chapter.

SOCIAL GROOMING

Let's start with grooming behavior among primates. While humans are relatively hairless, most other primates have thick fur all over their bodies. When left unchecked, this fur quickly becomes matted with dirt and debris. It also makes an attractive home for fleas, lice, ticks, and other parasites. As a result, primate fur needs periodic grooming to stay clean.

Individual primates can (and do) groom themselves, but they can only effectively groom about half their bodies. They can't easily groom their own backs, faces, and heads. So to keep their entire bodies clean, they need a little help from their friends.[1] This is called *social grooming*.[2]

Picture two male chimpanzees engaged in an act of social grooming. One chimp—the groomee—sits hunched over, exposing his full backside. The other chimp—the groomer—crawls up and begins examining the first chimp's fur. He'll typically spend a few minutes scratching and picking at it with his fingers, using his opposable thumbs to pull out bits of stray matter. It's a purposeful activity that requires a good deal of attention and focus.

If we could somehow ask the grooming chimp what he's doing, he might give a pragmatic explanation: "I'm trying to remove these bits and pieces from my friend's back." That's the purpose of the activity and what his attention is focused on. He might also cite the logic of straightforward reciprocity: "If I groom my friend's back, he's more likely to groom mine in return"—which is true; chimps form mutual grooming partnerships that are relatively stable over the course of their lives. At first blush, then, social grooming seems like an act of hygiene, a way to keep one's fur clean.

This is far from the complete picture, however. We can't take social grooming at face value. There are some puzzling facts that cast doubt on the simple hygienic function:

- Most primates spend far more time grooming each other than necessary for keeping their fur clean.[3] Gelada baboons, for example, devote a whopping 17 percent of their daylight hours to grooming each other.[4] Clearly this is overkill, as some primate species spend only 0.1 percent of their time grooming each other, while birds spend maybe 0.01 percent of their time on similar preening behaviors.[5]
- Even more puzzling is the fact that primates spend a lot more time grooming each other than they spend grooming themselves.[6] If the only purpose of grooming were hygiene, we'd expect to see more self-grooming in proportion to social grooming.
- Finally, we can correlate the average body size (of each primate species) with the amount of time they spend grooming. If grooming were strictly a hygienic activity, we'd expect larger species—those

with more fur—to spend more time grooming each other. But in fact there's no correlation.[7]

We might ask ourselves, "What's going on here?" There must be some other function at play.

The primatologist Robin Dunbar has spent much of his career studying social grooming, and his conclusion has since become the consensus among primatologists. Social grooming, he says, isn't just about hygiene—it's also about politics. By grooming each other, primates help forge alliances that help them in other situations.

An act of grooming conveys a number of related messages. The groomer says, "I'm willing to use my spare time to help you," while the groomee says, "I'm comfortable enough to let you approach me from behind (or touch my face)." Meanwhile, both parties strengthen their alliance merely by spending pleasant time in close proximity. Two *rivals*, however, would find it hard to let their guards down to enjoy such a relaxed activity.[8]

The bottom line: "Grooming," says Dunbar, "creates a platform off which trust can be built."[9]

This political function of grooming helps explain other data points that don't make sense according to the strictly hygienic function. For example, it explains why higher-ranked individuals receive more grooming than lower-ranked individuals.[10] When low-ranking primates choose to groom one of their superiors, they're less likely to be groomed in return—so they must be angling for some other kind of benefit (rather than simple reciprocity). Indeed, grooming partners are more likely to share food,[11] tolerate each other at feeding sites,[12] and support each other during confrontations with other members of the group.[13]

The political function of grooming also explains why grooming time across species is correlated with the *size of the social group*, but not the amount of fur.[14] Larger groups have, on average, greater political complexity, making alliances more important but also harder to maintain.

Note that these primates don't need to be *conscious* of their political motivations. As far as natural selection is concerned, all that matters is that primates who do more social grooming fare better than primates who do less. Primates are thereby endowed with instincts that make them feel good when they groom each other, without necessarily understanding *why* they feel good.[15]

It's also important to note that there's still *some* role for hygiene in explaining why primates groom each other. If hygiene were completely irrelevant, primates would simply give each other back massages instead of picking through each other's fur. But even though there's some hygienic value to social grooming, it doesn't explain why primates spend so much time doing it. Gelada baboons, for example, might be able to keep their fur clean with only 30 minutes of social grooming every day, but instead they spend 120 minutes. (This seems similar to a human showering four times a day.) Only politics explains why the geladas spend those additional, seemingly unnecessary 90 minutes.

COMPETITIVE ALTRUISM

Before we move on to human behavior, here is one more quick example.

The Arabian babbler, famously studied by Amotz Zahavi and a team of ornithologists at Tel Aviv University, is a small brown bird that lives in the arid brush of the Sinai Desert and parts of the Arabian Peninsula. Babblers live in small groups of 3 to 20 members who collectively defend a small territory of trees, shrubs, and bushes that provide much-needed cover from predators. Babblers who live as part of a group do well for themselves, whereas those who are kicked out of a group are in great danger. They're typically badgered away from other groups, have trouble finding food and shelter, and often fall prey to hawks, raptors, and snakes.[16]

The social life of the babbler is rather curious. For simplicity, we'll focus on the males, but similar behaviors can be found among the females. Male babblers arrange themselves into rigid dominance hierarchies. The alpha male, for example, consistently wins in small squabbles with the beta male, who in turn consistently wins against the gamma male. Very occasionally, a much more intense fight erupts between two babblers of adjacent rank, resulting in one babbler's death or permanent ejection from the group. Most of the time, however, the males get along splendidly with each other. In fact, they frequently help one another and the group in a variety of ways. Adults donate food to each other, bring food to their communal nestlings, attack predators and members of rival groups, and stand "guard duty" to watch for predators while the others look for food.

At first glance, these activities appear straightforwardly altruistic (i.e., self-sacrificing). A babbler who takes a stint at guard duty, for example, foregoes his own opportunity to eat. Likewise, a babbler who attacks an enemy assumes risk of serious personal injury. On more careful inspection, however, these activities turn out not to be as selfless as they seem.

First of all, babblers *compete* to help each other and the group—often aggressively so. For example, not only do higher-ranked babblers give food to lower-ranked babblers, sometimes they force it down the throats of unwilling birds! Similarly, when a beta male is standing guard duty at the top of a tree, the alpha will often fly up and harass the beta off his perch. The beta, meanwhile, isn't strong enough to bully the alpha from guard duty, but he will often stand insistently nearby, offering to take over if the alpha male allows it. Similar jockeying takes place for the "privilege" of performing other altruistic behaviors.

If the goal of these behaviors is to be helpful, why do the babblers waste effort competing to perform them? One hypothesis is that higher-ranked babblers are stronger, and therefore better able to forego food and fight off predators. And so, by taking on more of the burden (even if they have to fight for it), they're actually helping their weaker groupmates. The problem with this hypothesis is that babblers compete primarily with the birds immediately above or below them in the hierarchy. The alpha male, for example, almost never tries to replace the *gamma* male from guard duty; instead the alpha directs all of his competitive energies toward the beta. If the goal were to help weaker members, the alpha should be more eager to take over from the gamma than from the beta. Even more damning is the fact that babblers often *interfere* in the helpful behaviors of their rivals, for example, by trying to prevent them from feeding the communal nestlings. This makes no sense if the goal is to benefit the group as a whole.

So if these activities aren't altruistic, what's the point? What's in it for the individual babbler who competes to do more than his fair share of helping others?

The answer, as Zahavi and his team have carefully documented, is that altruistic babblers develop a kind of "credit" among their groupmates—what Zahavi calls *prestige status*. This earns them at least two different perks, one of which is mating opportunities: Males with greater prestige get to mate more often with the females of the group. A prestigious alpha, for example, may take all the mating opportunities for himself. But if the beta has earned high prestige, the alpha will occasionally allow him to mate with some of the females.[17] In this way, the alpha effectively "bribes" the beta to stick around.

The other perk of high prestige is a reduced risk of getting kicked out of the group. If the beta, for example, has earned lots of prestige by being useful to the group, the alpha is less likely to evict him. Here the logic is twofold. First, a prestigious beta has shown himself to be more useful to the group, so the alpha prefers to keep him around. Second, by performing more acts of "altruism," a babbler demonstrates his strength and fitness. An alpha who goes beak-to-beak with a prestigious beta is less likely to win the fight, and so gives the beta more leeway than he would give a beta with lower prestige.

Thus babblers compete to help others in a way that ultimately increases their own chances of survival and reproduction. What looks like altruism is actually, at a deeper level, competitive self-interest.

HUMAN BEHAVIORS

We can't always take animal behavior at face value—that's the main lesson to draw from the preceding examples. The surface-level logic of a behavior often belies deeper, more complex motives. And this is true even in species whose lives are much simpler than our own. So we can't expect human behaviors, like voting or making art, to be straightforward either.

Now, as we mentioned earlier, it would be a mistake to call these animal motives "hidden," at least in the psychological sense. When baboons groom each other, they may *happen* not to be thinking about the political consequences (perhaps they're simply acting on instinct), but their lack of awareness isn't *strategic*. They have no need to conceal the political intentions underlying their grooming behavior, and thus no need to suppress their own knowledge. Knowledge suppression is useful only when two conditions are met: (1) when others have partial visibility into your mind; and (2) when they're judging you, and meting out rewards or punishments, based on what they "see" in your mind.

These two conditions may hold for nonhuman primates in some situations. In the moments leading up to a fight, for example, both animals are struggling frantically to decipher the other's intentions.[18] And thus there can be an incentive for each party to deceive the other, which may be facilitated by a bit of self-deception. Just as camouflage is useful when facing an adversary with eyes, self-deception can be useful when facing an adversary with mind-reading powers. But the mind-reading powers of nonhuman primates are weak compared to our own, and so they have less need to obfuscate the contents of their minds.

We'll discuss this more thoroughly in later chapters. But before moving on, there's one last crucial point to make.

When we study the behavior of other species, we can't help putting ourselves in their shoes, in an attempt to feel what they feel and see the world through their eyes. But sometimes this method leads us astray, as when we find some animal behaviors "counterintuitive," and in such cases, it says more about *us* than the species whose behavior we struggle to understand. For more than a century after Charles Darwin first published his theory, for example, scientists would often appeal to "the good of the species" in order to explain seemingly altruistic animal behaviors, like the babblers volunteering for guard duty.[19] That's certainly the kind of thing *we* might say if we were in the babblers' shoes, but it's not a valid naturalistic explanation—either for their behavior or for our own.

To find out why we often misconstrue animal motives, including our own, we have to look more carefully at how our brains were designed and what problems they're intended to solve. We have to turn, in other words, to evolution.

Competition

Humans are a peculiar species. We're relatively hairless, we walk on our hind legs, we dance and sing like nobody's business. We laugh, blush, and shed tears. And our babies are among the most helpless in all the animal kingdom.

But perhaps our most distinctive feature is our intelligence. Relative to our body size, we have unusually large brains. Partly because of this, we're also the most behaviorally flexible creatures on the planet. But *why* are we so smart and flexible? And why did our brains grow so large, so quickly? (See Figure 2.)

Like the drunk who loses his keys and goes looking for them only under the streetlamp "because that's where the light is," people who study human evolution are more likely to search for explanations where the light (of evidence) is good. The archaeological record is biased toward objects that can endure, which means we get a pretty good picture of our ancestors' skeletons, stone tools, and some of their body paint (red ocher). But we have almost no way to recover their brain tissue, vocalizations, or body language.

This much is common sense. But in addition to biases in the evidence itself, *we* are also biased in the way we approach it. In this respect, we're not so much drunk as we are vain; we want our species to be seen in the most flattering light. There are facets of our evolutionary past that we spend less time poring over because we don't like how they make us look. In this sense, our problem isn't that the light is too *dim*, but that it's too *harsh*.

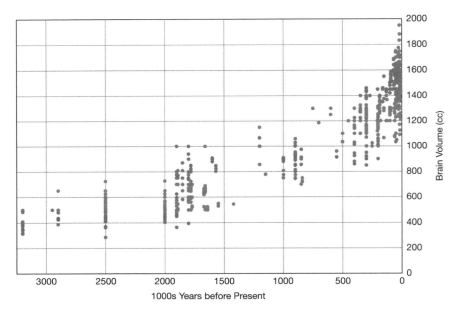

Figure 2. Human Ancestors' Brain Volume Over Time (de Miguel
and Henneberg 2001)

Consider these two broad "lights" where the keys to our big brains
might be found:

1. *Ecological challenges*, such as warding off predators, hunting big
   game, domesticating fire, finding new food sources, and adapting
   rapidly to new climates. These activities pit humans against their
   environment and are therefore *opportunities for cooperation*.
2. *Social challenges*, such as competition for mates, jockeying for
   social status, coalition politics (alliances, betrayals, etc.), intra-
   group violence, cheating, and deception. These activities pit humans
   against other humans and are therefore *competitive* and *potentially
   destructive*.

Many of us would prefer the keys to our intelligence to be found somewhere in the pleasing light of ecological challenges, implying that our

extra gray matter evolved in service of cooperation. "We grew smarter," the story would go, "so we could learn more, collaborate better against the harsh external world, and improve outcomes for everyone": win-win-win.

But many signs suggest that the keys to our intelligence lie in the harsh, unflattering light of social challenges, the arena of zero-sum games in which one person's gain is another's loss. It's not that we're completely unaware of these competitive, zero-sum instincts—we just tend to give them less prominence when explaining our behavior.

It's important to understand what we're actually afraid of here. Many kinds of competition are actually *easy* for us to acknowledge, even celebrate. We love playful competition, for example, as in games and sports. "There are no losers in wrestling," it's sometimes said, "only winners and learners." We also endorse competition in service of broader cooperative activities from which we all stand to gain, like when firms compete in the marketplace, driving down costs and spurring innovation. We're even comfortable acknowledging group versus group competition, up to and including war. It's not that we necessarily enjoy competing against other groups (although some of us do), but it isn't awkward or uncomfortable to talk about—because competition against Them highlights the shared interests among Us. However destructive, war tends to bring a nation together.

What's much harder to acknowledge are the competitions that threaten to drive wedges into otherwise cooperative relationships: sexual jealousy, status rivalry among friends, power struggles within a marriage, the temptation to cheat, politics in the workplace. Of course we acknowledge office politics in the abstract, but how often do we write about it on the company blog?

In general, we prefer explanations that make us look good, whether as individuals, families, communities, or nations. When it comes to our rivals, we're perfectly happy to entertain unflattering theories about their behavior, as long as the mud we fling at them doesn't spatter too much back at us.

These biases and psychological sore spots don't mean it's impossible for us to think clearly about competition, only that our job becomes more difficult. All else being equal, we'd prefer to look for the keys to human intelligence under the light of cooperation, a light that makes us look good. But if there's reason to believe the keys are elsewhere, we need to take a deep breath, roll up our sleeves, and start looking under the harsh light of competition.

PARABLE OF THE REDWOODS

Kevin's native California is home to the world's tallest tree species: *Sequoia sempervirens*, or the coastal redwood.

The tallest living specimen towers a lofty 379 feet (115 meters) above the forest floor. Historically some may have been even taller, with evidence of redwoods reaching 400 feet (122 meters) and beyond. This is approximately the height at which capillary action ceases to work; any taller and a tree can't get water from its roots to its topmost leaves. So redwoods are, in a sense, as tall as arboreally possible.[1]

Height, however, doesn't come cheap, whether for a redwood or any other tree. It takes a lot of energy and material to grow upward and remain standing in the face of wind and gravity—energy and material that could otherwise be put into developing stronger roots, growing horizontally to collect more sunlight, or making and dispersing more seeds in the hope of having more offspring.

So why bother? Why do trees put so much effort into vertical growth?

It depends on the species. Some grow tall to disperse their seeds more effectively. Other species do it to protect their leaves from terrestrial tree-eaters, like the acacia tree trying to stay out of reach from the giraffe. But for most trees, height is all about getting more sun. A forest is an intensely competitive place, and sunlight is a scarce but critical resource. And even when you're a redwood, the tallest of all tree species, you still have to worry about getting enough sun because you're in a forest of *other redwoods*.

Often a species' most important competitor is itself.

Thus the redwood is locked in an evolutionary arms race—or in this case, a "height race"—with itself. It grows tall because other redwoods are tall, and if it doesn't throw most of its effort into growing upward as fast as possible, it will literally wither and die in the shadows of its rivals.

Suppose we came upon a solitary redwood in an open meadow, towering far, far above the other plants and animals—a lanky giant standing all alone, reaching aggressively for the sky. This would look strange, even wrong, because it's not how nature usually does things. Why would a tree waste its energy growing so high above an open field? Wouldn't it get outcompeted by a shorter variant that threw more of its energy into reproduction? Yes. And so we can reasonably infer that an open field isn't the redwood's native environment. Instead, it must have evolved in a dense forest. Its height makes perfect sense, but only given the right context.

Now consider the human being. Like the redwood, our species has a distinctive feature: a huge brain. But if we think of *Homo sapiens* like the lone redwood in the open meadow, towering in intelligence over an otherwise brain-dead field, then we're liable to be puzzled. As shown in Figure 3, such intelligence would seem out of place, uncanny, unnecessary.

But of course, that's not the right way to think about it. We didn't evolve in the meadow (metaphorically speaking); we evolved in the dense forest. And like the redwood, we weren't competing primarily against other species, but against ourselves, as shown in Figure 4.

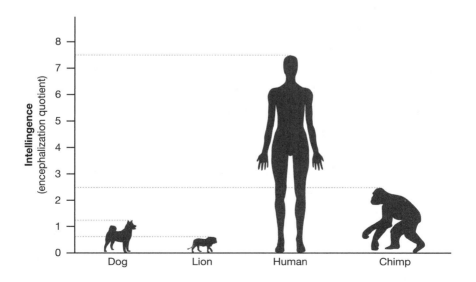

Figure 3. Human vs. Animal Intelligence

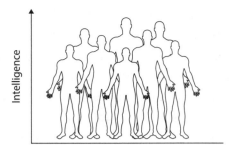

Figure 4. Humans Competing in Intelligence

"The worst problems for people," says primatologist Dario Maestripieri, "almost always come from other people."[2]

The earliest *Homo sapiens* lived in small, tight-knit bands of 20 to 50 individuals. These bands were our "groves" or "forests," in which we competed not for sunlight, but for resources more befitting a primate: food, sex, territory, social status. And we had to earn these things, in part, by outwitting and outshining our rivals.

This is what's known in the literature as the *social brain hypothesis*, or sometimes the *Machiavellian intelligence hypothesis*.[3] It's the idea that our ancestors got smart primarily in order to compete against each other in a variety of social and political scenarios.

"The way the brains of human beings have gotten bigger at an accelerating pace," writes Matt Ridley in his book on evolutionary biology, *The Red Queen*, "implies that some such within-species arms race is at work."[4] Steven Pinker and Paul Bloom also emphasize intra-species competition as an evolutionary cause of our intelligence. In an influential 1990 article on language evolution, they write: "Interacting with an organism of approximately equal mental abilities whose motives are at times outright malevolent makes formidable and ever-escalating demands on cognition."[5]

Robert Trivers goes even further. He argues that it was the arms race between lying and lie-detection that gave rise to our intelligence. "Both the detection of deception and often its propagation have been major forces favoring the evolution of intelligence. It is perhaps ironic that dishonesty has often been the file against which intellectual tools for truth have been sharpened."[6]

Of course, the social brain hypothesis isn't a complete account of how and why we evolved big brains.[7] But most scholars agree that intra-species competition was an important factor in shaping the kind of intelligence our species developed.

Now if, as we've been arguing, people are biased toward emphasizing cooperation and downplaying competition, then it will serve us well to temporarily reverse this bias. In what follows, let's emphasize and accentuate the more competitive aspects of our species' history. In particular, we're going to look at three of the most important "games" played by our ancestors: *sex, social status*, and *politics*.

SEX

A common tagline for natural selection is "survival of the fittest," but survival actually takes a back seat to reproduction. Yes, it's important not to get eaten by tigers. But consider that every creature alive today is the final link in an unbroken chain of ancestors who managed to reproduce—and yet many of those same ancestors died in the jaws of a predator (after they made some babies, of course). From the perspective of evolution, mating, not survival, is the name of the game.

Now, when discussing sex in our own species, it's easy to get distracted (often to the point of fixation) on sex *differences*: how men and women pursue different sexual strategies. Yes, it's true that there are biological differences between the sexes, and that they're important for understanding many aspects of human behavior. But here (and throughout the book), we're mostly going to be glossing over such differences.[8] To motivate our choice to lump men and women together, consider that when a species is pair-bonded and monogamous, the incentives for males and females converge.[9] Humans aren't perfectly pair-bonded and monogamous, of course, but it's a fair approximation. In fact, as Ridley says, "It is hard to overemphasize how unusual humans are in this respect."[10] Thus in sex, as in other areas of life, our approach will be to treat men and women as following the same general instincts, while perhaps giving them slightly different emphases.

Also remember that we're focusing on the *competitive* aspects of sex. Cooperative child-rearing is essential, to be sure, but it isn't our focus of attention here.

The main form of sexual competition is the competition for mates. Locally, this is largely a zero-sum competition, because within a given community, there are only a fixed number of mates to go around. Thus each of the two sexes faces competition primarily from other members of their sex. Every woman who wants to (monogamously) mate with a high-quality man has to compete with all the other women, while every man who wants to mate with a woman has to be chosen by her, ahead of all his rivals.

As in other competitions, like the competition for sunlight among the redwoods, mate competition in a sexually reproducing species leads to an evolutionary arms race. This is illustrated most iconically by the peacock's brilliant tail,[11] which serves as an advertisement of its owner's physical and genetic fitness. Similarly, among humans, the competitive aspect of courtship implies that both men and women will be keen to advertise themselves on the mating market. We want potential mates to know that we have good genes and that we'll make good parents.

The logic of this isn't particularly hard to understand, but the implications can be surprising. As Geoffrey Miller argues in *The Mating Mind*, "Our minds evolved not just as survival machines, but as courtship machines," and many of our most distinctive behaviors serve reproductive rather than survival ends. There are good reasons to believe, for example, that our capacities for visual art, music, storytelling, and humor function in large part as elaborate mating displays, not unlike the peacock's tail.

SOCIAL STATUS

Social status is traditionally defined as one's rank or position within a group—where you stand on society's totem pole. It's a measure of respect and influence. The higher your status, the more other people will defer to you and the better they'll tend to treat you.

As with the babblers we met in the previous chapter, social status among humans actually comes in two flavors: *dominance* and *prestige*.[12] Dominance is the kind of status we get from being able to intimidate others (think Joseph Stalin), and on the low-status side is governed by fear and other avoidance instincts. Prestige, however, is the kind of status we get from being an impressive human specimen (think Meryl Streep), and it's governed by admiration and other approach instincts. Of course, these two forms of status aren't mutually exclusive; Steve Jobs, for example, exhibited both dominance and prestige. But the two forms are analytically distinct strategies with different biological expressions. They are, as some researchers have put it, the "two ways to the top."[13]

Dominance is clearly the result of competition, which can often be vicious and destructive. It's all about strength and power, the ability to control others through force. But because only one person can come out on top in a dominance hierarchy, that person often has to knock others down in order to climb up, then continue to fight off contenders after earning the top spot. Stalin, for example, was notoriously paranoid and insecure in his hold on power, and during the Great Purge, he was responsible, directly or indirectly, for more than 600,000 deaths.[14]

Prestige, meanwhile, seems much less competitive, at least on the surface.[15] It's all about respect, which can't be taken by force, but rather must be freely conferred by admirers. Nevertheless, there's only so much respect to go around. In this regard, prestige is like a popularity contest, similar to the kind found in high schools around the world (only perhaps not quite as vapid). We earn prestige not just by being rich, beautiful, and good at sports, but also by being funny, artistic, smart, well-spoken, charming, and kind. These are all *relative* qualities, however. Compared to most other animals, every human is a certifiable genius—but that fact does little to help us in competitions within our own species. Similarly, even the poorest members of today's world are richer, by many material standards, than the kings and queens of yesteryear—and yet they remain at the bottom of the prestige ladder.

Another way to think about prestige is that it's your "price" on the market for friendship and association (just as sexual attractiveness is your "price" on the mating market). As in all markets, price is driven by supply and demand. We all have a similar (and highly limited) supply of friendship to offer to others, but the *demand* for our friendship varies greatly from person to person. Highly prestigious individuals have many claims on their time and attention, many would-be friends lining up at their door. Less prestigious individuals, meanwhile, have fewer claims on their time and attention, and must therefore offer their friendship at a discount. And everyone, with an eye to raising their price, strives to make themselves more attractive as a friend or associate—by learning new skills, acquiring more and better tools, and polishing their charms.

Now, our competitions for prestige often produce positive side effects such as art, science, and technological innovation.[16] But the prestige-seeking itself is more nearly a zero-sum game, which helps explain why we sometimes feel pangs of envy at even a close friend's success.

POLITICS

Aristotle famously called humans "the political animal," but it turns out, we aren't the only species who merit that title.[17]

In 1982, primatologist Frans de Waal published his influential book *Chimpanzee Politics*, which made a splash by ascribing *political* motives to nonhuman animals.[18] (It also introduced the word "Machiavellian" to the field of primatology.) De Waal's core insight was that human power struggles are structurally analogous to those that take place among chimpanzees. With the appropriate translations, chimps' political behaviors are intelligible to us; we recognize in them the same goals and motivations that *we* exhibit when we politick with our fellow humans.

What is it about the behavior of chimpanzees that inclines us to describe it as "political"? Like many other animals, chimps organize themselves into a dominance hierarchy, a more-or-less linear ordering from the strongest on top to the weakest on bottom, where stronger chimps make a habit of bullying the chimps below them in order to get better access to food, mates, and other opportunities. By itself, however, a dominance hierarchy is too simple and straightforward to warrant the label "politics." Chickens too have a dominance hierarchy—a pecking order—but few would accuse a chicken of scheming like Machiavelli.

So what turns an otherwise rigid, almost robotic dominance hierarchy into something teeming with politics? In a word: coalitions. Allies who wield power *together*. Here's de Waal again, from his later book *Our Inner Ape*:

> Two-against-one maneuvering is what lends chimpanzee power struggles both their richness and their danger. Coalitions are key. No male can rule by himself, at least not for long.[19]

In other words, if you're a male chimp in a community with other males, it's not enough simply to be strong or even the strongest. You also need to *gang up* with a team of other strong males. You need the ability to identify, attract, and retain good allies, and you need to be savvy enough to navigate the tumult as coalitions form, dissolve, and clash all around you.

Coalitions are what makes politics so *political*. Without the ability to form teams and work together toward shared goals, a species' "political" life will be stunted at the level of individual competition—every chicken for itself, pecking at every other chicken. But add just a dash of *cooperation* to the mix, and suddenly a species' political life begins to bloom.

Scientists have documented coalition politics in a variety of species. Primates, clearly, are a political bunch, as are whales and dolphins, wolves and lions, elephants and meerkats.[20] But we know of no species more political than our own. Just as human brains dwarf those of other species, both in size and in complexity, so too do our coalitions. These take many forms and go by many names. In government, coalitions appear as interest groups and political parties; in business, they are teams, companies, guilds, and trade associations. In high school, coalitions are called cliques or friends. On the street and in prison, they're called gangs. Sometimes they're simply called factions. They can be as small as two people voting a third off the island or as large as a globe-spanning religion. They have membership criteria (however formal or informal), the ability to recruit new members, and the ability to kick out current members.

Coalition politics is something we spend a *lot* of time doing. Whenever we anguish over the guest list for a party, we're playing politics. Whenever we join a church because we feel welcome there, or leave a job that isn't rewarding enough, we're following our political instincts. Finding and joining teams, dealing with the attendant headaches, and leaving them when necessary are behaviors that come as readily to us as pack-hunting to a wolf.[21]

Now, if you've read a biography of Henry Kissinger or Robert Moses, or watched *Survivor* or *Game of Thrones*, you know that coalition politics can get nasty. Winning tactics often include threats, counter-threats, betrayals, deceptions, and even violence; there's a reason "politics" is often used as a dirty word. But it would be a huge mistake to think that politics is all arm-twisting and backstabbing. It's also full of handshaking, backscratching, and even hugging.

This was an argument made by one of Niccolò Machiavelli's lesser-known but equally astute contemporaries, Baldassare Castiglione. Both men wrote books about how to navigate the political waters of 16th-century Italian city-states. Machiavelli's famous guidebook is *The Prince*, written for supreme rulers, while Castiglione wrote *The Book of the Courtier* for those of lesser nobility who sought favor at court. But although their subject matter is similar, in many ways, the two books are polar opposites. Machiavelli emphasizes the ruthless, amoral side of human politics, whereas Castiglione emphasizes the softer, more humane ways to curry favor. The ideal courtier, in Castiglione's opinion, should be well mannered and possessed of social graces. He should be skilled in horsemanship, poetry, music, and dance.[22] Rather than manipulating others through cunning and intimidation, the courtier should win their affections freely, through charm, flattery, and valuable companionship.[23]

Both Machiavelli and Castiglione are right, in their own ways. The two strategies they outline are both useful for succeeding in politics. It's important to note, however, that although Castiglione's methods are less *overtly* competitive, they nevertheless stem from similar incentives. Not every courtier can be the king's favorite; one man's fortune is his rival's setback. So it is ultimately the same drive—wanting to win at life's various competitions—that motivates both the scheming sociopath and the charming courtier.

STRUCTURAL SIMILARITIES

These three games—sex, politics, and social status—aren't perfectly distinct, of course. They overlap and share intermediate goals. Sometimes the prizes of one game become instruments in another. To succeed in the mating game, for example, it often pays to have high status and political clout—while an attractive mate can, in turn, raise one's social status.

The three games also share some important structural similarities. As we've mentioned, they're all competitive games where not everyone can win, and where unfettered competition has the potential to get nasty. This is especially true of both sex and social status in that there are only so many mates and friends to go around. But it's also true of politics. Despite the fact that it's possible to cooperate, politically, in ways that "enlarge the pie" for everyone, this is the exception rather than the rule—especially for our distant ancestors. In most contexts, for one coalition to succeed, others must fail. Importantly, however, members *within* a coalition can earn themselves a larger slice of pie by cooperating—a fact that makes politics such an intoxicating game.

The other important similarity is that each game requires two complementary skill sets: the ability to *evaluate potential partners* and the ability to *attract good partners*. In sex, the partners we're looking for are mates. In social status, we're looking for friends and associates. And in politics, we're looking for allies, people to team up with.

When we evaluate others, we're trying to estimate their value as partners, and so we're looking for certain traits or qualities. In our mates, we want those with good genes who will make good parents. In our friends and associates, we want those who have skills, resources, and compatible personalities—and the more loyal they are to us, the better. And we're looking for similar qualities in our political allies, since they're basically friends chosen for a specific purpose.

At the same time, in order to attract partners, we need to advertise our own traits—the same ones we're looking for in others. By displaying, accentuating, and even exaggerating these desirable traits, we raise our own value, helping to ensure that we'll be chosen by more and/or higher-quality mates, more and/or higher-status friends, and better coalitions. All of these competitions thereby result in arms races. Just as the redwoods are competing for light from the sun, we're competing for the "light" of attention and affection from potential mates, friends, and allies. And in each game, the way to win is to stand out over one's rivals.

In this context, the advice in Matthew 7:1—"Judge not, lest you be judged"—is difficult to follow. It goes against the grain of every evolved instinct we have, which is to judge others readily, while at the same time advertising ourselves so that we may be judged by others. To understand the competitive side of human nature, we would do well to turn Matthew 7:1 on its head: "Judge freely, and accept that you too will be judged."[24]

SIGNALS AND SIGNALING

Both of these tasks—judging and being judged—are mediated by *signals*.

A signal, in evolutionary biology,[25] is anything used to communicate or convey information. Unblemished skin or fur, for example, is a signal of a healthy organism; compare a prize-winning beagle to a mangy mutt. A growl is a signal of aggression—and the growl's depth is a signal of the creature's size.

Signals are said to be *honest* when they reliably correspond to an underlying trait or fact about the sender. Otherwise they are dishonest or deceptive.

The temptation to deceive is ubiquitous. Deception allows an agent to reap benefits without incurring costs. (See Chapter 5 for more on deception.) That's why the best signals—the most honest ones—are expensive.[26] More precisely, they are differentially expensive: costly to produce, but even more costly to fake.[27] A lion's loud, deep growl, for example, is an honest signal of a large body cavity, because it's impossible for a small creature, like a mouse, to make the same sound.

Sometimes it's even necessary to do something risky or wasteful in order to prove that you have a desirable trait. This is known as the *handicap principle*.[28] It explains why species with good defense mechanisms, like skunks and poison dart frogs, evolve high-contrast colors: unless it can defend itself, an animal that stands out quickly becomes another animal's lunch. For a nonbiological example, consider the difference between blue jeans and dress pants. Jeans are durable and don't need to be washed every day, whereas dress pants demand a bit more in terms of upkeep—which is precisely why they're considered more formal attire.

In the human social realm, honest signaling and the handicap principle are best reflected in the dictum, "Actions speak louder than words."[29] The problem with words is that they cost almost nothing; talk is usually too cheap. Which is a more honest signal of your value to a company: being told "great job!" or getting a raise?

We rely heavily on honest signals in the competitive arenas we've been discussing—that is, whenever we try to evaluate others as potential mates, friends, and allies. Loyal friends can distinguish themselves from fair-weather friends by visiting you in the hospital, for example. Healthy mates can distinguish themselves from unhealthy ones by going to the gym or running a marathon. Initiates who get gang tattoos thereby commit themselves to the gang in a way that no verbal pledge could hope to accomplish. Of course, we also use these honest signals whenever we wish to advertise our own value as a friend, mate, or teammate.

Note that we don't always need to be *conscious* of the signals we're sending and receiving. We may have evolved an instinct to make art, for example, as a means of advertising our artistic skills and free time (survival surplus)—but that's not necessarily what we're thinking about as we whittle a sculpture from a piece of driftwood. We may simply be thinking about the beauty of the sculpture (for more on art, see Chapter 11). Nevertheless, the deeper logic of many of our strangest and most unique behaviors may lie in their value as signals.[30]

One thing that makes signaling hard to analyze, in practice, is the phenomenon of *countersignaling*. For example, consider how someone can be either an enemy, a casual friend, or a close friend. Casual friends want to distinguish themselves from enemies, and they might use signals of warmth and friendliness—things like smiles, hugs, and remembering small details about each other. Meanwhile, close friends want to distinguish themselves from casual friends, and one of the ways they can do it is by being *unfriendly*, at least on the surface. When a close friend forgets his wallet and can't pay for lunch, you might call him an idiot. This works only when you're so confident of your friendship that you can (playfully) insult him, without worrying that it will jeopardize your friendship. This isn't something a casual friend can get away with as easily, and it may even serve to bring close friends closer together.

Thus signals are often arranged into a hierarchy, from non-signals to signals to counter-signals. Outsiders to an interaction may not always be able to distinguish non-signals from counter-signals. But insiders usually know how to interpret them, if only on an intuitive level.

When signals are used in competitive games, like sex, status, and politics, an arms race often results. In order to outdo the other competitors, each participant tries to send the strongest possible signal. This can result in some truly spectacular achievements: Bach's concertos, Gauguin's paintings, Shakespeare's sonnets and plays, Rockefeller's philanthropic foundation, and Einstein's theories of relativity. And sometimes, like the redwoods, humans too compete to reach for the sky, whether by climbing Mount Everest, building pyramids and skyscrapers, or launching rockets to the moon.

LOOKING AHEAD

As we think about our own ancestry and how we were shaped by it, it pays to keep the redwoods in mind. Faced with intense intra-species competition, they literally rose to the occasion, out of the darkness and into the light. So too with many of our most exaggerated features.

The problem with competitive struggles, however, is that they're enormously wasteful. The redwoods are so much taller than they need to be. If only they could coordinate not to all grow so tall—if they could institute a "height cap" at 100 feet (30 meters), say—the whole species would be better off. All the energy that they currently waste racing upward, they could instead invest in other pursuits, like making more pinecones in order to spread further, perhaps into new territory. Competition, in this case, holds the entire species back.

Unfortunately, the redwoods aren't capable of coordinating to enforce a height cap, and natural selection can't help them either. There's no equilibrium where all trees curtail their growth "for the good of the species." If a population of redwoods *were* somehow restraining themselves, it would take only a few mutations for one of the trees to break ranks and grab all the sunlight for itself. This rogue tree would then soak in more energy from the sun, and thereby outcompete its rivals and leave more descendants, ensuring that the next generation of redwoods would be even more rivalrous and competitive—until eventually they were all back to being as tall as they are today.

But our species is different. Unlike other natural processes, we *can* look ahead. And we've developed ways to avoid wasteful competition, by coordinating our actions using norms and norm enforcement—a topic we turn to in the next chapter.

Norms

Most of us have been in a situation like this: You're standing in line to buy a movie ticket, chatting quietly with a friend and minding your own business, when a group of strangers casually angles in ahead of you. Instantly, you flush with adrenaline. Your heart starts racing and you can feel the heat surge up your neck and into your face. "*Did they really just cut in line?*" you ask yourself as you brace for the moment-of-truth decision: Confront them, or let it slide?[1]

On the one hand, their behavior doesn't materially affect your life. It won't take more than an extra minute to get your movie ticket. Plus you'll never see these strangers again. And what if they're the violent sort? What if one of them picks a fight? What if they have a knife or a gun? Having to spend one extra minute in line doesn't justify any of this risk.

But on the other hand, *they cheated!* You can't let them walk all over you. What kind of self-respecting person lets others cut in line and get away with it?

This dilemma, and the strong physiological reaction that accompanies it, is part of a behavioral toolkit that's universal among humans, something we've inherited from our forager ancestors. Our behaviors and reactions may not always make sense in a modern context, but they evolved because our ancestors confronted situations like this all the time, and what was useful for them is still (mostly) useful for us, especially when we're facing people we know rather than strangers on the street.

As we saw in the previous chapter, redwood trees are trapped in unfettered competition with each other. Under natural selection, there's no way for them to curtail their growth "for the good of the species." But humans are different. Unlike the rest of nature, we *can* sometimes see ahead and coordinate to avoid unnecessary competition. This is one of our species' superpowers—that we're occasionally able to turn wasteful competition into productive cooperation. Instead of always bull-rushing to the front of a line, for example, we can wait patiently and orderly. But as the occasional line-cutter reminds us, there's always a temptation to cheat, and maintaining order isn't always easy.

For sociologists and anthropologists, conventions like queueing are known as *norms*. They're the rules or standards about how members of a community should behave. They range from loose, informal guidelines, like what to wear to a cocktail party, all the way to explicit, strictly enforced laws, like needing a license to drive on public roads. Table manners, sportsmanship, maritime law, the U.S. Tax Code, Robert's Rules of Order, and the use of "inside voices" at a library—these are but a few examples of the variety of norms that have proliferated in human cultures. And as we'll see in coming chapters, the desire to skirt and subvert norms is one of the key reasons we deceive ourselves about our own intentions.

Human groups develop norms because they (typically) benefit the majority of people in the group. Now, some norms, especially top-down laws, can be oppressive or extractive and an overall detriment to the societies that enforce them. But most norms—especially of the bottom-up, grassroots variety—are beneficial; they're one of the main ways we suppress competition and promote cooperation. In other words, we hold ourselves back, collectively, for our own good.

In *Debt*, the anthropologist David Graeber tells the story of Tei Reinga, a Maori villager and "notorious glutton" who used to wander up and down the New Zealand coast, badgering the local fishermen by asking for the best portions of their catch. Since it's impolite in Maori culture (as in many cultures) to refuse a direct request for food, the fishermen would oblige—but with ever-increasing reluctance. And so as Reinga continued to ask for food, their resentment grew until "one day, people decided enough was enough and killed him."

This story is extreme, to say the least, but it illustrates how norm-following and norm-enforcement can be a very high-stakes game. Reinga flouted an important norm (against freeloading) and eventually paid dearly for it. But just as tellingly, the fishermen who put him to death felt so duty-bound by a different norm (the norm of food-sharing) that they followed it even to the point of building up murderous resentment. "Couldn't you just have said no to Reinga's requests?!" we want to shout at the villagers. But similarly we should ask ourselves, "Can't we just let it go when someone cuts in line?" These instincts run deep.

Most norms, of course, aren't enforced on pain of death. In general, the punishment will be tailored to the crime. When you forget to zip up your fly, for example, no one's going to arrest you for public indecency; they're just going to snicker. For minor transgressions, then, we have an arsenal of soft sanctions we try to use before escalating to more serious forms of punishment. Instead of lashing out physically at a transgressor, we might roll our eyes or flash a disapproving scowl. If body language doesn't work, we might ask the transgressor to stop (politely or otherwise) or yell and demand an apology, perhaps in front of others.

But the threat of some kind of punishment must always be present, or a "norm" is little more than hot air. "Covenants," says Thomas Hobbes, "without the sword, are but words."[2] Similarly, you can't have enforcement without creating a de facto norm, regardless of whether you're willing to admit that it's a norm or not. In cults of personality, for example, such as those that formed around Mao Zedong or Steve Jobs, criticizing the leader is often frowned upon, and punished even by people other than the leaders themselves even if "criticizing the leader" isn't *officially* forbidden. The essence of a norm, then, lies not in the words we use to describe it, but in which behaviors get punished and what form the punishment takes.

OUR FORAGER ANCESTORS

Humans were the first animals on Earth to develop true norms. And even though we currently live in a world with a great variety of norms, including strict laws enforced by a complex legal system, our world (and our minds) grew out of an earlier, simpler world and still bears many features from that earlier period. For this reason, it's helpful to get acquainted with our species' upbringing.

Foraging, also known as hunting and gathering, is the lifestyle our ancestors practiced until the agricultural revolution starting around 10,000 B.C. Now, the portrait we're about to paint of the foraging lifestyle is actually a portrait of *modern* foragers, peoples who have maintained this way of life into the 20th and 21st centuries. Such groups are rare; perhaps as few as 20 are known to anthropologists. And no doubt they have been influenced by modernity in various ways, whether through contact with settled civilizations or simply by being relegated to environments that are unprofitable for farming, trading, and other "civilized" purposes. Even so, the data about this way of life is consistent enough, and corroborated by enough archaeological evidence and reasoning, for us to develop at least a rough sketch of how our ancestors probably lived.[3]

Foragers live a nomadic life in bands of 20 to 50 individuals. "Foraging," here, refers to their way of getting food—that is, extracting it from the natural environment, rather than by farming or herding. Most of their calories come from gathering fruit, nuts, and vegetables, but many groups supplement these gatherings with calories from fishing, hunting, and occasionally scavenging. Despite its prominence in the public imagination, big-game hunting is rarely the main source of calories.

Foragers are intensely reliant on each other for survival. To be without a band for more than a short time is effectively a death sentence. Everyone is expected to try to provide for themselves and to pitch in and help each other as they're able (no freeloading), but they can reasonably expect help from the rest of the band if they fall on hard times. At minimum, cooperative social life includes sharing food among the group, helping and learning from each other, hunting and scavenging in groups, coordinating to defend the band from predators and rival groups, and caring for each other when sick. Men, women, and children divide labor variously among themselves, but there's only a limited division of labor *within* each class. (In other words, most men do the same tasks as other men, and similarly for women and children.) Favors are traded freely,[4] but unlike in large modern economies, there are few gains to be made by trading material goods.

Each band moves throughout a large territory, setting up camp ("home base") in a particular location for a few weeks or a few months, and moving camp at least several times a year, when food becomes scarce or to take advantage of seasonal opportunities. Owing to their nomadism, foragers don't have much in the way of property; they own only as much as they can carry. They typically have loose associations with the small handful of neighboring bands, primarily for socializing. Bands usually don't see themselves as owning territory. Rivalries between groups do sometimes occur, sometimes even leading to (usually male) deaths, but all-out war is quite rare and tends to occur only in dense regions rich in resources. When to move camp and how to relate to other bands are all group-level decisions, discussed in open meetings where everyone has a say. Decisions are made by consensus, and dissenters are free to leave the band.

Foragers tend to be patrilocal, meaning that men stay in their native band, typically for their entire lives, while women move to another when they come of age. (Thus there are many kinship ties between neighboring bands.) Men and women don't typically mate for life, although they do practice years-long serial monogamy peppered with the occasional infidelity. A typical sexual relationship will produce at least one and perhaps a few children, and the father will help feed and raise his children for at least the first few years.

Despite occasional periods of hardship, foragers enjoy plenty of leisure time—more so than farmers, in fact—which they spend talking, joking, playing, singing, dancing, making art, and otherwise socializing among themselves.

The most striking feature of the nomadic foraging lifestyle, distinguishing it both from the chimpanzee lifestyle and our modern way of life, is its fierce egalitarianism. The main political actors within a band—which always includes adult men and sometimes adult women as well, depending on the culture—relate to each other as peers and equals. Relative to foragers, both chimps and farmers (and to a large extent industrial societies) are much more hierarchical and tolerant of direct authority and high degrees of overt inequality. Hierarchy, however, is alien to the forager way of life. Insofar as there are leaders within a forager band, they are people who are voluntarily respected by the rest of the band; think "council of elders" rather than an alpha strongman.

Egalitarianism among foragers is concerned primarily with preventing a single individual or coalition from dominating (and thereby making life miserable for) the rest of the group. This leads foragers to be vigilant for early warning signs of people who position themselves above others. This includes dominating or bullying individuals (outside the household or immediate family), bragging, seeking authority too eagerly, ganging up with other members of the group, and otherwise attempting to control others' behavior. Foragers would readily support the motto of the early American general Christopher Gadsden: "Don't tread on me."

Many of the norms that were common among our forager ancestors are by now deeply embedded in human nature. But these aren't our only norms. Most societies also teach their children norms specific to their society. This ability of societies to adopt differing norms is part of what has let humans spread across the Earth, by adopting norms better suited to each local environment.

This "cultural flexibility" also enabled our ancestors to implement the huge behavior changes required to turn hunters and gatherers into farmers and herders, roughly 10,000 years ago. Farmers have norms supporting marriage, war, and property, as well as rough treatment of animals, lower classes, and slaves. To help enforce these new norms, farmers also had stronger norms of social conformity, as well as stronger religions with moralizing gods.

WHY NORMS?

The insistent egalitarianism of our ancestors was arguably the world's first true norm. But how was it that our ancestors, and no other primate species, developed this characteristic political style?

Language is clearly a big factor. It's hard—although certainly not impossible—to imagine a community developing and enforcing norms without having language to express them. But before and beneath the communication challenge lies a more fundamental challenge: how to ensure that everyone, even the most powerful members of the community, abide by its norms.

It's important to distinguish what humans are doing, in following norms, from what other animals are doing in their related patterns of behavior. An animal that decides not to pick a fight is, in most cases, simply worried about the risk of getting injured—not about some abstract "norm against violence." Likewise, an animal that shares food with non-kin is typically just angling for future reciprocity—not following some "norm of food-sharing." The incentives surrounding true norms are more complex. When we do something "wrong," we have to worry about reprisal not just from the wronged party but also from third parties.[5] Frequently, this means the entire rest of our local group, or at least a majority of it. Big strong Albert could easily steal from wimpy Bob without fearing trouble from Bob himself, but in human groups, Albert would then face sanctions from the rest of the community. *Collective enforcement*, then, is the essence of norms. This is what enables the egalitarian political order so characteristic of the forager lifestyle.

If you refrain from hitting people because you're afraid they'll hit you back, that's not a norm. If you're afraid of speaking out against a dangerous regime because you're worried about retaliation from the regime itself, that's not a norm. But if you're worried that your neighbors might disapprove and even coordinate to punish you, then you're most likely dealing with a norm. It's this third-party, collective enforcement that's unique to humans.

Paul Bingham calls this "coalition enforcement," highlighting the fact that norm violators are punished by a coalition, that is, people acting in concert.[6] Christopher Boehm calls it a "reverse dominance hierarchy,"[7] where instead of the strongest apes dominating the group, in humans it's the rest of the group, working together, that's able to dominate the strongest apes and keep them effectively in check. What both thinkers identify as a key to enabling this kind of behavior, in our species and ours alone, is the use of deadly weapons (see Box 3).

Box 3: Weapons

Weapons are a game changer for two reasons. First, they level the playing field between weak and strong members of a group.[8] The earliest weapons were probably little more than sharp or heavy rocks, but still they would have sufficed to kill or seriously injure their targets. Without such weapons, the strong can physically dominate the weak without having to worry too much about retaliation. Even if a weaker chimp surprises a stronger chimp by attacking it while it's asleep, the weaker chimp is unlikely to get enough advantage (one or two extra blows or an extra bite) to tip the odds in its favor. With weapons, however, landing the first blow can yield a decisive advantage. A weaker human can maim or kill a stronger one with just a single large rock to the head or sharp rock to the neck.

Another way weapons alter the balance of power applies to projectile weapons like stones or spears. Such distance weapons make it much easier for a *coalition* to gang up on a single individual.[9] Without distance weapons, all violence must take place at close range in hand-to-hand combat. This ensures that there's little value in ganging up on a single individual with more than about three attackers; a fourth attacker would only get in the way. And a three-against-one melee still carries a big risk of serious injury for the attackers, especially if the one they're attacking is the strongest of the group. But with distance weapons, a coalition of five or seven can gang up on a despotic alpha individual with much lower risk to themselves, simply by surrounding the alpha while carrying heavy rocks or spears.

Once weapons enter the picture, physical strength is no longer the most crucial factor in determining a hominid's success within a group. It's still important, mind you, but not singularly important. In particular, political skill—being able to identify, join, and possibly lead the most effective coalition—takes over as the determining factor.

So, if Boehm, Bingham, and the others are right, it was learning to use deadly weapons that was the inflection point in the trajectory of our species' political behavior. Once our ancestors learned how to kill and punish each other collectively, nothing would be the same. Coalition size would balloon almost overnight. Politics would then become exponentially more complicated and require more intelligence to navigate, and brains would struggle to catch up for thousands of generations. And soon, norms would begin to proliferate, starting with the norm against being a too-dominant alpha, and continuing to this day as we invent new norms for every new context we develop (e.g., netiquette).

Theories about what happened among our distant ancestors are necessarily somewhat speculative. But whatever happened (and in what order), where we ended up as a species is clear: We are social animals who use language to decide on rules that the whole group must follow, and we use the threat of collective punishment to enforce these rules against even the strongest individuals. And although many rules vary from group to group, there are some—like those prohibiting rape and murder—that are universal to all human cultures.[10]

Even with our weapons and the ability to punish people collectively, however, norms can be very difficult to enforce. This important fact is often masked by our modern institutions—police, courts, prisons, and so forth—which work pretty smoothly, but only as the result of millennia of cultural evolution. For our distant ancestors, though, and for modern people in environments without strong oversight and governance, norm enforcement is a tricky business. This includes most of our social life, which is governed less by the threat of lawsuits and jail and more by the awkward (but mostly functional) norm-enforcement behaviors of our peers. It's more like keeping people from cutting in line than calling the police to deal with robbery.

That's why humans have at least two other tricks up our sleeves to incentivize good norm-following behavior: gossip and reputation.

GOSSIP AND REPUTATION

Among laypeople, gossip gets a pretty bad rap. But anthropologists see it differently. Gossip—talking about people behind their backs, often focusing on their flaws or misdeeds—is a feature of every society ever studied.[11] And while it can often be mean-spirited and hurtful, gossip is also an important process for curtailing bad behavior, especially among powerful people. If and when the North Korean regime is eventually toppled, for example, it will be in large part because citizens whispered in private about the failings of the "supreme leader."

Kevin experienced this benefit of gossip at a previous job, when he and his teammates accidentally hired a bully. They didn't immediately realize their mistake, as often happens in these situations, because the bully's bad behavior developed gradually, and only in proportion to how much influence he had gained at the company. But by the time it was clear that he was a bad apple, no one was willing to stand up to him. He had become too powerful, and it wasn't in anyone's individual self-interest to risk accusing him.

The solution was gossip. Through lots of two- and three-person discussions behind closed doors, Kevin and his teammates eventually settled on the consensus opinion that the bully had to go, and that they would all coordinate to make it happen. These conversations eventually led to his termination. But it took a lot longer than expected, and the outcome was far from certain. If the bully had been slightly more powerful, or slightly less troublesome, it might have turned out differently.

This kind of drama plays out in every kind of human community, from work teams and church groups to social clubs and political parties. In many of these cases, gossip is the way we coordinate on throwing someone out.

But gossip is important and useful even when it doesn't lead to formal sanctions, because it can substantially damage the reputation of whomever is being gossiped about. It's the threat of such reputational damage that provides an important check on bad behavior, especially in cases when direct punishment is too difficult or costly to enforce. Of course, the ability of gossip to damage someone's reputation is also why gossip is so often used maliciously. But when it comes to norm enforcement, it's important to see this as an abuse—a perversion—of an otherwise important sanctioning mechanism.

Reputation is also important for incentivizing people to help enforce norms. Standing up to norm violators can be risky, especially when they're powerful. It's rarely in people's best interests to stick out their necks to punish transgressors. But throw some reputation into the mix and it can suddenly become profitable. Someone who helps evict a cheater will be celebrated for her leadership. Who would you rather team up with: someone who stands by while rules are flouted, or someone who stands up for what's right?

When everyone is watching and judging everyone else—both for their individual behaviors and their efforts to punish cheaters—norms and their enforcement become viable enterprises (see Box 4).

Box 4: The Meta-Norm

Kevin's story illustrates that it's difficult to enforce norms because anyone who tries to mete out punishment faces the risk of retaliation. It doesn't seem worth it—and yet, somehow, humans manage to enforce a variety of norms. How can we resolve this puzzle?

One of the first scientists to study this formally was Robert Axelrod, a political scientist and game theorist who constructed a simple but illustrative model of norm-related behavior.[12] What Axelrod found is that, in most situations (involving a variety of different costs and benefits, including the costs of helping to punish), people have no incentive to punish cheaters.

However—and this was Axelrod's great contribution—the model can be made to work in favor of the good guys with one simple addition: *a norm of punishing anyone who doesn't punish others*. Axelrod called this the "meta-norm."

The meta-norm highlights how groups need to create an incentive for good citizens to punish cheaters. Whether that incentive comes by way of the stick or the carrot doesn't really matter. Axelrod framed it in terms of the stick, in that *not* standing up to a cheater is itself a punishable act. But a group may fare just as well by *positively* rewarding people who help to punish cheaters.

Many other scientists have replicated Axelrod's results in the lab, with human subjects playing various games that allow players to cheat and punish each other. And there's good evidence that many real communities employ a version of the meta-norm. In the United States, for example, it's unlawful to witness a crime without reporting it.

SUBTLE BUT IMPORTANT NORMS

As we've mentioned, humans have developed a wide variety of norms to constrain individual behavior. Many of these, like the norms against murder, rape, assault, and theft, are so obvious, and so strongly enforced, that they simply aren't relevant for this book. The norms we care about here are the subtle ones, violations of which are so hard to detect that we often don't notice even when we do it ourselves.

Typically, these are crimes of *intent*. If you just happen to be friendly with someone else's spouse, no big deal. But if you're friendly *with romantic or sexual intention*s, that's inappropriate. By targeting intentions rather than actions, norms can more precisely regulate the behavior patterns that cause problems within communities. (It would be ham-fisted and unduly cumbersome to ban friendliness, for example.) But regulating intentions also opens the door to various kinds of cheating, which we'll explore in Chapter 4.

Part of our thesis is that these weaker norms, the ones that regulate our intentions, are harder to notice, especially when we violate them ourselves, because we've developed that blind spot—the elephant in the brain. For this reason, it pays to dwell on a few of them, to remind ourselves that there's a lot of social pressure to conform to these norms, but that we *would* benefit from violating these norms freely, if only we could get away with it.

Bragging

Clearly we all enjoy tooting our own horns now and again, and so bragging (or showing off) is tolerated occasionally and in small doses. And in some contexts, bragging may even be celebrated—consider Muhammad Ali, for instance. But in most contexts, we start to bristle when people get too full of themselves. It's part of that forager aversion to dominance, since bragging is a way to increase one's influence and dominance within a community. We'd be wary of Daniel Kahneman, for example, if he went around introducing himself as a Nobel Prize–winner; we'd wonder why he felt the need to put himself above everyone else. For this reason, we actively celebrate people for being humble, and enjoy seeing arrogant people brought down a peg or two.

But note that there remains a strong incentive to brag and show off. We need people to notice our good qualities, skills, and achievements; how else will they know to choose us as friends, mates, and teammates? We want people to notice our charitable contributions, our political connectedness, and our prowess in art, sport, and school. If it weren't verboten, we'd post to Facebook every time we donated to charity, got a raise at work, or made friends with an important person. But because bragging is frowned upon, we have to be a little more discreet—a topic we'll explore in the next chapter.

Currying Favor

When a high-status person chooses someone as a mate, friend, or teammate, it's often seen as an endorsement of this associate, raising that person's status. This (among other things) creates an incentive to win the affections of people with high status.

But there are acceptable and unacceptable ways to do this. It's perfectly acceptable just to "be yourself," for example. If you're naturally impressive or likable, then it seems right and proper for others to like and respect you as well. What's *not* acceptable is sycophancy: brown-nosing, bootlicking, groveling, toadying, and sucking up. Nor is it acceptable to "buy" high-status associates via cash, flattery, or sexual favors. These tactics are frowned on or otherwise considered illegitimate, in part because they ruin the association signal for everyone else. We prefer celebrities to endorse products because they actually like those products, not because they just want cash. We think bosses should promote workers who do a good job, not workers who just sleep with the boss.

Nevertheless, these temptations exist.

Subgroup Politics

Like the norms against bragging and currying favor, the norm against subgroup politics is routinely violated. There are large areas of modern life where people are actively, aggressively political, such as in Washington, D.C. But the taboo against politics is typically strong in small-group settings. In most workplaces, for example, it's considered bad form, even a danger to the group, for someone to be openly "political." Warring factions can tear a group apart, or at least keep it from achieving its full potential.

Of course, as with bragging, there are gains to be had by individuals from acting politically; that's why the norm exists. But it also means we should expect to find the norm routinely violated, especially covertly.

Selfish Motives

Perhaps the most comprehensive norm of all—a catch-all that includes bragging, currying favor, and political behavior, but extends to everything else that we're supposed to do for prosocial reasons—is the norm against selfish motives. It's also the linchpin of our thesis. Consider how awkward it is to answer certain questions by appealing to selfish motives. Why did you break up with your girlfriend? "I'm hoping to find someone better." Why do you want to be a doctor? "It's a prestigious job with great pay." Why do you draw cartoons for the school paper? "I want people to like me."

There's truth in all these answers, but we systematically avoid giving them, preferring instead to accentuate our higher, purer motives.

GETTING OUR BEARINGS

In Chapter 2, we discussed how humans, like all animals, are competitive and selfish, and argued that competition was an important driving force in the evolution of our big brains. Then, in this chapter, we discussed how humans, *unlike* other animals, learned to limit wasteful intra-species competition by the use of norms.

Careful readers will have noticed the tension between these two facts. Specifically, if norms succeed at restricting competition, it reduces the incentive to be a clever competitor. For example, suppose our ancestors were successful in enforcing their "no politics" norm, nipping every political act right in the bud. In such a climate, there's little value in lugging around a big, politically savvy brain. In fact, big brains are extremely expensive; ours, for example, eats up one-fifth of our resting energy. So successful norm-enforcement should have caused human brains to shrink.

But of course our brains didn't shrink—they ballooned. And this wasn't in spite of our norms, but *because* of them. To find out why, we turn to the topic of cheating.

Cheating

Everybody cheats.

Let's just get that out up front; there's no use denying it. Yes, some people cheat less than others, and we ought to admire them for it. But no one makes it through life without cutting a few corners. There are simply too many rules and norms, and to follow them all would be inhuman.

Most of us honor the big, important rules, like those prohibiting robbery, arson, rape, and murder. But we routinely violate small and middling norms. We lie, jaywalk, take office supplies from work, fudge numbers on our tax returns, make illegal U-turns, suck up to our bosses, have extramarital affairs, and use recreational drugs. Your two coauthors, for example, will both confess to having committed more than half of these minor crimes.[1]

Why do we cheat? It's simple: cheating lets us reap benefits without incurring the typical costs. "Nearly 100% of elite competitive swimmers pee in the pool," says Carly Geehr, a member of the U.S. National Swim Team. "Some deny it, some proudly embrace it, but everyone does."[2] Why? Because it's too inconvenient to take bathroom breaks in the middle of practice.

Our ancestors did a lot of cheating. How do we know? One source of evidence is the fact that our brains have special-purpose adaptations for detecting cheaters.[3] When abstract logic puzzles are framed as cheating scenarios, for example, we're a lot better at solving them. This is one of the more robust findings in evolutionary psychology, popularized by the wife-and-husband team Leda Cosmides and John Tooby.[4]

But of course, if our ancestors needed to evolve brains that were good at cheater-*detection*, it's because their peers were routinely trying to cheat them—and those peers were also our ancestors. Thus early humans (and protohumans) were locked in an evolutionary arms race, pitting the skills of some at cheating against the skills of others at detecting cheating.

Human brains also have adaptations that help us cheat and evade norms. The most basic way to get away with something—whether you're stealing, cheating on your spouse, or just picking your nose—is simply to avoid being seen. One of our norm-evasion adaptations, then, is to be highly attuned to the gaze of others, especially when it's directed at us. Eyes that are looking straight at us jump out from a crowd.[5] Across dozens of experiments, participants who were being watched—even just by cartoon eyes—were less likely to cheat.[6] People also cheat less in full (vs. dim) light,[7] or when the concept of God, the all-seeing watcher, is activated in their minds.[8]

Perhaps more important is the emotion of *shame* and the behaviors that attend to it. Shame is the anguish we feel at being seen by others in degrading circumstances.[9] When we feel shame, like when we're the subject of scandal, we cover our faces, hang our heads, or avoid social contact altogether. And it's our *fear* of shame that prompts us either to refrain from cheating, or else to cover our tracks so others don't find out.

But we need to be careful here. If we focus too much on how cheaters avoid detection, it will distract us from a much more interesting type of cheating: doing it out in the open.

Consider these two very different norm-evasion scenarios:

1. *Cheating on a test.* When taking the test, you slip out to the bathroom to look up answers on your phone.
2. *Drinking in public.* In most parts of the United States, drinking alcohol in public is illegal. But there's a time-honored solution, which is to wrap your bottle in a brown paper bag.

In the first case—cheating on a test—your goal is simple: don't let the professor find out. The professor has a strong interest in keeping things fair, so in order to get away with cheating, you need to be as discreet and furtive as possible.

The incentives that govern drinking in public, however, are considerably more subtle. Crucially, it doesn't really fool anyone when you hide your booze in a paper bag—least of all the police. If the police want to cite you for public drinking, they can just waltz over, catch the smell of alcohol on your breath, and arrest you or issue a citation. But they usually won't bother.

Why not?

That's the puzzle we're going to study in this chapter—how we can often get away with cheating using only a modest amount of discretion. Again, this isn't true of all forms of cheating; people don't look the other way when they find a dead body. But there are many cases where the thinnest of pretexts, the most modest of fig leaves, can tip the scales of justice.

A QUICK CAVEAT

As we discuss cheating in the rest of this chapter (and the rest of the book), it's important not to get distracted by the urge to moralize about how wrong it is. There's a time and place for discussing how we *should* behave; in fact, we're so keen to moralize that we take almost every time and place as an opportunity to do so. But we need this book to be a judgment-free zone where we can admit to our bad tendencies and motives without worrying that we're falling short of our ideals. We need here to see ourselves as we are, not as we'd like to be.

Note also that, depending on your moral compass, some of these norm violations won't be considered "wrong." Recreational drug use is an oft-cited example. But regardless of whether it's wrong to do drugs, much of society still treats it as a form of cheating; drug users still have to take evasive maneuvers. So again, we'll be taking an amoral stance. We need to stay focused on how people break and skirt the rules, not whether their behavior is good or bad or whether the rules are just or unjust.

COMMON KNOWLEDGE

In Hans Christian Andersen's famous fairy tale "The Emperor's New Clothes," an emperor is swindled when two con men come to town offering to weave him an expensive new outfit. In fact, the "outfit" they weave is nothing more than thin air, but they tell the emperor that the clothes are invisible only to people who are stupid and incompetent. Anxious about his own intelligence, the emperor plays along, and so do all his subjects. "What fine, beautiful clothes!" they all say. Finally, during a procession through town, a small child blurts out the truth: "The emperor is naked!" And suddenly the spell is broken. Everyone decides that if an innocent child can't see the clothes, then there is nothing to see. They've all been duped.

The key to understanding this fairy tale, and much of what we're going to discuss in this book, is the concept of *common knowledge*.[10] For a piece of information to be "common knowledge" within a group of people, it's not enough simply for everyone to know it. Everyone must also know that everyone else knows it, and know that they know that they know it, and so on. It could as easily be called "open" or "conspicuous knowledge."

In his book *Rational Ritual*, the political scientist Michael Chwe illustrates common knowledge using email.[11] If you invite your friends to a party using the "To" and "Cc" fields, the party will be common knowledge—because every recipient can see every other recipient. But if you invite your guests using the "Bcc" field, even though each recipient *individually* will know about the party, it won't be common knowledge. We might refer to information distributed this way, in the "Bcc" style, as *closeted* rather than common.

Whether information is common or closeted can make a world of difference. In "The Emperor's New Clothes," the whole town knew that the king was being swindled by the con men, but this fact was crucially *not* common knowledge. Everyone saw the king was naked, but at the same time, everyone was worried that *other people* might believe the con men—so no adult was willing to speak up and risk looking like a fool. And yet, once the innocent child said what everyone was thinking, it broke the conspiracy of silence. And then, like water from a bursting dam, knowledge flooded out from the closets and into the commons.

Common knowledge is the difference between privately telling an individual and making a big public announcement; between a lesbian who's still in the closet (although everyone suspects her of being a lesbian), and one who's fully open about her sexuality; between an awkward moment that everyone tries to pretend didn't happen and one that everyone acknowledges (and can hopefully laugh about). Common knowledge is information that's fully "on the record," available for everyone to see and discuss openly.

Here's another way to think about it. We typically treat discretion or secret-keeping as an activity that has only one important dimension: how *widely* a piece of information is known. But actually there are two dimensions to keeping a secret: how *widely* it's known and how *openly*[12] or *commonly* it's known. And a secret can be widely known without being openly known—the closeted lesbian's sexuality, for example, or the fact that the emperor is naked.

Cheating is largely an exercise in discretion; in order to get away with something, you need to keep others from finding out about it. Sometimes only one dimension of secrecy is relevant. When you cheat on a test, for example, all that matters is whether one particular person—the professor—finds out. Conversely, when you drink alcohol on the street, it matters very little which particular people, or even how many of them, realize what you're doing; what matters more is how *openly* it's known. And this is where a thin brown bag can make all the difference.

If you brazenly flaunt an open beer bottle, the police are likely to give you trouble. This is because when you drink openly, it's clear not only to the *police* that you're breaking the law, but also to every passing citizen, including the most prudish members of the morality brigade (as well as impressionable children and their concerned parents). A police officer who turns a blind eye to *conspicuous* public drinking is open to a lot more criticism, from everyone involved, than an officer who ignores *discreet* public drinking. In this case, the brown paper bag doesn't fool the police officers themselves, but it provides them with just enough cover to avoid taking flak from their constituents.

WHEN A LITTLE DISCRETION GOES A LONG WAY

"Tickets! I need tickets! Anyone selling their tickets?!"

Scalping—the unauthorized reselling of tickets, typically at the entrance to concerts and sporting events—is illegal in roughly half of the states in the United States.[13] That's why you'll often hear scalpers hawking their goods with the counterintuitive (yet perfectly legal) request to *buy* tickets. Like wrapping alcohol in a paper bag, this practice doesn't fool the people who are charged with stopping it; the police and venue security personnel know exactly what's going on. And yet scalpers find it overwhelmingly in their interests to keep up the charade. This is another illustration of how even modest acts of discretion can thwart attempts at enforcing norms and laws.

Note that professional norm enforcers, such as police, teachers, and human resource managers, have a strong incentive to enforce norms: it's their job. Even so, they're often overworked or subject to lax over-sight, and therefore tempted to cut corners. Sometimes the threat of mere paperwork can be enough to keep police from enforcing minor infractions.[14]

Meanwhile, the rest of us—nonprofessionals—have even weaker incen-tives to enforce norms (as we discussed in Chapter 3). We may have to stand up against our peers or even our superiors, and we have to do it without any formal authority, so our cost–benefit calculation is already teetering on the edge of profitability, perched between red and black. All it takes is a gentle nudge to send it definitively into the red.

It's also important to remember that norm enforcement typically involves more than simply *detecting* that a norm violation has occurred. It also requires successfully *prosecuting* the violation, which means getting other members of the community to agree that a crime has taken place. Federal investigators might be arbitrarily certain that Tony Soprano is a Mafioso, for example, without having enough evidence to convict him in a court of law. Similarly, when your boss steals credit for your ideas at work, *you* can be certain of it—but good luck convincing your boss's boss. In general, it's much easier for firsthand witnesses to *detect* a crime than to convince others who are far removed.

The takeaway for the would-be cheater is that anything that hampers enforcement (or prosecution) will improve the odds of getting away with a crime. This is where discretion comes in. Such discretion can take many forms:

- *Pretexts.* These function as ready-made excuses or alibis.
- *Discreet communication.* Keeping things on the down-low.
- *Skirting a norm* instead of violating it outright.
- *Subtlety.* In honor cultures, an open insult is considered ample provocation for violence. In contrast, an insult that's subtle enough not to land "on the record" will often get a pass.

All of these techniques work by the same mechanism, in that they prevent a norm violation from becoming full common knowledge, which makes it more difficult to prosecute.

Let's look at a few of these techniques in greater detail.

PRETEXTS: READY-MADE EXCUSES

In 1527, King Henry VIII's marriage to Queen Catherine of Aragon seemed unlikely to give him the son he desperately needed, and at 38 years old, he was running out of options. Everyone at court knew that Henry wanted a younger woman—Anne Boleyn—as his wife. Unfortunately, his marriage to Catherine had been blessed by the previous pope, and the current pope was in no mood to grant an annulment.

What the king needed was a *pretext*, a false but plausible justification to distract from his real reason. So, nearly 20 years into his marriage to Catherine, the king suddenly "discovered" that she hadn't been a virgin on their wedding night, and that therefore their marriage was illegitimate.

As pretexts go, this was pretty ham-handed. But kings don't need their excuses to be particularly subtle or airtight; their power is enough of an incentive for most people to go along. In Henry's case, his pretext was enough to let him break from Roman Catholicism (thereby launching the English Reformation) and secure his annulment from the head of the new Anglican Church.[15]

Pretexts are a broad and useful tool for getting away with norm violations. They make prosecution more difficult by having a ready explanation for your innocence. This makes it harder for others to accuse and prosecute you. And as we've seen, a pretext doesn't need to fool everyone—it simply needs to be plausible enough to make people worry that *other people* might believe it.

Pretexts abound in human social life. Smoke shops sell drug paraphernalia—pipes, bongs, vaporizers—as devices for "smoking tobacco." Executives "voluntarily" step down to "spend more time with family." When a hotel invites its guests to "consider the environment" before leaving their used towels out to be washed, its primary concern isn't the environment but its bottom line. But to impose on guests merely to save money violates norms of hospitality—hence the pretext.[16]

DISCREET COMMUNICATION

> **conspire**, *v*. Make secret plans jointly to commit an unlawful or harmful act.

The word *conspire* has a fun etymology. It comes from the Latin *com-*, meaning together, plus *spirare*, meaning to breathe.

Picture two nobles conspiring to assassinate the king. They're hunched together in one of the castle hallways whispering—breathing together—to coordinate their activities. They keep their voices low, speak cryptically about "the plan" (rather than explicitly about "killing the king"), and keep their meeting as brief as possible before parting ways.

In communicating discreetly with each other, what are the nobles hoping to achieve? First, they're hoping not to be noticed at all. If they *are* noticed whispering together, they hope their voices aren't overheard. If their voices *are* overheard, they hope their words can't be made out. If their words *can* be made out, they hope the meaning is unclear. And finally, even if their meaning *is* clear to individual eavesdroppers, they hope their plans can remain closeted knowledge rather than becoming common knowledge.

Imagine two guards patrolling the castle together who happen to have overheard the nobles. Both guards might individually suspect a plot, but they might also be secretly happy about it. (Maybe the king has mistreated them.) Neither could openly admit to endorsing treason, but because the nobles were whispering, each guard can pretend not to have heard. If, instead, the nobles had been speaking loudly and openly, the plot would become common knowledge between the guards, and they would feel compelled to arrest the conspirators.

As a rule of thumb, whenever communication is discreet—subtle, cryptic, or ambiguous—it's a fair bet that the speaker is trying to get away with something by preventing the message from becoming common knowledge. Examples include

- *Body language.* A nod, a glance, a knowing smile, a quick roll of the eyes, or a friendly touch on the arm. In general, body language is discreet in a way that words aren't, because they are harder to interpret and quote to third parties. "The meaning of a wink," says Michael Chwe in *Rational Ritual*, "depends on it not being common knowledge."[17] We'll take a closer look at body language in Chapter 7.
- *Cryptic communication.* Using words or phrases whose meaning is obscure, but which are more easily understood by one's target audience than by hostile eavesdroppers. This is one reason we develop and use so much slang for bad, questionable, or illegal behavior. Terms like "hooking up" (sex), "420" (marijuana), and "gaming" (gambling) all proliferate partly in order to stay half a step ahead of the authorities (be they parents, police, or judgmental peers).[18]
- *Subtlety and subtext.* Indirection, hints, and innuendo. Such tactics allow us to convey meaning while retaining enough semantic elbow room to deny the message later, if need be. Examples include veiled threats ("It would be a shame if something happened to that pretty face of yours") and broaching bad behavior such as prostitution ("You looking to have a good time?") or drugs ("Do you like to party?").
- *Symbolism.* In her novel *Ethan Frome*, Edith Wharton cleverly symbolizes the sexual relationships between her main characters using two uncanny dinner items: pickles and donuts. More seriously, symbols can be used to rally resistance against a corrupt regime. If a resistance movement becomes associated with a particular color,

people can wear that color to support the resistance without making themselves as vulnerable to attack by the ruling regime.

- *Informal speech.* In general, the more formal your speech, the more the message is quotable and "on the record." And vice versa: less formal speech is typically "off the record."

These techniques can be useful even when there are only two people involved. Consider a man propositioning a woman for sex after a couple dates.[19] If he asks openly—"Would you like to have sex tonight?"—it puts both of their "faces" on the line; everything becomes less deniable. The solution is a little euphemism: "Want to come up and see my etchings?" Both parties have a pretty clear idea of what's being suggested, but crucially their knowledge doesn't rise to the status of common knowledge. He doesn't know that *she* knows that he was offering sex—at least not with certainty.

Still a question lingers: If both parties understand the proposition, why does it matter whether it's common knowledge? One way to model scenarios like this is to imagine a cast of peers waiting in the wings, eager to hear what happened on the date. This is the audience, real or imagined, in front of whom the couple is performing an act of cryptic communication, hoping to exchange a message—an offer of sex along with an answer—without its becoming common knowledge. Neither party needs to be consciously aware that they're performing in front of this imagined cast; this is simply how people, with years of practice, learn to act in order to save face.

An imagined audience—whether eavesdropping or learning about the scenario secondhand—is also a good way to model other norm-violation scenarios. When a crime boss says to one of his henchmen, "Take care of our friend over there," he's performing in front of a law enforcement system that might question him or his henchman at some later date. Of course, in talking this way, the boss accepts a small risk that he'll be misunderstood. Some of his "kill" orders won't be carried out, while other innocuous orders may be accidentally interpreted as orders to kill. This is the cost of doing business in the shadows.

SKIRTING NORMS

Real life norms have many gray areas and iffy boundary cases. This is because it's impossible to create standards everyone can agree on. Wittgenstein famously argued that it's impossible to define, in unambiguous terms, what constitutes a "game," and the same argument applies to all complex cultural concepts, including norms.

Gray areas are ripe for cheaters to test the limits, play in the margins, and push the envelope. In the United States, for example, the Federal Communications Commission imposes fines on television networks for violating standards of public decency. But what's considered indecent? In *Jacobellis v. Ohio*, Supreme Court Justice Potter Stewart refused to define obscenity, saying instead, "I know it when I see it"—but this kind of underspecification is exactly what allows a norm to be skirted.

The TV show *Seinfeld* was famous for pushing the boundaries of what could be discussed on network television. In one notorious episode, the characters made a bet to see who could hold out the longest without masturbating. And yet the word "masturbate" was very cleverly avoided throughout the show. Here's how the topic is introduced:

(George slowly enters. He's in a melancholy state)

. . .

JERRY: What's the matter?

GEORGE: My mother caught me.

JERRY: "Caught" you? Doing what?

GEORGE: You know . . . I was alone. . . . I stopped by [my parents'] house to drop the car off, and I went inside for a few minutes. Nobody was there — they're supposed to be working. My mother had a *Glamour* magazine, I started leafing through it. . . . So, one thing lead to another. . . .

Is that indecent? "I know it when I see it" is a hard criterion to apply to cases like this, in part because it depends on how vividly the censor is imagining the actions implied by the dialogue.

Other norms we like to skirt include dress codes, slacking off at work, flirting inappropriately, and acting politically in small social groups.

MINOR SINS

People have many reasons to fixate on celebrities and other power players, but one reason is to see what celebrities can get away with. Steve Jobs was famously abusive to his staff at Apple. John F. Kennedy had more mistresses than historians can confirm.[20] O. J. Simpson seemingly got away with murder.

We sometimes flatter ourselves that abusive CEOs and philandering presidents are a different breed of person from down-to-earth folks like us. But at least in the ways we evade norms, the difference is mostly a matter of degree. Celebrities may get away with violating big norms (occasionally even murder), but if a norm is weak enough, even everyday folks like us can violate it with impunity.

So we brag and boast, shirk and slack off, gossip and badmouth people behind their backs. We undermine our supposed teammates, suck up to our bosses, ogle and flirt inappropriately, play politics, and manipulate others for our own ends. In short, we're selfish. Not *irredeemably* selfish, just slightly more than our highest standards of behavior demand.

But of course we don't flaunt our selfishness; we don't gossip and shirk completely out in the open. (Even JFK had the decency to cheat on Jackie only behind closed doors.) When we brag, for example, we try to be subtle about it. It's crass to quote one's IQ or salary, but if those numbers are worth bragging about, we typically find a way to let our peers know—perhaps by using big, show-offy words or by buying conspicuous luxuries. We name-drop and #humblebrag. We show off our bodies by wearing flattering clothes. Or we let others boast on our behalves, as when we're being introduced as speakers.

We show similar discretion when we play small-scale politics, maneuvering for personal advantage in settings like church, the office, or our peer groups. We try to cultivate allies and undermine those who aren't allied with us; we angle to take credit for successes and avoid blame for failures; we lobby for policies that will benefit us, even when we have little reason to believe those policies will benefit the entire group. We tell people what they want to hear. But of course we don't do this out in the open. We don't say to our enemies, "I'm trying to undermine you right now." Instead we cloak our actions in justifications that appeal to what's best for everyone.

GETTING OUR BEARINGS

It takes a bit of cleverness to get away with cheating. This helps resolve the puzzle we identified at the end of Chapter 3: If norms are supposed to discourage competition, then why do we still need big brains? A plausible answer is that our norms are only partially enforced, so we need big brains to figure out how to cheat. In fact, norm-evaders and norm-enforcers are locked in a competitive arms race of their own—a game of cat and mouse—pushing each other ever upward in mental ability.

In the next chapter, we focus our attention on one particularly subtle and important form of cheating: self-deception. This will also address our book's central puzzle: Why are we *unconscious* of some of our motives?

Self-Deception

The red milksnake, utterly harmless, wears stripes to pose as a deadly coral snake. Some orchid species mimic other flowers in order to attract pollinating bees, but without providing any nectar in return.[1] Dozens of species use eye spots to trick other animals into thinking they're being watched. Possums, lizards, birds, and sharks "play dead," hoping to dissuade predators who are interested only in live prey. Even parasitic bacteria try to get in on the act, for example, by "wearing" certain molecules on their cell membranes in order to "look" like a native host cell, thereby fooling the host's immune system—a microscopic wolf in sheep's clothing.[2]

"Deception," says the evolutionary biologist Robert Trivers, "is a very deep feature of life. It occurs at all levels—from gene to cell to individual to group—and it seems, by any and all means, necessary."

And our species, of course, is no exception. Suffice it to say that deception is simply part of human nature—a fact that makes perfect sense in light of the competitive (selfish) logic of evolution. Deception allows us to reap certain benefits without paying the full costs. And yes, all societies have norms against lying, but that just means we have to work a little harder not to get caught. Instead of telling bald-faced lies, maybe we spin or cherry-pick the truth.

So far, so obvious. But here's the puzzle: we don't just deceive *others*; we also deceive *ourselves*. Our minds habitually distort or ignore critical information in ways that seem, on the face of it, counterproductive. Our mental processes act in bad faith, perverting or degrading our picture of the world. In common speech, we might say that someone is engaged in "wishful thinking" or is "burying her head in the sand"—or, to use a more colorful phrase, that she's "drinking her own Kool-Aid."

In his book *The Folly of Fools*, Trivers refers to self-deception as the "striking contradiction" at the heart of our mental lives. Our brains "seek out information," he says, "and then act to destroy it":

> On the one hand, our sense organs have evolved to give us a marvelously detailed and accurate view of the outside world . . . exactly as we would expect if truth about the outside world helps us to navigate it more effectively. But once this information arrives in our brains, it is often distorted and biased to our conscious minds. We deny the truth to ourselves. We project onto others traits that are in fact true of ourselves—and then attack them! We repress painful memories, create completely false ones, rationalize immoral behavior, act repeatedly to boost positive self-opinion, and show a suite of ego-defense mechanisms.[3]

We deceive ourselves in many different areas of life. One domain is sports. Consider how a boxer might purposely ignore an injury during a fight, or how a marathon runner might trick herself into thinking she's less fatigued than she "really" is.[4] A study of competitive swimmers found that those who were more prone to self-deception performed better during an important qualifying race.[5]

Another domain is personal health. You might suppose, given how important health is to our happiness (not to mention our longevity), it would be a domain to which we'd bring our cognitive A-game. Unfortunately, study after study shows that we often distort or ignore critical information about our own health in order to seem healthier than we really are.[6] One study, for example, gave patients a cholesterol test, then followed up to see what they remembered months later. Patients with the worst test results—who were judged the most at-risk of cholesterol-related health problems—were most likely to misremember their test results, and they remembered their results as better (i.e., healthier) than they actually were.[7] Smokers, but not nonsmokers, choose not to hear about the dangerous effects of smoking.[8] People systematically underestimate their risk of contracting HIV (human immunodeficiency virus),[9] and avoid taking HIV tests.[10] We also deceive ourselves about our driving skills, social skills, leadership skills, and athletic ability.[11]

These results are robust. There's a wide base of evidence showing that human brains are poor stewards of the information they receive from the outside world. But this seems entirely self-defeating, like shooting oneself in the foot. If our minds contain maps of our worlds, what good comes from having an inaccurate version of these maps?

OLD SCHOOL: SELF-DECEPTION AS DEFENSE

Broadly speaking, there are two schools of thought about why we deceive ourselves. The first—what we'll call the Old School—treats self-deception as a defense mechanism.

Sigmund Freud, along with his daughter Anna Freud, famously championed this school of thought. The Freuds saw self-deception as a (largely unconscious) coping strategy—a way for the ego to protect itself, especially against unwanted impulses.[12] We repress painful thoughts and memories, for example, by pushing them down into the subconscious. Or we deny our worst attributes and project them onto others. Or we rationalize, substituting good motives for ugly ones (more on this in Chapter 6).

According to the Freuds, the mind employs these defense mechanisms to reduce anxiety and other kinds of psychic pain. Later psychologists, following Otto Fenichel in the mid-20th century, reinterpreted the purpose of defense mechanisms as *preserving one's self-esteem*.[13] This has become the polite, common-sense explanation—that we deceive ourselves because we can't handle the truth. Our egos and self-esteem are fragile and need to be shielded from distressing information, like the fact that we probably *won't* win the upcoming competition, or the fact that we may be sick with some lurking cancer.

In a segment for the podcast *Radiolab*, Harold Sackeim—one of the first psychologists to experimentally study self-deception—explained it this way:

> SACKEIM: [Depressed people] see all the pain in the world, how horrible people are with each other, and they tell you everything about themselves: what their weaknesses are, what terrible things they've done to other people. And the problem is they're *right*. And so maybe the way we help people is to help them be *wrong*.
>
> ROBERT KRULWICH [*Radiolab* host]: It might just be that hiding ideas that we know to be true, hiding those ideas from ourselves, is what we need to get by.
>
> SACKEIM: We're so vulnerable to being hurt that we're given the capacity to distort *as a gift*.[14]

Poetic, maybe, but this Old School perspective ignores an important objection: Why would Nature, by way of evolution,[15] design our brains this way? Information is the lifeblood of the human brain; ignoring or distorting it isn't something to be undertaken lightly. If the goal is to preserve self-esteem, a more efficient way to go about it is simply to make the brain's self-esteem mechanism stronger, more robust to threatening information. Similarly, if the goal is to reduce anxiety, the straightforward solution is to design the brain to feel less anxiety for a given amount of stress.

In contrast, using self-deception to preserve self-esteem or reduce anxiety is a sloppy hack and ultimately self-defeating. It would be like trying to warm yourself during winter by aiming a blow-dryer at the thermostat. The temperature reading will rise, but it won't reflect a properly heated house, and it won't stop you from shivering.[16]

Alternatively, imagine you're the general in charge of a large army. You're outnumbered and surrounded by the enemy with no clear line of escape. As you contemplate your next move on a large paper map, you realize how easy it would be to erase the mountain range that's blocking your troops, or to draw a pass through the mountains where none actually exists. Having an escape route would certainly be a relief! But the map isn't the territory; you can't erase the actual mountains. Whatever you do to the map, the enemy will still have you surrounded. And by lying about reality, you're setting yourself up to make bad decisions that will lead to even worse outcomes.

A general who made a habit of indulging in such flights of fancy would quickly lose the war to one who didn't. And the same is true for our minds. We therefore need a better reason for deceiving ourselves than mere psychic comfort.

NEW SCHOOL: SELF-DECEPTION AS MANIPULATION

In recent years, psychologists—especially those who focus on evolutionary reasoning—have developed a more satisfying explanation for why we deceive ourselves. Where the Old School saw self-deception as primarily inward-facing, defensive, and (like the general editing the map) largely self-defeating, the New School sees it as primarily outward-facing, manipulative, and ultimately self-serving.

Two recent New School books have been Trivers' *The Folly of Fools* (2011) and Robert Kurzban's *Why Everyone (Else) Is a Hypocrite* (2013). But the roots of the New School go back to Thomas Schelling, a Nobel Prize–winning economist[17] best known for his work on the game theory of cooperation and conflict.

In his 1967 book *The Strategy of Conflict*, Schelling studied what he called *mixed-motive games*. These are scenarios involving two or more players whose interests overlap but also partially diverge. Thanks to the overlap, the players have an incentive to cooperate, but thanks to the divergence, they're also somewhat at odds with each other. If this sounds familiar, it's because humans (and our primate ancestors) have been playing mixed-motive games with each other for millions of years. It's what we do every day, what our minds were built for. Nevertheless, as Schelling demonstrated, mixed-motive games can incentivize strange, counterintuitive behavior.

A classic example is the game of chicken, typically played by two teenagers in their cars. The players race toward each other on a collision course, and the player who swerves first loses the game.[18] Traditionally it's a game of bravado. But if you really want to win, here's what Schelling advises. When you're lined up facing your opponent, revving your engine, *remove the steering wheel from your car and wave it at your opponent.* This way, he'll know that you're locked in, dead set, hell-bent— irrevocably committed to driving straight through, no matter what. And at this point, unless he wants to die, your opponent will *have to* swerve first, and you'll be the winner.

The reason this is counterintuitive is because it's not typically a good idea to limit our own options. But Schelling documented how the perverse incentives of mixed-motive games lead to option-limiting and other actions that seem irrational, but are actually strategic. These include

- *Closing or degrading a channel of communication.* You might purposely turn off your phone, for example, if you're expecting someone to call asking for a favor. Or you might have a hard conversation over email rather than in person.
- *Opening oneself up to future punishment.* "Among the legal privileges of corporations," writes Schelling, "two that are mentioned in textbooks are the right to sue and the 'right' to be sued. Who wants to be sued! But the right to be sued is the power to make a promise: to borrow money, to enter a contract, to do business with someone who might be damaged. If suit does arise, the 'right' seems a liability in retrospect; beforehand it was a prerequisite to doing business."[19]
- *Ignoring information*, also known as *strategic ignorance.* If you're kidnapped, for example, you might prefer not to see your kidnapper's face or learn his name. Why? Because if he knows you can identify him later (to the police), he'll be less likely to let you go. In some cases, knowledge can be a serious liability.
- *Purposely believing something that's false.* If you're a general who firmly believes your army can win, even though the odds are against it, you might nevertheless intimidate your opponent into backing down.

In other words, mixed-motive games contain the kind of incentives that reward self-deception.

There's a tension in all of this. In simple applications of decision theory, it's better to have more options and more knowledge. Yet Schelling has argued that, in a variety of scenarios, limiting or sabotaging yourself is the *winning move*. What gives?

Resolving this tension turns out to be straightforward. Classical decision theory has it right: there's no value in sabotaging yourself per se. The value lies in *convincing other players* that you've sabotaged yourself. In the game of chicken, you don't win because you're unable to steer, but because your opponent *believes* you're unable to steer. Similarly, as a kidnapping victim, you don't suffer because you've seen your kidnapper's face; you suffer when the kidnapper *thinks* you've seen his face. If you could somehow see his face without giving him any idea that you'd done so, you'd probably be better off.

By this line of reasoning, it's never useful to have *secret* gaps in your knowledge, or to adopt false beliefs that you keep entirely to yourself. The entire value of strategic ignorance and related phenomena lies in the way others act when they believe that you're ignorant. As Kurzban says, "Ignorance is at its most useful when it is most public."[20] It needs to be advertised and made conspicuous.

Another way to look at it is that self-deception is useful only when you're playing against an opponent who can take your mental state into account. You can't bluff the blind forces of Nature, for example. When a hurricane is roaring toward you, it's no use trying to ignore it; the hurricane couldn't care less whether or not you know it's coming. Sabotaging yourself works only when you're playing against an opponent with a theory-of-mind. Typically these opponents will be other humans, but it could theoretically extend to some of the smarter animals, as well as hypothetical future robots or aliens. Corporations and nation-states also use some of these self-sabotaging tactics vis-à-vis each other and the public at large. Self-deception, then, is a tactic that's useful only to social creatures in social situations.

It's hard to overstate the impact of what Schelling, Trivers, Kurzban, and others are arguing. Their conclusion is that we, humans, *must* self-deceive. Those who refuse to play such mind games will be at a game-theoretic disadvantage relative to others who play along. Thus we are often wise to ignore seemingly critical information and to believe easily refuted falsehoods—and then to prominently advertise our distorted thinking—because these are *winning moves*.

As Trivers puts it, "We deceive ourselves the better to deceive others."[21]

WHY DO WE BELIEVE OUR OWN LIES?

Still there's an important lingering question. If the goal of self-deception is to create a certain impression *in others*, why do we distort the truth to *ourselves*? What's the benefit of self-deception over a simple, deliberate lie?

There are many ways to answer this question, but they mostly boil down to the fact that lying is hard to pull off. For one thing, it's cognitively demanding. Huckleberry Finn, for example, struggled to keep his stories straight and was eventually caught in a number of lies. And it's even harder when we're being grilled and expected to produce answers quickly. As Mark Twain may have said elsewhere, "If you tell the truth, you don't have to remember anything."[22]

Beyond the cognitive demands, lying is also difficult because we have to overcome our fear of getting caught. People get angry when they're lied to—a reaction almost as universal as lying itself. (Even wasps who catch other wasps lying are known to retaliate in response.[23]) Therefore, aside from sociopaths and compulsive liars, most of us are afraid to tell bald-faced lies, and we suffer from a number of fear-based "tells" that can give us away. Our hearts race, our skin heats up, we start sweating and fidgeting. Maybe we have an eye twitch, nervous tic, awkward gulp, or cracking voice.[24]

In light of this, often the best way to get others to believe something is to make it a reality. When you're playing chicken, it won't do much good to yell at your opponent, "Hey, I've torn off my steering wheel!" He won't believe you until he sees that you've actually done it. Similarly, often the best way to convince others that we believe something is to *actually* believe it. Other people aren't stupid. They're aware that we often have an incentive to lie to them, so they're watching us, eagle-eyed, for any signs of deception. They're analyzing our words (often comparing them to things we said days, weeks, or months ago), scrutinizing our facial expressions, and observing our behaviors to make sure they conform to our stated motives.

The point is, our minds aren't as private as we like to imagine. Other people have partial visibility into what we're thinking. Faced with the translucency of our own minds, then, self-deception is often the most robust way to mislead others. It's not technically a lie (because it's not conscious or deliberate), but it has a similar effect. "We hide reality from our conscious minds," says Trivers, "the better to hide it from onlookers."[25]

Modeling the world accurately isn't the be-all and end-all of the human brain. Brains evolved to help our bodies, and ultimately our genes, get along and get ahead in the world—a world that includes not just rocks and squirrels and hurricanes, but also other human beings. And if we spend a significant fraction of our lives interacting with others (which we do), trying to convince them of certain things (which we do), why *shouldn't* our brains adopt socially useful beliefs as first-class citizens, alongside world-modeling beliefs?

Wear a mask long enough and it becomes your face.[26] Play a role long enough and it becomes who you are. Spend enough time pretending something is true and you might as well believe it.[27]

Incidentally, this is why politicians make a great case study for self-deception. The social pressure on their beliefs is enormous. Psychologically, then, politicians don't so much "lie" as regurgitate their own self-deceptions.[28] Both are ways of misleading others, but self-deceptions are a lot harder to catch and prosecute.

SELF-DECEPTION IN PRACTICE

There are at least four ways that self-deception helps us come out ahead in mixed-motive scenarios. We'll personify them in four different archetypes: the Madman, the Loyalist, the Cheerleader, and the Cheater.

The Madman

"I'm doing this *no matter what*," says the Madman, "so stay outta my way!"

When we commit ourselves to a particular course of action, it often changes the incentives for other players. This is how removing the steering wheel helps us win the game of chicken, but it's also why businesspeople, gang leaders, athletes, and other competitors try to psych out their opponents.

Rick Lahaye explains how athletes suffer when they don't play the Madman:

> Athletes use small cues of tiredness from close competitors to give themselves a boost and keep pushing forward during a race (e.g., a marathon runner thinking, "Do you see him breathe? He's almost done. Just keep pushing for one more bit and you will beat him."). Because of this, athletes conceal (negative) information about [themselves] to competitors. If you show any "signs of weakness," the opponent will see a chance for success and will be more willing to keep spending energy.[29]

It was also one of Richard Nixon's strategies for the war in Vietnam. As he explained to his chief of staff Bob Haldeman:

> I call it the Madman Theory, Bob. I want the North Vietnamese to believe I've reached the point where I might do anything to stop the war. We'll just slip the word to them that, "for God's sake, you know Nixon is obsessed about communism. We can't restrain him when he's angry — and he has his hand on the nuclear button" and Ho Chi Minh himself will be in Paris in two days begging for peace.[30]

Of course, Nixon's plan didn't work out as well as he hoped, but his reasoning was valid. People often defer to the crazy ones, and our minds respond to that incentive by being a little bit crazy ourselves.

The Loyalist

"Sure, I'll go along with your beliefs," says the Loyalist, thereby demonstrating commitment and hoping to earn trust in return.

In many ways, belief is a political act. This is why we're typically keen to believe a friend's version of a story—about a breakup, say, or a dispute at work—even when we know there's another side of the story that may be equally compelling. It's also why blind faith is an important virtue for religious groups, and to a lesser extent social, professional, and political groups. When a group's fundamental tenets are at stake, those who demonstrate the most steadfast commitment—who continue to chant the loudest or clench their eyes the tightest in the face of conflicting evidence—earn the most trust from their fellow group members. The employee who drinks the company Kool-Aid, however epistemically noxious, will tend to win favor from colleagues, especially in management, and move faster up the chain.

In fact, we often measure loyalty in our relationships by the degree to which a belief is irrational or unwarranted by the evidence. For example, we don't consider it "loyal" for an employee to stay at a company when it's paying her twice the salary she could make elsewhere; that's just calculated self-interest. Likewise, it's not "loyal" for a man to stay with his girlfriend if he has no other prospects. These attachments take on the color of loyalty only when someone remains committed despite a strong temptation to defect. Similarly, it doesn't demonstrate loyalty to believe the truth, which we have every incentive to believe anyway. It only demonstrates loyalty to believe something that we *wouldn't* have reason to believe *unless* we were loyal.

There's a famous Chinese parable illustrating the Loyalist function of our beliefs:

> Zhao Gao was a powerful man hungry for more power. One day he brought a deer to a meeting with the emperor and many top officials, calling the deer a "great horse." The emperor, who regarded Zhao Gao as a teacher and therefore trusted him completely, agreed that it was a horse—and many officials agreed as well. Others, however, remained silent or objected. This was how Zhao Gao flushed out his enemies. Soon after, he murdered all the officials who refused to call the deer a horse.[31]

Zhao Gao's ploy wouldn't have worked if he had called the deer a deer. The truth is a poor litmus test of loyalty.

The Cheerleader

"I know this is true," the Cheerleader says. "Come on, believe it with me!"

This kind of self-deception is a form of propaganda. As Kurzban writes, "Sometimes it is beneficial to be . . . wrong in such a way that, if everyone else believed the incorrect thing one believes, one would be strategically better off."[32]

The goal of cheerleading, then, is to change other people's beliefs. And the more fervently we believe something, the easier it is to convince others that it's true. The politician who's confident she's going to win *no matter what* will have an easier time rallying supporters than one who projects a more honest assessment of her chances. The startup founder who's brimming with confidence, though it may be entirely unearned, will often attract more investors and recruit more employees than someone with an accurate assessment of his own abilities.

When we deceive ourselves about personal health, whether by avoiding information entirely or by distorting information we've already received, it *feels* like we're trying to protect ourselves from distressing information. But the reason our egos need to be shielded—the reason we evolved to feel pain when our egos are threatened—is to help us maintain a positive social impression. We don't personally benefit from misunderstanding our current state of health, but we benefit when *others* mistakenly believe we're healthy. And the first step to convincing others is often to convince ourselves. As Bill Atkinson, a colleague of Steve Jobs, once said of Jobs's self-deception, "It allowed him to con people into believing his vision, because he has personally embraced and internalized it."[33]

The Cheater

"I have no idea what you're talking about," the Cheater says in response to an accusation. "My motives were pure."

As we discussed in Chapter 3, many norms hinge on the actor's intentions. Being nice, for example, is generally applauded—but being nice *with the intention to curry favor* is the sin of flattery. Similarly, being friendly is generally considered to be a good thing, but being friendly *with romantic intentions* is flirting, which is often inappropriate. Other minor sins that hinge on intent include bragging, showing off, sucking up, lying, and playing politics, as well as selfish behavior in general. When we deceive ourselves about our own motives, however, it becomes much harder for others to prosecute these minor transgressions. We'll see much more of this in the next chapter.

In other cases, it's not our *intentions* that determine whether a norm was violated, but our *knowledge*. Learning about a transgression sometimes invokes a moral or legal duty to do something about it.[34] If we see a friend shoplift, we become complicit in the crime. This is why we might turn a blind eye or strive to retain plausible deniability—so that, when questioned later, we'll have nothing to hide.

* * * * *

Again, in all of these cases, self-deception works because other people are attempting to read our minds and react based on what they find (or what they think they find). In deceiving ourselves, then, we're often acting to deceive and manipulate others. We might be hoping to intimidate them (like the Madman), earn their trust (like the Loyalist), change their beliefs (like the Cheerleader), or throw them off our trail (like the Cheater).

Of course, these aren't mutually exclusive. Any particular act of self-deception might serve multiple purposes at once. When the mother of an alleged murderer is convinced that her son is innocent, she's playing Loyalist to her son and Cheerleader to the jury. The prizefighter who is grossly overconfident about his odds of winning is playing both Cheerleader (to his fans, teammates, and other supporters) and Madman (to his opponent).

MODULARITY

The benefit of self-deception is that it can, in some scenarios, help us mislead others. But what about its costs?

As we've mentioned, the main cost is that it leads to suboptimal decision-making. Like the general who erases the mountain range on the map,
then leads the army to a dead end, self-deceivers similarly run the risk of
acting on false or missing information.

Luckily, however, we don't have to bear the full brunt of our own deceptions. Typically, at least part of our brain continues to know the truth. In
other words, our saving grace is inconsistency.

"To understand most important ideas in psychology," says social psychologist Jonathan Haidt in *The Happiness Hypothesis*, "you need to
understand how the mind is divided into parts that sometimes conflict."
He goes on:

> We assume that there is one person in each body, but in some ways we
> are each more like a committee whose members have been thrown
> together working at cross purposes.[35]

There are dozens of schemes for how to divide up the mind. The Bible
identifies the head and the heart. Freud gives us the id, ego, and super-
ego. Iain McGilchrist differentiates the analytical left brain from the holis-
tic right brain,[36] while Douglas Kenrick gives us seven "subselves": Night
Watchman, Compulsive Hypochondriac, Team Player, Go-Getter,
Swinging Single, Good Spouse, and Nurturing Parent.[37] Meanwhile, the
next generation is growing up on Pixar's *Inside Out*, which portrays the
mind as a committee of five different emotional personalities.

None of these schemes is unequivocally better or more accurate than
the others. They're just different ways of slicing up the same complex
system—the reality of which is even more fragmented than the "committee" metaphor suggests. Psychologists call this *modularity*. Instead of a single monolithic process or small committee, modern psychologists see the
brain as a patchwork of hundreds or thousands of different parts or "modules," each responsible for a slightly different information-processing task.
Some modules take care of low-level tasks like detecting edges in the visual
field or flexing a muscle. Others are responsible for medium-sized opera-
tions like walking and conjugating verbs. Still higher-level modules (which

are themselves composed of many lower-level modules) are responsible for things like detecting cheaters[38] and managing our social impressions.

The point is that there are many different systems in the brain, each connected to other systems but also partially isolated from each other. The artificial intelligence researcher Marvin Minsky famously described this arrangement as the "society of mind."[39] And like a society, there are different ways to carve it up for different purposes. Just as America can be broken down in terms of political factions (liberals vs. conservatives), geography (urban vs. rural, coastal vs. heartland), or generations (Baby Boomers, Gen Xers, Millennials), the mind can also be carved up in many different ways.

And crucially, as Haidt stressed, the different parts don't always agree. A fact might be known to one system and yet be completely concealed or cut off from other systems. Or different systems might contain mutually inconsistent models of the world.

This is illustrated rather dramatically by the rare but well-documented condition known as *blindsight*, which typically follows from some kind of brain damage, like a stroke to the visual cortex. Just like people who are conventionally blind, blindsighted patients swear they can't see. But when presented with flashcards and forced to guess what's on the card, they do better than chance. Clearly some parts of their brains are registering visual information, even if the parts responsible for conscious awareness are kept in the dark.[40]

What this means for self-deception is that it's possible for our brains to maintain a relatively accurate set of beliefs in systems tasked with *evaluating potential actions,* while keeping those accurate beliefs hidden from the systems (like consciousness) involved in *managing social impressions.* In other words, we can act on information that isn't available to our verbal, conscious egos. And conversely, we can believe something with our conscious egos without necessarily making that information available to the systems charged with coordinating our behavior.

No matter how fervently a person believes in Heaven, for example, she's still going to be afraid of death. This is because the deepest, oldest parts of her brain—those charged with self-preservation—haven't the slightest idea about the afterlife. Nor should they. Self-preservation systems have no business dealing with abstract concepts. They should run on autopilot and be extremely difficult to override (as the difficulty of committing suicide attests[41]). This sort of division of mental labor is simply good mind design. As psychologists Douglas Kenrick and Vladas Griskevicius put it, "Although we're aware of some of the surface motives for our actions, the deep-seated evolutionary motives often remain inaccessible, buried behind the scenes in the subconscious workings of our brains' ancient mechanisms."[42]

Thus the very architecture of our brains makes it possible for us to behave hypocritically—to believe one set of things while acting on another. We can know *and* remain ignorant, as long as it's in separate parts of the brain.[43]

SELF-DISCRETION

Self-*discretion* is perhaps the most important and subtle mind game that we play with ourselves in the service of manipulating others. This is our mental habit of giving less psychological prominence to potentially damaging information. It differs from the most blatant forms of self-deception, in which we actively lie to ourselves (and believe our own lies). It also differs from strategic ignorance, in which we try our best not to learn potentially dangerous information.

Picture the mind as a society of little modules, systems, and subselves chattering away among themselves. This chatter is largely what constitutes our inner mental life, both conscious and unconscious. Self-discretion, then, consists of *discretion among different brain parts*. When part of the brain has to process a sensitive piece of information—wanting to get the upper hand in a particular interaction, for example—it doesn't necessarily make a big conscious fuss about it. Instead, we might just feel vaguely uneasy until we've gained the upper hand, whereupon we'll feel comfortable ending the conversation. At no point does the motive "Get the upper hand" rise to full conscious attention, but the same result is accomplished discreetly.

Information is sensitive in part because it can threaten our self-image and therefore our social image. So the rest of the brain conspires—whispers—to keep such information from becoming too prominent, especially in consciousness. In this sense, the Freuds were right: the conscious ego needs to be protected. But not because we are fragile, but rather to keep damaging information from leaking out of our brain and into the minds of our associates.

Self-discretion can be very subtle. When we push a thought "deep down" or to the "back of our minds," it's a way of being discreet with potentially damaging information. When we spend more time and attention dwelling on positive, self-flattering information, and less time and attention dwelling on shameful information, that's self-discretion.

Think about that time you wrote an amazing article for the school paper, or gave that killer wedding speech. Did you feel a flush of pride? That's your brain telling you, "This information is good for us! Let's keep it prominent, front and center." Dwell on it, bask in its warm glow. Reward those neural pathways in the hope of resurfacing those proud memories whenever they're relevant.

Now think about the time you mistreated your significant other, or when you were caught stealing as a child, or when you botched a big presentation at work. Feel the pang of shame? That's your brain telling you not to dwell on that particular information. Flinch away, hide from it, pretend it's not there. Punish those neural pathways, so the information stays as discreet as possible.[44]

GETTING OUR BEARINGS

In summary, our minds are built to sabotage information in order to come out ahead in social games. When big parts of our minds are unaware of how we try to violate social norms, it's more difficult for others to detect and prosecute those violations. This also makes it harder for us to calculate optimal behaviors, but overall, the trade-off is worth it.

Of all the things we might be self-deceived about, the most important are *our own motives*. It's this special form of self-deception that we turn to in the next chapter.

Counterfeit Reasons

"Reason is . . . the slave of the passions, and can never pretend to any other office than to serve and obey them."—David Hume[1]

"A man always has two reasons for doing anything: a good reason and the real reason."—J. P. Morgan[2]

Let's briefly take stock of the argument we've been making so far. In Chapter 2, we saw how humans (and all other species for that matter) are locked in the game of natural selection, which often rewards selfish, competitive behavior. In Chapter 3, we looked at social norms and saw how they constrain our selfish impulses, but also how norms can be fragile and hard to enforce. In Chapter 4, we looked at the many and subtle ways that humans try to cheat by exploiting the fragility of norm enforcement, largely by being discreet about bad behavior. In Chapter 5, we took a closer look at the most subtle and intriguing of all these norm-evasion techniques: self-deception. "We deceive ourselves," as Robert Trivers says, "the better to deceive others"—in particular, to make it harder for others to catch and prosecute us for behaving badly.

Together, these instincts and predispositions make up the elephant in the brain. They're the facts about ourselves, our behaviors, and our minds that we're uncomfortable acknowledging and confronting directly. It's not that we're entirely or irredeemably selfish and self-deceived—just that we're often rewarded for acting on selfish impulses, but less so for acknowledging them, and that our brains respond predictably to those incentives.

In this chapter, we turn our attention to one particular type of self-deception: the fact that we're strategically ignorant about our own *motives*. In other words, we don't always know the "whys" behind our own behavior. But as we'll see, we certainly pretend to know.

"I WANTED TO GO GET A COKE"

In the 1960s and early 1970s, neuroscientists Roger Sperry and Michael Gazzaniga conducted some of the most profound research in the history of psychology—a series of experiments that would launch Gazzaniga into an illustrious career as the "grandfather" of cognitive neuroscience,[3] and for which Sperry would eventually win the Nobel Prize in 1981.

In terms of method, the experiments were fairly conventional: an image was flashed, some questions were asked, that sort of thing. What distinguished these experiments were their subjects. These were patients who had previously, for medical reasons, undergone a *corpus callosotomy*—a surgical severing of the nerves that connect the left and right hemispheres of the brain. Hence the nickname for these subjects: *split-brain patients*.

Until Sperry and Gazzaniga's experiments, no one had noticed anything particularly strange about split-brain patients. They were able to walk around leading seemingly normal lives. Neither their doctors nor their loved ones—nor the patients themselves—had noticed that much was amiss.

But things *were* amiss, in a rather peculiar way, as Sperry and Gazzaniga were about to find out.

In order to understand their research, it helps to be familiar with two basic facts about the brain. The first is that each hemisphere processes signals from the *opposite* side of the body. So the left hemisphere controls the right side of the body (the right arm, leg, hand, and everything else), while the right hemisphere controls the left side of the body. This is also true for signals from the ears—the left hemisphere processes sound from the right ear, and vice versa. With the eyes it's a bit more complicated, but the upshot is that when a patient is looking straight ahead, everything to the right—in the right half of the visual field—is processed by the left hemisphere, and everything to the left is processed by the right hemisphere.[4]

The second key fact is that, after a brain is split by a callosotomy, the two hemispheres can no longer share information with each other. In a normal (whole) brain, information flows smoothly back and forth between the hemispheres, but in a split-brain, each hemisphere becomes an island unto itself—almost like two separate people within a single skull.[5]

Now, what Sperry and Gazzaniga did, in a variety of different experimental setups, was ask the *right hemisphere* to do something, but then ask the *left hemisphere* to explain it.

In one setup, they flashed a split-brain patient two different pictures at the same time, one to each hemisphere. The left hemisphere, for example, saw a picture of a chicken while the right hemisphere saw a picture of a snowy field. The researchers then asked the patient to reach out *with his left hand* and point to a word that best matched the picture he had seen. Since the right hemisphere had seen the picture of the snowy field, the left hand pointed to a shovel—because a shovel goes nicely with snow.

No surprises here. But then the researchers asked the patient to *explain* why he had chosen the shovel. Explanations, and speech generally, are functions of the left hemisphere, and thus the researchers were putting the left hemisphere in an awkward position. The *right hemisphere* alone had seen the snowy field, and it was the right hemisphere's unilateral decision to point to the shovel. The *left hemisphere*, meanwhile, had been left completely out of the loop, but was being asked to justify a decision it took no part in and wasn't privy to.

From the point of view of the left hemisphere, the only legitimate answer would have been, "I don't know." But that's not the answer it gave. Instead, the left hemisphere said it had chosen the shovel because shovels are used for "cleaning out the chicken coop." In other words, the left hemisphere, lacking a real reason to give, *made up a reason on the spot*. It pretended that it had acted on its own—that it had chosen the shovel because of the chicken picture. And it delivered this answer casually and matter-of-factly, fully expecting to be believed, because it had no idea it was making up a story. The left hemisphere, says Gazzaniga, "did not offer its suggestion in a guessing vein but rather as a statement of fact."[6]

In another setup, Sperry and Gazzaniga asked a patient—by way of his right hemisphere (left ear)—to stand up and walk toward the door. Once the patient was out of his chair, they then asked him, out loud, what he was doing, which required a response from his left hemisphere. Again this put the left hemisphere in an awkward position.

Now, *we* know why the patient got out of his chair—because the researchers asked him to, via his right hemisphere. The patient's left hemisphere, however, had no way of knowing this. But instead of saying, "I don't know why I stood up," which would have been the only honest answer, it made up a reason and fobbed it off as the truth:

"I wanted to go get a Coke."

RATIONALIZATION

What these studies demonstrate is just how effortlessly the brain can rationalize its behavior. Rationalization, sometimes known to neuroscientists as *confabulation*, is the production of fabricated stories made up without any conscious intention to deceive. They're not *lies*, exactly, but neither are they the honest truth.

Humans rationalize about all sorts of things: beliefs, memories, statements of "fact" about the outside world. But few things seem as easy for us to rationalize as our own motives. When we make up stories about things *outside* our minds, we open ourselves up to fact-checking. People can argue with us: "Actually, that's not what happened." But when we make up stories about our own motives, it's much harder for others to question us—outside of a psychology lab, at least. And as we saw in Chapter 3, we have strong incentives to portray our motives in a flattering light, especially when they're the subject of norm enforcement.

Rationalization is a kind of epistemic forgery, if you will. When others ask us to give reasons for our behavior, they're asking about our true, underlying motives. So when we rationalize or confabulate, we're handing out *counterfeit reasons* (see Box 5). We're presenting them as an honest account of our mental machinations, when in fact they're made up from scratch.

Box 5: "Motives" and "Reasons"

When we use the term "motives," we're referring to the underlying causes of our behavior, whether we're conscious of them or not. "Reasons" are the verbal explanations we give to account for our behavior. Reasons can be true, false, or somewhere in between (e.g., cherry-picked).

Even more dramatic examples of rationalization can be elicited from patients suffering from *disability denial*,[7] a rare disorder that occasionally results from a right-hemisphere stroke. In a typical case, the stroke will leave the patient's left arm paralyzed, but—here's the weird part—the patient will completely deny that anything is wrong with his arm, and will manufacture all sorts of strange (counterfeit) excuses for why it's just sitting there, limp and lifeless. The neuroscientist V. S. Ramachandran recalls some of the conceptual gymnastics his patients have undertaken in this situation:

> "Oh, doctor, I didn't want to move my arm because I have arthritis in my shoulder and it hurts." Or this is from another patient: "Oh, the medical students have been prodding me all day and I don't really feel like moving my arm just now."
>
> When asked to raise both hands, one man raised his right hand high into the air and said, when he detected my gaze locked onto his motionless left hand, "Um, as you can see, I'm steadying myself with my left hand in order to raise my right."[8]

Apart from their bizarre denials, these patients are otherwise mentally healthy and intelligent human beings. But no amount of cross-examination can persuade them of what's plainly true—that their left arms are paralyzed. They will confabulate and rationalize and forge counterfeit reasons until they're blue in the face.

Meanwhile, the rest of us—healthy, whole-brained people—are confronted every day with questions that ask us to explain our behavior. *Why did you storm out of the meeting? Why did you break up with your boyfriend? Why haven't you done the dishes? Why did you vote for Barack Obama? Why are you a Christian?* Each of these questions demands a reason, and in most cases we dutifully oblige. But how many of our explanations are legitimate, and how many are counterfeit? Just how pervasive is our tendency to rationalize?

INTRODUCING THE PRESS SECRETARY

We need to be careful about drawing abrupt conclusions from research on brain-damaged subjects. The fact that stroke victims and split-brain patients confabulate doesn't necessarily imply that healthy, whole-brained humans do the same. The brain is an intricate organ, and it's no surprise that destroying some of its parts, whether by stroke or by surgery, can cause it to behave strangely—to do things it was never designed to do.

So what *is* the brain designed to do?

Well, what Gazzaniga concludes from his years of research, including later work on healthy patients, is that all human brains contain a system he calls the "interpreter module."[9] The job of this module is to interpret or make sense of our experiences by constructing explanations: stories that integrate information about the past and present, and about oneself and the outside world. This interpreter works to the best of its abilities given the information available to it. So in whole-brained patients, when information is flowing freely between the two hemispheres, the explanations produced by the interpreter typically make a lot of sense. But when the information flow breaks down, whether because of brain damage or any other reason, the interpreter is forced to weave more tenuous, inventive explanations, or even whole-cloth fabrications.

The key question regarding the interpreter is this: For whom does it interpret? Is it for an *internal* audience, that is, the rest of the brain, or for an *external* audience, that is, other people? The answer is both, but the outward-facing function is surprisingly important and often underemphasized. This has led many thinkers, including Dan Dennett, Jonathan Haidt, and Robert Kurzban, to give the interpreter module a more memorable name: the Press Secretary (see Box 6).

Box 6: "Press Secretary"

When we capitalize "Press Secretary," we're referring to the *brain module* responsible for explaining our actions, typically to third parties. The lowercase version of "press secretary" refers to the job held by someone in relation to a president or prime minister.

The idea here is that there's a structural similarity between what the interpreter module does for the brain and what a traditional press secretary does for a president or prime minister. Here's Haidt from *The Righteous Mind*:

> If you want to see post hoc reasoning [i.e., rationalization] in action, just watch the press secretary of a president or prime minister take questions from reporters. No matter how bad the policy, the secretary will find some way to praise or defend it. Reporters then challenge assertions and bring up contradictory quotes from the politician, or even quotes straight from the press secretary on previous days. Sometimes you'll hear an awkward pause as the secretary searches for the right words, but what you'll never hear is: "Hey, that's a great point! Maybe we should rethink this policy."

Press secretaries can't say that because they have no power to make or revise policy. They're simply told what the policy is, and their job is to find evidence and arguments that will justify the policy to the public.[10]

Press secretaries—along with their corporate cousins, public relations teams—fill an interesting niche at the boundary between organizations and the outside world. They're close enough to the actual decision-makers to be privy to *some* important details, but not close enough to get the full scoop. In fact, many press secretaries excel at their jobs with remarkably little contact with the president.[11] Crucially, however, when talking to the press, they don't differentiate between answers based on privileged information and answers that are mere educated guesses. They don't say, "I *think* this is what the administration is doing." They speak authoritatively—like the left hemisphere of the split-brain patient who declared, "I wanted to go get a Coke." In fact, press secretaries actively exploit this ambiguity, hoping their educated guesses will be taken for matters of fact. Their job is to give explanations that are sometimes genuine and sometimes counterfeit, and to make it all but impossible for their audiences to tell the difference.

Press secretaries also provide a buffer between the president and reporters probing for sensitive, potentially damaging information. Remember how knowledge can sometimes be dangerous? Press secretaries can use strategic ignorance to their advantage in ways that a president, who must typically remain informed, can't. In particular, what press secretaries don't know, they can't accidentally betray to the press. "I do my best work," says William Bailey, the fictional press secretary on TV's *The West Wing*, "when I'm the least-informed person in the room."

This is what makes the role of press secretary so hazardous—epistemically if not also morally. It's structured to deliver counterfeit explanations, but also to make those explanations hard to detect, which is as close as you can get without actually lying.

Press secretaries and public relations teams exist in the world because they're incredibly useful to the organizations that employ them. They're a natural response to the mixed-motive incentives that organizations face within their broader ecosystems. And the argument that Kurzban, Dennett, and others have made is that our brains respond to the same incentives by developing a module analogous to a president's press secretary.

Above all, it's the job of our brain's Press Secretary to avoid acknowledging our darker motives—to tiptoe around the elephant in the brain. Just as a president's press secretary should never acknowledge that the president is pursuing a policy in order to get reelected or to appease his financial backers, our brain's Press Secretary will be reluctant to admit that we're doing things for purely personal gain, especially when that gain may come at the expense of others. To the extent that we have such motives, the Press Secretary would be wise to remain strategically ignorant of them.

What's more—and this is where things might start to get uncomfortable—there's a very real sense in which *we* are the Press Secretaries within our minds. In other words, the parts of the mind that we identify with, the parts we think of as our conscious selves ("I," "myself," "my conscious ego"), are the ones responsible for strategically spinning the truth for an external audience.

This realization flies in the face of common sense. In everyday life, there's a strong bias toward treating the self as the mind's ultimate decision-maker—the iron-fisted monarch, or what Dennett calls the mind's Boss or Central Executive.[12] As Harry Truman said about his presidency, "The buck stops here"—and we often imagine the same is true of the self. But the conclusion from the past 40 years of social psychology is that the self acts less like an autocrat and more like a press secretary. In many ways, its job—*our* job—isn't to make decisions, but simply to defend them. "You are not the king of your brain," says Steven Kaas. "You are the creepy guy standing next to the king going, 'A most judicious choice, sire.' "

In other words, even *we* don't have particularly privileged access to the information and decision-making that goes on inside our minds. We think we're pretty good at introspection, but that's largely an illusion. In a way we're almost like outsiders within our own minds.

Perhaps no one understands this conclusion better than Timothy Wilson, a social psychologist who's made a long career studying the perils of introspection. Starting with an influential paper published in 1977[13] and culminating in his book *Strangers to Ourselves*, published in 2002, Wilson has meticulously documented how shockingly little we understand about our own minds.

Wilson writes about the "adaptive unconscious," the parts of the mind which lie outside the scope of conscious awareness, but which nevertheless give rise to many of our judgments, emotions, thoughts, and even behaviors. "To the extent that people's responses are caused by the adaptive unconscious," writes Wilson, "they do not have privileged access to the causes and must infer them." He goes on:

Despite the vast amount of information people have, their explanations about the causes of their responses are no more accurate than
the explanations of a complete stranger who lives in the same culture.[14]

This, then, is the key sleight-of-hand at the heart of our psychosocial
problems: We pretend we're in charge, both to others and even to ourselves, but we're less in charge than we think. We pose as privileged insiders, when in fact we're often making the same kind of educated guesses
that any informed outsider could make. We claim to know our own minds,
when, as Wilson says, we're more like "strangers to ourselves."

The upshot is that every time we give a reason, there's a risk we're just
making things up. Every "because" clause, every answer to a "Why?" question, every justification or explanation of a motive—*every one of these is
suspect*. Not all will turn out to be rationalizations, but any of them could
be, and a great many are.

SNEAKING PAST THE GATEKEEPER

For those of us who want to understand what's really going on in our
minds, the Press Secretary module poses a problem. It acts as a gatekeeper,
an information broker, helping the rest of the brain (the "administration")
conceal its secrets by presenting the most positive, defensible face to the
outside world. We'd like to peer inside the mind—to understand what the
administration is up to—but the Press Secretary controls so much of the
information flow, and it's a notorious spin doctor.

Our challenge in this chapter, then, as well the rest of the book, is to
sneak past the gatekeeper,[15] to catch a glimpse of what's really going on in
the mind, behind the Press Secretary's smoke screen. We've already seen
one fruitful approach: studying split-brain patients and stroke victims. In
such patients, the Press Secretary is partially incapacitated, cut off from
vital sources of information that would normally be available to it. But
there's another time-honored approach to sneaking past the gatekeeper—
misdirecting it.

One of the striking facts about social psychology is how many experiments rely on an element of misdirection. It's almost as if the entire field is based on the art of distracting the Press Secretary in order to expose its rationalizations.

In one classic study, researchers sent subjects home with boxes of three "different" laundry detergents, and asked them to evaluate which worked best on delicate clothes.[16] All three detergents were identical, though the subjects had no idea. Crucially, however, the three *boxes* were different. One was a plain yellow, another blue, and the third was blue with "splashes of yellow."

In their evaluations, subjects expressed concerns about the first two detergents and showed a distinct preference for the third. They said that the detergent in the yellow box was "too strong" and that it ruined their clothes. The detergent in the blue box, meanwhile, left their clothes looking dirty. The detergent in the third box (blue with yellow splashes), however, had a "fine" and "wonderful" effect on their delicate clothes.

Here again, as in the split-brain experiments, *we* (third parties with privileged information) know what's really going on. The subjects simply preferred the blue-and-yellow *box*. But because they were asked to evaluate the *detergents*, and because they thought the detergents were actually different, their Press Secretaries were tricked into making up counterfeit explanations.

Analogous studies involving other products, like wine and pantyhose, have found similar results.[17] The experimental deception in all these studies is the same: An identical product is presented as many "different" products in order to measure how suggestible people are to packaging, presentation, brand, and other framing effects. In each case, the Press Secretary makes up reasons it thinks are legitimate: "Oh, *this* wine is a lot sweeter," or "*These* pantyhose are so smooth." But since the products are identical, we know the reasons must be rationalizations.[18]

In an even more deceptive experiment, researchers showed male subjects pairs of photos of female faces. For each pair, the subjects were asked to point to the face they found more attractive. What the subjects didn't realize is that, after they pointed to their chosen photograph, the researcher used sleight of hand to slip them the *other* photograph, the one they *didn't* choose. The subjects were then asked to explain their "choice." Not only did a clear majority of participants fail to notice the switch, but after being given the wrong photograph, they often proceeded to give concrete and specific reasons for their "choice." "She looks like an aunt of mine I think, and she seems nicer than the other one." Or "She's radiant. I would rather have approached her at a bar than the other one. I like earrings!" (The other woman, the subject's actual choice, was not wearing earrings.) Even under the best conditions—unlimited time to make the choice, pairs of women with different hair colors or styles—the subjects realized they had been deceived only about a third of the time. In most trials, the subject's Press Secretary was perfectly happy to rationalize a decision the subject didn't actually make.[19]

Another technique involves detecting counterfeit reasons *statistically*. Here the idea is to split people into two groups, vary a parameter or two between the groups, then notice how the groups give conflicting reasons for their behavior. Richard Nisbett and Timothy Wilson gave a great demonstration of this technique in the 1977 study we mentioned earlier ("Telling More Than We Can Know"). Subjects were split into two groups. Each group watched a short video of a teacher with a foreign accent, then rated the teacher's overall likability as well as his appearance, mannerisms, and accent. The only difference between the two groups was the way the teacher related to his students. In one group, he was warm and friendly; in the other group, cold and hostile. Otherwise his appearance, mannerisms, and accent were the same.

Subjects in the warm condition obviously liked the teacher more—and, because of the halo effect, they also rated his other attributes higher. But when subjects were asked whether the teacher's overall likability had influenced their judgments about his other attributes, they strongly denied it. In fact, many of them said it was the other way around—that it was the teacher's appearance, mannerisms, and accent that determined whether they liked him. In other words, subjects couldn't "see" that it was actually the teacher's behavior that had influenced their judgments, and so instead many of them made up bogus explanations for how they had formed their opinions.[20]

RATIONALIZATION IN REAL LIFE

We've seen how to catch rationalizations in the lab. Now our task is to spot this kind of behavior in the wild.

Let's start with a simple case involving Kevin's nephew Landon. Here's the scene: It's 8 p.m. and time for Landon to go to bed. He's three years old and in the midst of potty training. His mom asks if he needs to use the toilet before tucking him in for the night. Landon says no, so she gives him a kiss, turns out the light, and shuts the door. Five minutes later he calls out, "Mommy, I need to go potty!" She takes him to the bathroom and then back to bed. But five minutes later he's calling again, "Mommy, I need to go potty!"

At this point, we can roll our eyes. Clearly Landon doesn't need to use the bathroom. And he's far from alone in this behavior. On parenting forums, some moms even describe perfectly potty-trained children who, after being denied their third or fourth consecutive bathroom request, will wet themselves (just a bit) to prove how serious they are. But they aren't fooling anyone; no one with a healthy bladder needs to pee that frequently. Instead these toddlers simply don't want to go to sleep—that's their true motive—and they're using "potty" as a bedtime stalling tactic. It's an excuse, a pretext, a counterfeit reason.

Adults, of course, are more cunning about their counterfeit reasons, and it's commensurately harder to catch them in the act. Adult Press Secretaries are highly trained professionals, their skills honed through years of hard experience; above all, they know how to give rationalizations that are *plausible*. And thus when we (outsiders) are faced with a suspicious reason, it's almost impossible to prove that it's counterfeit. Remember people are often convinced they're telling the truth, and they'll sometimes go to great lengths to prove it—not unlike a toddler wetting herself to "prove" that her bathroom need was legitimate.

We, your two coauthors, can also give examples from our own lives. Robin, for example, has often said his main goal in academic life is to get his ideas "out there" in the name of intellectual progress. But then he began to realize that whenever he spotted his ideas "out there" without proper attribution, he had mixed feelings. In part, he felt annoyed and cheated. If his main goal was actually to advance the world's knowledge, he should have been celebrating the wider circulation of his ideas, whether or not he got credit for them. But the more honest conclusion is that he wants individual prestige just as much as, if not more than, impersonal intellectual progress.

Shortly after his 23rd birthday, Kevin was diagnosed with Crohn's disease. For a while he was extremely reluctant to talk about it (except among family and close friends), a reluctance he rationalized by telling himself that he's simply a "private person" who doesn't like sharing private medical details with the world. Later he started following a very strict diet to treat his disease—a diet that eliminates processed foods and refined carbohydrates. Eating so healthy quickly became a point of pride, and suddenly Kevin found himself perfectly happy to share his diagnosis, since it also gave him an opportunity to brag about his diet. Being a "private person" about medical details went right out the window—and now, look, here he is sharing his diagnosis (and diet!) with perfect strangers in this book.

These two examples illustrate one of the most effective ways to rationalize, which is telling half-truths. In other words, we cherry-pick our most acceptable, prosocial reasons while concealing the uglier ones. Robin really *does* want to get his ideas out there, and Kevin really *is* a private person. But these two explanations aren't the full story.

To identify other examples, we'll have to relax our standards of proof. It's hard to accuse a particular reason of being counterfeit—that's the whole point; we can never be perfectly certain—but here we appeal to our readers' common sense and lived experience. We all know that this happens. And even if some of these examples aren't airtight, we hope they'll give the general flavor of how people use and abuse reasons:

- Parents will often enforce kids' bedtimes "for their own good," when a self-serving motive seems just as likely—that parents simply want an hour or two of peace and quiet without the kids. Of course, many parents genuinely believe that bedtimes are good for their children, but that belief is self-serving enough that we should be skeptical that it's the full story.

- Minor impediments are often exaggerated to avoid unwanted social encounters: "I'm not feeling well today" as an excuse not to go work, for example, or "I'm too busy" to decline a meeting. Typically there's a grain of truth to these reasons, but it's often exaggerated, and meanwhile other reasons (e.g., "I simply don't want to") are conveniently omitted.

- People who download copyrighted material—songs, movies, books— often rationalize their actions by saying, "Faceless corporations take most of the profits from artists anyway." The fact that most of these people wouldn't dream of stealing CDs or DVDs from Best Buy (an equally faceless corporate entity) attests to a different explanation for their behavior, which is that online, they feel anonymous and are less afraid of getting caught.

The point is, we have many reasons for our behaviors, but we habitually accentuate and exaggerate our pretty, prosocial motives and downplay our ugly, selfish ones.[21]

GETTING OUR BEARINGS

So far in this book, our focus has been mostly theoretical. We've tried to explain *why* we often hide our motives, even from ourselves. But merely knowing that hidden motives exist doesn't tell us how widespread they are, nor how big are their effects. For that, we have to turn outward to our behavior and institutions.

In the chapters that follow, we'll examine many different areas of life. For each area, we'll suggest that our visible motives—the usual motives we claim to have—don't seem adequate to explain our behaviors, and that other quite different motives often explain our behaviors better.

As you read the chapters that make up Part II of this book, feel free to jump around. Each chapter stands more or less on its own, so you can read what interests you and skip what doesn't. To recap the relevant section from the table of contents:

(And don't forget the conclusion in Chapter 17 at the very end.)

For better or worse, this book is extremely wide-ranging. In most of the fields we discuss, we—your two coauthors—are relative amateurs. We've tried our best to learn the relevant literature, but we could only read so much; no doubt we're missing a lot of important information. Most of our claims, therefore, and especially the controversial ones, are taken from experts in each field. Of course, we realize that a few expert opinions don't necessarily reflect a consensus among all experts—nor, it should be noted, is consensus opinion necessarily the truth. If we seem to have selectively chosen our sources and evidence, then it's probably because we have. So we are no doubt wrong in many places, not just in the details, but also in some larger conclusions.

Our main goal is to demonstrate that hidden motives are common and important—that they're more than a minor correction to the alternate theory that people mostly do things for the reasons that they give. For this purpose, we don't need to be right about everything. In fact, we expect most readers to buy only about 70 percent of what we're selling—and we're OK with that. Where we're lacking in perspective, we expect that others will widen our view and point out our mistakes. But we hope our overall thesis can withstand these individual corrections.

That said, let's now set out to investigate specific behaviors and institutions, starting with body language.

PART II

Hidden Motives in Everyday Life

Body Language

I n schools across the country, from the first day of kindergarten through high school graduation, children will spend thousands of hours practicing the skills of verbal communication. They'll learn to listen, speak, read, and write—to express their own thoughts and to decipher the expressions of others. Many of these children, however, will receive *not a single hour* of instruction on how to communicate with body language.

Now, it's wrong to say (as many have mistakenly repeated) that "over 90 percent of communication is nonverbal."[1] But the myth persists in part because it alludes to something true, which is that, for social creatures like us, body language is very important. Our bodies convey vital information about our emotions—serenity and anxiety, excitement and boredom, pride and shame—as well as our social attitudes—trust and distrust, self-assurance and self-doubt, intimacy and formality, loyalty and defiance. And we use body language (see Box 7) to coordinate some of our most meaningful activities: making friends, falling in love, and negotiating our position in a hierarchy.

Box 7: "Body Language"

When we say "body language," we're referring not just to arm movements and torso positioning, but more generally to all forms of "nonverbal communication." In fact, we're using these terms synonymously. The concept includes facial expressions, eye behaviors, touch, use of space, and everything we do with our voices besides uttering words: tone, timbre, volume, and speaking style.[2]

We can see the importance of nonverbal skills even from a very early age. One study of 60 kindergarteners, for example, found that children who were better at reading emotions (from photographs of both adults and children) were also more popular among their classmates. The savvier the child, the more likely he or she was to be chosen as an activity partner.[3] These are just correlations, but we also know from personal experience how useful it can be to read body language well.

So why is it left out of the curriculum?

Let's set this question aside for a moment to consider another, related puzzle: the fact that we're largely unconscious of the messages we're sending with our bodies.[4] Certainly we're aware of some of these messages, but not nearly to the extent that we're aware of our spoken messages. And given the importance of nonverbal communication, we might expect to be hyper-aware of it. But in fact the opposite is true. With hardly any deliberate thought, we manage to deftly position our limbs and torsos, flash meaningful facial expressions, laugh at all the right moments, take up an appropriate amount of space, modulate our tone of voice, make or break eye contact as needed, and decipher and react to all these behaviors in others. As physicist-turned-psychologist Leonard Mlodinow says in *Subliminal*, "Much, if not most, of the nonverbal signaling and reading of signals is automatic and performed outside our conscious awareness and control."[5]

It's not just that we *happen* to be partially oblivious to our body language. In many ways, we seem to prefer it this way. We feel it's appropriate for people to act spontaneously. When body language becomes a deliberate performance, it seems forced, perhaps even creepy. Consider the glad-handing salesman who (perhaps after reading a book on body language) starts greeting his customers with a clasp on the shoulder in an attempt to cultivate intimacy and affection. Thankfully, this is the exception rather than the rule; most body language remains involuntary.

In addition to being unaware of our own body language, we're also (although perhaps to a lesser extent) unaware of what *others* are doing with their bodies. "I'm pretty sure Sally doesn't like me," you might tell your spouse, but when asked to justify your impression, you come up blank. "I don't know, it's just a feeling. I can't quite put my finger on it." Even Charles Darwin noticed this. In his pioneering work on nonverbal communication, *The Expression of the Emotions in Man and Animals*, he writes, "It has often struck me as a curious fact that so many shades of expression are instantly recognized without any conscious process of analysis on our part."[6] We're generally aware of the overall gist of one another's body language, but we often struggle to identify the specific behaviors that give rise to our impressions. (See Box 8.)

The question, as always, is "why?" Why are we largely unaware of these signals?

One answer is that consciousness is simply too *slow* to manage the frenetic give-and-take of body language. When an enemy lunges in your direction, your body needs to react instantly; a delay of even a few hundred milliseconds might prove fatal.[7] Consciousness is also too *narrow*. We can focus our spotlight attention on only a small handful of things at once. But in order to weave through a crowd, for example, our brains need to monitor dozens, hundreds, or even thousands of things simultaneously—a task only the unconscious can perform.

But these are only partial answers. Even if we grant that consciousness isn't capable of managing body language in real time, that doesn't explain why consciousness *remains* largely in the dark. Our egos—Press Secretaries—could easily arrange to become better informed about what's going on, even if only after the fact. Indeed, this is exactly what happens to those who study body language professionally, like actors and police interrogators. A more comprehensive answer, then, needs to explain why our conscious minds seem by default to *ignore* what our bodies are up to.

Given what was discussed in Part I, the answer we provide in this chapter should come as no surprise: humans are strategically blind to body language because it often betrays our ugly, selfish, competitive motives. To acknowledge the signals sent by our bodies "feels dangerous to some people," say Alex Pentland and Tracy Heibeck, "as if we were admitting that we are ruled by some base animal nature."[8] Well, so be it. We *are* ruled by an animal nature: human nature.

Box 8: Signals versus Cues

In biology, a *signal* is a behavior or trait used by one animal, the "sender,"
to change the behavior of another animal, the "receiver."[9] Some signals
are deceptive and used to manipulate the receiver, but most are honest,
providing benefit to *both* senders and receivers.[10] A peacock's luxurious tail, for example, conveys information about the health and fitness
of the male sender to one or more female receivers, and both parties
benefit by using the signal to find mates.

A *cue* is similar to a signal, in that it conveys information, except that
it benefits only the receiver.[11] In other words, a cue conveys information the sender might wish to conceal. Sometimes we refer to cues in
the human realm as "tells"—like in the poker movie *Rounders*, when
one character unconsciously twists open an Oreo whenever he has a
winning hand. Other cues or tells can include sweaty palms (indicating
nervousness), shortness of breath (indicating windedness from exer-
tion), and pacifying behaviors such as rubbing one's neck (indicating
anxiety or discomfort).[12]

Cues are important for many students of body language, especially
those—like poker players or police interrogators—who are hoping to
read minds and sniff out deception. In this chapter, however, we're concerned with (honest) signals, that is, traits or behaviors that help both
senders and receivers coordinate their actions.

HONEST SIGNALS: WHY ACTIONS SPEAK
LOUDER THAN WORDS

"No, I can't explain the dance to you. If I could say it, I wouldn't have to
dance it."—Isadora Duncan[13]

Body language differs from spoken language—words—in at least one
crucial regard. In spoken language, the mapping between symbols and
meanings is mostly arbitrary. Words have a fanciful, airy-fairy quality to
them; they aren't anchored to anything fundamental. The only reason we

express gratitude by saying "thank you," instead of "merci" or "arigatou" or "uggawuggawugga," is because that's the way our people have always done it.

Body language, however, is mostly *not* arbitrary.[14] Instead, nonverbal behaviors are meaningfully, functionally related to the messages they're conveying. We show emotional excitement, for example, by being *physically* excited: making noise, waving our arms, dancing up and down.[15] Or we show interest by widening our eyes and looking toward the thing we're interested in, the better to take in visual information. Unlike words, which vary from language to language, most of these signals are shared across cultures.[16] No society arbitrarily decides to convey interest by *closing* their eyes, for example, because the very meaning of interest implies a desire to pay attention and learn more.[17] By the same principle, closing one's eyes or looking away tends to convey some kind of aversion, like boredom or disgust.

The point is, body "language" isn't just a way to communicate. It's also functional; it has material consequences. If we lunge aggressively toward another person, for instance, we better be prepared to fight. And owing to these consequences, body language is *inherently more honest* than verbal language. It's easy to talk the talk, but harder to walk the walk.

This is the principle of honest signaling, which we encountered in Chapter 2.[18] Signals need to be expensive so they're hard to fake. More precisely, they need to be *differentially expensive*—more difficult to fake than to produce by honest means.[19]

Consider how male koalas use mating calls to attract females. Larger and healthier males are capable of making deeper, louder, and more frequent calls—both because large males have bigger body cavities, and because, relative to smaller and weaker males, they have less to fear from rivals and predators. In this way, loud and frequent mating calls are *differentially expensive*. They're expensive to produce (even large, healthy males run the risk of being preyed upon), but they're even more expensive for small and weak males. This helps guarantee their honesty, ensuring that females can use them as a reliable signal for choosing mates.

Back in the human realm, we find honest signals underlying much of our body language. An open posture makes a person vulnerable, for example, which is more dangerous (i.e., costly) for people in tense situations than for people in calm situations. An open posture is therefore an honest signal of comfort. Similarly, it's dangerous to hug someone when you feel threatened by them, ensuring that a hug remains an honest signal of trust and friendship.

And so it's this quality—honesty—that makes body language an ideal medium for coordinating some of our most important activities. It's simply too easy, too tempting, to lie with words. So in matters of life, death, and finding mates, we're often wise to shut up and let our bodies do the talking.

Let's now turn our attention to how we use (honest) body language to navigate the often treacherous waters of human social life. As we do, keep in mind that people may have differing levels of awareness in different domains. What's obvious to you might be revelatory to someone else, and vice versa. Books on "how to read body language" are popular precisely because we *don't* all have perfect intuitive awareness of these things.

SEX

Considering that our ancestors were mating for millions of years before learning to speak, it's no surprise we use body language to coordinate this crucial activity. Intercourse itself is mostly nonverbal, of course, but so are many of the events leading up to it: flirting, come-ons, playing coy, seduction (see Box 9).

All cultures have norms encouraging sexual modesty. Both men and women are expected not to advertise their sexual intentions too prominently and to conduct their sexual activities in private.[20] These norms are crucial to keeping the peace, especially in light of the powerful interests each of us has in the sexual activities of others—husbands and wives guarding their mates, ex-lovers jealous of new lovers, and parents trying to restrict the sexual activities of their teenage children. Nevertheless, we often find ourselves negotiating sex in places that aren't as private as we might like, so we find ways to skirt the norm of modesty. We do this by flirting discreetly, dressing suggestively, and otherwise coordinating to run off for a more private rendezvous.[21]

Imagine a stereotypical one-night stand: Alison and Ben meet for the first time at a bar and end up having sex with each other later that night. Let's set aside the issue of what makes Ben attractive to Alison and vice versa. The question we're interested in is this: Supposing they're both attracted to each other, how do they convey their interest and coordinate to go home with each other? How do they move from strangers to lovers in just a few short hours?

It's possible they'll exchange a small handful of explicit messages on the topic: "I think you're cute," "Do you have a boyfriend?" "Want to come back to my place?" But just as often these messages go unstated, and the entire *pas de deux* is choreographed nonverbally—a carefully negotiated escalation of intimacy.[22]

To begin with, eye contact. Few behaviors convey the message "I'm attracted to you" as convincingly as a lingering come-hither stare. The more intense and prolonged the eye contact, the more it signals that both partners are interested in each other—and comfortable enough to advertise their interest, at least to each other. (Note that eye behaviors are especially hard for third parties to notice, making them ideal for use as discreet signals.) Eye contact will be complemented by body language that says, "I'm open to further interaction." Alison, for example, may uncross her arms, smile invitingly, and turn her body toward Ben.[23]

Even in conversation, what Alison and Ben say to each other may be less significant than how they interact physically. As they develop a rapport, they'll begin to mirror each other's posture. They'll lean in and broach the bubble of personal space that mere strangers are reluctant to violate.[24] They'll even begin to touch each other, perhaps starting with light contact on the back, shoulder, or elbow, then moving to areas reserved for greater intimacy: hands, legs, neck. At some point they may head out to the dance floor, to further escalate physical contact and to see if their bodies (via their brains) can synchronize to a rhythm.[25] If they dance well together, it bodes well for their activities later in the evening.

Now, if this were a romantic comedy—emphasis on *comedy*—Ben might remain oblivious to Alison's come-ons, until finally she's forced to blurt it out: "Take me home already!" But this strikes us as funny only because most people *don't* need words to get the message.

All of this assumes that both partners do, in fact, want to go home with each other. More commonly, one or both participants don't actually know their own full intentions. And much of the thrill and drama of courtship lies in struggling to decipher the other's mixed signals. Women, for example, sometimes instinctively "play coy," attempting to hide or downplay their interest, thereby requiring men to put more effort into courtship.[26]

Sexual jealousy is another cross-cultural human universal,[27] giving rise to the phenomenon of mate-guarding.[28] A couple out on a date, for example, will often use "tie-signs"—handholding, arm-on-shoulder, and so forth—to signal their romantic connection to their partner. These signals are intended not just for each other, but also for third parties, that is, potential rivals. One research team approached and interviewed couples waiting in line to buy movie tickets and found that men performed more tie-signs with their dates when the interviewer posed a greater romantic threat—when the interviewer was male instead of female, for example, or when he asked personal instead of impersonal questions.[29]

Box 9: Love in the Air?

Pheromones are chemical signals secreted by one animal that influence the behavior of other animals, often via the nose. They're an important communication mechanism for many species, from ants and bees to pigs and dogs, and frequently play a role in sexual attraction. Farmers, for example, can buy a pheromone that causes female pigs to assume a mating stance. But what role do pheromones play in human attraction?[30]

The research here is tantalizing. Women asked to smell T-shirts worn by different men were more attracted to men who had complementary immune systems (which would benefit their potential children).[31] Meanwhile, gay men preferred the sweat of other gay men to the sweat of straight men.[32] Scientists debate whether these effects are caused by specific pheromones, but it's clear there's at least *some* chemical basis to human attraction, and that the effects are largely unconscious.[33]

POLITICS

Another domain in which body language plays a surprisingly central role is *politics*. By conveying trust, loyalty, leadership, and followership (as well as distrust, betrayal, and defiance), nonverbals provide richly expressive tools to help us coordinate our coalitions—though we're often unaware of exactly how we use these tools.

Like the nonverbals of sex, the nonverbals of politics run deep in our ancestry. As we saw in Chapter 1, social grooming among primates isn't just a hygienic activity; it also serves a political function. By picking dirt and parasites from each other's fur, primates forge alliances that pay off in other scenarios as well, such as confrontations with other members of the group.

Humans, of course, are a relatively hairless species, so we don't need to spend as much time monitoring each other for dirt and parasites.[34] But we still use proximity and touch to develop friendship and other social bonds.[35] Perhaps the human behaviors most analogous to social grooming are back massages along with brushing, braiding, and other haircare activities. "In traditional cultures," writes Robin Dunbar, "such as the !Kung San hunter-gatherers of southern Africa, women form very distinct haircare cliques who exclusively plait each other's hair."[36] But we also pat, pet, cuddle, hug, shake hands, clasp shoulders, and kiss each other affectionately on the cheek. Boys may wrestle playfully, while girls play "patty cake." The logic here is the same that underlies social grooming in other primates. When we feel comfortable around others, we touch them and allow ourselves to be touched. When we sense hostility, however, we're much more skittish about these violations of personal space.

Of course, our politically charged body language extends far beyond proximity and touch—just as one might expect from the most intensely political species on the planet. When we feel threatened, for example, we naturally adopt an alert and defensive posture. We hunch our shoulders or cross our arms. We sit forward with feet planted firmly on the floor, the better to stand up quickly if tensions escalate. Conversely, when we're in the presence of trusted friends, we let our guards down—by maintaining an open, vulnerable posture, by showing our palms, or by relaxing our shoulders and leaving our necks exposed. "It has always been my impression," says Joe Navarro, a Federal Bureau of Investigation interrogator and body-language expert, "that presidents often go to Camp David to accomplish in polo shirts what they can't seem to accomplish in business suits forty miles away at the White House. By unveiling themselves ventrally (with the removal of coats) they are saying, 'I am open to you.'"[37]

We also coordinate politically with our eyes. We narrow our eyelids when we perceive a threat, for example, or give a quick nod and "eyebrow flash" when we recognize friends or friendly strangers.[38] When situations get tense, we often look to our leaders—literally—for guidance, to gauge their reactions and to potentially follow their lead.

More generally, any act of following or copying another person's behavior—from mimicry on the dance floor to the call-and-response routines common in religious ceremonies—demonstrates a leader's ability to inspire others to follow. In modern workplaces, for example, it's almost always the boss who initiates the end of a meeting, perhaps by being the first to stand up from the table. It would be a *faux pas* for a subordinate to get up and leave before the boss signaled that everyone was free to go.

Our metaphorical use of language also encodes many of these nonverbal political signals.[39] When we betray someone, we "turn our backs" on them, figuratively if not literally. When we confide, we "open up." We're "warm" and "close" with our friends and family, but give the "cold shoulder" to people we dislike. We "stand firm" or "give ground" in confrontations. Body language even shows up in the etymologies of many words that are now entirely abstract. "Confrontation," for example, derives from Latin words meaning "foreheads together."[40]

It's instructive to compare and contrast two greeting rituals: the *handshake*, currently the predominant greeting ritual in Western countries, and the *hand-kiss*, which was popular among European aristocrats in the 18th and 19th centuries (but which has since fallen out of fashion).[41] Both are gestures of trust and amity, but they differ in their political implications. Shaking hands is symmetric and fundamentally egalitarian; it's a ritual between supposed equals. Hand-kissing, however, is inherently asymmetric, setting the kisser apart from, and subordinate to, the recipient of the kiss. The kisser must press his lips on another person's (potentially germ-ridden) hands, while simultaneously lowering his head and possibly kneeling. This gesture is submissive, and when it's performed freely, it's an implicit pledge of loyalty. Even when the ritual is somewhat coerced, it can send a powerful political message. Kings and popes, for example, would often "invite" their subjects to line up for public kiss-the-ring ceremonies, putting everyone's loyalty and submission on conspicuous display and thereby creating common knowledge of the leader's dominance.

We offer one final example of nonverbal political behavior. Imagine yourself out to dinner with a close friend. At some point, the conversation may turn to gossip—discussing and judging the behavior of those who aren't present. But before your friend makes a negative remark about someone, he's liable to glance over his shoulder, lean in, and lower his voice. These are nonverbal cues that what he's about to say requires discretion. He's letting you know that he trusts you with information that could, if word got out, come back to bite him.

SOCIAL STATUS

> "Suddenly we understood that every inflection and movement implies a status, and that no action is due to chance, or really 'motiveless.' It was hysterically funny, but at the same time very alarming. All our secret manoeuvrings were exposed."—Keith Johnstone[42]

Of all the signals sent and received by our bodies, the ones we seem least aware of are those related to social status. And yet, we're all downright obsessed with our status, taking great pains to earn it, gauge it, guard it, and flaunt it. This is a source of great dramatic irony in human life.

Because of their privileged position, high-status individuals have less to worry about in social situations.[43] They're less likely to be attacked, for example, and if they are attacked, others are likely to come to their aid. This allows them to maintain more relaxed body language. They speak clearly, move smoothly, and are willing to adopt a more open posture. Lower-status individuals, however, must constantly monitor the environment for threats and be prepared to defer to higher-status individuals. As a result, they glance around, speak hesitantly, move warily, and maintain a more defensive posture.

High-status individuals are also willing to call more attention to themselves. When you're feeling meek, you generally want to be a wallflower. But when you're feeling confident, you want the whole world to notice. In the animal kingdom, this "Look at me!" strategy is known as *aposematism*.[44] It's a quintessentially honest signal. Those who call attention to themselves are more likely to get attacked—unless they're strong enough to defend themselves. If you're the biggest male lion on the savanna, go ahead, roar your heart out. The same principle explains why poisonous animals, like coral reef snakes and poison dart frogs, wear bright warning colors. They may not look too tough, but they're packing heat.

In the human realm, aposematism underlies a wide variety of behaviors, such as wearing bright clothes, sparkling jewelry, or shoes that clack loudly on the pavement. Wearing prominent collars, headdresses, and elaborate up-dos and swaggering down the street with a blaring boom box all imply the same thing: "I'm not afraid of calling attention to myself, because I'm powerful."

But status is more than just an individual attribute or attitude—it's fundamentally an act of *coordination*. When two people differ in status, both have to modify their behavior.[45] Typically the higher-status person will take up more space, hold eye contact for longer periods of time (more on this in just a moment), speak with fewer pauses, interrupt more frequently, and generally set the pace and tenor of interaction.[46] The lower-status person, meanwhile, will typically defer to the higher-status person in each of these areas, granting him or her more leeway, both physically and socially. In order to walk together, for example, the lower-status person must accommodate to match the gait of the higher-status person.

Most of the time, these unconscious status negotiations proceed smoothly. But when people *disagree* about their relative status, nonverbal coordination breaks down—a result we perceive as social awkwardness (and sometimes physical awkwardness as well). Most of us have had these uncomfortable experiences, as, for example, when sitting across from a rival colleague, not quite knowing how to position your limbs, whether it's your turn to talk, or how and when to end the interaction.

An especially unconscious behavior is how we change our tone of voice in response to the status of our conversation partners. One study used a signal-processing technique to analyze 25 interviews on the *Larry King Live* show. The study found that Larry King adjusted his vocal patterns to match those of his higher-status guests, while lower-status guests adjusted their patterns to match his.[47] A similar analysis was able to predict U.S. presidential election results. During debates, the relative social status of the two candidates—as measured by tone-of-voice accommodation—accurately predicted who would win the popular vote (if not the electoral college vote).[48]

In humans, just as with the Arabian babbler we encountered in Chapter 1, status comes in two distinct varieties: dominance and prestige. *Dominance* is the kind of status we get from being able to intimidate others—think Vladimir Putin or Kim Jong-un. Dominance is won by force, through aggression and punishment. In the presence of a dominant person, our behavior is governed by *avoidance* instincts: fear, submission, and appeasement.[49]

Prestige, however, is the kind of status we get from doing impressive things or having impressive traits—think Meryl Streep or Albert Einstein. Our behavior around prestigious people is governed by *approach* instincts. We're attracted to them and want to spend time around them.[50]

Depending on the type of status at play in a given interaction—dominance or prestige—the participants will adopt different patterns of body language. This becomes especially clear when we consider eye contact.

In contexts governed by dominance, eye contact is considered an act of aggression. It's therefore the prerogative of the dominant to stare at whomever he or she pleases, while submissives must refrain from staring directly at the dominant. When a dominant and a submissive make eye contact, the submissive must look away first. To continue staring would be a direct challenge. Now, submissives can't avoid looking at dominants entirely. They need to monitor them to see what they're up to (e.g., in order to move out of their space). So instead, submissives resort to "stealing" quick, furtive glances.[51] You can think of personal information as the key resource that dominant individuals try to monopolize for themselves. They use their eyes to soak up personal info about the other members of the group, but try to prevent others from learning about them.

In contexts governed by prestige, however, eye contact is considered a gift: to look at someone is to elevate that person. In prestige situations, lower-status individuals are ignored, while higher-status individuals bask in the limelight.[52] In this case, attention (rather than information) is the key resource, which lower-status admirers freely grant to higher-status celebrities.

Many interactions, of course, involve both dominance and prestige, making status one of the trickier domains for humans to navigate. When Joan the CEO holds a meeting, for example, she's often both the most dominant *and* the most prestigious person in the room, and her employees must rely on context to decide which kinds of eye contact are appropriate. Whenever Joan is talking, she's implicitly asking for attention (prestige), and her employees oblige by looking directly at her. When she stops talking, however, her employees may revert to treating her as dominant, issuing the kind of furtive glances characteristic of submissives who hesitate to intrude on her privacy, and yet still wish to gauge her reactions to what's happening in the meeting.

Social status influences how we make eye contact, not just while we listen, but also when we speak. In fact, one of the best predictors of dominance is the *ratio* of "eye contact while speaking" to "eye contact while listening." Psychologists call this the *visual dominance ratio*.

Imagine yourself out to lunch with a coworker. When it's your turn to talk, you spend some fraction of the time looking into your coworker's eyes (and the rest of the time looking away). Similarly, when it's your turn to listen, you spend some fraction of the time making eye contact. If you make eye contact for the *same* fraction of time while speaking and listening, your visual dominance ratio will be 1.0, indicative of high dominance. If you make *less eye contact while speaking*, however, your ratio will be less than 1.0 (typically hovering around 0.6), indicative of low dominance.[53]

In *Subliminal*, Mlodinow summarizes some of these findings:[54]

> What is so striking about the data is not just that we subliminally adjust our gazing behavior to match our place on the hierarchy but that we do it so consistently, and with numerical precision. Here is a sample of the data: when speaking to each other, ROTC officers exhibited ratios of 1.06, while ROTC cadets speaking to officers had ratios of 0.61;[55] undergraduates in an introductory psychology course scored 0.92 when talking to a person they believed to be a high school senior who did not plan to go to college but 0.59 when talking to a person they believed to be a college chemistry honor student accepted into a prestigious medical school;[56] expert men speaking to women about a subject in their own field scored 0.98, while men talking to expert women about the women's field, 0.61; expert women speaking to nonexpert men scored 1.04, and nonexpert women speaking to expert men scored 0.54.[57] These studies were all performed on Americans. The numbers probably vary among cultures, but the phenomenon probably doesn't.

Our brains manage all these behaviors almost effortlessly. Rarely do we have to ask ourselves, consciously, "How should I hold my arms? Should I make or break eye contact? What tone of voice should I use?" It all comes to us quite naturally, because our ancestors who were adept at it fared better than those of our (non-)ancestors who were less naturally skilled.

WHY WE'RE UNAWARE OF BODY LANGUAGE

Let's now circle back to our original question: Why does so much of our nonverbal signaling take place outside the spotlight of conscious awareness?

The three areas of social life we've examined in this chapter—sex, politics, and status—are laced with norms governing our behavior.[58] What we may hope to accomplish in each area is often at odds with the interests of others, which can easily lead to conflict. That's why societies have so many norms to regulate behavior in these areas, and why we (as individuals) must take pains to conduct ourselves discreetly.

As a medium of communication, body language gives us just the cover we need. Relative to spoken language, it's considerably more ambiguous. While the overall *patterns* of body language may be consistent, any isolated behavior will have many interpretations.[59] Such ambiguity, as we've seen in earlier chapters, can be a feature rather than a bug—especially when we're trying to hide our intentions from others.

Consider how we use our bodies to "say" a lot of things we'd get in trouble for saying out loud. It would be appallingly crass to announce, "I'm the most important person in the room"—but we can convey the same message, discreetly, simply by splaying out on a couch or staring at people while talking to them. Similarly, "I'm attracted to you," is too direct to state out loud to someone you just met—but a smile, a lingering glance, or a friendly touch on the wrist can accomplish the same thing, with just enough plausible deniability to avoid ruffling feathers.

The point is, relative to spoken messages, nonverbal messages are much harder to pin down precisely, making it easier to avoid accusations of impropriety. In a meeting at work, for example, Peter may use nonverbals to marginalize his rival Jim (e.g., by ignoring him while he speaks). But if Peter is accused of acting "politically," he'll quickly deny it, arguing that his accuser has misread the situation. Later, at a party, he may use body language to flirt with another woman. But if his wife accuses him, he's likely to explain that he was merely being friendly.

Peter himself may not even be fully aware of what he's doing. At work he may simply think, "Jim is always ruining things," and not consider his own behavior to be "political." Similarly, at the party, he may truly believe he's just being friendly, without any conscious intention to flirt. Nevertheless, in both cases his behavior deserves to be questioned. Whether or not he acknowledges it, part of Peter's mind would love to see Jim fired, and part of his mind is attracted to the other woman and is curious to see what might happen if he continues "being friendly."

If Peter introspected carefully enough, he could probably bring himself to notice these motives lurking in the back of his mind—but why bother calling attention to them? The less his Press Secretary knows about these motives, the easier it is to deny them with conviction. And meanwhile, the rest of his brain is managing to coordinate his self-interest just fine.

Body language also facilitates discretion by being *less quotable* to third parties, relative to spoken language. If Peter had explicitly told a colleague, "I want to get Jim fired," the colleague could easily turn around and relay Peter's agenda to others in the office. Similarly, if Peter had asked his flirting partner out for a drink, word might get back to his wife—in which case, bad news for Peter.

This is the magic of nonverbal communication. It allows us to pursue illicit agendas, even ones that require coordinating with other people, while minimizing the risk of being attacked, accused, gossiped about, and censured for norm violations. This is one of the reasons we're strategically unaware of our own body language, and it helps explain why we're reluctant to teach it to our children.[60]

Not all of our nonverbal messages are taboo in this way, of course. We're all perfectly aware that droopy eyes mean we're feeling tired, outstretched arms mean we're feeling proud, and smiles mean we're feeling happy. It doesn't fluster us to admit these meanings or to comment on them in conversation. But as soon as someone points out our sex-, politics-, or status-related body language, we begin to fumble about self-consciously. And like a murder suspect turning suddenly awkward during an interrogation, we're uncomfortable because we have something to hide.

Laughter

Humans can be strange. And of all our strange behaviors, surely among the strangest is our tendency to erupt into wild fits of rhythmic gasping and grunting. We contort our faces, clutch our sides, and double over as if in anguish. But far from being painful, this curious activity is considered the height of pleasure. We actively seek it out. We gather in large crowds, eager to experience it together. We even judge our friends, our lovers, and our leaders by their ability to elicit it from us.

Laughter[1]—chuckles, chortles, giggles, and guffaws—is an innate and universal behavior. We start laughing almost as soon as we're out of the womb, months before we learn to talk or sing.[2] Even infants born blind and deaf, who can't copy behaviors from their parents or siblings, instinctively know how to laugh.[3] And while each culture develops its own distinct language and singing style, laughter sounds pretty much the same in every remote village and bursting metropolis on the planet. As they say, it needs no translation.

Laughter is an involuntary behavior. It's not something we actively decide to do; our brains simply do it, naturally and spontaneously. In this way, laughter is similar to other involuntary behaviors like breathing, blinking, flinching, hiccuping, shivering, and vomiting. But whereas these are merely physiological, laughter is an involuntary *social* behavior.[4] We use laughter to flirt, bond with friends, mock our enemies, probe social norms, and mark the boundaries of our social groups. It's a response to social cues, laced with interpersonal significance, and yet "we"—the conscious, deliberate, willful parts of our minds—don't get to decide when we do it.[5]

As if that weren't strange enough, we're also astonishingly unaware of what laughter means and why we do it. Speculation abounds, but much of it is erroneous, and not just among laypeople. For more than two millennia, many of the Western world's brightest minds—from Plato and Aristotle to Hobbes and Descartes, and even Freud and Darwin—have been completely mistaken about why we laugh (see Box 10).

Box 10: A Brief History of Laughter

Prior to 1930, according to philosopher John Morreall, there were three main theories of laughter and humor.[6]

According to the *superiority theory* (Plato, Aristotle, Thomas Hobbes, and René Descartes[7]), laughter is fundamentally mean-spirited, a form of mockery, derision, or scorn. The superiority theory says that we laugh primarily *at* other people, because we feel superior to them. The problems with this theory are that it can't explain why we laugh when we're tickled, or why we *don't* laugh when we see a beggar on the street.

According to the *relief theory* (Sigmund Freud, Herbert Spencer), laughter is a physiological process. We laugh whenever a situation initially causes the brain to summon "nervous energy" (to deal with a perceived threat or negative emotion), but then takes away the need for such energy. Unused, the excess energy somehow needs to be dissipated, and convulsive laughter does the trick. In other words, laugher = tension + relief. The main problem with this theory is that there's no such thing as "nervous energy" sloshing around in our brains. Our brains aren't hydraulic processes; they're chemical and electrical. And modern analogs to "nervous energy"—hormones like epinephrine and cortisol—don't need to be dissipated through laughter.

Finally, the *incongruity theory* (Immanuel Kant, Arthur Schopenhauer) says we laugh when our expectations are violated, especially in a pleasing way. Incongruity explains why most jokes take the form of a setup followed by a punchline: the setup creates an expectation, which is then violated by the punchline. The main problem with this theory is that it doesn't explain why incongruity causes us to make sounds[8] or how those sounds are used socially.

As we'll see, there are grains of truth in all these theories. But none of them captures the essence of laughter as an *evolved social behavior.*

For a behavior we perform every day, it's shocking how alien laughter is to our conscious minds. But while "we" may not understand or control our laughter, our brains are experts at it. They know when to laugh, at which stimuli, and they get it right most of the time, with inappropriate laughter bursting forth only on occasion. Our brains also instinctively know how to interpret the laughter of others, whether by laughing in return or otherwise reacting appropriately. It's only to "us"—our conscious, introspective minds—that laughter remains a mystery.

On the surface, laughter seems to be all fun and games, an expression of joy. Picture an infant giggling at a game of peekaboo with her father—what could be more wholesome and innocent? But from earlier chapters, we know that ignorance often serves a deceptive purpose; our brains hide certain things from us in order to hide them more effectively from others. This suggests there may be a hidden dark side to laughter. Consider how we often use humor as an excuse to trot out our most taboo subjects: race, sex, politics, and religion. Or how we laugh at people who are different from us or people who aren't in the room. We can say things in the comedic register that we'd never dream of saying in a straight-faced discussion. The paradox of laughter is that it puts us at ease in social situations, and yet its meaning and purpose seem to reside squarely in our introspective blind spot.

In this chapter we're going to demystify laughter—to "crack the code" and explain it as clearly as possible. (It turns out there's a very crisp, satisfying answer.) Then we'll turn our attention to the darker side of laughter, to investigate what our brains are hiding from us.

THE BIOLOGY OF LAUGHTER

Why *do* we laugh?

When we're asked this question in real life—upon laughing at a joke, for example—we might say, "Because it was funny." In other words, it's our perception of something humorous that causes us to laugh. This fits the stimulus–response pattern underlying many of our behaviors, especially the involuntary ones, and it has a lot of intuitive appeal. Just as we smile when we're happy and cry when we're sad, so too must we laugh in response to some psychological state triggered by humor.

This line of thinking might lead us to wonder about the psychology of humor—a topic fruitfully explored in the book *Inside Jokes*, for example. But for our purpose in investigating laughter, humor turns out to be a wild goose chase. In part, this is because whatever "humor" turns out to be, we're still left with the question of why we emit *giggles* and *chuckles* in response. Beyond that, we also need to explain why we laugh at *nonhumorous* stimuli like tickling, pillow fights, and roller coasters—or when, as children, we get to explore a new physical environment like snow, water, or a big pile of leaves.

In order to explain laughter, then, we'll have to look beyond the psychology of humor. And that's our cue to introduce Robert Provine, a professor of neurobiology at the University of Maryland. Now, Provine wasn't the first to crack the code of laughter; others, like Max Eastman, had conjectured the solution half a century earlier. But Provine's research has done more to solidify our understanding of laughter than the legion of armchair theorists who preceded him.

In the 1990s, Provine noticed that the literature on laughter was full of speculative theorizing, but preciously short on actual data. So he resolved to fix this by studying laughter empirically, both in the lab and out "in the wild"—in shopping malls, parks, and other public spaces in contemporary America. He decided to treat laughter as an animal behavior, not unlike a dog's bark or a bird's song. "In the spirit of Jane Goodall heading out to Gombe Stream Preserve to study chimpanzees," writes Provine, "three undergraduate assistants and I set forth on an urban safari to study humans in their natural habitat."[9]

This empirical, biological study of laughter produced a few key observations. The most important observation is that we laugh far more often in social settings than when we're alone—30 times more often, in Provine's estimate.[10] It's not that we never laugh by ourselves; clearly, sometimes, we do. But laughter is designed, or at least optimized, for social situations. This is one reason TV and radio producers developed "laugh tracks" for their shows. Even canned laughter tricks our brains into thinking we're in a more social setting than we actually are—and so we're more likely to laugh.[11]

The second key observation about laughter is that it's a vocalization, a sound. And across the animal kingdom, sounds serve the purpose of *active communication*. Cobras hiss to scare off predators. Dogs bark as a warning sign. Male birds sing to attract females, while baby birds chirp to let their parents know they're hungry. In all these cases, animals make noise because they want to be heard—because they want to affect their listeners in predictable ways. And so too with laughter. When Provine studied 1,200 episodes of laughter overheard in public settings, his biggest surprise was finding that *speakers laugh more than listeners*—about 50 percent more, in fact. This makes little sense if we think of laughter as a passive reflex, but becomes clear when we remember that laughter is a form of active communication. Even infants seem to use laughter intentionally, to communicate their emotional state to their interaction partners. Provine describes the "duet" that takes place between mother and baby, where the mother first provides some stimulation, typically in the form of a touch or a tickle, and the baby responds either by laughing ("More! More!") or by crying, defending, or fussing ("Too much! Stop!").[12] Similarly, an early study at Yale demonstrated that infants laugh much more readily when tickled by their mothers than when tickled by a stranger.[13] This kind of laughter isn't just a knee-jerk physiological reaction; it's a message used to regulate social interaction.

The final key observation is that laughter occurs even in other species. Specifically, it's found in all five of the "great apes"—orangutans, gorillas, bonobos, chimpanzees, and humans—although not in any other primates, suggesting an origin in our common ancestor, 12 to 18 million years ago. This evolutionary account is corroborated by the acoustic properties of laughter. By analyzing recorded laughs from each of the great-ape species, researchers were able to reconstruct the same "family tree" of species relationships that we know from genetics. In other words, the more closely related two species are, the more their laughs sound alike.[14]

Our ape cousins also laugh in many of the same situations as we do—when being tickled by a friendly familiar, for example, or during rough-and-tumble play.[15] The chimp Lucy, reared among humans, has even been caught laughing while drunk on alcohol and making funny faces at herself in the mirror.[16] And chimps, like humans, laugh more with others than when they're alone.[17]

All of this suggests that laughter serves a concrete biological function rooted in animal communication. But what kind of message is so important that our distant ape ancestors evolved an innate signal to convey it?

LAUGHTER IS A PLAY SIGNAL

"Both in man and his primate relatives, laughter marks the boundary of seriousness."—Alexander Kozintsev[18]

"I am convinced that a majority of the learned philosophers who have written treatises on laughter and the comic never saw a baby."—Max Eastman[19]

According to legend, Archimedes had his iconic "Eureka!" moment in a public bath. Newton had his moment under an apple tree. And Eastman—an American journalist and roving intellectual—had his flash of insight about laughter while playing with an infant. Here's how he describes that insight in his 1936 book *The Enjoyment of Laughter*:

The next time you are called upon to entertain a baby, I will tell you what to do. Laugh, and then make a perfectly terrible face. If the baby is old enough to perceive faces . . . he will laugh too. But if you make a perfectly terrible face all of a sudden, without laughing, he is more likely to scream with fright. In order to laugh at a frightful thing he has to be in a mood of play.[20]

The core idea here is that laughter is necessarily coupled with play. If the mood is serious, a terrible face will elicit a scream, but if the mood is playful, the very same stimulus will elicit a laugh. As Eastman says, "No definition of humor, no theory of wit, no explanation of comic laughter, will ever stand up, which is not based upon the distinction between *play-ful* and *serious*."[21]

Play, according to zoologists, is a mode of behavior in which animals, especially young ones, explore the world and practice skills that will be important later in life. It's a voluntary, nonfunctional (i.e., impractical[22]) activity undertaken in a safe, relaxed setting.[23] And it's extremely common in the animal kingdom. Every mammal engages in play—think wrestling or play biting—and many birds do as well. Even reptiles and amphibians have been caught in the act.

But while we humans often play by ourselves (e.g., with Legos), recall that we laugh mostly in the presence of others. So what *communicative* purpose does laughter serve in the context of play?

Gregory Bateson, a British anthropologist, figured it out during a trip to the zoo. He saw two monkeys engaged with each other in what looked like combat, but clearly wasn't real. They were, in other words, merely *play fighting*. And what Bateson realized was that, in order to play fight, the monkeys needed some way to communicate their playful intentions— some way to convey the message, "We're just playing." Without one or more of these "play signals," one monkey might misconstrue the other's intentions, and their playful sparring could easily escalate into a real fight.[24]

At the time, it wasn't clear to Bateson exactly how the monkeys were telegraphing their playful intentions to each other, just that they must have had some means of doing it. But biologists have since studied these play signals in detail, and it's not only primates who use them. "We're just playing" is such an important message, it turns out, that many species have developed their own vocabulary for it.[25] Dogs, for example, have a "play bow"—forearms extended, head down, hindquarters in the air— which they use to initiate a bout of play.[26] Chimps use an open-mouthed "play face," similar to a human smile,[27] or double over and peer between their legs at their play partners.[28] And many animals, in addition to using specific gestures, will also move slowly or engage in exaggerated or unnec-essary movement, as if to convey playful intent by conspicuously wasted effort that no animal would undertake if it were in serious danger. All of these signals serve to reassure playmates of one's happy mood and friendly intentions.

And humans, in the same vein, have laughter. But not *just* laughter—we also use smiling, exaggerated body movements, awkward facial expressions (like winking), and a high-pitched, giddy "play scream." All of these signals mean roughly the same thing: "We're just playing." This message allows us to coordinate *safe social play* with other humans, especially when we're playing in ways that hint at or border on real danger.

We can actually distinguish two closely related meanings of laughter, depending on context. When we laugh at our own actions, it's a signal to our playmates that our *intentions* are ultimately playful (although we may seem aggressive). This is the kind of laugh a young child might give after play hitting an adult or other child,[29] or that adults give when they're gently poking fun at someone. It's the behavioral equivalent of "Just kidding!" or a winking emoji at the end of a text message ☺. When we laugh in response to *someone else's* actions, however, it's a statement not about intentions but about perceptions. It says, "I perceive your actions as playful; I know you're only kidding around." This is reactive laughter, the kind elicited in response to an external stimulus. Jokes and other forms of humor are one such stimulus, but being tickled, chased, or surprised in a game of peekaboo all work the same way.[30]

Both uses of laughter function as reassurances: "In spite of what might seem serious or dangerous, I'm still feeling playful." And the "in spite of" clause is important. We don't laugh continuously throughout a play session, only when there's something potentially unpleasant to react to. Like all acts of communication, laughter must strive to be relevant.[31] When it's obvious that everyone is safe and happy—while quietly playing Monopoly, for example—there's no need to belabor the obvious. We need to reinforce that "We're just playing" only when circumstances arise which might, if not for the laughter, be mistaken for too serious or dangerous[32] (see Box 11).

This helps explain why an element of danger is so important for getting a laugh. Now, danger isn't strictly required—we sometimes laugh at harmless wordplay, for example.[33] But danger certainly helps. A pun is a lot funnier when it's a sexual double-entendre told in the presence of children. ("How many flies does it take to screw in a light bulb? Two.") And when there's not enough danger, attempts at humor often fall flat. The comic strips *Marmaduke* and *The Family Circus*, for instance, are so timid and toothless (to many sensibilities) as to be considered boring.

Box 11: Kevin Fires a Shotgun

The first time I fired a shotgun and felt the recoil, I started laughing—somewhat hysterically, in fact. I realize that makes me sound crazy, but here's what I think happened. A firearm is a taboo object in my culture. I was raised without any contact with guns, and so when I fired one as an adult at a shooting range, I was already perched at the psychological boundary between safety and danger. Then, given the surprise of the blast and the violent recoil, I was plunged into terror for a fraction of a second—not unlike the initial jump of a skydiver. But I quickly realized that I was perfectly safe, and my brain's response to all this, evidently, was to laugh—to let my friends know that I felt safe and comfortable, and that I wanted to try it again.

The play-signal theory also explains many of the instances when we *don't* laugh. When a clown "trips" and falls down the stairs, you might chuckle, knowing that he's just playing and is actually OK. But when your aging grandmother stumbles and falls, everything is decidedly *not* OK; her accident represents acute danger. It's only after you've rushed to her side and discovered that she's perfectly safe that *maybe* it becomes reasonable to laugh about the situation—especially if she starts laughing first. In fact, the logic of laughter explains why her laughter is likely to trigger yours, rather than the other way around. If she laughs first, it means she feels safe, so you can feel safe too. But if you laugh first, she's liable to take offense. How could you feel safe when she hasn't given the "all clear" (you insensitive clod)? It must mean you don't really care what happens to her.

In light of all this, we're now equipped to think about the relationship between laughter and humor. In any given comedic situation, humor precedes and causes laughter, but when we step back and take a broader perspective, the order is reversed. Our propensity to laugh comes first and provides the necessary goal for humor to achieve.[34] Humor can thus be seen as an art form, a means of provoking laughter subject to certain stylistic constraints. Humorists, in general, work in the abstract media of words and images. They don't get credit, as humorists, for provoking laughter by physical means— by tickling their audiences, for example. They're also generally discouraged from eliciting contagious laughter, that is, by laughing themselves.

In this way, humor is like opening a safe. There's a sequence of steps that have to be performed in the right order and with a good deal of precision. First you need to get two or more people together.[35] Then you must set the mood dial to "play." Then you need to jostle things, carefully, so that the dial feints in the direction of "serious," but quickly falls back to "play." And only then will the safe come open, releasing the precious laugher locked inside.[36]

Different cultures may put different constraints on how a humorist is allowed to interact with the safe, or they may set a different "combination," that is, by defining "playful" and "serious" in their own idiosyncratic ways such that one culture's humor might not unlock a foreigner's safe. But the core locking mechanism is the same in every human brain, and we come straight out of the factory ready to be tickled open, literally and metaphorically.

THE DARK SIDE OF LAUGHTER

> "In everything that we perceive as funny there is an element which, if we were serious and sufficiently sensitive, and sufficiently concerned, would be unpleasant."—Max Eastman[37]

As we mentioned earlier, people are profoundly ignorant about laughter's meaning and purpose (at least in our default state, before learning the science). But where does this ignorance come from? Why does introspection fail us so spectacularly here?

It's not simply because laughter is involuntary, outside our conscious control. Flinching, for example, is also involuntary, and yet we understand perfectly well why we do it: to protect ourselves from getting hit. Thus our ignorance about *laughter* needs further explanation.

As we've hinted, such ignorance may be strategic; our brains may be trying to hide something. And yet the meaning of laughter—"We're playing!"—seems entirely innocent and aboveboard.

Perhaps it's not what laughter *is* that makes us uncomfortable, but rather *how we use it*. In this regard, laughter is like money. It doesn't bother us to "admit" that money is a medium of exchange,[38] but we might well be embarrassed to reveal our credit card statements to the entire world. When the *New York Times* reported that Target can predict whether a woman is pregnant simply by analyzing her recent purchases, it caused quite a stir among privacy advocates, for obvious reasons.[39] Similarly, if our brains kept a log of all the specific situations that ever jiggled a laugh out of us, we might be just as nervous about opening those records up for the world to inspect. As Provine points out, "Laughter . . . is a powerful probe into social relationships."[40] But often we don't want to be probed. We crave privacy and plausible deniability, and our natural ignorance about laughter may provide just the cover we need.

To understand what laughter reveals (that we might prefer to keep hidden), we need to consider two important factors: norms and psychological distance.

NORMS

As young children, most of our play concerns the physical world. And what we laugh at is similarly physical or physiological. Common triggers for laughter among infants and toddlers include mock aggression (tickling, chasing), mock danger (being thrown in the air by a caretaker), and carefully crafted surprises (peekaboo).

As we age, however, we start paying more attention to the *social* world and its attendant dangers, many of which revolve around *norms*. In Chapter 3, we saw how norm violations can be serious business. When we violate a norm, we have to worry about getting caught and punished. And when someone else seems to violate a norm, we have to ask ourselves, "Is this a threat? Do I need to step in and regulate?" Our actions in these situations carry real risks. If we misstep, we might face disapproval from our peers or censure from authority figures—or worse. Remember the Maori villager who was killed for too much freeloading?

But where there's danger, there's also an opportunity for exploratory play. And just as the physical danger of a roller coaster tickles our physiological funny bone, flirting with norm-related danger tickles our social funny bone.[41]

Consider a five-year-old girl who finds potty humor hilarious. She knows it's rude to perform (or talk about) certain bodily functions in front of others, and that she risks being punished if she does. But at the same time, she can't take every rule at face value; she needs to probe her boundaries. Just how serious are these norms, really? If she soils her pants, of course, she may feel legitimately ashamed—and thus, no laughter. But if she merely farts, she'll quickly learn that the danger is quite small; her parents may scowl, but they're not going to send her to her room. And this realization—that farting can be safe, even though it's officially discouraged—is liable to provoke some laughter. And a whoopie cushion may be even funnier to the young girl, since it produces only *fake* fart noises, and is entirely benign.

At some point during her development, however, she'll exhaust the learning opportunities around bodily norms, and they'll cease to be a fertile source of play. And soon she'll graduate to the grown-up world, where we're concerned mostly with social, sexual, and moral norms. These are an endless source of fascination, in part because there are so many of them, with so many nuances, that we can never hope to learn all of their boundaries and edge cases. But they're also fascinating because they're always shifting around as circumstances and attitudes change. Just as guides to etiquette need to be refreshed every few years, so too must our humor evolve to keep up with changing norms. What was once a sweet spot for comedy can evolve into a genuine sore spot, a cultural bruise—or vice versa. The shifting political landscape can neuter what was once a deadly serious accusation ("Commie!"), turning it into a playful insult. Tech innovations, such as the cell phone, turn old norms upside down and force new ones to come into being. Only some of these norms are ever written down—and when they are, they're often obsolete as soon as the ink is dry. They vary widely across different communities and contexts. And sometimes, as with sexual norms, they're uncomfortable to discuss in precise terms or in serious settings. All of these factors make them ripe for play, and therefore laughter.

In the broadest sense, there are at least two ways to use the danger of norms for comedic effect. The first is to feint across the norm boundary, but then retreat back to safety without actually violating it. The second way is to step across the boundary, violating the norm, and then to realize, like a child jumping into snow for the first time, "It's safe over here! Wheee!"

Here, for example, is a joke that flirts with, but doesn't actually consummate, a norm violation:

MARY: What do you call a black man flying a plane?
JOHN: Uh . . . I don't know. . . .
MARY: A pilot. What did you think, you racist?!

The humor here plays off the norm against racism. After Mary's setup, John starts to squirm uncomfortably, afraid his friend is about to tell an offensive joke. But when Mary delivers the punchline, it's sweet, safe relief. She wasn't telling a racist joke after all. She was just playing! And a hearty chuckle ensues.[42]

This joke uses the norm against racism only to provide the sense of danger, and achieves safety (and laughter) by *not* violating it. In this way, the joke ultimately reinforces the norm. But other jokes don't pull back from the norm violation, and must achieve safety by other means, which often subverts the norms that they're playing with.

In September 2012, for example, the French satirical magazine *Charlie Hebdo* published irreverent cartoons of the prophet Muhammad, including a few nude caricatures. While many secular liberals found the cartoons humorous, some fundamentalist Muslims most definitely did not. These divergent attitudes are a reflection of how seriously each group treats the norms against mocking religion (in general) or depicting Muhammad (in particular). Secularists feel that such "norms" shouldn't have much sway in public life, while fundamentalists would like them to be enshrined as law.

What our brains choose to laugh at, then, reveals a lot about our true feelings in morally charged situations. It says, "I realize something is supposedly considered 'wrong' here, but I'm not taking it seriously." If we laugh at cartoon drawings of Muhammad, our brains reveal that we're only weakly committed to the norm in question. What seems like a mere cartoon is actually a proxy for much deeper issues.

A real danger of laughter, then, is the fact that we don't all share the same norms to the same degree. What's sacred to one person can be an object of mere play to another. And so when we laugh at norm violations, it often serves to weaken the norms that others may wish to uphold. This helps explain why people charged with maintaining the highest standards of propriety—schoolmarms, religious leaders, the guardians in Plato's *Republic*, the Chinese officials who banned puns in 2014[43]—have an interest in tamping down on laughter and humor.

When two people laugh at the same joke for the same reasons, it brings them closer together. But when we laugh at another person's sacred cow, it ceases to be all fun and games.

PSYCHOLOGICAL DISTANCE

The other kind of sensitive information our brains "leak" through laughter is how we feel toward those who become the objects of our comedy, the butts of our jokes. The less we care about people, the easier is it to laugh when bad things happen to them.

Actually two variables are important here. The first is, simply, *how much pain* is involved. We're more likely to laugh at a pinprick than at a broken bone, and more likely to laugh at a broken bone than a violent death.

The second variable is *psychological distance*.[44] When people are "farther" from us, psychologically, we're slower to empathize with them, and more likely to laugh at their pain. "Tragedy," said Mel Brooks, "is when *I* cut my finger. Comedy is when *you* walk into an open sewer and die."[45]

According to this measure, friends are closer than acquaintances, who in turn are closer than enemies. But our perception of psychological distance depends on many other factors. For example, events that take place in the make-believe space of fiction are more psychologically distant than events that happen in real life, and cartoon comedies are more remote than live-action dramas. Similarly, ancient history is more psychologically remote than recent history. In an episode of *South Park*, the characters joke about whether enough time has passed for AIDS to be considered funny.[46] Or as Carol Burnett said, "Comedy is tragedy plus time."[47]

Together these two variables determine how much pain we feel, sympathetically, upon learning about someone else's misfortune. When someone close to us suffers terribly, we feel it in our marrow; it *hurts*. But when a distant stranger suffers only a scratch, it hardly registers for us. In between, of course, are all the interesting edge cases: a close friend who spills wine on her lap, or a second-cousin who breaks his arm doing something stupid. Whether or how hard we laugh at such edge cases says a lot about our relationship to the person experiencing pain.

Imagine a group of three popular middle-school girls standing by their lockers in the hallway. One of their unpopular classmates, Maggie, walks by and trips, spilling her books and papers everywhere—and the popular girls start pointing and laughing.

Clearly this laughter is rude, perhaps even aggressive. When someone gets hurt, the humane response is to break from a playful mood into a serious mood, to make sure they're OK. The popular girls' laughter, then, reveals that they don't take Maggie's suffering seriously. They're treating her pain as an object of play—a mere plaything.

Note that this isn't a different *type* of laughter than the kind we saw earlier. It means the same thing: "In spite of what just happened, I'm feeling safe." Or "I realize something is supposedly 'wrong' here, but it doesn't bother me." It's the *context* that makes this laughter rude and mean-spirited.

Now, we need to be careful how we moralize about what these popular girls are doing. It would be easy to condemn them for laughing at the misfortune of another human being. But that's not the real problem; we all laugh at other people in this way. Consider the *Darwin Awards*, a website that "commemorates those who improve our gene pool by removing themselves from it." It's a catalog of gruesome deaths (usually involving irony, stupidity, or both), played entirely for laughs. But although the accidents described in the *Darwin Awards* are vastly more serious than Maggie's stumble, we find it funny because the victims are strangers, and thus their pain doesn't register as serious for us. For better or worse, this is how we're wired.

To give an even more disturbing example, consider how often we joke and laugh about prison rape—"Don't drop the soap!" for example. On sober reflection, we may realize these jokes are distasteful, if not morally odious; rape should be universally condemned, no matter who the victims are. And yet, when the victims are convicted criminals, our brains don't send us the same "danger!" signals that they would send if the victims were innocent citizens. People behind bars are remote, both socially and psychologically, and we tend not to empathize with them to the same degree we empathize with our friends and neighbors.

When the popular girls laugh at Maggie, then, their brains are running the same algorithm that ours are running when we laugh at prison rape or the *Darwin Awards*.[48]

If we insist on moralizing about what the popular girls are doing, we should focus on the fact that their laughter itself contributes to further suffering. Most of us strive to laugh only in situations where our laughter is harmless, or even (on occasion) helpful. When a friend spills wine on her shirt, we want to laugh, ideally, only after she's given us the "all clear" by laughing herself. Or we might take a risk and laugh preemptively, hoping that our laughter will help her to appreciate the non-seriousness of the situation. But such laughter needs to be very gentle indeed, and we'll want to back off if she shows any sign of taking offense, lest our laughter be the cause of further suffering.

Teasing hinges on a similar dynamic. To tease is to provoke a small amount of suffering in a playful manner, often accompanied by laughter. The interesting cases lie between *good-natured teasing*, which strengthens a relationship, and *mean-spirited teasing*, which weakens it. Teasing is good-natured when it provokes only light suffering, and when the offense is offset by enough warmth and affinity that the person being teased generally feels more loved than ridiculed. The fact that it's hard to tease strangers—because there's no preexisting warmth to help mitigate the offense—means that the people we tease are necessarily close to us. Knowing and sensing this is partly what gives teasing its power to bring people closer together.

Teasing can become mean-spirited, however, when it provokes too much suffering, or when it's not offset with enough good, warm feelings. And when there's no affinity whatsoever, teasing turns into bullying or simply abuse. This kind of bullying can be especially effective (for the bully) or frustrating (for the victim), because the bully has a built-in excuse: "I'm only kidding! Can't you take a joke?" (more on this in the next section).

It's worth reiterating that our brains do most of this on autopilot. We rarely make *conscious* calculations about the strength of our relationships, or how much suffering is too much to laugh at—but our brains perform these calculations all the same, automatically and unconsciously. As Provine points out, it's precisely because laughter is involuntary that it's such a powerful probe into social relationships.

* * * * *

Thus we use laughter to gauge and calibrate social boundaries—both behavioral boundaries (norms) and group membership boundaries (who deserves how much of our empathy). But this calibration is a delicate act. We need deniability.

DENIABILITY

"Laughter in no way strives to be verbalized or explained; in fact, it goes all out to avoid verbalization and explanation."—Alexander Kozintsev[49]

"The meaning of a wink depends on it not being common knowledge."—Michael Chwe[50]

Try to imagine (or remember) what it's like to be a wide-eyed 14-year-old anxious to learn about sex. Beyond the basic mechanics covered in sex education, the topic has remained pretty murky for you, and you have a lot of pressing questions. When are you allowed to talk about sex? How explicit can you be in front of different audiences (friends, grandparents, younger children, mixed company)? Which aspects of sex are truly dangerous, and which are merely taboo? Which practices are considered appropriate versus slightly deviant versus beyond the pale?

Amid all this uncertainty, it's clear that the adults aren't giving you the full story. So where should you turn?

One thing you've noticed is that while the adults may not talk openly about sex, they're willing and even eager to joke about it. So if you keep your ears open and pay careful attention, you might be able to glean enough hints to piece together a reasonably accurate picture.

You might be especially intrigued, for example, by the *Seinfeld* episode "The Contest" in which the characters wager to see who can hold out the longest without masturbating. The dialogue is careful to dance around the actual word "masturbate," but you weren't born yesterday; you know what they're talking about. And the fact that masturbation is played for *laughs* tells you most of what you need to know about the topic: first, that it's a taboo, not something you'll want to discuss in front of grandma; and second, that it's commonplace and more or less acceptable, at least in the eyes of mainstream TV-watching Americans. Society may not fully condone it, but it won't get you labeled a deviant. It's a norm violation, but also benign.

Laughter, then, shows us the boundaries that language is too shy to make explicit. In this way, humor can be extremely useful for exploring the boundaries of the social world. The sparks of laughter illuminate what is otherwise murky and hard to pin down with precision: the threshold between safety and danger, between what's appropriate and what's transgressive, between who does and doesn't deserve our empathy. In fact, what laughter illustrates is precisely the fact that our norms and other social boundaries aren't etched in stone with black-and-white precision, but ebb and shift through shades of gray, depending on context.

For this task, language just doesn't cut it. It's too precise, too quotable, too much "on the record"—all of which can be stifling and oppressive, especially when stated norms are too strict. In order to communicate in this kind of environment, we (clever primates) turn to a medium that gives us "wiggle room" to squirm out of an accusation, to defy any sticklers who would try to hold us accountable.

Laughter may not be nearly as expressive as language, but it has two properties that make it ideal for navigating sensitive topics. First, it's relatively *honest*. With words, it's too easy to pay lip service to rules we don't really care about, or values that we don't genuinely feel in our gut. But laughter, because it's involuntary, doesn't lie—at least not as much. "*In risu veritas*," said James Joyce; "In laughter, there is truth."[51] Second, laughter is *deniable*. In this way, it gives us safe harbor, an easy out. When someone accuses us of laughing inappropriately, it's easy to brush off. "Oh, I didn't really understand what she meant," we might demur. Or, "Come on, lighten up! It was only a joke!" And we can deliver these denials with great conviction because we really *don't* have a clear understanding of what our laughter means or why we find funny things funny. Our brains just figure it out, without burdening "us" with too many damning details.

The comedian Bill Burr has preemptively used the "lighten up" defense on a number of occasions. On the topic of comedians getting attacked for their jokes, Burr said:

> I'm worried every time I see a comedian apologize. [Addressing a hypothetical attacker:] Just because *you* took what I said seriously doesn't mean *I* meant it. You don't get to decide that you're in my head and that you know my intent. If I'm joking, I'm *joking*."[52]

In another interview he says, "I don't think it's fair to get offended by comedians."[53] And yet what fans say they love about Burr is that he's honest—"refreshingly," "brutally," "devastatingly" honest.

So which is it? Is he just joking or telling the truth?

The beauty of laughter is that it gets to be both. The safe harbor of plausible deniability is what allows Burr and other comedians to get away with being honest about taboo topics. As Oscar Wilde said,[54] "If you want to tell people the truth, make them laugh; otherwise they'll kill you."

Conversation

For linguists and evolutionary psychologists, the origins of human language are a fascinating mystery—and so seductive that the Paris Linguistic Society famously had to ban discussion of the topic in 1866 to avoid getting mired in speculative debates.[1] In this chapter, however, we'll be taking our linguistic faculties as a given in order to focus on a different (but related) question: What motivates us to actually *use* our language faculties—as, for example, in casual conversation? We'll start with personal conversations, but then move on to consider conversations in the mass media and academia.

SHARING INFORMATION

According to one estimate, we spend roughly 20 percent of our waking lives engaged in conversation,[2] and we spend that time doing a great many different things. We ask questions, give commands, make promises, declare rules, and deliver insults. Often we engage in idle small talk; occasionally we tell stories or recite poetry. We also argue, brag, flatter, threaten, and joke. (And none of this includes the deceptive uses of language.[3]) But for most observers, one function stands out above all others: *sharing information*. This is arguably the primary function of language.[4] It's what we do every time we state a fact, explain a theory, or spread some news. Much of what we *write* also falls into this category: books, blog posts, how-to manuals, news articles, and academic papers. Even gossip is just a way to share a particular type of information, that is, social information.

There's a nonverbal analog to the info-sharing function of speech, namely, pointing something out. *Look over there*, we "say" using an index finger. *Isn't that interesting?* Or we can physically show an interesting object to a viewer by presenting it with our hands. These behaviors appear in human infants between 9 and 12 months of age.[5] The infants aren't asking for any kind of help; they simply want to direct the adult's attention to an interesting object, and are satisfied when the adult responds by paying attention. And so it is with most of our speech acts.

Now, it can be tempting to overemphasize the value of sharing information. We fixate on this function of language in part because it's the basis for all our greatest achievements, especially as modern humans living in large agrarian or industrial civilizations. It's through language that we've managed to accumulate culture and wisdom, to engage in math, science, and history, to run businesses and govern nations. It's what enables us, in the words of Isaac Newton, to "stand on the shoulders of giants," to build off the past and improve it.

But we need to be careful not to let these awe-inspiring modern miracles cloud our thinking,[6] because our instincts for using language didn't evolve to help us do science or build empires. Language evolved among our foraging ancestors at least 50,000 years ago (if not far earlier), long before we became the undisputed masters of the planet.[7] As we dig into our conversational motives, it pays to keep in mind that our ancestors were animals locked in the competitive struggle to survive and reproduce. Whatever they were doing with language had to help them achieve biologically relevant goals in their world, and to do so more effectively than their peers.

COSTS AND BENEFITS

To understand any behavior, it's essential to understand its cost–benefit structure. And since conversation is a two-way street, we actually need to investigate the costs and benefits of two behaviors: speaking and listening.

In what follows, we're going to lean heavily on the insights of the psychologist Geoffrey Miller, whom we met in the introduction, as well as the computer and cognitive scientist Jean-Louis Dessalles. Their two books (*The Mating Mind* and *Why We Talk,* respectively) provide thoughtful perspectives on conversation as a *transaction* between speakers and listeners—a transaction constrained, crucially, by the laws of economics and game theory.[8]

Let's start with listening, which is the simpler of the two behaviors. Listening costs very little,[9] but has the large benefit of helping us learn vicariously, that is, from the knowledge and experience of others. (This isn't the only benefit, as we'll see, but it *is* important.) As listeners, we get to see through other people's eyes, hear through their ears, and think through their brains. If your friend spots a tiger before you do, he can yell, "Watch out!" and you'll be spared a vicious mauling. If grandma remembers what happened to the tribe 60 years ago, before the rest of us were around, she can share stories that might spare us the repetition of historical errors.

But if we focus too much on the benefits of listening, we can be seduced into thinking that the evolution of language was practically inevitable, when in fact (as far as we know), complex language evolved only in one species.[10] So let's turn our attention to the speaking side of the transaction, focusing first on the costs.

In a naive accounting, speaking seems to cost almost nothing—just the calories we expend flexing our vocal cords and firing our neurons as we turn thoughts into sentences. But this is just the tip of the iceberg. A full accounting will necessarily include two other, much larger costs:

1. *The opportunity cost of monopolizing information.* As Dessalles says, "If one makes a point of communicating every new thing to others, one loses the benefit of having been the first to know it."[11] If you tell people about a new berry patch, they'll raid the berries that could have been yours. If you show them how to make a new tool, soon everyone will have a copy and yours won't be special anymore.

2. *The costs of acquiring the information in the first place.* In order to have interesting things to say *during* a conversation, we need to spend a lot of time and energy foraging for information *before* the conversation.[12] And sometimes this entails significant risk. Consider

the explorer who ventures further than others, only to rush home and broadcast her hard-won information, rather than keeping it for herself. This requires an explanation.

In light of these costs, it seems that a winning strategy would be to relax and play it safe, lettings others do all the work to gather new information. If they're just going to share it with you anyway, as an act of altruism, why bother?

But that's not the instinct we find in the human animal. We aren't lazy, greedy listeners. Instead we're both intensely curious *and* happy to share the fruits of our curiosity with others. In order to explain why we speak, then, we have to find some benefit large enough to offset the cost of acquiring information and devaluing it by sharing. If speakers are giving away little informational "gifts" in every conversation, what are they getting in return?

THE BENEFITS OF SPEAKING: RECIPROCITY?

A simple but incomplete answer is that speakers benefit by a quid pro quo arrangement: "I'll share something with you if you return the favor."[13]

Let's call this the reciprocal-exchange theory. In this view, speakers and listeners alternate roles, not unlike two traders who meet along the road and exchange goods with each other. At first, this arrangement appears to balance the books by providing enough benefit to offset the speaker's costs. But on more careful inspection, there are a number of puzzling behaviors that the reciprocal-exchange theory has trouble explaining.

Puzzle 1: People Don't Keep Track of Conversational Debts

If the act of speaking were a favor, then we would expect speakers to keep track of which listeners owed them information in return.[14] This kind of bookkeeping is manageable when it comes to simple or discreet favors like sharing food, but starts to break down when things get complex and ambiguous, as it does in conversation. Is one juicy piece of gossip worth 10 pieces of trivia? 100? There's no way to tell.

More to the point, however, is the fact that we don't actually seem to keep track of conversational debts. We don't resent our friends who are quieter than average, for example. Instead we speak freely, asking for little more than to be heard and understood. Similarly, we can talk to a whole roomful of people or write an article read by millions, without feeling the need for our listeners or readers to give anything back.[15]

Puzzle 2: People Are More Eager to Talk Than Listen

If exchanging information were the be-all and end-all of conversation, then we would expect people to be *greedy listeners* and *stingy speakers*.[16] Instead, we typically find ourselves with the opposite attitude: eager to speak at every opportunity.[17] In fact, we often *compete* to have our voices heard, for example, by interrupting other speakers or raising our voices to talk over them. Even while we're supposed to be listening, we're frequently giving it a halfhearted effort while our brains scramble feverishly thinking of what to say next.

We're so eager to speak, in fact, that we have to curb our impulses via the norms of conversational etiquette. If speaking were an act of giving, we would consider it *polite* for people to "selflessly" monopolize conversations. But in fact, it's just the opposite. To speak too much or "hog the mic" is considered rude, while the opposite behavior—inviting someone else to take the floor, or asking a dinner guest about one of her hobbies—is considered the epitome of good manners.

These seemingly inverted priorities are reflected not only in our behavior, but also our anatomy. Here's Miller again:

> If talking were the cost and listening were the benefit of language, then our speaking apparatus, which bears the cost of our information-altruism, should have remained rudimentary and conservative, capable only of grudging whispers and inarticulate mumbling. Our ears, which enjoy the benefits of information-acquisition, should have

evolved into enormous ear-trumpets that can be swivelled in any direction to soak up all the valuable intelligence reluctantly offered by our peers. Again, this is the opposite of what we observe. Our hearing apparatus remains evolutionarily conservative, very similar to that of other apes, while our speaking apparatus has been dramatically re-engineered. The burden of adaptation has fallen on speaking rather than listening.[18]

The takeaway from all these observations is that our species seems, somehow, to derive more benefit from speaking than from listening.

Puzzle 3: The Criterion of Relevance

According to the reciprocal-exchange theory, conversations should be free to bounce around willy-nilly, as speakers take turns sharing new, unrelated information with each other. A typical conversation might go something like this:

A: FYI, Alex and Jennifer are finally engaged.
B: Thanks. Have you heard that the President is trying to pass a new healthcare bill?
A: Yeah, I already knew that.
B: Oh. In that case, um . . . a new Greek restaurant just opened on University Avenue.
A: That's new information to me. Thanks.

Either listener might ask follow-up questions, of course. But as soon as their curiosity had been satisfied, they might be expected to turn around and share some new information of their own, regardless of whether it pertained to the previous discussion.

But this is not what human conversation looks like. Instead we find that speakers are tightly constrained by the criterion of *relevance*.[19] In general, whatever we say needs to relate to the topic or task at hand. Conversations can meander, of course, but the ideal is to meander gracefully. Speakers who change the topic too frequently or too abruptly are considered rude, even if they're providing useful information.

Puzzle 4: Suboptimal Exchanges

One final problem with the reciprocal-exchange theory is that we seem to neglect the most profitable exchanges of information. When two people meet for the first time, they rarely talk about the most important topics they know—even though this would be the biggest win from an info-exchange perspective. We rarely ask our friends and family members, "What are the biggest, most important lessons you've learned in life?" Nor do we spontaneously offer this information. It may come up occasionally, but most of the time we prefer to exchange news (more on this in a moment), discuss the latest TV shows, or languish in friendly, comfortable chitchat.

RESOLUTION: SEX AND POLITICS

To resolve these puzzles, both Miller and Dessalles suggest that we stop looking at conversation as an exchange of information, and instead try to see the benefits of speaking as something other than receiving more information later down the road.[20]

Specifically, both thinkers argue that speaking functions in part as an act of *showing off*. Speakers strive to impress their audience by consistently delivering impressive remarks. This explains how speakers foot the bill for the costs of speaking we discussed earlier: they're compensated not in-kind, by receiving information reciprocally, but rather by raising their social value in the eyes (and ears) of their listeners.

Now, in Miller's theory, speakers are primarily trying to impress potential *mates*, while for Dessalles, the primary audience is potential *allies*. Though seemingly at odds, these two accounts are, for the most part, mutually compatible. In fact, we can treat Miller's mating theory as a special case of Dessalles' more general alliance theory. In other words, a mate is just a particular kind of ally—one that we team up with for making and raising children, rather than for social, professional, or political gain.[21]

Here's a thought experiment that might help. Imagine that every human being carries around a magical backpack full of tools. At any point, you can reach into your backpack and pull out a tool, and (here's the magic) it will be *copied* as you pull it out, so the original gets to stay in the backpack. Every time you reach in, you get a new copy — but you can only get copies of tools you already possess. In this way, tool-sharing between backpacks works like information-sharing between brains: you can give something away without losing it for yourself.

Now, suppose you meet up with an old acquaintance from school—let's call him Henry—and the two of you start sharing tools with each other. Broadly speaking, you have two stances you can take toward Henry. You can treat him either as a *trading partner* or as a *potential ally* (whether as a mate or otherwise). If you're looking to trade, you care mostly about the tools he can give you in any one exchange—specifically, the tools you don't already own. But if you're looking for an ally, you care less about the specific tools you receive from him, and much more about the *full extent of his toolset*— because when you team up with Henry, you effectively get access to *all* his tools. The ones he gives you during any individual exchange may be useful, but you're really eyeing his backpack. And while you can't look directly inside it, you can start to gauge its contents by the variety of tools he's able to pull from it on demand. The more tools he's able to produce, the more he probably has tucked away in the backpack. And again, you're looking for a backpack full of tools that are both *new* to you and *useful* to the things you care about. If Henry can consistently delight you with new, useful artifacts, it speaks to the quality of his backpack and therefore his value as an ally.

And so it is with conversation. Participants evaluate each other not just as trading partners, but also as potential allies. Speakers are eager to impress listeners by saying new and useful things, but the facts themselves can be secondary. Instead, it's more important for speakers to demonstrate that they have abilities that are attractive in an ally. In other words, speakers are eager to show off their backpacks.

Now, your skill as a speaker can manifest itself in a variety of ways. You might simply have encyclopedic knowledge about many topics. Or you might be intelligent, able to deduce new facts and explanations on the fly.

Or you might have sharp eyes and ears, able to notice things that other people miss. Or you might be plugged into valuable sources of information, always on top of the latest news, gossip, and trends. But listeners may not particularly care *how* you're able to impress, as long as you're consistently able to do so. If you're a reliable source of new information, you're likely to make a good teammate, especially as the team faces unforeseeable situations in the future. In other words, listeners care less about the tools you share with them; they're really salivating over your backpack.

Here's another way to look at it. Every remark made by a speaker contains two messages for the listener: *text* and *subtext*. The text says, "Here's a new piece of information," while the subtext says, "By the way, I'm the *kind of person* who knows such things." Sometimes the text is more important than the subtext, as when a friend gives you a valuable stock tip.[22] But frequently, it's the other way around. When you're interviewing someone for a job, for example, you aren't trying to learn new domain knowledge from the job applicant, but you might discuss a topic in order to gauge the applicant as a potential coworker. You want to know whether the applicant is sharp or dull, plugged-in or out of the loop. You want to know the size and utility of the applicant's backpack.[23]

In casual conversation, listeners have a mixture of these two motives. To some extent we care about the text, the information itself, but we also care about the subtext, the speaker's value as a potential ally. In this way, every conversation is like a (mutual) job interview, where each of us is "applying" for the role of friend, lover, or leader (see Box 12.).

Conversation, therefore, looks on the surface like an exercise in sharing information, but subtextually, it's a way for speakers to show off their wit, perception, status, and intelligence, and (at the same time) for listeners to find speakers they want to team up with. These are two of our biggest hidden motives in conversation.

Box 12: Lovers and Leaders

"Much of human courtship," writes Miller about lovers, "is verbal courtship."[24] He estimates that most couples exchange on the order of a million words before they conceive a child (if in fact they do).[25] That's a lot of talking. And for a decision as high-stakes as choosing a mate, we want to learn as much as we can about our partners. Some of what we learn will be explicit information delivered through the channel of language: "So, tell me about your childhood." But a lot of it will be information we infer about our partners by listening to what they say and how they say it. When William Shakespeare writes, "All the world's a stage," the poem tells us not just about the world and its staginess, but also about Shakespeare himself—his linguistic virtuosity and possibly, by extension, his genetic fitness.

Conversational and oratorical skills are also prized attributes of leaders around the world. Of course, we also value leaders who are brave, generous, physically strong, and politically well connected—but speaking ability ranks up there in importance. We rarely join companies where the CEO is the least articulate person in the room, nor do we routinely elect mumbling, stuttering, scatter-brained politicians. We want leaders who are sharp and can prove it to us.[26] "In most or all societies," writes Robbins Burling, "those who rise to positions of leadership tend to be recognized as having high linguistic skills."[27]

The competition to show off as a potential lover or leader also helps explain why language often seems more elaborate than necessary to communicate ideas—what the linguist John Locke calls "verbal plumage."[28] Plain speech just isn't as impressive as elevated diction.

PUZZLES REVISITED

This view of talking—as a way of showing off one's "backpack"—explains the puzzles we encountered earlier, the ones that the reciprocal-exchange theory had trouble with. For example, it explains why we see people jockeying to speak rather than sitting back and "selfishly" listening—because the spoils of conversation don't lie primarily in the information being exchanged, but rather in the subtextual value of finding good allies and advertising oneself as an ally. And in order to get credit in this game, you have to speak up; you have to show off your "tools."

It also explains why people don't keep track of conversational debts—because there *is* no debt. The act of speaking is a reward unto itself, at least insofar as your remarks are appreciated. You can share information with 10 or 100 people at once, confident that if you speak well, you'll be rewarded at the subtextual level.

But why do speakers need to be *relevant* in conversation? If speakers deliver high-quality information, why should listeners care whether the information is related to the current topic? A plausible answer is that it's simply too easy to rattle off memorized trivia. You can recite random facts from the encyclopedia until you're blue in the face, but that does little to advertise your *generic facility* with information. Similarly, when you meet someone for the first time, you're more eager to sniff each other out for this generic skill, rather than to exchange the most important information each of you has gathered to this point in your lives. In other words, listeners generally prefer speakers who can impress them *wherever a conversation happens to lead*, rather than speakers who steer conversations to specific topics where they already know what to say.

If we return to the backpack analogy, we can see why relevance is so important. If you're interested primarily in trading, you might ask, "What do you have in your backpack that could be useful to me?" And if your partner produces a tool that you've never seen, you'll be grateful to have it (and you'll try to return the favor). But anyone can produce a curiosity or two. The real test is whether your ally can consistently produce tools that are both *new* to you and *relevant* to the situations you face. "I'm building a birdhouse," you mention. "Oh, great," he responds, "here's a saw for cutting wood," much to your delight. "But how will I fix the wood together?" you ask. "Don't worry, I also have wood glue." Awesome! "But now I need something to hold birdseed," you say hopefully. Your ally thinks for a minute, rummaging through his backpack, and finally produces the perfect plastic feeding trough. Now you're *seriously* impressed. He seems to have all the tools you need, right when you need them. His backpack, you infer, must be chock-full of useful stuff. And while you could—and will—continue to engage him in useful acts of trading, you're far more eager to team up with him, to get continued access to that truly impressive backpack of his.[29] We want allies who have an entire Walmart in their backpacks, not just a handful of trinkets.[30]

This also helps to explain why listeners aren't tempted to deceive speakers by downplaying the quality or novelty of new information that they learn by listening. If conversation were primarily about reciprocal exchange, we'd be tempted to habitually deprecate what our partners were offering, in order to "owe" less in return. "I already knew that," we might say (even if it wasn't true), like a pawnbroker belittling an old ring as "worthless" (when in fact it's worth a great deal). Because speakers can't peer into listeners' brains directly, they'd have no way of verifying. But listeners rarely try to shortchange speakers in this way. Instead, we're typically happy to give speakers an appropriate amount of credit for their insightful remarks—credit we pay back not in terms of other information, but rather in terms of respect. And we're incentivized to give them exactly as much respect as they deserve because we're evaluating them as potential allies rather than as trading partners.[31]

PRESTIGE

So far we've been using the language of politics—shopping for allies—to explain our conversational behavior. Speakers, we've said, are trying to advertise their value as allies, and conversely, listeners evaluate speakers as potential allies. This is one way to talk about a more general concept we introduced in Chapter 2: *prestige*. And although there are many different ways to look at prestige, we can treat it as synonymous with "one's value as an ally."

Thus, speaking well is one way to increase our prestige—but of course there are many other ways. In fact, one of the most important "tools" that people have is the respect and support of others. So you can gain prestige not just by directly showing impressive abilities yourself (e.g., by speaking well), but also by showing that other impressive people have chosen you as an ally. You might get this kind of "reflected" or second-order prestige by the fact that an impressive person is willing to talk to you, or (even more) if they've chosen to reveal important things to you before revealing them to others. Even listeners stand to gain prestige, then, simply by association with prestigious speakers.

For our distant ancestors, this kind of politicking mainly happened face to face. For example, you could hear someone talk in person, and then, if you liked what you heard, you could try to form or upgrade your personal relation with the speaker right on the spot. Or if you didn't like what you heard, you could try to distance yourself or downgrade your relationship.

In the modern world, thanks to printing, television, and the Internet, we now have far more ways to talk, listen, and associate with others. And thus a great many new kinds of conversations are now possible, along with ways to establish and gain from reflected prestige. Let's now look in more detail at two common types of larger conversations: news and academic research. Our motives regarding each of them seem to have a lot in common with our motives in personal conversation.

NEWS

"The man who reads nothing at all is better educated than the man who reads nothing but newspapers."—Thomas Jefferson (attributed)[32]

People today may seem to have an unprecedented obsession with news. Rather than waiting for a daily paper or the six o'clock TV broadcast, we can get up-to-the-minute reports, 24 hours a day, from tiny computers we keep in our pockets and purses—just pull to refresh. But although the *way* we consume news has changed, our preoccupation with it is nothing new. Here's Mitchell Stephens from his classic text *A History of the News*:

It might be surprising to learn that more than 275 years ago the English—though they had no radio, television, satellites or computers, and though men obtained much of their news at the coffeehouse— thought their era was characterized by an obsession with news. . . . Nor were the English the only people before us who thirsted after news.

In the middle of the fourth century B.C., for example, Demosthenes portrayed his fellow Athenians as preoccupied with the exchange of news. . . . Observers have often remarked on the fierce concern with news that they find in preliterate or semiliterate peoples.[33]

Why have humans long been so obsessed with news? When asked to justify our strong interest, we often point to the virtues of staying apprised of the important issues of the day. During a 1945 newspaper strike in New York, for example, when the sociologist Bernard Berelson asked his fellow citizens, "Is it very important that people read the newspaper?" almost everyone answered with a "strong 'yes,'" and most people cited the "'serious' world of public affairs."[34] And yet (according to Stephens), Berelson learned that readers

> have other less noble-sounding uses for their newspapers: They use them as a source of pragmatic information—on movies, stocks, or the weather; they use them to keep up with the lives of people they have come to "know" through their papers—from the characters in the news stories to the authors of the columns; they use them for diversion—as a "time-filler"; and they use them to prepare themselves to hold their own in conversations.[35]

Now, it did make some sense for our ancestors to track news as a way to get practical information, such as we do today for movies, stocks, and the weather. After all, they couldn't just go easily search for such things on Google like we can. But notice that our access to Google hasn't made much of a dent in our hunger for news; if anything we read more news now that we have social media feeds, even though we can find a practical use for only a tiny fraction of the news we consume.

There are other clues that we aren't mainly using the news to be good citizens (despite our high-minded rhetoric). For example, voters tend to show little interest in the kinds of information most useful for voting, including details about specific policies, the arguments for and against them, and the positions each politician has taken on each policy.

Instead, voters seem to treat elections more like horse races, rooting for or against different candidates rather than spending much effort to figure out who *should* win. (See Chapter 16 for a more detailed discussion on politics.)

We also show surprisingly little interest in the accuracy of our news sources. While prices in financial and betting markets can plausibly give very timely, accurate, and unbiased information, we continue to let legal obstacles hinder such information on most topics outside of business.[36] One of us (Robin) was told by a reliable source a few years ago that a major media firm based in Washington, D.C., had several people working for several months on a project to score prominent pundits on the accuracy of their predictions. The project was canceled, however, soon after results came back showing how depressingly inaccurate most pundits actually are. If consumers truly cared about pundit accuracy, there might well be more "exposés" like this—the better for us to find and pay attention to those rare pundits whose predictions tend to come true. Instead, we seem content with just the veneer of confidence and expertise, as long as our pundits are engaging, articulate, connected to us, and have respected pedigrees.

These patterns in behavior may be puzzling when we think of news as a source of useful information. But they make sense if we treat news as a larger "conversation" that extends our small-scale conversation habits. Just as one must talk on the current topic in face-to-face conversation, our larger news conversation also maintains a few "hot" topics—a focus so strong and so narrow that policy wonks say that there's little point in releasing policy reports on topics not in the news in the last two weeks. (This is the criterion of relevance we saw earlier.) And for our part, as consumers of news, we compete to learn information on these hot topics before others, so we aren't confused in conversation and so our talk can seem more impressive. We also prefer news written by and about prestigious people, as it helps us to affiliate with them.

Meanwhile, the slow decline of professional journalism has been more than offset by the army of amateurs rising to the occasion (in quantity, if not in quality). Think of all the time people spend writing blogs and sharing links on Twitter and Facebook. Few are getting paid financially for their efforts, but they're getting compensated all the same.

ACADEMIC RESEARCH

"It still seems remarkable to me how often people bypass what are more important subjects to work on less important ones."—Robert Trivers[37]

Researchers at universities, think tanks, and corporate labs are not shy about explaining why their work deserves funding: Research increases the world's insight and understanding on important topics, leading to more innovation and economic growth. And it's true that research does often help the world in these ways. But such benefits are probably overstated,[38] and we have reasons to doubt whether these are in fact the main motivations that drive academia.

Like news and personal conversations, academic "conversations" are full of people showing off to impress others.[39] Even if they sometimes claim otherwise, researchers seem overwhelmingly motivated to win academic prestige. They do this by working with prestigious mentors, getting degrees from prestigious institutions, publishing articles in prestigious journals, getting proposals funded by prestigious sponsors, and then using all of these to get and keep jobs with prestigious institutions. As Miller points out, "Scientists compete for the chance to give talks at conferences, not for the chance to listen."[40]

But that's all on the supply side, to explain why academics are motivated to produce research. What of the *demand* for research? Here we also see a preference for prestige, rather than a strict focus on the underlying value of the research. To most sponsors and consumers of research, the "text" of the research (what it says about reality and how important and useful that information is) seems to matter less than the "subtext" (what the research says about the prestige of the researcher, and how some of that glory might reflect back on the sponsor or consumer).

College students, for example, are willing to pay more to attend schools where the professors are famous for their research (and as alumni they donate more money to such schools), even though few students actually read or engage with their professors' work. (Even fewer students study the quality of research at colleges when deciding where to go.) And of course the prestige of a professor has little to do with teaching ability.

Meanwhile, other academics consume research by reading it and citing it in their own work. And, like news and ordinary conversation, these research "conversations" tend to cluster around a few currently hot (relevant) topics. Perversely, however, the reliability of research *decreases* with the popularity of a field.[41] Not only can these topic fashions last for decades, but research that's done outside these clusters is often neglected (though there's little to suggest it's less valuable). In fact, there's likely *more* insight to be gleaned where others aren't looking—it just won't seem as relevant to the current conversation.[42] And thus, on average, researchers who are "out in the weeds" can expect fewer citations (even if a small number of them will make big, juicy discoveries).

Consider also how research sponsors might better achieve research insight at a lower cost by offering prizes for pre-specified accomplishments, like the X Prize or the DARPA Grand Challenge,[43] instead of the usual up-front grants.[44] One problem with prizes, from a sponsor's point of view, is that sponsoring prizes leaves the sponsor less room for discretion; they must give money to the winners, no matter who they are. So there's less opportunity for sponsors and researchers to develop a relationship with one another (like art patrons and artists do), so that donors can earn prestige by association.

Finally, consider the academic referees who evaluate research for publication and funding. Referees are perhaps the most important gatekeepers to academic prestige, so we might hope they're rewarding only the most deserving papers and proposals, those whose "text" is most valuable. Unfortunately, here too we see the biases characteristic of a political species. Referees seem to care more about prestige indicators of the work they accept, and how it will reflect on them and their organization, than about the work's substance and social value.

To start with, referees largely can't agree on which research is good enough to accept; their judgments are highly idiosyncratic.[45] But to the extent that they do agree on what's "good," much of it comes from a tendency to recognize and favor already prestigious insiders. (These insiders can be recognized by name or, in the case of a blind peer review process, by sleuthing and educated guesswork.) For example, when articles previously published in a journal were resubmitted soon afterward with new obscure names and institutions, only 10 percent of them were noticed as having been published before, and of the remaining 90 percent, only 10 percent were accepted under the new names.[46]

Of course, the peer review process *does* sometimes reward the work of new and/or outside researchers. But in the long experience of one of us (Robin), the judgments of referees in these cases typically focus on whether a submission makes the author seem impressive. That is, referees pay great attention to spit and polish—whether a paper covers every possible ambiguity and detail. They show a distinct preference for papers that demonstrate a command for difficult methods. And referees almost never discuss a work's long-term potential for substantial social benefit.

Many possible reforms, such as a review process that's blind to a paper's conclusions, could help journals to increase the accuracy of their publications.[47] But such reforms would limit journals' ability to select papers more likely to bring prestige, so we see surprisingly little interest in them.

THE ELEPHANT IN THE BOOK

In case it's not clear by now, this chapter helps explain Kevin and Robin's "hidden" motives for writing and publishing this book. To put it baldly, we want to impress you; we're seeking prestige. We hope the many things we've said so far testify to the size and quality of our "backpacks."

As an academic, Robin will be judged by the number and influence of his publications, and we hope this book will serve as a nice line item on his resume. Meanwhile, as an academic outsider, Kevin has undertaken this book largely as a vanity project. It's unlikely to help him much in his engineering career, and he could probably have more impact by building software—but he's always wanted his name on the cover of a book. Of course, this project has also been fun, an excuse to read and discuss many fascinating topics. And we hope readers will enjoy and perhaps profit from the fruits of our labor. But there's no way we would have done all this work without the hope of garnishing our reputations.[48]

No doubt we've made many trade-offs in service of this motive and at the expense of more prosocial motives like delivering maximum value to our readers. Perhaps the book is too long, for example; speakers do like to speak, after all. Certainly we could have used simpler language in many places, making the book easier to digest, though at the risk of appearing less scholarly. And of course, we could have released this as a free (or cheap) self-published e-book, but we wanted the prestige of a printed book from a respected publisher. We hope you'll forgive us these trespasses, as we have tried hard not to moralize (too much) about the selfish motives of others.

Consumption

I n 1930, in an essay titled, "Economic Possibilities for our Grandchildren," the economist John Maynard Keynes made a famous prediction. Observing the breakneck pace of innovation and economic growth during the 19th and early 20th centuries, Keynes reasoned that within the next hundred years, the economy would produce so much stuff, so cheaply and easily, that all our material needs would be satisfied. Workers in the 21st century, then, would be clocking in at less than 15 hours per week, free to dedicate the rest of their time to art, play, friends, and family—in other words, the good life.[1]

The year 2030 is fast approaching, but clearly we are not on track to meet Keynes's prediction of a leisure society. In fact, many of us today work nearly as many hours as our great-great-grandparents did a hundred years ago.[2] And yet, as many observers have pointed out, even some of the poorest among us live better than kings and queens of yore.

So why do we continue working so hard?

One of the big answers, as most people realize, is that we're stuck in a rat race. Or to put it in the terms we've been using throughout the book, we're locked in a game of competitive signaling. No matter how fast the economy grows, there remains a limited supply of sex and social status—and earning and spending money is still a good way to compete for it.[3]

The idea that we use purchases to flaunt our wealth is known as *conspicuous consumption*. It's an accusation that we buy things not so much for purely personal enjoyment as for showing off or "keeping up with the Joneses." This dynamic has been understood since at least 1899, when Thorstein Veblen published his landmark book *The Theory of the Leisure*

Class.[4] It remains, however, an underappreciated idea, and explains a lot more of our consumer behavior than most people realize.

When you think about people two or three rungs above you on the social ladder, especially the nouveau riche, it's easy to question the utility of their ostentatious purchases. Does anyone really *need* a 10,000-square-foot house, a $30,000 Patek Philippe watch, or a $500,000 Porsche Carrera GT? Of course not, but the same logic applies to much of your own "luxurious" lifestyle—it's just harder for you to see.[5]

Consider taking the perspective of a mother of six from the slums of Kolkata. To her, your spending habits are just as flashy and grotesque as those of a Saudi prince are to you. Do you really need to spend $20(!!) at Olive Garden to have a team of chefs, servers, bussers, and dishwashers cater to your every whim? Twenty dollars may be more than the family in Kolkata spends on food in an entire week. Of course, it doesn't *feel*, to you, like conspicuous consumption. But when a friend invites you out to dinner, it's nice being able to say yes. (If you had to decline because you couldn't afford to eat out, you might feel a twinge of shame.) And at the end of the meal, when you leave two uneaten breadsticks on the table, it doesn't feel at all like conspicuous waste. You're just thinking, "Why bother?" In fact, you might feel silly asking the waiter to pack them up for you, those two measly pieces of bread.

One way or another, we're all conspicuous consumers. But it's a lot more than wealth and class that we're trying to show off with our purchases.

BEYOND WEALTH

Consider why people buy environmentally friendly "green" products. Electric cars typically cost more than gas-powered ones. Disposable forks made from potatoes cost more than those made from plastic, and often bend and break more easily.

Conventional wisdom holds that consumers buy green goods—rather than non-green substitutes that are cheaper, more functional, or more luxurious—in order to "help the environment." But of course we should be skeptical that such purely altruistic motives are the whole story.

In 2010, a team of psychologists led by Vladas Griskevicius under-
took some experiments to tease out some of these ulterior motives.[6] The
researchers gave subjects a choice between two equivalently priced goods,
one of them luxurious but non-green, the other green but less luxurious. For example, they gave subjects a choice between two car models,
both $30,000 versions of the Honda Accord. The non-green model was a
top-of-the-line car with a sporty V-six engine replete with leather seats,
GPS navigation system, and all the luxury trimmings. The green model
had none of the nice extras, but featured a more eco-friendly hybrid
engine. Subjects were also given a choice between two household clean-
ers (high-powered vs. biodegradable) and two dishwashers (high-end vs.
water-saving).

Subjects in the control group, who were simply asked which product
they'd rather buy, expressed a distinct preference for the luxurious (non-
green) product. But subjects in the experimental group were asked for
their choice only after being primed with a status-seeking motive.[7] As a
result, experimental subjects expressed significantly more interest in the
green version of each product.

In another experiment, Griskevicius and his team asked subjects to
consider buying green or non-green products in two different shopping scenarios. One group was asked to imagine making the purchase
online, in the privacy of their homes, while another group was asked
to imagine making the purchase *in public*, out at a store. What they
found is that, when subjects are primed with a status motive, they show
a stronger preference for green products when shopping in public, and
a weaker preference for green products when shopping online. Clearly
their motive isn't just to help the environment, but also to *be seen* as
being helpful.[8]

Savvy marketers at Toyota, maker of the popular Prius brand of hybrid
cars, no doubt had this in mind when they designed the Prius's distinctive
body. For the U.S. market, they chose to produce a hatchback instead of
a sedan, even though sedans are vastly more popular.[9] Why change two
things at once, both the engine and the body? A likely reason is that a distinctive body makes the car more conspicuous.[10] Whether out on the road

or parked in a driveway, a Prius is unmistakable. If the Prius looked just like a Camry, fewer people would notice it.

Discussions of conspicuous consumption often focus on how we use products to signal wealth and social status. But the expressive range is actually much wider. Hybrid owners, for example, probably aren't trying to advertise their wealth per se. A Prius doesn't cost much more than a standard combustion car, and doesn't have the high-end cachet of a BMW or Lexus. Instead, what Prius owners are signaling is their *prosocial attitude*, that is, their good-neighborliness and responsible citizenship. They're saying, "I'm willing to forego luxury in order to help the planet." It's an act of conspicuous altruism, which we'll see much more of in Chapter 11, on charitable behavior.

Other desirable traits that consumers are keen to signal include the following:

- *Loyalty to particular subcultures.* A Boston Bruins cap says, "I support my local hockey team, and by extension, the entire community of other fans and supporters." An AC/DC T-shirt says, "I'm aligned with fans of hard rock (and the countercultural values it stands for)." These products function as badges of social membership.
- *Being cool, trendy, or otherwise "in the know."* Sporting the latest fashions or owning the hottest new tech gadgets shows that you're plugged into the zeitgeist—that you know what's going to be popular before everyone else does.
- *Intelligence.* A Rubik's Cube isn't just a cheap plastic toy; it's often an advertisement that its owner knows how to solve it, a skill that requires an analytical mind, not to mention a lot of practice.

These, again, are just a few of the many traits our purchases can signal.[11] Others include athleticism, ambition, health-consciousness, conformity (or authenticity), youth (or maturity), sexual openness (or modesty), and even political attitudes. Blue jeans, for example, are a symbol of egalitarian values, in part because denim is a cheap, durable, low-maintenance fabric that make wealth and class distinctions harder to detect.[12]

And it's not just the products themselves that signal our good traits, but also the stories we tell about how or why we acquired them. Depending on what kind of story we tell, the same product can send different messages about its owner. Consider three people buying the same pair of running shoes. Alice might explain that she bought them because they got excellent reviews from *Runner's World* magazine, signaling her conscientiousness as well as her concern for athletic performance. Bob might explain that they were manufactured without child labor, showing his concern for the welfare of others. Carol, meanwhile, might brag about how she got them at a discount, demonstrating her thrift and nose for finding a good deal.

The fact that we often discuss our purchases also explains how we're able to use services and experiences, in addition to material goods, to advertise our desirable qualities.[13] A trip to the Galápagos isn't something we can tote around like a handbag, but by telling frequent stories about the trip, bringing home souvenirs, or posting photos to Facebook, we can achieve much of the same effect. (Of course, we get plenty of personal pleasure from travel, but some of the value comes from being able to share the experience with friends and family.) Buying experiences also allows us to demonstrate qualities that we can't signal as easily with material goods, such as having a sense of adventure or being open to new experiences. A 22-year-old woman who spends six months backpacking across Asia sends a powerful message about her curiosity, open-mindedness, and even courage. Similar (if weaker) signals can be bought for less time and money simply by eating strange foods, watching foreign films, and reading widely.

Now, as consumers, we're aware of many of these signals. We know how to judge people by their purchases, and we're mostly aware of the impressions our own purchases make on others. But we're significantly less aware of the *extent* to which our purchasing decisions are driven by these signaling motives.

When clothes fit well, we hardly notice them. But when anything is out of place, it suddenly makes us uncomfortable. So too when things "fit"— or don't—with our social and self-images. Any deviation from what's considered appropriate to our stations and subcultures is liable to raise eyebrows, and without a good reason or backstory, we're unlikely to feel good about it. If you're a high-powered executive, imagine wearing your old high school backpack to work. If you're a bohemian artist, imagine bringing the *Financial Times* to an open-mic night. If you're a working-class union member, imagine ordering kale salad with tofu at a restaurant. (Please forgive the contrived examples; we hope you get the point.) In cases like these, the discomfort you might feel is a clue to how carefully you've constructed your lifestyle to make a particular set of impressions.[14]

INCONSPICUOUS CONSUMPTION

To get a better sense for just how much of our consumption is driven by signaling motives (i.e., conspicuous consumption), let's try to imagine a world where consumption is entirely *inconspicuous*.

Suppose a powerful alien visits Earth and decides to toy with us for its amusement. The alien wields a device capable of reprogramming our entire species. With the push of a little red button, a shock wave will blast across the planet, transfiguring every human in its wake. It will transform not only our brains, but also our genes, so that the change will persist across generations.

The particular change the alien has in mind for our species is peculiar. (But we should be grateful; other planets have fared worse.) The alien is going to render us *oblivious to each other's possessions*. Everything else about our psychology will remain the same, and specifically, we'll still be able to enjoy our own possessions. But after getting blasted, we'll cease being able to form meaningful impressions about *other people's* things—their clothes, cars, houses, tech gadgets, or anything else. It's not that these objects will become literally invisible to us. We'll still be able to perceive and interact with them. We'll just, somehow, no longer care. In particular, we won't be able to judge anyone by their possessions, nor will anyone be able to judge us. No one will comment on our clothes anymore or notice if we stop washing our cars.[15] It will render all our purchases completely inconspicuous. And, for what it's worth, we'll be completely aware of these changes; we will fully understand the effect the alien had on our species.

Let's call this Obliviation. (Not to be confused with the Harry Potter spell of the same name, which causes memory erasure.) Here's the big question: How does Obliviation change our behavior as consumers?

First of all, it's unlikely to change much overnight. We all have entrenched habits that we developed long before the alien's intervention, many of which will stick with us for a long time, even if they no longer make sense. But after a few years, and certainly after a generation or two, life will look very different.

One important consequence is that whole categories of products will disappear as the demand for them slowly evaporates. In *Spent*, Geoffrey Miller distinguishes between products we buy for *personal use*, like scissors, brooms, and pillows, and products we buy for *showing off*, like jewelry and branded apparel[16] (see Table 1). In an Obliviated world, clearly there's no use for anything in the "showing off" category.[17]

But most products offer a mix of personal value and signaling value. A car, for example, is simultaneously a means of transport and, in many cases, a coveted status symbol. (Witness the wide eyes and fawning coos of friends and family whenever you buy a new car, even a relatively modest one.) After Obliviation, then, we'll continue to buy cars for transportation, but we'll base our decisions entirely on functionality, reliability, comfort,

Table 1. Products for personal use versus for showing off

More for Personal Use	More for Showing Off
Scissors	Jewelry
Brooms	Branded apparel
Blankets	Wristwatches
Mattresses	Shoes
Cleaning products	Cars
Underwear	Mobile phones
Gasoline	Restaurants
Life insurance	Living room furniture

and (low) price. Hummers, which are expensive and comically impractical, will lose almost all of their appeal. Lexuses, BMWs, and other higher-
end cars may continue to be valued for their quality, but consumers today
also pay a premium for the luxury brand—a premium that would soon
disappear.

Clothes are another product category that's part function, part fashion.
In an Obliviated world, the fashion component will lose all its value. What
remains is likely to be the merest fraction of the bewildering variety of
clothing items available today. Think about what you wear when you're
home alone—not tight jeans or delicate silk shirts, but comfortable, inexpensive items like T-shirts, sweatpants, and slippers. Today it's considered
inappropriate to wear sweatpants to a dinner party or around the office. But
in an Obliviated world, where no one is even capable of noticing, why not?

Housing would also change substantially after Obliviation. Today we're
keenly aware that our homes make impressions on visiting friends and
family.[18] So as we shop around for a new house or apartment, we wonder
silently to ourselves, "What will my friends think of this place? Is it nice
enough? Is it in the right kind of neighborhood?" Similarly, when we buy
new rugs, paintings, or furniture, we often do so hoping they'll be admired.

We don't make these decisions strictly (or even primarily) for others, of
course; our homes provide an enormous amount of personal enjoyment.
But in an Obliviated world, spared from having to worry about what others
think, we'll certainly do many things differently. At the margin, we'll choose
to live in smaller, cheaper homes that require less upkeep. We'll clean them
less, decorate them less, and furnish them more comfortably and cheaply.
Living rooms—which are often decorated lavishly with guests in mind, then
used only sparingly—will eventually disappear or get repurposed. We'll also
keep smaller yards, landscaped for functionality and ease of maintenance.
Many yards, even front yards, will simply be left to the birds.

PRODUCT VARIETY

Perhaps the most surprising consequence of Obliviation is that a lot of
product *variety* would dry up.

Consider the question of what to wear. In an Obliviated world, we'll soon shift to the most functional and comfortable clothes. But we'll also start wearing the same outfits, day in and day out. And if we happen to wear the same thing as our friends, family, and coworkers, it won't bother us because we won't even notice.[19] Today there's a stigma to wearing uniforms, in part because it suppresses our individuality. But the very concept of "individuality" is just signaling by another name.[20] The main reason we like wearing unique clothes is to differentiate and distinguish ourselves from our peers. In this way, even the most basic message sent by our clothing choices—"I'm my own person, in charge of my own outfit"—would have no place or value in an Obliviated society.

Similar standardization would occur in other product categories like cars and houses. Today, many people cringe at the idea of cookie-cutter homes. It's somehow less dignified to live in a house that's identical to all the other houses in the neighborhood, or to drive the same car as everyone else on the road. It conjures an image of a totalitarian society where everyone is forced to conform to the same, tired "choices." In an Obliviated world, however, our choices wouldn't be restricted by an oppressive government, but simply by our own indifference.

Another compelling reason to switch to standardized goods is that they'd be significantly cheaper. The costs of manufactured goods can be broken down into *fixed costs* and *marginal* (or *per-unit*) *costs*. Fixed costs include things like designing the good and setting up the factory. Marginal costs include the price of raw materials and the energy and labor costs associated with running the factory. When a factory produces 10,000 goods to serve a niche market, the cost of the final product is dominated by fixed up-front costs. If the same factory instead cranks out 10 million copies, the fixed costs are amortized and the final cost plummets.

To give one example, consider the difference between a basic black Hanes T-shirt, which you can buy for $4 through Amazon,[21] and a uniquely designed, custom-printed T-shirt, which will cost you more than $20 through CustomInk. That's a fivefold difference. If all of us were willing to wear identical black T-shirts, manufacturers could keep the same looms spinning out the same items at a tiny fraction of the cost.

The cost of variety is even greater when you consider distribution costs. Whenever you go to the store to buy clothes, for example, you're paying for a lot more than the fabric. You're also paying for the *opportunity* to choose from among all the latest fashions. Retailers have to throw away (or sell at steep discounts) all the goods that don't sell in a given season. Major cities today offer dozens, hundreds, or even thousands of boutique outfitters, each catering to a different niche audience. All this variety adds up. Meanwhile, centralized warehouse-stores like Costco Wholesale and IKEA can offer deep discounts on their standardized wares by unlocking economies of scale and centralized distribution. If we weren't such conspicuous consumers, choosing fashions to carefully match our social and self-images, we could enjoy these same economies of scale for many more of our purchases.

After Obliviation, there will continue to be some variety, of course, even in the most social product categories. Clothes still need to come in different shapes and sizes, made out of different materials for different climates. Rich people will still prefer to spend some of their money on more expensive, higher-quality goods. (They won't get any style points for wearing cashmere, but it still feels great on the skin.) And for strictly personal goods like brooms and pillows, Obliviated consumers will likely demand the same variety they do today. But the variety in many product categories will soon collapse into a few standardized models.

It's worth discussing, briefly, what we're likely to do with all the money we'll save by buying fewer, cheaper, and more standardized goods. Will we stash it all in the bank for a rainy day? Ha! Recall that the alien's intervention makes us oblivious only to each other's *possessions*. Crucially, it doesn't render us altogether incapable of judging one another. So, after getting Obliviated, we'll continue striving to make good impressions—just not by showing off our material goods. We'll still play sports and spend money on gym memberships. We'll still buy books so we can read and discuss them. We'll continue giving to charity (see Chapter 12) and trying to earn fancy degrees from exclusive schools (see Chapter 13). Given the kind of creatures we are—ever striving to impress others—we would likely channel a lot of our savings, although perhaps not all of it, into these other activities.

ADVERTISING

Let's now leave the Obliviation thought experiment and return to the real world for one final question: How does *advertising* affect us as conspicuous consumers—as creatures who use products to signal our good traits?

In fact, there are a few different mechanisms by which ads coax us to buy things, and not all of them appeal to our signaling instincts. Many of them target us as rational consumers who make individual purchases for strictly personal enjoyment.

One of these mechanisms is simple and straightforward: *providing information*. You're more likely to buy a product when you know what its features are, where you can buy it, and how much it will cost. When you do a web search for "buy shoes online" and an ad for Zappos pops up, for example, the ad simply informs or reminds you that Zappos is a good place to "buy shoes online." You don't need to be a conspicuous consumer for this kind of ad to influence your behavior.

Another important ad mechanism is *making promises*. Sometimes these promises are made explicitly, in the form of a guarantee or warranty. But just as often they're made implicitly, as part of a brand's overall persona. These are called "brand promises." When a company like Disney makes a name for itself as a purveyor of family-friendly entertainment, customers come to rely on Disney to provide exactly that. If Disney were ever to violate this trust—by putting swear words in its movies, for instance—consumers would get angry and buy fewer of Disney's products in the future. So the effect of these promises, whether they're conveyed explicitly or implicitly, is that the brand becomes incentivized to fulfill them. And consumers respond, quite sensibly, by buying more from brands who put their reputations on the line in this way.

But there's at least one type of advertising that can't be explained by any of these straightforward mechanisms. Consider this ad for Corona beer: An attractive couple lounges by a sun-lit ocean, a light breeze blowing in their hair, Coronas in hand, and not a care in the world. The ad's caption: "Find your beach."

Something strange is going on here. This ad says nothing at all about the taste of Corona, its price, its alcohol content, or any other features that might distinguish it from other beers. Nor is the ad making any kind of promise. The ad is simply trying to associate Corona with the idea of relaxing at the beach—an association which is almost entirely arbitrary.[22] There's nothing intrinsic to Corona that makes it more relaxing than any other beer. We could imagine the same ad being used to sell Budweiser or Heineken—except that it might clash with the arbitrary images those other brands have been using previously to market their beers.

Let's call this *lifestyle advertising* (sometimes known as *image advertising*). It's an attempt to link a brand or product with a particular set of cultural associations. This technique is used to sell a variety of products, including liquor, soda, cars, shoes, cosmetics, mobile phones, and of course clothing fashion brands. Before the recent crackdown on tobacco advertising, cigarettes were famously advertised with lifestyle associations. Recall the notorious Marlboro Man, a rugged, independent cowboy. With a different twist of fate, he could have been used to sell Camel or Lucky Strike cigarettes. Like Corona's beach, he was a more-or-less arbitrary choice grafted onto a commodity product.

A popular explanation for this kind of ad is that it works by targeting our individual emotions.[23] Just as Ivan Pavlov trained his dogs to associate an arbitrary stimulus, a ringing bell, with the promise of food, lifestyle ads train consumers to associate a brand or product with positive emotions, like relaxation in the case of Corona or rugged, manly spirit in the case of Marlboro. With the help of a little repetition, these associations slowly work their way into our unconscious minds. Later, when we're shopping for a product, the positive associations come flooding back to us, and we'll be more favorably disposed to buying the product. These ads are brainwashing us (the explanation goes), and they're doing it to us as *individuals*.

Now, certainly some amount of Pavlovian training is responsible for why these lifestyle ads are so effective. But given everything we've seen in this book, it should come as no surprise that something more subtle and *social* is going on as well.

To understand the social component of lifestyle advertising, we need to turn to an influential 1983 paper by the sociologist W. Phillips Davison. Davison was interested in how our perceptions and behavior can be manipulated by different forms of persuasive mass media—not just advertising, but also propaganda, political rhetoric, and news coverage of current events. He noticed that people often claim *not* to be influenced by a particular piece of media, and yet believe that *other people* will be influenced. For example, when New Yorkers heard a message from one gubernatorial candidate attacking another candidate, they said it had only a small effect on their personal voting decisions, but estimated that it would have a greater effect on the average New Yorker.[24]

Davison dubbed this the "third-person effect," and it goes a long way toward explaining how lifestyle advertising might influence consumers. When Corona runs its "Find Your Beach" ad campaign, it's not necessarily targeting you directly—because *you*, naturally, are too savvy to be manipulated by this kind of ad. But it might be targeting you indirectly, by way of your peers.[25] If you think the ad will change *other people's* perceptions of Corona, then it might make sense for you to buy it, even if you know that a beer is just a beer, not a lifestyle. If you're invited to a casual backyard barbecue, for example, you'd probably prefer to show up with a beer whose brand image will be appealing to the other guests. In this context, it makes more sense to bring a beer that says, "Let's chill out," rather than a beer that says, "Let's get drunk and wild!"

Unless we're paying careful attention, the third-person effect can be hard to notice. In part, this is because we typically assume that ads are targeting us directly, as individual buyers; indirect influence can be harder to see. But it's also a mild case of the elephant in the brain, something we'd rather not acknowledge. All else being equal, we prefer to think that we're buying a product because it's something we want for ourselves, not because we're trying to manage our image or manipulate the impressions of our friends. We want to be cool, but we'd rather be seen as naturally, effortlessly cool, rather than someone who's trying too hard.

Our blind spot notwithstanding, the third-person effect is pervasive in advertising. The next time you see a brand advertisement for a popular consumer product, try asking yourself how the ad might be preying on your signaling instincts.

Again, this can be subtle. Consider, for example, a public health ad that ran in the New York subway in 2009. The ad depicted a sugary cola being poured out of a bottle and into a glass, transforming along the way from a dark brown liquid into oozing globs of fat. The effect was arresting, even nauseating. Who wants all that fat in their body? The ad cemented its message with the tagline, "Are you pouring on the pounds?"[26]

On the surface, this ad seems to be appealing directly to you as an individual. It's making a kind of rational argument: "If you drink sugary beverages, you're liable to get fat." But consider also the effect this ad is likely to have on social creatures who judge each other based on what they consume. The campaign ran for three months and was seen by millions of New Yorkers. If you saw the ad, chances are good most of your peers saw it too. In light of this, how likely will you be to bring soda to a friend's birthday party? How self-conscious will you be slurping a Big Gulp at the office all-hands meeting? Those globs of fat have stuck in everyone's mind. Maybe better to reach for water or diet soda instead. Peer pressure is a powerful force, and advertisers know how to harness it to their advantage.

Some of our readers may fancy themselves immune to lifestyle advertising. Certainly Kevin did for many years. Then one day he saw an ad for Axe body spray.[27] This ad, like many in Axe's campaign, featured a young male protagonist who, after using the body spray, suddenly found himself being mobbed by a horde of attractive young women. Clearly this is intended to be a positive association for many viewers, but in Kevin's case, the ad actually backfired. There's nothing wrong with the product itself; it smells great and masks body odor effectively. But the cultural associations were enough to dissuade Kevin from using the product. This shows how arbitrary images can turn customers *away*, but by similar principles, other lifestyle ads must be having an opposite, positive effect. Such positive effects might be weaker and harder to detect, especially for strategic self-deceivers, but they're influencing us all the same.

* * * * *

The hypothesis we've been considering is that lifestyle or image-based advertising influences us by way of the third-person effect, rather than (or in addition to) Pavlovian training. Now, what evidence is there that this is actually what's happening?

Let's look at some predictions made by this hypothesis, to see if they're borne out in the real world.

Prediction: Lifestyle ads will be used to sell social products more than personal products

If lifestyle ads worked primarily by Pavlovian training, then we'd expect all product categories to make liberal use of them—even strictly personal products like brooms, peanut butter, and gasoline. A household cleaner like Lysol, for example, might market itself as high-end and luxurious, the kind of product that celebrities and upper-class people use to keep their homes in tip-top condition. Consumers would then, presumably, form an emotional association between Lysol and luxurious living, and be willing to pay a premium for it.

But we rarely find such ads for personal products. Instead, a good rule of thumb is that the easier it is to judge someone based on a particular product, the more it will be advertised using cultural images and lifestyle associations.[28] Keep in mind that a product doesn't need to be literally visible to be judged. If you're wearing perfume, someone might ask about it. When you go on vacation, you're expected to tell stories about it. A digital music library is hard for others to "see," but "What are your favorite bands?" is a common enough question, bringing the relevant information to the surface where it can be evaluated.

Prediction: Lifestyle ads work better with larger contiguous audiences

If lifestyle ads worked entirely by Pavlovian training, then the only thing an advertiser would care about is how many viewers saw the ad. It wouldn't matter whether those viewers knew that anyone else had seen the ad. You might be the only person on the planet to see the Corona "Find Your Beach" ad, but if it worked by Pavlovian training, it would still convince you to buy Corona.

If lifestyle ads work by the third-person effect, however, then you *will* care whether other people have seen the ad. Therefore, such an ad will be more effective if it's displayed in front of larger audiences. You need to see the ad *and* be confident that others have seen it too.

This is the difference between a Super Bowl commercial, which reaches some 50 million households in a single broadcast,[29] and a direct-mail campaign where flyers are sent to 50 million households separately (and unbeknownst to each other).[30] The Super Bowl audience is more than the sum of its parts, and lifestyle advertisers happily pay a premium for it.

This is what Michael Chwe found when he studied ad pricing across different TV shows and product categories. Advertisers must spend more per person to advertise on popular TV shows relative to less popular shows, and those selling social products are willing to pay this premium to reach larger contiguous audiences. Taken to the extreme during major TV events like the Super Bowl, the majority of ads are selling social goods.[31]

Prediction: Some lifestyle ads will target third parties who aren't potential buyers

If lifestyle ads work entirely by Pavlovian training, then it would never make sense to advertise to an audience that's unable or unlikely to buy the product. Brands would try to target their ads as narrowly as possible to their purchasing demographic. Why pay to reach a million viewers if only 10,000 of them can afford your product? But if lifestyle ads work by the third-person effect, then there will be some products for which it makes good business sense to target a wider audience, one that includes both buyers and non-buyers.[32]

One reason to target non-buyers is to create envy. As Miller argues, this is the case for many luxury products. "Most BMW ads," he says, "are not really aimed so much at potential BMW buyers as they are at potential

BMW coveters."[33] When BMW advertises during popular TV shows or in mass-circulation magazines, only a small fraction of the audience can actually afford a BMW. But the goal is to reinforce for *non-buyers* the idea that BMW is a luxury brand. To accomplish all this, BMW needs to advertise in media whose audience includes both rich and poor alike, so that the rich can see that the poor are being trained to appreciate BMW as a status symbol.

Naturally this feels manipulative, and it is. But the same tactics can be used for more honorable purposes as well. The U.S. Marine Corps, for example, advertises itself as a place to build strength and character. In doing so, it's not advertising only to potential recruits; it's also reminding *civilians* that the people who serve in the Marines have strength and character. This helps to ensure that when soldiers come home, they'll be respected by their communities, offered jobs by employers, and so forth.

* * * * *

To sum up, we are conspicuous consumers in more varied and subtle ways than most of us realize. Advertisers understand this part of human nature and use it to their advantage. But ads aren't necessarily preying on our irrational emotions, brainwashing us into buying things that aren't useful to us. Instead, by creating associations that exist out in the broader culture—not just in our own heads, but in the heads of third parties—ads turn products into a vocabulary that we use to express ourselves and signal our good traits.

Art

H umans are animals. This has been a central theme of this book, but it's a fact we often lose sight of in everyday life. It's too easy to get caught up in all the ways we're *different* from other animals: language, reasoning, music, technology, religion. And yet even in our uniqueness, humans were forged by the same processes responsible for all animal behaviors: natural and sexual selection, the relentless imperative to survive and reproduce.

In this chapter we're going to focus on art, one of the most peculiar and celebrated of all human behaviors. We've been making art for a long time. Early humans in Europe were painting cave walls and fashioning Venus figurines between 15,000 and 35,000 years ago.[1] Halfway around the world in Indonesia, the earliest rock art appeared some 40,000 years ago.[2] Stretching even farther back, in South Africa, red ocher engravings have been dated to 100,000 years ago, and the use of red ocher as body paint likely extends even farther back.[3] Art is also a human universal.[4] Every human culture on the planet makes art, whether by painting, styling their hair, adorning their bodies, decorating their living spaces, whittling sculptures out of wood, or making music and poetry.

Art poses a challenge for evolutionary thinkers. It's a *costly* behavior, both in time and energy,[5] but at the same time it's *impractical*[6] (see Box 13). Art doesn't put food on your table, look after your children, or keep you warm at night—at least not directly. So art, on its face, seems like a waste of time and energy. And natural selection doesn't look kindly on waste. How, then, did our instincts for art evolve?

Box 13: What Is Art?

Surely this is an important question, especially for a chapter that takes "art" as its subject matter. But frankly, we'd like to avoid the disputes that rage over the definition. The Scottish philosopher Walter Bryce Gallie famously called art an "essentially contested concept," implying that people will never fully agree on what it means.[7] Our goal is simply to investigate *why people make and enjoy art*. We aren't trying to change anyone's mind about what art is, and especially not what it should be.

Nevertheless, we need to describe the range of behaviors that we'll be considering in this chapter. And here we'd like to take a generous attitude, admitting many different forms under the "art" umbrella. These forms include:

- *Visual arts*, such as cave art, pigment on canvas, chiseled stone, and graphic design
- *Performing arts*, such as music, dance, theater, film, and comedy
- *Language arts*, such as poetry and fiction
- *Body art*, such as fashion, tattoos, piercings, cosmetics, and jewelry
- *Domestic arts*, such as interior design, gardening, cooking, and decorative crafts

To hazard a definition, we're partial to Ellen Dissanayake's characterization of art as anything "made special," that is, not for some functional or practical purpose but for human attention and enjoyment.[8] A clay pot, for example, is highly functional, and therefore not "art." But to the extent that it's been painted, etched, distinctively shaped, or otherwise embellished with non-functional elements, we will consider it "art."

In his book *The Mating Mind*, the evolutionary psychologist Geoffrey Miller gives a promising answer. Miller argues that while ecological selection (the pressure to survive) abhors waste, sexual selection often favors it. The logic, as you may recall from Chapter 2, is that we prefer mates who can *afford* to waste time, energy, and other resources (see Box 14). What's valuable isn't the waste itself, but what the waste says about the survival surplus—health, wealth, energy levels, and so forth—of a potential mate.

To appreciate the power of this idea, let's turn once again to the nonhuman world.

Box 14: Art: Adaptation or Evolutionary Byproduct?

Human bipedalism is an *adaptation*: a functional trait evolved and/or maintained by natural selection. Our ability to read, however, *isn't* an adaptation, because natural selection had no hand in developing it. It's merely a byproduct of other adaptations—vision, language, tool use, and so on.[9]

So what about art? Is it an adaptation or a byproduct? Many evolutionary psychologists consider art to be an adaptation. In other words, it was evolved and/or maintained by natural selection (including sexual selection) for its role in contributing to our biological fitness.[10] Not everyone agrees; Steven Pinker, for example, famously refers to music as "auditory cheesecake," pleasurable but not particularly useful.[11] But most evolutionary thinkers credit our propensity to make and enjoy art as adaptive, somehow or other.

Here's the quick argument for art as an adaptation. First, it's a *human universal*: every culture makes and enjoys art.[12] Second, art is *costly*: it takes a lot of time and energy to make.[13] But nature aggressively weeds out costly behaviors unless they somehow pay for themselves by providing survival or reproductive advantages. In other words, if a costly behavior is universal, it typically indicates positive selection pressure.[14] Finally, art is old enough, in evolutionary terms, for selection to have had plenty of time to work its magic.[15]

Note that this *doesn't* mean there are genes specifically for art. Art may have arisen, originally, as a byproduct of other adaptations. But how the behavior arose isn't as important as the fact that it's persisted over many generations in spite of its high cost. That's what suggests that it's an adaptation.

PARABLE OF THE BOWERBIRD

If we didn't recognize its behavior as familiar to our own, the bowerbird would be one of the most astonishing creatures on the planet.

Bowerbirds are a family of 20 species scattered across the forests and shrub lands of Australia and New Guinea.[16] What's distinctive about these birds are their eponymous *bowers*—the elaborate structures built by the males of the species to attract females. Different species build their bowers in different shapes and sizes. Some are long avenue-like walkways flanked by walls of vertically placed sticks. Others are more like a maypole, circular structures propped up against a small sapling. Perhaps most impressive are the expansive gazebo-like bowers built by the humble (10-inch long) Vogelkop bowerbird. These structures tower up to nine feet off the ground, with an opening large enough (as Miller puts it) "for David Attenborough to crawl inside."[17] The zoologists who first encountered these structures couldn't believe they'd been built by such a tiny bird, assuming instead that the local villagers had built them for their children to play in.[18]

As if these architectural feats weren't impressive enough, the male bowerbird takes the incredible further step of *decorating* his bower. This is where the parallels to human art become especially pronounced. Some species daub the walls of their bowers with a blueish "paint" that they regurgitate through their beaks. Others amass large collections of rare and visually fascinating objects—round pebbles, snail shells, flower petals, shiny beetles—and spend hours arranging them meticulously around their bowers. Satin bowerbirds have a preference for blue objects: feathers, berries, flowers, and even industrial artifacts like bottle caps and ballpoint pens.

These bowers serve only a single purpose: they're built by the males to attract females. Crucially, they *aren't* used by the females for laying eggs and raising young. After mating with a male, the female flies off to build her own (much smaller) cup-shaped nest up in a tree, and she raises her chicks entirely on her own, without any help from her mate.

From the perspective of the female, then, the male bowerbird exists only to provide his half of the genome. This may seem like a waste. Why

doesn't he help raise his chicks, like the males of so many other bird species? But in fact, the bowerbird male provides more than just cheap sperm;
crucially, he provides *battle-tested* sperm. Sperm that comes with a seal
of approval from Mother Nature, certifying that the male in question is
physically and (by implication) genetically fit. To construct and decorate
a bower, a male must spend most of his free time scouring the forest for
materials and arranging them meticulously into place. When his ornaments fade, he must collect new ones. He also needs to defend his bower
against attack by his rivals, who are keen to sabotage his structure and
steal his more impressive ornaments.[19] "During the breeding season,"
writes Miller, "males spend virtually all day, every day, building and maintaining their bowers." The reward for all this effort is more mating opportunities. A successful male bowerbird can mate with as many as 30 females
in a single mating season.[20] The flip side, of course, is that some males with
less-impressive bowers don't attract any females, and as a result their inferior genes don't get passed along to the next generation.

It's instructive to consider this behavior from the perspective of both
males and females. The male illustrates the virtue of the handicap principle.[21] Bower-building is difficult, but that's precisely the point. If it were easy,
every male could do it; fit males demonstrate their fitness only by doing
things that unfit males can't do. Take the satin bowerbird, for instance. By
focusing his collecting efforts on *blue* ornaments, which are exceedingly
rare in nature, a satin male can prove his fitness more reliably than by using
ornaments of any other color. Even a sickly male could decorate his hut
with green or brown, colors that abound in the forest, but only the heartiest
males can find enough blue to impress their potential mates. They collect
blue objects not in spite of the difficulty, but because of it.

Female bowerbirds, in turn, illustrate the importance of *discernment*
in evaluating the displays of their male suitors.[22] A female bowerbird will
visit up to eight males before choosing her favorite to mate with.[23] If she
didn't shop around, she might inadvertently decide to mate with a less-
fit male. This is especially important considering that environments can
vary. If a satin bowerbird population happens to live in a forest with an
abundance of blue-colored objects, even a relatively unfit male might be

able to muster a display that would be impressive in a blue-scarce environ-ment. It's only by shopping around for the *most* impressive displays that the female can ensure she's mating with the fittest male.

ART IN HUMANS

Now, there are intriguing parallels between bowerbird behavior and human art. But it's also important to mention some of the key differences.

Crucially, in our species, males don't have a monopoly on making art—nor do females have a monopoly on enjoying it. Both sexes are avid artists, and both are art aficionados. Insofar as we use art for courtship, then, it goes both ways: men impressing women with their art and vice versa.[24] This makes perfect sense for a species, like ours, in which even males invest a lot in their offspring and, consequently, need to be choosy about their mates.

But the bigger difference is that human art is more than just a *court-ship display*, that is, an advertisement of the artist's value as a poten-tial mate. It also functions as a general-purpose *fitness display*, that is, an advertisement of the artist's health, energy, vigor, coordination, and overall fitness.[25] Fitness displays can be used to woo mates, of course, but they also serve other purposes like attracting allies or intimidating rivals.[26] And humans use art for all of these things. In *One Thousand and One Nights*, for example, Scheherazade uses her artful storytelling to stave off execution and win the affections of the king. Maya Angelou, in contrast, managed not to woo Bill Clinton with her poetry, but rather to impress him—so much so that he invited her to perform at his presiden-tial inauguration in 1993. Intimidating rivals is perhaps a lesser function of human art, but even here, we find examples in graffiti (as when gangs tag walls to mark their territory) as well as in stand-up comedy (as when comedians use wit to humiliate hecklers). The point is simply that art is an impressive display, and humans have many reasons for wanting to impress others.

Importantly, human artists don't need to be conscious of this motive.[27] Humans, as we've seen many times throughout the book, are adept at acting on unconscious motives, especially when the motive in question (e.g., showing off) is antisocial and norm-violating. What's important isn't whether we're *aware* that we're using art as a fitness display, but rather the fact that art *works* as a fitness display. It serves a useful and important purpose, both to artists and consumers, so we shouldn't be surprised to find ourselves endowed with instincts both to make and enjoy art.

There's a lot of conventional wisdom, not to mention a long philosophical literature, about what art is and what it should be. In some accounts, it's primarily about portraying beauty and inducing pleasure. In others, it's about self-expression or communicating with an audience—conveying ideas, emotions, and experiences that the consumer wouldn't otherwise have access to. Art should challenge us, push the envelope, and strive to effect political change. These functions aren't mutually exclusive, nor are they incompatible with the fitness display theory. There's no doubt that observing art often induces strong feelings that we deeply crave, such as awe and an appreciation of beauty, and that creating art often gives us a strong sense of accomplishment and connection.

The argument we're making in this chapter is simply that "showing off" is *one* of the important motives we have for making art, and that many details of our artistic instincts have been shaped substantially by this motive. Not only do artists want to show off, but consumers simultaneously use art as a means to judge the artist. That's one of the big reasons people appreciate art, and we can't understand the full range of phenomena unless we're willing to look at art as a fitness display.

Remember, we need to explain how artists and consumers get *concrete advantages* out of making and enjoying art, especially given how much effort it takes and how much attention we pay to it. Art is an animal behavior, after all, and we need something like the fitness-display theory to explain how art pays for itself in terms of enhanced survival and reproduction, especially in the primitive ("folk art") context of our foraging ancestors.

To better understand the phenomena that make sense only according to the fitness display theory, it helps to introduce an important distinction between the "intrinsic" and "extrinsic" properties of a work of art:

- *Intrinsic properties* are the qualities that reside "in" the artwork itself, those that a consumer can directly perceive when experiencing a work of art. We might also think of them as perceptual properties. The intrinsic or perceptual properties of a painting, for example, include everything visible on the canvas: the colors, textures, brush strokes, and so forth.[28]
- *Extrinsic properties*, in contrast, are factors that reside outside of the artwork, those that the consumer *can't* perceive directly from the art itself. These properties include who the artist is, which techniques were used, how many hours it took, how "original" it is, how expensive the materials were, and so on. When observing a painting, for example, consumers might care about whether the artist copied the painting from a photograph. This is an extrinsic property insofar as it doesn't influence our perceptual experience of the painting.

Now we're ready to understand the most important difference between the conventional view of art (in any of its forms: beauty, communication, etc.) and the fitness-display theory. The difference is that the conventional view locates the vast majority of art's value in its *intrinsic* properties, along with the experiences that result from perceiving and contemplating those properties. Beauty, for example, is typically understood as an experience that arises from the artwork itself. According to the conventional view, artists use their technical skills and expressive power to create the final physical product, which is then perceived and enjoyed by the consumer. The *extrinsic* properties, meanwhile, are mostly an aside or an afterthought; in the conventional view, they aren't crucial to the transaction.

In contrast, in the fitness-display theory, extrinsic properties are crucial to our experience of art. As a fitness display, art is largely a statement about the *artist*, a proof of his or her virtuosity. And here it's often the extrinsic properties that make the difference between art that's impressive, and which therefore succeeds for both artist and consumer, and art that falls flat. If a work of art is physically (intrinsically) beautiful, but was made too easily (like if a painting was copied from a photograph), we're likely to judge it as much less valuable than a similar work that required greater skill to produce. One study, for example, found that consumers appreciate the same artwork less when they're told it was made by multiple artists instead of a single artist—because they're assessing the work by how much effort went into it, rather than simply by the final result.[29]

The importance of extrinsic properties becomes especially clear when we contemplate the idea of a hypothetical "replica museum"—a gallery stocked entirely with *copies* of the world's masterpieces. If the replicas are sufficiently accurate, they will be indistinguishable from the originals. Maybe artists and art students would care more about seeing the originals, but the rest of us should (according to the conventional view) be perfectly happy to visit a replica museum. Because replicas are cheap relative to the originals, we'll pay less to see a much wider variety—and in the convenience of our hometowns, rather than scattered around the world in Paris, London, Venice, and New York. Of course, replica museums don't exist, and the idea strikes us as a bit silly[30]—but that's precisely the point. Our disdain for replicas strongly suggests that we often use art as something other than a trigger for sensory or intellectual experiences.

Consider Leonardo da Vinci's *Mona Lisa*, celebrated for its beautiful detail, the surreal backdrop, and of course the subject's enigmatic smile. More visitors have seen the *Mona Lisa* in person—on display behind bulletproof glass at the Louvre—than any other painting on the planet. But when researchers Jesse Prinz and Angelika Seidel asked subjects to consider a hypothetical scenario in which the *Mona Lisa* burned to a crisp, 80 percent of them said they'd prefer to see the *ashes* of the original rather than an indistinguishable replica.[31] This should give us pause.

THE IMPORTANCE OF EXTRINSIC PROPERTIES

Imagine that one of your friends, an artist, invites you over to see her latest piece. "It's a sculpture of sorts," she says. "Smooth swirls punctuated by sharp spikes. Rich pinks and oranges. Pretty abstract, but I think you'll like it." It sounds interesting, so you drop by her workshop, and there, perched on a pedestal in the center of the room, is the sculpture. It's a delicate seashell-looking thing, and your friend is right, it's beautiful. But as you move in for a closer look, you begin to wonder if it might actually *be* a seashell. *Did she just pick it up off the beach, or did she somehow make it herself?* This question is now absolutely central to your appreciation of this "sculpture." Here your perceptual experience is fixed; whatever its provenance, the thing on the pedestal is clearly pleasing to the eye. But its value *as art* hinges entirely on the artist's technique. If she found it on the beach: meh. If she used a 3D printer: cool. And if she made it by manually chiseling it out of marble: whoa!

This way of approaching art—of looking beyond the object's intrinsic properties in order to evaluate the effort and skill of the artist—is endemic to our experience of art. In everything that we treat as a work of "art," we care about more than the perceptual experience it affords. In particular, we care about how it was constructed and what its construction says about the virtuosity of the artist.

Consider our emphasis on originality in works of art. We prize originality and spurn works that are too derivative, however pleasing they might otherwise be to our senses or intellect. Here again, we betray our concern for using art to evaluate the artist. Insofar as art is a perceptual experience, it shouldn't matter whether the artist copied another artist in producing the work, but it makes a world of difference in gauging the artist's skill, effort, and creativity.

"We find attractive," says Miller, "those things that could have been produced only by people with attractive, high-fitness qualities such as health, energy, endurance, hand–eye coordination, fine motor control, intelligence, creativity, access to rare materials, the ability to learn difficult skills, and lots of free time."[32]

Artists, in turn, often respond to this incentive by using techniques that are more difficult or demanding, but which don't improve the intrinsic properties of the final product. "From an evolutionary point of view," writes Miller, "the fundamental challenge facing artists is to demonstrate their fitness by making something that lower-fitness competitors could not make, thus proving themselves more socially and sexually attractive."[33] Artists routinely sacrifice expressive power and manufacturing precision in order to make something more "impressive" as a fitness display.

One place we find this sacrifice is in the performing arts. For example, by almost any measure of technical control, film exceeds live theater. Film directors can fuss endlessly over lighting, set design, and camera angles; they can demand retake after retake until their actors get everything just right. The camera can zoom in to capture movement and facial expressions of great subtlety. Mistakes can often be fixed by editors in post-production. And the results are frequently sublime, which is one reason film has become the most popular dramatic and comedic medium of our time. And yet consumers continue to relish live performances, shelling out even for back-row seats at many times the price of a movie ticket. Why? In part, because performing live is a *handicap*. With such little margin for error, the results are that much more impressive. A similar trade-off arises for musicians (e.g., lip synching is anathema) and standup comics, and for improv versus sketch-comedy troupes. A live performance, or even more so an improvised one, won't be as technically perfect as a prerecorded one, but it succeeds by putting the artists' talents on full display.

Consider another application of the handicap principle: the appeal of *constraints* in a given art form. Poets who adhere to strict meter and rhyme schemes prevent themselves from using words that don't fit. Sculptors who work with marble don't allow themselves to patch up their mistakes with putty or glue. And consumers appreciate it. We enjoy art not in spite of the constraints that artists hold themselves to, but because those constraints allow their talents to shine.

WHEN EXTRINSIC FACTORS CHANGE

We can also catch art being used as a fitness display by observing "natural experiments": historical scenarios in which the extrinsic (production) factors change, while everything else remains more or less the same. In the conventional view of why we appreciate art (beauty, etc.), it's only the intrinsic properties that matter. If we leave the intrinsic factors the same, then, we shouldn't expect our appreciation to change much, even if the extrinsic factors change. But in fact, our experiences change dramatically.

Consider the lobster—as David Foster Wallace invites us to do in an essay of the same name. "Up until sometime in the 1800s," writes Wallace,

> lobster was literally low-class food, eaten only by the poor and insti-tutionalized. Even in the harsh penal environment of early America, some colonies had laws against feeding lobsters to inmates more than once a week because it was thought to be cruel and unusual, like making people eat rats. One reason for their low status was how plen-tiful lobsters were in old New England. "Unbelievable abundance" is how one source describes the situation.[34]

Today, of course, lobster is far less plentiful and much more expensive, and now it's considered a delicacy, "only a step or two down from caviar."

A similar aesthetic shift occurred with skin color in Europe. When most people worked outdoors, suntanned skin was disdained as the mark of a low-status laborer. Light skin, in contrast, was prized as a mark of wealth; only the rich could afford to protect their skin by remaining indoors or else carrying parasols. Later, when jobs migrated to factories and offices, lighter skin became common and vulgar, and only the wealthy could afford to lay around soaking in the sun.[35]

Now, lobster and suntans may not be "art," exactly, but we neverthe-less experience them aesthetically, and they illustrate how profoundly our tastes can change in response to changes in extrinsic factors. Here, things that were once cheap and easy became precious and difficult, and there-fore more valued. Typically, however, the extrinsic factors change in ways that make things *easier* rather than more difficult.

Prior to the Industrial Revolution, when most items were made by hand, consumers unequivocally valued *technical perfection* in their art objects. Paintings and sculptures, for example, were prized for their realism, that is, how accurately they depicted their subject matter. Realism did two things for the viewer: it provided a rare and enjoyable sensory experience (intrinsic properties), *and* it demonstrated the artist's virtuosity (extrin-sic properties). There was no conflict between these two agendas. This was true across a variety of art forms and (especially) crafts. Symmetry,

smooth lines and surfaces, the perfect repetition of geometrical forms—
these were the marks of a skilled artisan, and they were valued as such.[36]

Then, starting in the mid-18th century, the Industrial Revolution ush-
ered in a new suite of manufacturing techniques. Objects that had previously been made only by hand—a process intensive in both labor and
skill—could now be made with the help of machines. This gave artists and
artisans unprecedented control over the manufacturing process. Walter
Benjamin, a German cultural critic writing in the 1920s and 1930s, called
this the Age of Mechanical Reproduction, and it led to an upheaval in
aesthetic sensibilities.[37] No longer was intrinsic perfection prized for its
own sake. A vase, for example, could now be made smoother and more
symmetric than ever before—but that very perfection became the mark
of cheap, mass-produced goods. In response, those consumers who could
afford handmade goods learned to prefer them, not only in spite of, but
because of their imperfections.

In *The Theory of the Leisure Class*, Thorstein Veblen invites us to consider the case of two spoons: an expensive, handmade silver spoon and
a factory-made spoon cast from cheap aluminum.[38] As utensils, the two
spoons are equally serviceable; both convey food to the mouth, no problem. And yet consumers vastly prefer the silver spoon to the aluminum
spoon. Is it because silver is more beautiful than aluminum? Many consumers would say so. But imagine showing the spoons to an untrained
forager from the Amazonian forests, someone who knows nothing of
modern manufacturing or the scarcity of different metals. Both spoons,
being polished and shiny, will catch and please the forager's eye; the slight
differences in grain and color won't matter much. The silver spoon may be
heavier, but the forager may just as well prefer the lighter spoon. Perhaps
the most salient difference will be the fact that the aluminum spoon is
made to a more exacting standard, with nary an imperfection on its surface, whereas the silver spoon will have minor defects from the silver-
smith's hammer. After attending to all the perceptual qualities of the two
spoons, the forager might easily prefer the aluminum one.

What's "missing" from the forager's experience is nowhere to be found
in the spoons themselves, as physical objects. The key facts, so relevant

to modern consumers, are entirely extrinsic to the spoons. *We* know that aluminum is common and cheap, while silver is rare and precious. And we know that factory-made goods are available to everyone, while only the wealthy can afford one-of-a-kind goods handcrafted by loving artisans. Once these key facts are known, savvy consumers—those with refinement and taste—quickly learn to value everything about the silver spoon that differentiates it from its more vulgar counterpart, imperfections and all.

The advent of photography wreaked similar havoc on the realist aesthetic in painting. Painters could no longer hope to impress viewers by depicting scenes as accurately as possible, as they had strived to do for millennia. "In response," writes Miller, "painters invented new genres based on new, non-representational aesthetics: impressionism, cubism, expressionism, surrealism, abstraction. Signs of handmade authenticity became more important than representational skill. The brush-stroke became an end in itself."[39]

These technological and aesthetic trends continue well into the present day. Every year, new technology forces artists and consumers to choose between the difficult "old-fashioned" techniques and the easier, but more precise, new techniques. Photographers have to decide whether to use digital cameras and photo-editing software. Musicians have to decide whether to use electronic synthesizers and pitch correction. Couples have to decide which jewels should adorn their engagement rings: mined diamonds, synthetic diamonds, moissanite, or cubic zirconia.[40]

As both artists and consumers, we're often eager to jump in and explore the expressive and aesthetic possibilities of each new medium and manufacturing technique. But just as often, we hold out. Whenever we prefer things made "the old-fashioned way"—handwritten instead of printed, homemade instead of store-bought, live instead of prerecorded—we're choosing to celebrate the skill and effort of an artist over the intrinsically superior results of a more mechanical process.

Our standards for art also evolve in response to what we *know* about the extrinsic factors involved in a given art form. Roman Mars explores this idea at length in his design podcast *99% Invisible*. In one episode, for example, he focuses on brutalism, an architectural movement characterized by its use of concrete. Popular during the 1950s and 1960s, brutalism is now notorious for having produced some of the world's most reviled buildings. Among the lay public, brutalist architecture is considered intrinsically cold, inhuman, and even hideous. And yet, says Mars, "as with any art form—whether opera or painting or literature—the more you know about it, the more you appreciate it." Not surprisingly, then, brutalism has plenty of admirers among architects and students of architecture. "They know that concrete requires a great deal of skill and finesse to work with. Every little detail has to be calculated out in advance, because once the concrete is poured, there's no going back to make adjustments."[41]

* * * * *

Hopefully by now we've demonstrated that art is valued for more than its intrinsic beauty and expressive content. It's also fundamentally a statement about the artist, that is, a fitness display.

In the following sections, we briefly explore some of the more interesting consequences of this idea.

WHY ART IS IMPRACTICAL

The fitness-display theory helps us understand why art needs to be impractical in order to succeed as "art."

Consider a well-made kitchen knife: sturdy, solid, and sharp. As many commentators have pointed out, there's something delightful, even beautiful, about an object perfectly suited to its purpose. And yet, however exquisite the knife's craftsmanship, however pleasing it is to the senses, it doesn't qualify as "art" unless it has decorative, non-functional elements.

The fitness-display theory explains why. Art originally evolved to help us advertise our survival surplus and, from the consumer's perspective, to gauge the survival surplus of others. By distilling time and effort into something *non*-functional, an artist effectively says, "I'm so confident in my survival that I can afford to *waste* time and energy."

The waste is important. It's only by doing something that serves no concrete survival function that artists are able to advertise their survival surplus. An underground bunker stocked with food, guns, and ammo may have been expensive and difficult to build (especially if it was built by hand), and it may well reflect the skills and resources of its maker. But it's not attractive in the same way art is. The bunker reflects a kind of desperation of an animal worried about its survival, rather than the easy assurance of an animal with more resources than it knows what to do with.

Thus *impracticality* is a feature of all art forms. But we can see it with special clarity in those art forms that need to distinguish themselves from closely related practical endeavors. Consider the difference between *clothing*, which is a necessity, and *fashion*, which is a luxury. Fashion often distinguishes itself from mere clothing by being conspicuously impractical, non-functional, and sometimes even uncomfortable. "The history of European costume," writes Alison Lurie, "is rich in styles in which it was literally impossible to perform any useful function: sleeves that trailed on the floor, . . . powdered wigs the size, color and texture of a large white poodle, . . . and corsets so tight that it was impossible to bend at the waist or take a normal breath."[42] Even today we encumber ourselves in the name of style. High heels, for example, are awkward for walking and brutal on the feet—which is precisely how they're able to convey the message, "I care about fashion." Neckties are utterly superfluous, of course, as are dangly earrings and elaborate updos. Meanwhile, durable, low-maintenance fabrics, like cotton or denim, don't have nearly the same cachet as fabrics that are delicate and hard to clean, like silk, lace, or wool. And *polyester*? Please.[43]

Food—as an art form—also needs to distinguish itself as something more than mere nourishment and a source of gustatory pleasure. Cakes, for example, are easy to make and almost always taste great. But however delicious, no one will pay $1,000 for a wedding cake unless it's exquisitely decorated. Haute cuisine also differentiates itself from takeout by virtue of its artful arrangement (a sprig of fresh rosemary), elaborate preparations (tableside flambé), and specially sourced ingredients (not just any lemons, but *Meyer* lemons). None of these especially improves the taste, but we appreciate them nonetheless.

DISCERNMENT

The fitness-display theory also helps us understand why artistic *discernment*—the skill of the savvy consumer or critic—is an important adaptive skill.

Discernment helps us answer a question we're often asking ourselves as we navigate the world: "Which way is high status?" Like the female bowerbird, we use art as one of our criteria for choosing mates (and team-mates). But without the ability to distinguish "good" art from "bad" art, we run the risk of admiring less fit, lower-status artists. So just as the female bowerbird needs to inspect all the local bowers to improve her discernment, humans also need to consume a lot of art in order to calibrate our judgments, to learn which things are high status.

It's only by shopping around and sampling a wide variety of art that we learn to appreciate which skills are common (banging two rocks together) and which are rare (elaborate rhythms). An unrefined palate won't appreciate a Michelin-starred restaurant. An untrained ear can't appreciate the genius of Bach. Only the princess, accustomed as she'd become to royal fineries, could feel the pea beneath 20 mattresses and 20 featherbeds. In this way, discernment becomes important not only for differentiating high quality from low quality (and good artists from mediocre ones), but also as a fitness display unto itself. The fact that the princess could feel the pea, even under the mattresses (i.e., when handicapped), is itself an impressive feat, a mark of her high birth.

We spend an incredible amount of our leisure time refining our critical faculties in this way. Rarely are we satisfied simply to sit back and passively enjoy art (or any other type of human achievement for that matter). Instead we lean forward and take an active role in our experiences. We're eager to evaluate art, reflect on it, criticize it, calibrate our criticisms with others, and push ourselves to new frontiers of discernment. And we do this even in art forms we have no intention of practicing ourselves. For every novelist, there are 100 readers who care passionately about fiction, but have no plans ever to write a novel.

Thus discernment, artistic or otherwise, is a critical skill, and yet it can be something we take for granted, in part because we do it so effortlessly. Think about how rarely we're impressed by truly unimpressive people. When it happens, we feel as though we've been taken in by a charlatan. It can even be *embarrassing* to demonstrate poor aesthetic judgment. We don't want others to know that we're inept at telling good art from bad, skilled artists from amateurs. This suggests that we evaluate each other not only for our first-order skills, but for our skills at evaluating the skills of others.

Human social life is many layered indeed.

Charity

I n 1972, Peter Singer—a man the *New York Times* would describe decades later as "perhaps the world's most controversial ethicist"[1]— made a splash among moral philosophers with an essay titled, "Famine, Affluence, and Morality." His argument began with a simple premise: If you notice a boy drowning in a shallow pond right in front of you, you have a moral obligation to try to rescue him. To do otherwise—to stand by and let him drown—would be unconscionable.

So far, this isn't particularly controversial. But Singer went on to argue that you have the exact same moral obligation to rescue children in developing countries who are dying of starvation, even though they're thousands of miles away. The fact that they aren't dying right in your backyard isn't justification enough to ignore their plight.[2]

Singer's conclusion tends to make people uncomfortable, especially since most of us *don't* help starving children in far-off places with the same urgency we would help a boy drowning in the local pond. (Your two coauthors certainly don't.) The argument implies that every time we take a vacation, buy an expensive car, or remodel the house, it's morally equivalent to letting people die right in front of us. According to one calculation, for the cost of sending a kid through college in America, you could instead save the lives of more than 50 children (who happen to live in sub-Saharan Africa).[3] Yes, many of us *do* try to help people in extreme need, but we also spend a lot on personal indulgences.

What Singer has highlighted with this argument is nothing more than simple, everyday human hypocrisy—the gap between our stated ideals (wanting to help those who need it most) and our actual behavior (spending money on ourselves). By doing this, he's hoping to change his readers' minds about what's considered "ethical" behavior. In other words, he's trying to moralize.

Our goal, in contrast, is simply to investigate what makes human beings tick. But we will still find it useful to document this kind of hypocrisy, if only to call attention to the elephant. In particular, what we'll see in this chapter is that *even when we're trying to be charitable*, we betray some of our uglier, less altruistic motives.

EFFECTIVE ALTRUISM

To appreciate the contrast between our ideals and our actual behavior, it helps to portray what ideal charitable behavior looks like. Luckily, others have done this job for us.

In 2006, Holden Karnofsky and Elie Hassenfeld were working as hedge fund analysts in Connecticut. After making a comfortable living for a few years, they decided to donate a good portion of their earnings to charity. But they wanted to make sure their donations would be used effectively, so they began researching charities the same way they'd been trained to research investment opportunities, namely, by asking for data.

Along with a few friends, Karnofsky and Hassenfeld drafted up a list of promising charities and began reaching out for information. For each charity, they wanted to know how their donations would be spent, and more importantly, how the outcomes would be measured. They wanted to gauge how efficient the whole process was, in order to get the best bang for their charity buck. In financial terms, they were looking to maximize their return on investment (ROI)—or in this case, return on donation (ROD)—and were simply doing due diligence.[4]

The response from the charities they contacted was disheartening. Some simply sent glossy brochures with photos of smiling children and a few pat assurances that good work was being done. Other charities were hostile. One accused Karnofsky and Hassenfeld of attempting to steal confidential information on behalf of a competitor. (Take a moment to consider why a philanthropist might want to keep a "trade secret.") Almost none of the charities responded with the kind of hard, outcome-oriented data that would satisfy a financial analyst.[5]

Eventually they realized that they weren't getting the information they wanted "because the charities themselves didn't have it."[6] But still Karnofsky and Hassenfeld thought the data was important, and they thought other donors would want it too. So in 2007, they decided to leave their jobs and start GiveWell, an organization dedicated to doing (and publicizing) quantitative research on different charities in order to determine which are the most effective, that is, have the highest ROD. This is similar in spirit to the approach taken by Consumer Reports or the Motley Fool, but instead of researching cars and cameras or stocks and bonds, GiveWell researches charities.

GiveWell now sits at the center of a growing social movement called *effective altruism*. Inspired by the work of Singer (along with Karnofsky, Hassenfeld, and others), effective altruists hope to change how people donate their time, effort, and money to good causes. And they're using reason and evidence where others have relied mostly on emotion and gut instinct. This is a hard-nosed, data-driven approach that looks above all for *results*. In deciding how to give, effective altruists follow their heads, not their hearts.

This approach sounds sensible enough, but it can lead to some strange conclusions. In 2015, for example, GiveWell listed these as its three most effective charities:

1. *The Against Malaria Foundation*, which brings mosquito nets to sub-Saharan Africa.
2. *GiveDirectly*, an organization that distributes cash directly to people in need, no strings attached(!).
3. *The Schistosomiasis Control Initiative*, which helps treat people infected with a particular parasitic worm.

These are hardly the most popular or paradigmatic charities. They aren't nearly as high-profile as the United Way, Salvation Army, or Make-A-Wish

Foundation, for example. But they get results. According to GiveWell's estimates, the Against Malaria Foundation can save a life for about $3,500.[7]

Now, you may or may not agree that effective altruism is the *ideal* approach to charity. Among other things, the movement has been criticized for taking an overly narrow view of what makes a given charity "effective."[8] GiveWell, in particular, focuses almost exclusively on charities whose impact can be reliably measured, which causes it to ignore charities that try to effect more nebulous (political or cultural) changes. Still, by taking a rigorously results-oriented approach, effective altruism highlights how traditional charities have *not* been taking this kind of approach.

If we're going to give money to charity, don't we want our donations to be as useful as possible? Isn't that the whole point? Unfortunately, when we start to look at real-world altruism, helping people efficiently doesn't seem to be our top priority.

REAL-WORLD ALTRUISM

Taken at face value, Americans are a fairly generous people. Nine out of 10 of us donate to charity every year.[9] In 2014, these donations amounted to more than $359 billion—roughly 2 percent of the country's GDP.[10] Some of this comes from corporations or charitable foundations, but more than 70 percent is donated by individuals—men and women who tithe at church, sponsor public radio, support children's hospitals, and give back to their alma maters (see Table 2). Of course, it's not just Americans; citizens of other developed countries are similarly generous, give or take.

In this chapter we're focusing on *monetary* donations. People also donate their time (e.g., by volunteering at soup kitchens), professional expertise (pro bono work), and even body parts like blood, kidneys, and bone marrow—not to mention all the small daily kindnesses that go largely undocumented. We're limiting our scope to financial donations only because they're well studied and easy to measure, but we expect that similar arguments apply to all forms of charity.

The striking thing about real-world altruism is how sharply it deviates from effective altruism. The main recipients of American charity are

Table 2.   U.S. Charitable Donations, 2014

($ billions)

Where the money comes from			Where the money goes		
Individuals	$259	72%	Religion	$115	32%
Foundations	$54	15%	Education	$55	15%
Bequests	$28	8%	Human services	$42	12%
Corporations	$18	5%	Foundations	$42	12%
Total	*$359 billion*		Health	$30	8%
			Society-benefit organizations	$26	7%
			Arts and culture	$17	5%
			International affairs	$15	4%
			Animals and the environment	$11	3%
			Individuals	$6	2%
			Total	*$359 billion*	

SOURCE: Giving USA 2015

religious groups and educational institutions. Yes, some of what we give to religious groups ends up helping those who desperately need it, but much of it goes toward worship services, Sunday school, and other ends that aren't particularly charitable. Giving to educational institutions is arguably even less impactful (as we'll argue in Chapter 13 when we take a closer look at schools). Overall, no more than 13 percent[11] of private American charity goes to helping those who seem to need it most: the global poor.

In addition to inefficient allocation at the national level, we also show puzzling behavior when making individual choices. For example, one recent survey found that[12]

- The majority of Americans (85 percent) say that they care about nonprofit performance, but only 35 percent do research on any charitable gift in the course of a calendar year.

- Of those that research, most (63 percent) do so to validate the non-profit they're seeking to give to.
- Only 3 percent of donors do comparative research to find the best nonprofit to give to.

Occasionally, we're even happy to donate without knowing the most basic facts about a charity, like what its purpose is or how donations will be spent. "Within two weeks of Princess Diana's death in 1997," writes Geoffrey Miller, "British people had donated over £1 billion to the Princess of Wales charity, long before the newly established charity had any idea what the donations would be used for, or what its administrative overheads would be."

When we analyze donation as an economic activity, it soon becomes clear how little we seem to care about the impact of our donations. Whatever we're doing, we aren't trying to maximize ROD. One study, for example, asked participants how much they would agree to pay for nets that prevent migratory bird deaths. Some participants were told that the nets would save 2,000 birds annually, others were told 20,000 birds, and a final group was told 200,000 birds. But despite the 10- and 100-fold differences in projected impact, people in all three groups were willing to contribute the same amount.[13] This effect, known as *scope neglect* or *scope insensitivity*, has been demonstrated for many other problems, including cleaning polluted lakes, protecting wilderness areas, decreasing road injuries, and even preventing deaths.[14] People are willing to help, but the amount they're willing to help doesn't scale in proportion to how much impact their contributions will make.

People also prefer to "diversify" their donations, making many small donations rather than a few strategic large ones to the most useful charities.[15] Diversification makes sense for investors in capital markets (like the stock market), but not for philanthropists in the charity "market." The main reason to diversify is to hedge against risk to the beneficiary of the portfolio. But society (the presumed beneficiary of charitable giving) is already thoroughly diversified. There are thousands of well-funded charities taking almost every conceivable approach to helping people. Whether individual donors spread out or concentrate their donations does little to affect the overall allocation. And meanwhile, as the effective altruists convincingly demonstrate, some charities are vastly more effective than others. Giving $3,500 to the Against Malaria Foundation will save a whole human life, while the same amount divided across 100 different charities might go entirely to waste, hardly covering the administrative overhead necessary to collect and process all those separate donations.

When we evaluate charity-related behaviors, gross inefficiencies don't seem to bother us. For example, wealthy people often perform unskilled volunteer work (and are celebrated for it), even when their time is worth vastly more on the open market.[16] Here's Miller again:

> The division of labor is economically efficient, in charity as in business. Instead, in most modern cities of the world, we can observe highly trained lawyers, doctors, and their husbands and wives giving up their time to work in soup kitchens for the homeless or to deliver meals to the elderly. Their time may be worth a hundred times the standard hourly rates for kitchen workers or delivery drivers. For every hour they spend serving soup, they could have donated an hour's salary to pay for somebody else to serve soup for two weeks.[17]

These behaviors don't make sense if we try to explain charity-related behaviors as an attempt to maximize ROD. Something else is going on— but what, exactly? What might we be trying to accomplish with our generosity, if not helping others as efficiently as possible? Are we simply failing in our goals, or do we have other motives?

"WARM GLOW" THEORY

In 1989, to explain some of these inefficiencies, the economist James Andreoni proposed a different model for why we donate to charity. Instead of acting strictly to improve the well-being of others,[18] Andreoni theorized, we do charity in part because of a selfish psychological motive: it makes us happy. Part of the reason we give to homeless people on the street, for example, is because the *act* of donating makes us feel good, regardless of the results.[19]

Andreoni calls this the "warm glow" theory. It helps explain why so few of us behave like effective altruists. Consider these two strategies for giving to charity: (1) setting up an automatic monthly payment to the Against Malaria Foundation, or (2) giving a small amount to every panhandler, collection plate, and Girl Scout. Making automatic payments to a single charity may be more efficient at improving the lives of others, but the other strategy—giving more widely, opportunistically, and in smaller amounts—is more efficient at generating those warm fuzzy feelings.[20] When we "diversify" our donations, we get more opportunities to feel good.

As an ultimate explanation for our behavior, however, the warm glow theory is just a stopgap.[21] The much more interesting and important question is *why* it feels good when we donate to charity. Digging beneath the shallow psychological motive (pursuing happiness), what deeper incentives are we responding to?

To figure this out, we're going to examine five factors that influence our charitable behavior:

1. *Visibility*. We give more when we're being watched.
2. *Peer pressure*. Our giving responds strongly to social influences.
3. *Proximity*. We prefer to help people locally rather than globally.
4. *Relatability*. We give more when the people we help are identifiable (via faces and/or stories) and give less in response to numbers and facts.
5. *Mating motive*. We're more generous when primed with a mating motive.

This list is far from comprehensive, but taken together, these factors help explain why we donate so inefficiently, and also why we feel that warm glow when we donate. Let's briefly look at each factor in turn.

VISIBILITY

Perhaps the most striking bias in how we do charity is that *we give more when we're being watched*. One study found that when door-to-door solicitors ask for donations, people give more when there are two solici-tors than when there's just one.[22] But even when it's a lone solicitor, peo-ple donate significantly more when the solicitor makes eye contact with them.[23] People also give more when the solicitor can see their donations, compared to when their donations are tucked away in an envelope.[24] Even just an image of abstract, stylized "eyespots" makes people more generous.[25]

Charities know that people like to be recognized for their contribu-tions. That's why they commemorate donors with plaques, using larger and more prominent plaques to advertise more generous donations. Exceptionally generous donations are honored by chiseling the benefac-tor's name in stone at the top of a building. For smaller contributions, charities often reward donors with branded paraphernalia—pins, T-shirts, tote bags, pink ribbons, yellow wristbands—all of which allow donors to demonstrate to their peers that they've donated to worthy causes. (They can literally wear their generosity on their sleeves.) Even blood donors typically walk away with a sticker that says, "I gave blood today." Other charities help their donors by hosting conspicuous events—places to see and be seen. These include races, walk-a-thons, charity balls, benefit con-certs, and even social media campaigns like the "ice bucket challenge." By helping donors advertise their generosity, charities incentivize more donations.[26]

Conversely, people prefer *not* to give when their contributions *won't* be recognized. Anonymous donation, for example, is extremely rare. Only around 1 percent of donations to public charities are anonymous.[27] Similarly, in lab experiments, people who donate seldom choose to remain anonymous.[28] And even when people donate "anonymously" to public charities, we should be skeptical that their identities are kept completely hidden. "A London socialite once remarked to me that she knew many anonymous donors," writes Miller. "They were well known within their social circle . . . even though their names may not have been splashed across the newspapers."[29] At the very least, most "anonymous" donors dis-cuss their donations with their spouses and close friends.

Often charities bracket donations into tiers and advertise only which tier a given donor falls into (rather than an exact dollar amount). For example, someone who gives between $500 and $999 might be called a "friend" or "silver sponsor," while someone who gives between $1,000 and $1,999 might be called a "patron" or "gold sponsor." If you donate $900, then, you'll earn the same label as someone who donates only $500. Not surprisingly, the vast majority of donations to such campaigns fall exactly at the lower end of each tier.[30] Put another way: very few people give more than they'll be recognized for.

PEER PRESSURE

Another strong influence on our charitable giving is *peer pressure*. Although donors often deny this influence,[31] the evidence says otherwise. First of all, solicitation works: people donate when they're asked for money, especially by friends, neighbors, and loved ones. People seldom initiate donations on their own; up to 95 percent of all donations are given in response to a solicitation.[32] In-person solicitations, like when someone comes to your door or passes the collection plate at church, work better than impersonal solicitations like direct mail or TV advertisements.[33] People are especially likely to donate when the solicitor is a close associate.[34]

Certainly some of these effects are due to endorsements: When a friend asks for a donation, it's likely to be a good cause, whereas if a stranger makes the request, you might suspect it of being fraudulent or otherwise unworthy. But even when a charitable cause is fully vetted, *peer* pressure is more effective than *non-peer* pressure. Universities, for example, often solicit donations from alumni by having other alumni *from the same class* call them up.[35] This kind of solicitation is even more effective when the solicitor is a former roommate.[36] Here the main relevant variable is the social distance between donor and solicitor.

Peer pressure plays a big role in many areas of life, of course, but it's an especially strong influence on charitable decisions. Contrast how we make donations versus other financial decisions like investments and purchases. If we invested like we donate, we'd make 95 percent of our investments in response to a direct request from a friend, family member, church buddy, or even a stranger on the phone. Instead, when friends or strangers solicit investment ("a ground-floor opportunity!"), we typically eye it with suspicion. Similarly, if we made *purchases* like we donate to charity, we'd see a lot more companies doing door-to-door or in-home sales, like Cutco knife demonstrations or Tupperware parties. Instead these social-selling strategies are the exception rather than the rule; we typically prefer to initiate purchases ourselves in anonymous markets.

PROXIMITY

We're more disposed to help people who are closer to us, not just physically but socially. We'd sooner help people in our local communities than strangers in far-off places. Remember the drowning boy in Peter Singer's thought experiment? Most of us are eager to save him, but few are as eager to help dying children in other countries. Partly this is because the drowning boy is *identifiable* (more on this in the next section), but partly it's due to distance.

Jonathan Baron and Ewa Szymanska call this bias *parochialism*. When they surveyed people about their willingness to help people in their own country (the United States) versus children in India, Africa, or Latin America, people showed a distinct preference for helping others in their own country. As one subject commented, "There are just as many needy children in *this* country and I would help them *first*."[37]

These survey results are borne out in the data on actual giving. In 2011, Americans donated $298 billion to charity, of which only an estimated 13 percent ($39 billion) went to help foreigners.[38] This is hardly the profile of effective charity, since even the neediest Americans are typically better off than many people in developing countries.

To be fair, parochialism is an inescapable part of human nature, and it's written all over our behavior. We treat close family better than friends, and friends better than strangers—so it's no surprise that we often privilege our fellow citizens over people in foreign countries.

RELATABILITY

According to Singer, one of the most well-confirmed findings in behavioral studies of altruism is that we're much more likely to help someone we can identify—a specific individual with a name,[39] a face, and a story. First investigated by Thomas Schelling in 1968,[40] this phenomenon has since come to be known as the *identifiable victim effect*. The corresponding downside, of course, is that we're *less* likely to help victims who *aren't* identifiable. As Joseph Stalin is reported to have said, "A single death is a tragedy; a million deaths is a statistic."[41]

Charities that raise a lot of money understand this, which is why they engage in so much storytelling. "Meet Liz Cintron," the United Way website proudly proclaims, "a senior at Georgetown University and a shining example of how helping one person realize their dreams is a victory for all of us."[42] Liz's story, perched beneath her bright, beaming smile, is chockfull of personal details. As the charity that raises more money each year than any other charity, United Way clearly knows what it's doing.[43]

Another charity that makes great use of biographical details is the microlending site Kiva.org, which allows donors to make interest-free loans to people in developing countries. Visitors to the website are presented with a wide array of photos, each of which gives way to a human story and a concrete request for help. For example, Maria is a 44-year-old rice farmer from the Philippines asking for $325 to purchase fertilizer for her crops.[44] These are real people facing eminently relatable problems.

Contrast this with the Against Malaria Foundation. Although it saves hundreds of lives every year, it can't offer names or faces of the people it helps, because it saves only *statistical* lives. Since it takes roughly 500 mosquito nets to save one life (on average),[45] there's no single individual a donor can point to and say, "I saved *this man's* life." This kind of statistical approach to lifesaving may be effective, but it doesn't tug as strongly at our heartstrings.

MATING MOTIVE

One final factor influencing our generosity is the opportunity to impress potential mates. Many studies have found that people, especially men, are more likely to give money when the solicitor is an attractive member of the opposite sex.[46] Men also give more to charity when nearby observers are female rather than male.[47]

A particularly illuminating study was carried out in 2007 by the psychologist Vladas Griskevicius along with some of his colleagues.[48] Subjects, both male and female, were asked about whether they would engage in various altruistic behaviors. Before hearing the questions, however, they were divided into experimental and control groups and given different tasks to perform. The experimental subjects were primed with a mating mindset, for example, by being asked to imagine an ideal first date.[49] The control subjects, meanwhile, were given a similar task, but one completely unrelated to romantic motives.

Relative to subjects in the control group, subjects in the experimental group (who were primed with mating cues) were significantly more likely to report altruistic intentions.[50] The thought of pursuing a romantic partner made them more eager to do good deeds. This, however, was true only of *conspicuous* good deeds, like teaching underprivileged kids or volunteering at a homeless shelter. When asked about *inconspicuous* forms of altruism, like taking shorter showers or mailing a letter someone had dropped on the way to the post office, the experimental group was no more likely than the control group to report an interest in such activities.

APPEARANCES MATTER

In light of all this evidence, the conclusion is pretty clear. We may get *psychological* rewards for anonymous donations, but for most people, the "warm fuzzies" just aren't enough. We also want to be *seen* as charitable.

Griskevicius calls this phenomenon "blatant benevolence." Patrick West calls it "conspicuous compassion."[51] The idea is that we're motivated to *appear* generous, not simply to *be* generous, because we get social rewards only for what others notice. In other words, charity is an advertisement, a way of showing off.

Now, this is hardly a revelation. Many observers have noticed that people crave recognition for their good deeds. "A millionaire does not really care whether his money does good or not," said George Bernard Shaw, "provided he finds his conscience eased and his social status improved by giving it away."[52] "Take egotism out," said Ralph Waldo Emerson, "and you would castrate the benefactors."[53]

But while we can recognize this in the abstract, when we actually go to donate money or help people, we strongly prefer *not* to acknowledge that we're doing it for the credit or glory. To donate with credit in mind hardly seems like charity at all. In fact, many people feel that the only "true" acts of charity are the perfectly anonymous ones.[54] And yet, we mostly don't donate anonymously; we *are* concerned (at least at an unconscious level) with getting credit. So let's dig a bit deeper into our showing-off motive. By giving to charity, who, exactly, are we hoping to impress? And which qualities are we trying to advertise?

Let's start with the first question. As Griskevicius and Miller argue, one of our primary audiences is potential mates. Giving to charity is, in part, a behavior designed to attract members of the opposite sex.[55] Stinginess isn't sexy. We want mates who will be generous with us and, perhaps more importantly, our future offspring. Note that charities that help children, like Shriners children's hospitals and the Make-A-Wish Foundation, are especially celebrated.

But potential mates aren't our only intended audience. Anecdotally, both men and women are impressed when they learn about a donor's generosity, irrespective of the donor's gender.[56] Women actively celebrate the generosity of Princess Diana and Mother Teresa,[57] for example, while men actively celebrate the generosity of Warren Buffett and Bill Gates. In addition, women who have gone through menopause (and therefore have no mating incentive) are as generous as any other demographic, and perhaps even more so. They volunteer, donate money, and run charitable foundations—even when they're happily married with no chance of having further children. It's also telling that people advertise their philanthropic activities on resumes and in capsule biographies, and that colleges ask students about volunteer work during the admissions process. Politicians also trumpet their generosity when running for office. (In fact, generosity is a prized attribute of leaders around the world.[58]) In other words, charity serves to impress not just potential mates, but also social and political gatekeepers.

We can imagine running Griskevicius's experiment, but instead of priming people with a mating motive, try priming them with a *team-joining* or *social-climbing motive*. For example, rather than asking subjects to describe an ideal romantic evening, ask them to imagine running for local office or interviewing at a prestigious company. Then see how willing they are to engage in acts of (conspicuous) generosity. We predict that subjects primed with these other social motives will show a similar increase in their willingness to donate and perform other self-sacrificing acts.

The other important question to ask is *"Why* does charity make us attractive to mates, teammates, and social gatekeepers?" In other words, which qualities are we demonstrating when we donate, volunteer, or otherwise act selflessly? Here again there are a few different answers.

The most obvious thing we advertise is *wealth*, or in the case of volunteer work, spare time.[59] In effect, charitable behavior "says" to our audiences, "I have more resources than I need to survive; I can give them away without worry. Thus I am a hearty, productive human specimen." This is the same logic that underlies our tendency toward conspicuous consumption, conspicuous athleticism, and other fitness displays. All else being equal, we prefer our associates—whether friends, lovers, or leaders—to be well off. Not only does some of their status "rub off" on us, but it means they have more resources and energy to focus on our mutual interests. Those who are struggling to survive don't make ideal allies.

Charity also helps us advertise our *prosocial orientation*, that is, the degree to which we're aligned with others. (We might also call it "good-neighborliness.") Contrast charity with conspicuous consumption, for example. Both are great ways to show off surplus wealth, but consumption is largely selfish, whereas charity is the opposite. When we donate to a good cause, it "says" to our associates, "Look, I'm willing to spend my resources for the benefit of others. I'm playing a positive-sum, cooperative game with society." This helps explain why generosity is so important for those who aspire to leadership. No one wants leaders who play zero-sum, competitive games with the rest of society. If *their wins* are *our losses*, why should we support them? Instead we want leaders with a prosocial orientation, people who will look out for us because we're all in it together.

This is one of the reasons we're biased toward local rather than global charities. We want leaders who look out for their immediate communities, rather than people who need help in far-off places. In a sense, we *want* them to be parochial. In some situations, it borders on *antisocial* to be overly concerned with the welfare of distant strangers. A politician who campaigns to forego local projects in order to donate taxpayer money to Indian farmers is unlikely to be elected. Remember the comment from earlier: "There are just as many needy children in *this* country and I would help them *first*."

The fact that we use charity to advertise our prosocial orientation helps explain why, as a general rule, we do so little original research to determine where to donate. Original research generates *private* information about which charities are worthy, but in order to signal how prosocial we are, we need to donate to charities that are *publicly* known to be worthy. Imagine that, after doing some research, you determine that the best charity is the "Iodine Global Network,"[60] so you write them a $500 check and compose a (tasteful) Facebook post mentioning your contribution. Unfortunately, none of your friends have heard of the Iodine Global Network. Is it even a real charity? For all they know, you're only supporting it because your sister works there. These suspicions reduce the amount of social credit you get for supporting this charity. If instead you donated to breast cancer research or the United Way, no one would second-guess your good intentions.

There's one final quality that charity allows us to advertise: the spontaneous, almost involuntary concern for the welfare of others. Variations on this trait go by various names—empathy, sympathy, pity, compassion. When we notice someone suffering and immediately decide to help them, it "says" to our associates, "See how easily I'm moved to help others? When people near me are suffering, I *can't help* wanting to make their situation better; it's just who I am." This is a profoundly useful trait to advertise; it means you'll make a great ally. The more time other people spend around you, the more they'll get to partake of your spontaneous good will.

It's this function of charity that accounts for a lot of the puzzles we discussed earlier. For one, it explains why we donate so opportunistically. Most donors don't sketch out a giving strategy and follow through as though it were a business plan. Instead we tend to donate spontaneously—in response to a solicitation, for example, or when we see homeless people shivering on the street, or after a devastating hurricane or earthquake. Why? Because spontaneous giving demonstrates how little choice we have in the matter, how it's simply part of our character to help the people in front of us.[61] This also helps explain why we respond to individual faces and stories more than we respond to dry statistics, however staggering the numbers.

For the psychologist Paul Bloom, this is a huge downside. Empathy, he argues, focuses our attention on single individuals, leading us to become both parochial and insensitive to scale.[62] As Bertrand Russell is often reported to have said, "The mark of a civilized man is the capacity to read a column of numbers and weep,"[63] but few of us are capable of truly *feeling* statistics in this way. If only we could be moved more by our heads than our hearts, we could do a lot more good.

And yet the incentives to show empathy and spontaneous compassion are overwhelming. Think about it: Which kind of people are likely to make better friends, coworkers, and spouses—"calculators" who manage their generosity with a spreadsheet, or "emoters" who simply can't help being moved to help people right in front of them? Sensing that emoters, rather than calculators, are generally preferred as allies, our brains are keen to advertise that *we* are emoters. Spontaneous generosity may not be the most effective way to improve human welfare on a global scale, but it's effective where our ancestors needed it to be: at finding mates and building a strong network of allies.

MISSING FORMS OF CHARITY

To summarize: We have many motives for donating to charity. We want to help others, but we also want to be *seen* as helpful. We therefore use charity, in part, as a means to advertise some of our good qualities, in particular our wealth, prosocial orientation, and compassion.

This view helps explain why some activities that help others *aren't* celebrated as acts of charity. One such unsung activity is giving to people in the far future. Instead of donating money now, we might put it in a trust and let the magic of compound interest work for 50 or 500 years, stipulating how it should be put to use after it's grown to a much larger size. These have been called "Methuselah trusts," the most famous of which were set up by Benjamin Franklin. On his death, he gave two gifts of £1,000 each to the cities of Boston and Philadelphia, and he instructed the funds to be invested for 100 years before being used to sponsor apprenticeships for local children.[64]

Insofar as the goal of charity is to help others, Methuselah trusts are a potentially great way to do it. But very few people give to such trusts. In part, this is because helping people in the far future doesn't showcase our empathy or prosocial orientation. We're rewarded (by our peers) for giving in the here and now, to people who are part of our local communities. There's something suspect about wanting to help people who are too remote in space or time.

Another activity that isn't celebrated as charity is what Robin has called "marginal charity."[65] Here the idea is to nudge our personal decisions just slightly (marginally) in the direction that's beneficial to others. Normally we try to optimize for our own private gain. When a property development firm is planning to build a new apartment complex, for example, they'll crunch a few numbers to determine the most profitable height for the building—10 stories, say. But what's optimal for the developer isn't necessarily optimal for the neighborhood. Regulations, for example, might make it difficult to get building permits, which can result in housing shortages. So if the developer built 11 stories instead of 10, it would reduce their profit by only a tiny amount, but it would add a bunch of new apartments to the neighborhood.

In terms of providing value to others, marginal charity is *extremely* efficient. It does a substantial amount of good for others at very little cost to oneself. (In other words, it has an incredible ROD.) But at the same time, marginal charity utterly fails as a way to advertise good qualities. First of all, there's no way to demonstrate to others that you've engaged in an act of marginal charity; it's almost perfectly invisible. Second, it's extremely analytical. Instead of showcasing your spontaneous compassion, it showcases your facility with abstract economic principles. For these reasons, while some people may practice marginal charity, it's not celebrated or rewarded as a legitimate way to help others.

WRAPPING UP

Singer may be right that there's no *moral* principle that differentiates between a child drowning nearby and another one starving thousands of miles away. But there are very real *social* incentives that make it more rewarding to save the local boy. It's a more visible act, more likely to be celebrated by the local community, more likely to result in getting laid or making new friends. In contrast, writing a check to feed foreign children offers fewer personal rewards.

This is the perverse conclusion we must accept. The forms of charity that are most effective at helping others *aren't* the most effective at helping donors signal their good traits. And when push comes to shove, donors will often choose to help themselves.

If we, as a society, want more and better charity, we need to figure out how to make it more rewarding for individual donors. There are two broad approaches we can take—both of which, Robin and Kevin humbly acknowledge, are far easier said than done.

One approach is to do a better job marketing the most effective charities. Given that donors use charities as ways to signal wealth, prosocial orientation, and compassion, anything that improves their value as a signal will encourage more donations.

The other approach is to learn to celebrate the qualities that make someone an effective altruist. As Bloom points out, it's easy (perhaps too easy) to celebrate empathy; for millions of years, it was one of the first things we looked for in a potential ally, and it's still extremely important. But as we move into a world that's increasingly technical and data-driven, where fluency with numbers is ever more important, perhaps we can develop a greater appreciation for those who calculate their way to helping others.

Education

Why do students go to school?

Our society's standard answer is so obvious that it seems hardly worth discussing. It is almost shouted from every school transcript and class syllabus: to learn the material. Students attend lectures and read books showing them new facts and methods on specific topics. Then they do projects and homework assignments to practice their new skills, and take tests to gauge their mastery of the new material. Years later, particular jobs require particular degrees, as if to say, "Obviously, you wouldn't want to be treated by a doctor who hadn't gone to medical school, or drive over a bridge designed by someone who hadn't gone to engineering school."

More generally, we might say that students go to school to improve themselves, typically with an eye to their future careers.[1] And employers, in turn, are happy to pay a premium for workers who have spent so many years improving themselves. This explanation is simple, clear, and plausible—and no doubt partially true. But we all know it isn't the full story. It may be what parents and teachers like to say at school board meetings and what lawmakers proclaim as they sign a new education bill. Meanwhile, in other contexts—over drinks with friends, say—most of us aren't particularly reluctant to admit that school serves other, less noble functions. In this way, our "hidden" motives in education aren't buried very deep. But we still feel pressure, especially in the public sphere, to pay lip service to feel-good, prosocial motives like learning.

In what follows (much of which is cribbed from Bryan Caplan's excellent new book *The Case Against Education*), we'll show how "learning" doesn't account for the full value of education, and we'll present a variety of alternative explanations for why students go to school and why employers value educated workers.

LEARNING PUZZLES

It's very hard to get into our most exclusive colleges, and they charge high tuitions. Stanford University, for example, accepts less than 5 percent of its applicants and charges more than $45,000 in tuition alone (not counting room, board, and books).[2] However, it turns out that anyone can get a tuition-free education from Stanford—*if* they're willing to skip the official transcript and degree. If you just sit respectfully in class, join the discussions, and maybe turn in assignments, most professors are happy to treat you like other students. In fact, they're flattered to see you so eager to learn from them.

One of us, Robin, actually did this at Stanford 25 years ago when he worked nearby at the National Aeronautics and Space Administration (NASA). One of his professors even wrote him a letter of recommendation when he applied to graduate school. And Stanford isn't unusual in this regard; most colleges are like this. But if an exclusive education is so valuable, why are people like Robin allowed to steal it so easily? Apparently, so few people ever try this tactic that colleges don't even notice a problem.

Consider what happens when a teacher cancels a class session because of weather, illness, or travel. Students who are there to learn should be upset; they're not getting what they paid for! But in fact, students usually celebrate when classes are canceled. Similarly, many students eagerly take "easy A" classes, often in subjects where they have little interest or career plans. In both cases, students sacrifice useful learning opportunities for an easier path to a degree. In fact, if we gave students a straight choice between getting an education without a degree, or a degree without an education, most would pick the degree—which seems odd if they're going to school mainly to learn.

But it's perfectly natural for students to value a degree without necessarily valuing every fact and skill they had to learn to get it. The degree is just an approximate measure of how much they learned, so they might be tempted to cut corners along the way. What's more puzzling is the extent to which *employers* value the degree, above and beyond all the learning that went into earning it. We can see this from the salaries that employers pay to students who finish their degrees, relative to students who drop out partway through school. If employers value learning per se, they should reward students (with higher salaries) in direct proportion to the number of years of school they complete. Instead, we find that employers care much more about the final year (and the resulting degree). This has been called the "sheepskin effect," named after the kind of paper (i.e., vellum) on which diplomas are traditionally printed.

Today in the United States, students who complete one additional year of high school or college earn, on average, about 11 percent more for the rest of their lives. However, not all years are the same. Each of the first three years of high school or college (the years that don't finish a degree) are worth on average only about a 4 percent salary bump. But the last year of high school and the last year of college, where students complete a degree, are each worth on average about a 30 percent higher salary. Yet the classes that students take during senior year aren't crammed with much more learning than are classes in other years. Employers seem to care about something besides what students learn in classes.

Being a graduate is valued even in jobs that don't seem to require any formal education. For example, bartenders with a high school diploma make 61 percent more, and those with a college diploma make an additional 62 percent, relative to their less credentialed peers. For waiters, these gains are 135 percent and 47 percent, and for security guards, they are 60 percent and 29 percent.[3] Yet high school and college teach little that is useful for being a bartender, waiter, or security guard. Why do employers pay so much for unused learning?

In addition to the puzzling behavior of students and employers, we also find things at the systems level that cast doubt on the simple "learning" function.

For example, much of what schools bother to teach is of little use in real jobs. Reading, writing, and arithmetic are clearly useful. But high school students spend 42 percent of their time on rarely useful topics such as art, foreign language, history, social science, and "personal use" (which includes physical education, religion, military science, and special education).[4] Math tends to be more applicable, but even many math classes, such as geometry or calculus, are irrelevant for most students' future employers. Similarly, science classes are largely a waste, except for the minority who pursue careers in scientific fields.

In college we find a similar tolerance for impractical subjects. For example, more than 35 percent of college students major in subjects whose direct application is rare after school: communications, English, liberal arts, interdisciplinary studies, history, psychology, social sciences, and the visual and performing arts.[5] Certainly some students find jobs in these areas, but the vast majority do not. Even engineering majors, whose curriculum is more narrowly targeted to their future trade, never use many of the topics they study in school; employers mostly see themselves as having to train new engineering graduates from scratch.

(Of course, there's much more to life than becoming a productive worker, and school could conceivably help in these regards, e.g., by helping to make students "well-rounded" or to "broaden their horizons." But this seems like a cop-out, and your two coauthors are extremely skeptical that schools are mostly trying to achieve such functions. We ask ourselves, "Is sitting in a classroom for six hours a day really the best way to create a broad, well-rounded human being?")

Even more troubling for the "learning" story, however, is the fact that even when useful material is taught, students don't retain it long enough to apply it later in life. They may cram well enough to pass their final exams, but if they're given the same exam years later, they won't do much better than students who never took the class. For example, while most high school students must take two years of a foreign language, less than 7 percent of adults report that they can speak a foreign language better than "poorly" as a result of schooling (and less than 3 percent can speak it "well"). In general surveys, only 38 percent of American adults can pass the U.S. citizenship test, only 32 percent know that atoms are bigger than electrons, and barely half can compute that saving $0.05 per gallon on 140 gallons of oil yields $7.00 of savings. And yet, at some point, these were basic facts and skills that almost everyone learned.

Furthermore, even if we could remember what we learn in school, decades of research have shown that we're bad at transferring our knowledge to the real world. In school, when a teacher lectures on a sample problem, and then assigns a modestly different homework problem, most students can figure out how the homework is like the lecture. But decades later, almost no one can reliably recognize a complex real-world problem as similar enough to a school problem to successfully apply school learning.

School advocates often argue that school teaches students "how to learn" or "how to think critically." But these claims, while comforting, don't stand up to scrutiny. "Educational psychologists," writes Caplan, "have measured the hidden intellectual benefits of education for over a century. Their chief discovery is that education is narrow. As a rule, students only learn the material you specifically teach them."[6]

Another systems-level failure is that schools consistently fail to use better teaching methods, even methods that have been known for decades. For example, students learn worse when they're graded, especially when graded on a curve.[7] Homework helps students learn in math, but not in science, English, or history.[8] And practice that's spaced out, varied, and interleaved with other learning produces more versatility, longer retention, and better mastery. While this feels slower and harder, it works better.[9] Instead, most schools grade students frequently (often on curves), give homework, and lump material together in ways that make it feel like students are learning faster, when in fact they're learning less.

Students, especially teenagers, also learn more in school when classes don't start so early.[10] In a North Carolina school district, a one-hour delay in school start time—for example, from 7:30 a.m. to 8:30 a.m.—resulted in a 2 percentile gain in student performance.[11] And yet most school districts, at least in the United States, start school earlier for teenagers than for preteens.[12]

Perhaps the most damning puzzle of all, however, is the finding that education isn't nearly as valuable at the national level as at the individual level. The data are a little messy, but here's how it works. Individual students can expect their incomes to rise roughly 8 to 12 percent for each additional year of school they complete. Nations, however, can expect their incomes to rise by only 1 to 3 percent for each additional year of school completed by their citizens on average.[13] If schooling actually works by improving individual students, then we would expect the improvements for individual students to be cumulative across a nation. But nations don't seem to benefit as much from educating their citizens. Something, as they say, doesn't add up.

A SIGNALING EXPLANATION

In 2001, the Nobel Prize was awarded to economist Michael Spence for a mathematical model of one explanation for these puzzles: signaling.[14] The basic idea is that students go to school not so much to learn useful job skills as to *show off* their work potential to future employers. In other words, the value of education isn't just about learning; it's also about credentialing. Of course, this idea is much older than Spence; he's just famous for expressing the idea in math.

In the signaling model, each student has a hidden quality—future work productivity—that prospective employers are eager to know.[15] But this quality isn't something that can be observed easily over a short period, for example, by giving job applicants a simple test. So instead, employers use school performance as a proxy. This works because students who do better in school, over the long run, tend to have greater work potential. It's not a perfect correlation, of course, and there are many exceptions, but by and large, school performance predicts future work performance (and therefore earnings).

People often talk as if intelligence were the key element underlying both school and work performance. But ordinary IQ can't be the whole story, because we have cheap and fast tests to reveal IQ. More to the point, however, raw intelligence can only take you so far. If you're smart but lazy, for example, your intelligence won't be worth very much to your employer. As Caplan argues, the best employees have a whole bundle of attributes—including intelligence, of course, but also conscientiousness, attention to detail, a strong work ethic, and a willingness to conform to expectations. These qualities are just as useful in blue-collar settings like warehouses and factories as they are in white-collar settings like design studios and cubicle farms. But whereas someone's IQ can be measured with a simple 30-minute test, most of these other qualities can only be demonstrated by consistent performance over long periods of time.

Imagine interviewing a 22-year-old college grad for a position at your firm. Glancing down at her resume, you notice she got an A in the biology class she took during her sophomore year. What does this tell you about the young woman in front of you? Well, it doesn't necessarily mean she understands biology; she *might* have retained that knowledge, but statistically speaking, she's probably forgotten a lot of it. More precisely, it tells you that she's the kind of person who's capable of getting an A in a biology class. This is more than just a tautology. It implies that she has the ability to master a large body of new concepts, quickly and thoroughly enough to meet the standards of an expert in the field—or at least well enough to beat most of her peers at the same task. (Even if the class wasn't graded on a strict curve, most professors calibrate their courses so that only a minority of students earn A's.) In addition to what the A tells you about her facility with concepts, it also tells you that she's the kind of person who can consistently stay on top of her workload. Every paper, project, and homework assignment has a deadline, and she met most if not all of them. Every test fell on a specific date, and she studied and crammed enough to perform well on those tests—all while managing a much larger workload from other classes, of course. If she got good grades in those courses too— wow! And if she did lots of extracurricular activities (or a small number at a very high level), her good grades shine even brighter. All of this testifies quite strongly to her ability to get things done at your firm, and none it depends on whether she actually remembers anything from biology or any of her other classes.[16]

In other words, educated workers are generally better workers, but not necessarily because school *made* them better. Instead, a lot of the value of education lies in giving students a chance to advertise the attractive qualities they *already* have.

Caplan offers a helpful analogy. Suppose you inherit a diamond from your grandma, and you want to turn around and sell it. What can you do to fetch a good price? On the one hand, you could take steps to improve the diamond, perhaps by polishing it or cutting it into a more attractive shape. On the other hand, you could take the diamond to be inspected by a professional, who will then issue a certificate attesting to its quality. This will also raise the price, since most buyers can't judge a diamond themselves, and without a certificate, they're worried about getting swindled.

The traditional view of education is that it raises a student's value via *improvement*—by taking in rough, raw material and making it more attractive by reshaping and polishing it. The signaling model says that education raises a student's value via *certification*—by taking an unknown specimen, subjecting it to tests and measurements, and then issuing a grade that makes its value clear to buyers.

Of course, these two processes aren't mutually exclusive. While labor economists tend to downplay the signaling model, it's well known as an explanation and is popular among sociologists of education. No one claims that signaling explains the entire value of education. Some learning and improvement certainly does take place in the classroom, and some of it is critical to employers. This is especially true for technical and professional fields like engineering, medicine, and law. But even in those fields, signaling is important, and for many other fields, signaling may completely eclipse the learning function. Caplan, for example, estimates that signaling is responsible for up to 80 percent of the total value of education.

IMPLICATIONS OF THE SIGNALING MODEL

"I have never let my schooling interfere with my education."—Mark Twain[17]

The signaling model can explain all the puzzles we saw earlier. Clearly it explains why both students and employers are more interested in credentials (getting good grades and degrees from good colleges) than learning per se, even though, like Robin, they could get top-quality learning entirely for free. It also explains why no one is particularly bothered when curricula are impractical or when students forget what they learn—because it's not the knowledge itself that's as important as showing that you have the *generic ability* to learn and complete schoolwork. Signaling also explains the sheepskin effect, where actually earning a diploma is more valuable than the individual years of learning that went into it—because employers prefer workers who stick around and finish what they start.

As is often the case with these "hidden motive" explanations, things that seem like flaws (given the official function) actually turn out to be features (for the hidden function). For example, the fact that school is boring, arduous, and full of busywork might hinder students' ability to learn. But to the extent that school is primarily about credentialing, its goal is to separate the wheat (good future worker bees) from the chaff (slackers, daydreamers, etc.). And if school were *easy* or *fun*, it wouldn't serve this function very well. If there were a way to fast-forward all the learning (and retention) that actually takes place in school—for example, by giving students a magic pill that taught them everything in an instant—we would *still* need to subject them to boring lectures and nitpicky tests in order to credential them.

Signaling also explains a lot of things we *don't* see (that we might expect to see if school were primarily about learning). For example, if the value of a college degree were largely a function of what you learned during your college career, we might expect colleges to experiment with giving students a comprehensive "exit exam" covering material in all the courses they took. Sure, it would be difficult, and there's no way to test the material in the same depth as final exams given at the end of each semester. But if employers actually cared about knowledge, they'd want to know how much students actually retain. Instead, employers seem content with information about students' generic ability to learn things (and complete assignments on time).

Remember the puzzle where nations don't get as much value out of school as individual students do? Well the signaling model explains why. The more school is about credentialing (rather than learning), the less the nation as a whole stands to benefit from more years of it. If only a small amount of useful learning takes place, then sending every citizen to an extra year of school will result in only a small increase in the nation's overall productivity.

Meanwhile, when you're an individual student within a nation, getting more school can substantially increase your future earnings—not because of what you've learned, but because the extra school helps distinguish you as a better worker. And, crucially, it distinguishes you *from other students*. Thus, to the extent that education is driven by signaling rather than learning, it's more of a *competition* than a cooperative activity for our mutual benefit. Sure, we'd *like* school to be a place where we can all get better together, but the signaling model shows us that it's more of a competitive tournament where only so many students can "win."

"Higher education," says Peter Thiel, a tech billionaire famously critical of college,

> sorts us all into a hierarchy. Kids at the top enjoy prestige because they've defeated everybody else in a competition to reach the schools that proudly exclude the most people. All the hard work at Harvard is done by the admissions officers who anoint an already-proven hyper-competitive elite. If that weren't true—if superior instruction could explain the value of college—then why not franchise the Ivy League? Why not let more students benefit? It will never happen because the top U.S. colleges draw their mystique from zero-sum competition.[18]

All of this suggests that we reconsider our huge subsidies and encouragements of school. Yes, there are benefits to credentialing and sorting students—namely, the economic efficiency that results from getting higher-skilled workers into more important jobs. But the benefits seem to pale next to the enormous monetary, psychic, and social waste of the education tournament.[19]

BEYOND SIGNALING

Signaling certainly goes a long way toward explaining why we value education and why schools are structured the way they are. But if schools today mainly function as a credentialing apparatus, it seems like there should be cheaper, less wasteful ways to accomplish the same thing. For example, an enterprising young man could drop out of school and work an entry-level job for a few years, kind of like an apprenticeship. If he's smart and diligent, he could conceivably get promoted to the same level he would have been hired at if he'd taken the time to finish his degree—and meanwhile, he'd be making a salary instead of studying and doing homework for free. So why don't we see more young people doing this?

A partial (but unsatisfying) answer is that going to school is simply the norm, and therefore anyone who deviates from it shows their unwillingness to conform to societal expectations. It's all well and good for Bill Gates or Steve Jobs to drop out of college, but most of us aren't that talented. And what employer wants to risk hiring someone who was too antsy to complete a degree? A desire to break the mold may be attractive in a CEO, but not necessarily for someone working at a bank or paper company. By this logic, school isn't necessarily the best way to show off one's work potential, but it's the equilibrium our culture happened to converge on, so we're mostly stuck with it.

But if school is really such a waste, we might expect to see people eagerly innovating to come up with alternatives. Certainly there are some efforts in this direction, like online courses and Thiel's sponsorship for talented students to forego college.[20] But by and large, most of us accept that school is a reasonable use of our time and money, in part because school serves a wide variety of useful functions, even beyond learning skills and signaling work potential.

For young children, for example, school plays a valuable role simply as day care. Not only is it typically subsidized by the government, but the kid-to-"babysitter" ratio is quite high. Additionally, both primary and secondary schools give students an opportunity to socialize with, and be socialized by, their peers—an opportunity that homeschooled children, for example, must pursue by other means. Meanwhile, for young adults, college serves all sorts of useful functions that aren't typically considered "educational." College campuses are a great place to network, making friends and contacts that can be valuable later in life, both professionally and socially. It's also a great place to meet a future husband or wife. In the

United States today, roughly 28 percent of married college grads attended the same college as their spouse.[21] And even when students don't find their soulmates at college, simply going to college and graduating makes them more likely to marry someone else with a college degree, which can substantially increase their household earnings.[22]

These functions of college—networking and dating—can be seen as *investments* in a student's future. But there's also a sense in which going to college is an act of *consumption*. In other words, some appreciate college in part because for them, it's simply fun—like a summer camp that lasts four years. It's a place to join clubs, go to parties, and experiment with drugs and alcohol. For a more limited set of students, even the classes themselves might be fun (shocking, we know). Looking back, most adults remember their college days with fondness. Beyond intrinsic personal enjoyment, college may also serve as *conspicuous* consumption—a way to signal your family's wealth and social class (in addition to your own qualities as a worker). Many private universities seem awfully expensive relative to their rankings, and if students cared strictly about learning, they'd get a lot more bang for their buck at an inexpensive state school.

Now, none of these "hidden" functions of school are all that hidden. It doesn't particularly bother us to admit that primary school works well as day care or that college is a great social scene. Nevertheless, these functions get short shrift in public discourse. All else being equal, we prefer to emphasize the most prosocial motive, which is that school is a place for students to learn. It costs us nothing to *say* that we send kids to school "to improve themselves," which benefits society overall, and meanwhile we get to enjoy all the other benefits (including the signaling benefits) without having to appear quite so selfish and competitive.

But there are at least two other functions of school that we're substantially less comfortable admitting to.

PROPAGANDA

Schools have been around for a long time. Our word "academic," for example, comes from Plato's famous Academy, named after the olive grove in which scholars met privately for lectures and discussions.[23] But schools today look very little like Plato's Academy. Specifically, our modern K–12 school system is both *compulsory* and largely *state sponsored*. How did we get here?

Compulsory state-sponsored education traces its heritage to a relatively recent, and not particularly "scholarly," development: the expansion of the Prussian military state in the 18th and 19th centuries. Prussian schools were designed to create patriotic citizens for war, and they apparently worked as intended. But the Prussian education system had many other attractive qualities (like teacher training) that made it appealing to other nations. By the end of the 1800s, the "Prussian model" had spread throughout much of Europe.[24] And in the mid-1800s, American educators and lawmakers explicitly set out to emulate the Prussian system.

This suggests that public K–12 schools were originally designed as part of nation-building projects, with an eye toward indoctrinating citizens and cultivating patriotic fervor. In this regard, they serve as a potent form of propaganda. We can see this function especially clearly in history and civics curricula, which tend to emphasize the rosier aspects of national issues. The American Pledge of Allegiance, which was composed in the late 1800s and formally adopted by Congress in 1942, further cements the propaganda function.[25]

We see statistical evidence of the propaganda function in history. Countries have made large investments in state primary education systems when they face military rivals or threats from their neighbors.[26] And just as powerful governments have sought to control mass media outlets like newspapers and TV stations, they have similarly sought state control over schools. Today, governments that control larger wealth transfers (like totalitarian regimes) tend to control and fund more schools than less powerful governments, as well as more TV stations—but not more hospitals.[27] It seems that the governments that most need to indoctrinate their citizens do in fact pay for more school.

Yes, this might be a waste from a global perspective, but at least we can understand why nations don't coordinate internally to avoid this sort of school. All-in-all, though, propaganda probably plays only a modest role in how students are educated (even if it helps explain why governments are eager to fund schools). Meanwhile, there's another hidden function of education that more directly affects the day-to-day life of a student.

DOMESTICATION

The modern workplace is an unnatural environment for a human creature. Factory workers stand in a fixed spot performing repetitive tasks for hours upon hours, day after day. Knowledge workers sit at their desks under harsh fluorescent lights, paying sustained, focused attention to intricate (and often mind-numbing) details. Everyone has to wake up early, show up on time, do what they're told, and submit to a system of rewards and punishments.

One of the main reasons so few animals can be domesticated is that only rare social species let humans sit in the role of dominant pack animal.[28] And we, too, naturally resist submitting to other humans. Recall from Chapter 3 that our ancient hunter-gatherer ancestors were fiercely egalitarian and fought hard to prevent even the appearance of taking or giving orders. And while many women throughout history have been bossed around within their families, prior to the Industrial Revolution, most men were free; outside of childhood and war, few had to regularly take direct orders from other men.

In light of this, consider how an industrial-era school system prepares us for the modern workplace. Children are expected to sit still for hours upon hours; to control their impulses; to focus on boring, repetitive tasks; to move from place to place when a bell rings; and even to ask permission before going to the bathroom (think about that for a second). Teachers systematically reward children for being docile and punish them for "acting out," that is, for acting as their own masters. In fact, teachers reward discipline independent of its influence on learning, and in ways that tamp down on student creativity.[29] Children are also trained to accept being measured, graded, and ranked, often in front of others. This enterprise, which typically lasts well over a decade, serves as a systematic exercise in human domestication.

Schools that are full of regimentation and ranking can acclimate students to the regimentation and ranking common in modern workplaces.[30] This theory is supported by the fact that managers of modern workplaces, like factories, have long reported that workers worldwide typically resist regimentation, unless the local worker culture and upbringing are unusually modern.[31] This complaint was voiced in England at the start of the industrial revolution, and also in developing nations more recently.

The main symptom is that unschooled workers don't do as they're told. For example, consider the data on cotton mill "doffers," workers who remove full spools of yarn from cotton spinning machines. In 1910, doffers in different regions around the world had a productivity that varied by a factor of six, even though they did basically the same job with the same material and machines.[32] In some places, each doffer managed six machines, while in other places only one machine. The problem was that workers in less-developed nations just refused to work more machines:

> Moser, an American visitor to India in the 1920s, is even more adamant about the refusal of Indian workers to tend as many machines as they could " . . . it was apparent that they could easily have taken care of more, but they won't . . . They cannot be persuaded by any exhortation, ambition, or the opportunity to increase their earnings." In 1928 attempts by management to increase the number of machines per worker led to the great Bombay mill strike. Similar stories crop up in Europe and Latin America.[33]

The reluctance of unschooled workers to follow orders has taken many forms. For example, workers won't show up for work reliably on time, or they have problematic superstitions, or they prefer to get job instructions via indirect hints instead of direct orders, or they won't accept tasks and roles that conflict with their culturally assigned relative status with coworkers, or they won't accept being told to do tasks differently than they had done them before.

Modern schools also seem to change student attitudes about fairness and equality. While most fifth graders are strict egalitarians, and prefer to divide things up equally, by late adolescence, most children have switched to a more meritocratic ethos, preferring to divide things up in proportion to individual achievements.[34]

Now, some of this may seem heavy-handed and forebodingly authoritarian, but domestication also has a softer side that's easier to celebrate: civilization. Making students less violent. Cultivating politeness and good manners. Fostering cooperation. In France, for example, school was seen as a way to civilize "savage" peasants and turn them into well-behaved citizens. Here's historian Eugen Weber:

Schools set out "to modify the habits of bodily hygiene and cleanliness, social and domestic manners, and the way of looking at things and judging them." Savage children were taught new manners: how to greet strangers, how to knock on doors, how to behave in decent company. . . . [35] Where schooling did not take hold, "ways are coarse, characters are violent, excitable, and hotheaded, troubles and brawls are frequent."[36]

So it's a mixed bag. Schools help prepare us for the modern workplace and perhaps for society at large. But in order to do that, they have to break our forager spirits and train us to submit to our place in a modern hierarchy. And while there are many social and economic benefits to this enterprise, one of the first casualties is *learning*.[37] As Albert Einstein lamented, "It is . . . nothing short of a miracle that modern methods of instruction have not yet entirely strangled the holy curiosity of inquiry."[38]

Medicine

A mericans today spend more than $2.8 trillion a year on medicine.[1] That's 17 percent of GDP and more than the entire economic output of almost any other country. One out of every $6 spent in the United States goes toward paying for doctors' visits, diagnostic tests, hospital stays, surgeries, and prescription drugs (see Box 15).

Box 15: "Medicine"

In this chapter, we're using the word "medicine" to refer, in aggregate, to all practices for diagnosing, treating, or preventing illness. This includes almost everything you might be billed for by the healthcare system: drugs, surgeries, diagnostic tests, emergency treatments, and visits to the doctor or hospital.

We're also treating medicine as an economic good, so we're going to use phrases like "medical consumers," "the demand for medicine," and even "marginal medicine." The latter refers to the medicine that some people get that others don't, or that some individuals might get if they choose to spend more. In developed countries, for example, since almost everyone has access to vaccines and emergency room medicine, those treatments are not marginal.

The question of why we spend so much on medicine—or any economic good, for that matter—has two components: supply and demand. Much of the public discussion to date has focused on the supply side: Why does medicine *cost* so much to provide? And how can we provide it more cheaply to more people? But in this chapter, we're going to focus on the demand side: Taking costs as a given, why do we, as consumers, *want* so much medicine?

Ask people on the street why they go to the doctor and they'll give a simple, straightforward answer: to get healthy. They might even flash you a funny look for asking about something so obvious. But if we've learned anything from this book, it's that these "obvious" motives are rarely the full story.

In the introduction, we asked readers to consider the case of a toddler who stumbles and scrapes his knee, then runs over to his mother for a kiss. The kiss has no therapeutic value, and yet both parties appreciate the ritual. The toddler finds comfort in knowing his mom is there to help him, especially if something more serious were to happen, and the mother is happy to deepen her relationship with her son by showing that she's worthy of his trust.

The thesis we will now explore in this chapter is that a similar ritual lurks within our modern medical behaviors, even if it's obscured by all the genuine healing that takes place. In this ritual, the patient takes the role of the toddler, grateful for the demonstration of support. Meanwhile, the role of the mother is played not just by doctors, but everyone who helps along the way: the spouse or parent who drives the patient to the hospital, the friend who helps look after the kids, the coworkers who cover for the patient at work, and—crucially—the people and institutions who sponsor the patient's health insurance in the first place. These sponsors include spouses, parents, employers, and national governments. Each party is hoping to earn a bit of loyalty from the patient in exchange for helping to provide care. In other words, medicine is, in part, an elaborate adult version of "kiss the boo-boo."

Like the conspicuous behaviors we've seen in other chapters, we're going to call this the *conspicuous caring* hypothesis.

The healing power of medicine can make it hard to see the conspicuous caring transaction. But Jeanne Robertson, a comedian from North Carolina, puts it on full display when she describes the ritual of taking food to sick friends and family:

In our area of the country, when somebody gets sick, we take over food. Have you noticed this? Now you can *buy* that food at the grocery store or the deli. But write this down on the big list of important things for life: *you get a lot more credit if you make it yourself.* You can put it on your grandmother's platter, but the women in the kitchen will say, "*I know where she got that chicken.*" I'm telling you, it works out that way.[2]

If the goal of bringing food is simply to help feed the family during their time of need—to save them the trouble of making their own dinner— then a store-bought chicken would be just as useful as a homemade one. But that's not the only goal. We also want to show the sick family that we took time out of our busy schedule to help. Only the conspicuous effort of making a dish from scratch allows us to show how much we care.

THE EVOLUTIONARY ARGUMENT

To understand why humans have these instincts, it helps to consider the ancestral conditions in which our caring behaviors likely evolved. Crucially, our distant ancestors didn't have much in the way of effective (therapeutic) medicine. But caring for the sick and injured was still an important activity, crucial to survival and reproduction.

Imagine yourself living in a band of foragers 1 million years ago. You're out picking berries when you stumble on a branch, badly spraining your ankle. It's painful, but that's the least of your worries. First you'll need help getting back to the camp. Luckily you went foraging with friends, so they lend their shoulders and help you hobble back home. But your bigger challenge now is how to survive the next week or two while your ankle heals.

Among other things, you need food, both for yourself and for your family. If you were living as a farmer, you might have supplies of food saved up—but farming won't be invented for another 990,000 years, give or take. And meanwhile, foragers don't accumulate resources; they own little more than they can carry, and most food is perishable. So again, you'll need to rely on your allies—family, friends, and other people in your support network.[3]

The same logic applies when you're stricken with the flu. Your allies can't treat your illness, but they can support you (and your family) while your body heals on its own.

In addition to needing *physical* support, however, you're also going to need *political* support—people to look after your interests while you're incapacitated. Your allies can help in a number of ways: advocating on your behalf in camp decisions, monitoring your mate for fidelity, and protecting you from enemies who might otherwise use your illness to move against you.

These political issues help explain why you might want *conspicuous* support. If rivals have been eyeing your mate, for example, they're less likely to make an advance if they notice that you have allies looking out for you. Similarly, if you've made enemies—for example, by being too domineering or by cheating with someone else's mate—then they're less likely to attack you when they can see that others have your back.

Consider what it would say about you if no one came to your aid. It would show that you don't have many allies, that you're not a respected member of your group. And even if you heal, people won't treat you the same. They'll have seen that you're socially and politically weak. Before you fell sick, you may have succeeded in giving everyone the impression that you were well liked, but maybe people were simply afraid of retribution. Your illness showed everyone your true standing in the camp.

The dangers of being abandoned when ill—both material and political dangers—explain why sick people are happy to be supported, and why others are eager to provide support. In part, it's a simple quid pro quo: "I'll help you this time if you'll help me when the tables are turned." But providing support is also an advertisement to third parties: "See how I help my friends when they're down? If you're my friend, I'll do the same for you." In this way, the conspicuous care shown in our medical behaviors is similar to the conspicuous care shown in charity; by helping people in need, we demonstrate our value as an ally.

MEDICINE IN HISTORY

In addition to understanding our likely evolutionary environment, it helps to take a historical view of medicine. How did humans approach medicine before it became the effective science it is today?

The historical record is clear and consistent. Across all times and cultures, people have been eager for medical treatments, even without good evidence that such treatments had therapeutic benefits, and even when the treatments were downright harmful.[4] But what these historical remedies lacked in scientific rigor, they more than made up for through elaborate demonstrations of caring and support from respected, high-status specialists.

In fact, healers were one of the first specialized roles in tribal cultures. The shaman—part priest, part doctor—performed a variety of healing rituals on behalf of sick patients. Some of these rituals involved useful herbs, but many, like dances, spells, and prayers, are things we now recognize as entirely superstitious.

Medical textbooks from ancient Egypt show a medical system surprisingly like our own, with expensive doctors who matched specific detailed symptoms to complex treatments, most of which were not very useful.

And of course, many treatments were actually harmful. In his book *Strange Medicine*, Nathan Belofsky describes some of the gruesome and injurious treatments commonly practiced by physicians across the ages. Leeching and bloodletting are just two of the better-known examples. Others include trepanation (boring holes to the skull to release evil spirits), burning candles in the mouth (to kill invisible "toothworms"), and lining lovesick patients with lead shields.[5] One particularly harmful (yet all-too-common) practice was known as "counter-irritation": cutting into the patient, inserting foreign objects like dried peas or beans, and then periodically reopening the wound to make sure it didn't heal.[6]

The logic of conspicuous caring is especially clear in what happened to England's King Charles II, who fell inexplicably ill on February 2, 1685.

The records of the king's treatment were released by his physicians, who wanted to convince the public that they had done everything in their power to save the king. And what, exactly, did this entail? After a pint and a half of blood was drawn, according to Belofsky,

> His Royal Majesty was forced to swallow antimony, a toxic metal. He vomited and was given a series of enemas. His hair was shaved off, and he had blistering agents applied to the scalp, to drive any bad humors downward.
>
> Plasters of chemical irritants, including pigeon droppings, were applied to the soles of the royal feet, to attract the falling humors. Another ten ounces of blood was drawn.
>
> The king was given white sugar candy, to cheer him up, then prodded with a red-hot poker. He was then given forty drops of ooze from "the skull of a man that was never buried," who, it was promised, had died a most violent death. Finally, crushed stones from the intestines of a goat from East India were forced down the royal throat.[7]

Not surprisingly, the king died on February 6. But notice all the *conspicuous effort* in this story. If Charles's physicians had simply prescribed soup and bed rest, everyone might have questioned whether "enough" had been done. Instead, the king's treatments were *elaborate* and *esoteric*. By sparing no expense or effort—by procuring fluids from a torture victim and stones from exotic goat bellies—the physicians were safe from accusations of malpractice. Their heroic measures also reflected well on their employers, that is, the king's family and advisers.

On Charles's part, receiving these treatments was proof that he had the best doctors in the kingdom looking after him. And by agreeing to the especially painful treatments, he demonstrated that he was resolved to get well by any means necessary, which would have inspired confidence among his subjects (at least until his untimely demise).

This third-party scrutiny of medical treatments isn't just a historical phenomenon. Even today, there are strong incentives to *be seen* receiving the best possible care. Consider what happened to Steve Jobs. When he died of pancreatic cancer in 2011, the world mourned the loss of a tech-industry titan. At the same time, many were harsh in condemning Jobs for refusing to follow the American Medical Association's best practices for treating his cancer. "Jobs's faith in alternative medicine likely cost him his life," said Barrie Cassileth, a department chief at the Memorial Sloan Kettering Cancer Center. "He essentially committed suicide."[8]

Now, imagine that, hypothetically, Jobs's *son* had come down with pancreatic cancer. If the Jobs family had pursued the same line of alternative treatment, the public outrage would have been considerably more severe. Cassileth's remark that Jobs "essentially committed suicide," for example, would turn into the accusation that he "essentially committed murder." We see a similar accusation leveled at Christian Scientists when they refuse mainstream medical treatment for their children.[9]

The point here is that whenever we fail to uphold the (perceived) highest standards for medical treatment, we risk becoming the subject of unwanted gossip and even open condemnation. Our seemingly "personal" medical decisions are, in fact, quite public and even political.

MEDICINE TODAY: TOO MUCH

Now, the evolutionary and historical perspectives suggest that our ancestors had reasons to value medicine apart from its therapeutic benefits. But medicine today is different in one crucial regard: it's often very effective. Vaccines prevent dozens of deadly diseases. Emergency medicine routinely saves people from situations that would have killed them in the past. Obstetricians and advanced neonatal care save countless infants and mothers from the otherwise dangerous activity of childbirth. The list goes on.

But the fact that medicine is often effective doesn't prevent us from *also* using it as a way to show that we care (and are cared for). So the question remains: Does modern medicine function, in part, as a conspicuous caring ritual? And if so, how important is the hidden caring motive relative to the overt healing motive? For example, if conspicuous caring were only 1/100th as important as the therapeutic motive, then we could, for all practical purposes, safely ignore it. However, if the conspicuous caring motive is half as strong as the healing motive, then it could make a huge difference to our medical behaviors.

To find out just how important conspicuous caring really is, we will need to look at some actual data on our medical behaviors.

The biggest prediction of the conspicuous caring hypothesis is that we'll end up consuming too much medicine, that is, more than we need strictly for health purposes. After all, this is what usually happens when products or services are used as gifts. When people buy chocolates for their sweethearts on Valentine's Day, for example, they usually buy special fancy chocolates in elaborate packaging, not the standard grocery-store Hershey's bar. A feast usually offers more and better food than people eat at a typical meal. And Christmas gifts are usually more expensive, and often less useful, than items you would have bought for yourself.[10] (Though, yes, some kids do get socks.)

Medical treatments vary greatly, in both their costs and potential health benefits. If patients are focused entirely on getting well, we should expect them to pay only for treatments whose expected health benefits exceed their costs (whether financial costs, time costs, or opportunity costs). But when there's another source of demand (i.e., conspicuous caring), then we should expect consumption to rise past the point where treatments are cost-effective, to include treatments with higher costs and lower health benefits. Thus conspicuous care is to some extent excessive care.

(There's another way to look at it, of course, which is that we *are* getting our money's worth when we buy medicine, but the value isn't just health; it's also the opportunity to demonstrate support. It only looks like we're getting ripped off if we measure the health benefits but ignore the social benefits.)

We will now look to see if people today consume too much medicine. For the most part, we won't be looking at individual treatments. It's easy to find specific drugs or surgeries that don't work particularly well, but that won't tell us much about the overall impact of medical spending. Instead we're going to step back and examine the *aggregate* relationship between medicine and health. Given the treatments that people choose to undergo, across a wide range of circumstances, does more spending lead on average to better health outcomes? We're also going to restrict our investigation to *marginal* medical spending. It's not a question of whether some medicine is better than no medicine—it almost certainly is—but whether, say, $7,000 per year of medicine is better for our health than $5,000 per year, given the treatment options available to us in developed countries.[11]

One place to start this investigation is by comparing health outcomes across different regions of the same country. As it happens, there are often huge differences in how the same medical conditions are treated in different regions. In the United States, for example, the surgery rates for men with enlarged prostates vary more than fourfold across different regions, and the rates of bypass surgery and angioplasty vary more than threefold. Total medical spending on people in the last six months of life varies fivefold.[12] These differences in practice are largely arbitrary; medical communities in different regions have mainly just converged on different standards for how to treat each condition.[13]

These variations result in a kind of natural experiment, allowing us to study the effects of *regionally marginal medicine*, that is, the medicine consumed in high-spending regions but not consumed in low-spending regions. And the research is fairly consistent in showing that the extra medicine doesn't help. Patients in higher-spending regions, who get more treatment for their conditions, don't end up healthier, on average, than patients in lower-spending regions who get fewer treatments. These results hold up even after controlling for many factors that affect both medical use and health—things like age, sex, race, education, and income.

One of the earliest of these studies was published in 1969.[14] It found that variations in death rates[15] across the 50 U.S. states were predicted by variations in income, education, and other variables, but *not* by variations in medical spending. A later study looked at 18,000 Medicare patients across the country who were diagnosed with the same condition, but who received different levels of treatment.[16] Yet another study did the same for Veterans Affairs' patients.[17] All these studies found that patients treated in higher-spending places were no healthier than other patients.

Perhaps the largest study of regional variations looked at end-of-life hospital care for 5 million Medicare patients across 3,400 U.S. hospital regions. We might hope to see that patients live longer when local hospitals decide to keep them in the intensive care unit (ICU) for longer periods of time, relative to patients in hospitals that kick them out sooner. What the study found, however, was the opposite. For each extra day in the ICU, patients were estimated to live roughly 40 *fewer* days.[18] The same study also estimated that spending an additional $1,000 on a patient resulted in somewhere between a *gain of 5 days* and a *loss of 20 days* of life.[19] In short, the researchers found "no evidence that improved survival outcomes are associated with increased levels of spending."[20]

These studies—along with many others (but not all[21])—show that patients who receive more medicine don't achieve better health outcomes. Still, these are just *correlational* studies, leaving open the possibility that some hidden factors are influencing the outcomes, and that somehow (despite the absence of correlation) more medicine really does improve our health. To really make a strong case, then, we need to turn to the scientific gold standard: the randomized controlled study. This can better reveal if increased medical care actually *causes* better outcomes.

Spoiler alert: it doesn't.

THE RAND HEALTH INSURANCE EXPERIMENT

Between 1974 and 1982, the RAND Corporation, a nonprofit policy think tank, spent $50 million to study the causal effect of medicine on health. It was, and remains, "one of the largest and most comprehensive social science experiments ever performed in the United States."[22]

Here's how the RAND experiment worked. First, 5,800 non-elderly adults were drawn from six U.S. cities. Within each city, all participants were given access to the same set of doctors and hospitals, but they were randomly assigned different levels of medical subsidies. Some patients received a full subsidy for all medical visits and treatments; they could consume as much medicine as they wanted without paying a dime. Other patients received discounts ranging from 75 percent to 5 percent off their total bill.[23] Note that a 5 percent discount is effectively unsubsidized, but the researchers needed to give patients some incentive to enroll in the study. Patients remained in the program between three and five years.[24]

As expected, patients whose medicine was fully subsidized (i.e., free) consumed a lot more of it than other patients. As measured by total spending, patients with full subsidies consumed 45 percent more than patients in the unsubsidized group.[25] This 45 percent difference constituted the marginal medicine examined in this study, that is, the medicine that some people got that others did not.

Despite the large differences in medical consumption, however, the RAND experiment found almost no detectable health differences across these groups. To measure health, comprehensive physical exams were given to all participants both before and after the study.[26] These exams included 22 physiological measurements like blood pressure, lung capacity, walking speed, and cholesterol levels. The exams also used extensive questionnaires to gauge five measures of overall well-being: physical functioning, role functioning (i.e., at work), mental health, social health, and general health perception.[27]

For the five measures of overall well-being, all groups fared the same.[28] Of the 22 physiological measurements, only one—diastolic blood pressure—showed a statistically significant improvement in the fully subsidized group (relative to the other groups).[29] But this is an outcome we should expect purely by chance. Out of 20 noisy measurements, on average, 1 of them will randomly appear to differ from zero (at a 95 percent confidence interval), even if all the underlying values are actually zero.

Needless to say, the RAND experiment researchers were surprised by their results. To look more closely, they wondered if their fully subsidized patients were choosing treatments that were less effective than the treatments chosen by other patients. For example, maybe the fully subsidized patients decided to get unnecessary surgeries, or to visit the doctor when they had milder symptoms. Unfortunately, this wasn't the case. Doctors who were asked to look at patient records couldn't tell the difference between the fully subsidized and unsubsidized patients. Severity of diagnosis and appropriateness of treatment were statistically indistinguishable

between the two groups.[30] The marginal medicine wasn't "less useful medicine," at least in the eyes of trained professionals.

Now, put yourself in the shoes of someone chosen to participate in the
RAND study. Imagine getting assigned to the unsubsidized group, while
a lucky friend of yours is assigned a full subsidy. Naturally you're going
to feel disappointed. For the next three to five years, you'll have to pay
for all of your medicine, while your friend gets everything for free. But
in addition to the financial burden, you might also *fear for your health*.
If you have a persistent cough, for example, you might decide not to go
to the clinic, hoping your cough will clear up on its own. Or you might
decide that you can't afford the cholesterol medication recommended by
your doctor.

This fear, however, is misplaced. The RAND study tells us that, on
average, you're going to end up *just as healthy* as your friend. Your bank
account may suffer, but your body will be just fine.

The only other large, randomized study like the RAND experiment is
the Oregon Health Insurance Experiment. In 2008, the state of Oregon
held a lottery to decide who was eligible to enroll in Medicaid. This gave
researchers the opportunity to compare the health outcomes of lottery
winners and losers.[31]

Like in the RAND study, lottery winners ended up consuming more
medicine than lottery losers.[32] Unlike the RAND study, however, the
Oregon study found two areas where lottery winners fared significantly
better than lottery losers. One of these areas was mental health: lottery
winners had lower incidence of depression.[33] The other area was subjective: winners reported that they *felt* healthier. Surprisingly, however,
two-thirds of this subjective benefit appeared immediately following the
lottery, before the winning patients had any chance to avail themselves of
their newly subsidized healthcare.[34] In other words, lottery winners experienced something akin to the placebo effect.

In terms of physiological health, however, the Oregon study echoes the
RAND study. By all objective measures, including blood pressure, lottery
winners and losers ended up statistically indistinguishable.[35]

BUT! . . . BUT! . . .

We've now arrived at the unpalatable conclusion that people in the United States currently consume too much medicine. We could probably cut back our medical consumption by a third without suffering a large adverse effect on our health.[36]

This conclusion is more or less a consensus among health policy experts, but it isn't nearly as well-known or well-received by the general public. Many people find the conclusion hard to reconcile with the extraordinary health gains we have achieved over the past century or two. Relative to our great-great-grandparents, today we live longer, healthier lives—and most of those gains are due to medicine, right?

Actually, no. Most scholars don't see medicine as responsible for most improvements in health and longevity in developed countries.[37] Yes, vaccines, penicillin, anesthesia, antiseptic techniques, and emergency medicine are all great, but their *overall* impact is actually quite modest. Other factors often cited as plausibly more important include better nutrition, improvements in public sanitation, and safer and easier jobs. Since 1600, for example, people have gotten a lot taller, owing mainly to better nutrition.

More to the point, however, the big historical improvements in medical technology don't tell us much about the value of the *marginal* medicine we consume in developed countries. Remember, we're not asking whether some medicine is better than no medicine, but whether spending $7,000 in a year is better for our health than spending $5,000. It's perfectly consistent to believe that modern medicine performs miracles *and* that we frequently overtreat ourselves.

People also find it hard to reconcile the unpalatable conclusion with all the stories we hear from the media about promising new medical research. Today, it's a better drug for reducing blood pressure. Tomorrow, a new and improved surgical technique. Why don't these individual improvements add up to large gains in our aggregate studies?

There's a simple and surprisingly well-accepted answer to this question: *most published medical research is wrong.*[38] (Or at least overstated.)

Medical journals are so eager to publish "interesting" new results that they don't wait for the results to be replicated by others. Consequently, even the most celebrated studies are often statistical flukes. For example, one study looked at the 49 most-cited articles published in the three most prestigious medical journals. Of the 34 of these studies that were later tested by other researchers, only 20 were confirmed.[39] And these were among the best-designed and most respected studies in all of published medical research. Less-celebrated research would probably be confirmed even less often.

Another hang-up some people have (toward the unpalatable conclusion) is their belief in the value of *specific* marginal treatments. For example, if your uncle was helped by a pacemaker, but many people can't afford pacemakers, you might think, "*This* marginal treatment has great value, so how could marginal medicine on average have no value?" The problem is that marginal medical treatments are just as likely to do harm as good. Prescription drugs almost always have side effects, some of them quite nasty. Surgeries often come with complications. Staying in the hospital puts patients at higher risk of contracting infections and communicable diseases. According to the Centers for Disease Control and Prevention, improper catheter use alone is responsible for 80,000 infections and 30,000 deaths every year.[40] Few medical treatments are without risk.

TESTING CONSPICUOUS CARE

The fact that we consume too much medicine has many possible explanations. Perhaps the most tempting is the idea that health is so important to us that we're willing to try anything, even if it's unlikely to help much (like the RAND experiment shows).

To show that our medical behaviors are driven by the conspicuous caring motive, rather than "health at any cost," we have to look at other predictions made by the conspicuous caring hypothesis.

Prediction 1: Keeping Up with the Joneses

To the extent that medicine functions as a caring signal, it's going to be sensitive to context. If everyone around you spends a lot on medical care, you'll need to spend a lot too, or risk looking like someone who doesn't care enough.

Economists have found exactly this kind of "keeping up with the Joneses" effect. When they compare people with similar incomes and wealth who happen to live in different countries, those who live in richer countries (where their neighbors are richer) spend more on medicine, while those who live in poorer countries (where their neighbors can't afford as much medicine) spend less.[41] In other words, if your income stayed the same as you moved from being a relatively rich person in a poor nation to being a relatively poor person in a rich nation, you would likely increase your medical consumption.

This makes little sense if medicine is a simple transaction where you pay to try to get better health outcomes. For a given dollar amount, you might expect to get similar health benefits regardless of what country you're in. But it makes perfect sense if one of the benefits you're paying for is a social benefit: convincing others that you care (or are well cared for). To get these social benefits, you need to spend roughly as much as your "Jones" neighbors.

Prediction 2: Preference for Treatments Requiring Visible Effort and Sacrifice

To maximize social credit for giving a gift, you need other people to see how much you sacrificed for it. (Recall the disapproval Robertson knew she would receive if she brought a store-bought chicken.) Thus conspicuous care prefers gifts that can be more easily *seen* as requiring effort and sacrifice.

When we consume medicine for the simple, private goal of getting well, we shouldn't care how much it costs or how elaborate it is, as long as it works. However, to the extent that we use medicine to show how much we care (and are cared for), the conspicuous effort and expense are crucial.

Patients and their families are often dismissive of simple cheap remedies, like "relax, eat better, and get more sleep and exercise." Instead they prefer expensive, technically complicated medical care—gadgets, rare substances, and complex procedures, ideally provided by "the best doctor in town." Patients feel better when given what they think is a medical pill, even when it is just a placebo that does nothing. And patients feel even better if they think the pill is more expensive.[42]

This bias is especially pronounced in how we treat patients who are terminally ill, and even more so for elderly family members. Roughly 11 percent of all medical spending in the United States, for example, goes toward patients in their final year of life.[43] And yet it's one of the least effective (therapeutic) kinds of medicine. Even where it succeeds in prolonging life, it rarely succeeds in helping the patient achieve a reasonable quality of life; heroic end-of-life care is rarely pleasant for the patient.[44] Unfortunately few family members are willing to advocate for lesser care, fearing it will be seen as tantamount to abandoning their beloved relative.

Prediction 3: Focus on Public Rather Than Private Signs of Medical Quality

When you buy something for personal use, you will be equally open to private and public signals of its quality. It doesn't matter *how* you know that something is good, as long as it is. In contrast, when using something as a gift, you need your audience to see widely accepted signs of your gift's quality, in order to maximize the social credit you get for giving it. Observers can't appreciate quality that they can't see.

This is the same bias we saw in Chapter 12, where donors rarely do their own research about the effectiveness of different charities, preferring instead to give to charities that are widely seen as good causes.

Similarly, in medicine more than other industries, we focus less on local performance track records, and more on standard and widely visible credentials and reputations. For example, even though randomized trials have found nurse practitioners to be just as medically effective as general practice doctors,[45] we only let the doctors treat patients. When choosing between doctors, people typically focus on the prestige of their school or hospital, instead of their individual track records for patient outcomes.

In fact, patients show surprisingly little interest in private information on medical quality. For example, patients who would soon undergo a dangerous surgery (with a few percent chance of death) were offered private information on the (risk-adjusted) rates at which patients died from that surgery with individual surgeons and hospitals in their area. These rates were large and varied by a factor of three. However, only 8 percent of these patients were willing to spend even $50 to learn these death rates.[46] Similarly, when the government published risk-adjusted hospital death rates between 1986 and 1992, hospitals with twice the risk-adjusted death rates saw their admissions fall by only 0.8 percent.[47] In contrast, a single high-profile news story about an untoward death at a hospital resulted in a 9 percent drop in patient admissions at that hospital.[48]

Prediction 4: Reluctance to Openly Question Medical Quality

When something functions as a gift, it's often considered rude and ungrateful to question its quality. ("Don't look a gift horse in the mouth," as the saying goes.) So if you want to seem grateful to those who help pay for your medicine, you will be reluctant to openly question the quality of that medicine. After all, it's the thought (and effort) that counts.

Skeptical attitudes toward medicine seem to be a mild social taboo today (as readers may notice if they discuss this chapter with friends or relatives). Many people are quite uncomfortable with questioning the value of modern medicine. They'd rather just trust their doctors and hope for the best.

And yet medicine deserves its share of public scrutiny—as much, if not more so, than any other area of life. One of the simplest reasons is the prevalence and high cost of medical errors, which are estimated to cause between 44,000 and 98,000 deaths in the United States every year.[49] As Alex Tabarrok puts it, "More people die from medical mistakes each year than from highway accidents, breast cancer, or AIDS and yet physicians still resist and the public does not demand even simple reforms."[50]

Such simple reforms might include

- Regulating catheter use. Studies have found that death rates plummet when doctors are required to consistently follow a simple five-step checklist.[51]

- Requiring autopsies. Around 40 percent of autopsies reveal the original cause-of-death diagnosis to have been incorrect.[52] But autopsy
  rates are way down, from a high of 50 percent in the 1950s to a current rate of about 5 percent.[53]
- Getting doctors to wash their hands consistently. Compliance for best
  handwashing practices hovers around 40 percent.[54]

Some of these problems are downright scandalous, and yet, as Tabarrok
points out, they're largely ignored by the general public. We'd rather not
look our medical gift horse in the mouth.

Another way we're reluctant to question medical quality is by getting
second opinions. Doctors frequently make mistakes, as we've seen, and
second opinions are often useful—for example, for diagnosing cancer,[55]
determining cancer treatment plans,[56] and avoiding unnecessary surgery.[57] And yet we rarely seek them out.

Prediction 5: A Focus on Helping during Dramatic Health Crises

If our goal is really "health at any cost," then we should expect to pursue
the most effective health strategies, whatever form they may take. If we're
using medicine as a signal of support, however, then we'll provide and
consume more of it during a patient's times of crisis, when they are more
grateful for support.

And this is exactly what we find. The public is eager for medical interventions that help people when they're sick, but far less eager for routine
lifestyle interventions. Everyone wants to be the hero offering an emergency cure, but few people want to be the nag telling us to change our
diets, sleep and exercise more, and fix the air quality in our big cities—
even though these nagging interventions promise much larger (and more
cost-effective) health improvements.

One study, for example, tracked 3,600 adults over seven and a half
years. Investigators reported that people who reside in rural areas lived
an average of 6 years longer than city dwellers, nonsmokers lived 3 years

longer than smokers, and those who exercised a lot lived 15 years longer than those who exercised only a little.[58] In contrast, most studies that look similarly at how much medicine people consume fail to find any significant effects. Yet it is medicine, and not these other effects, that gets the lion's share of public attention regarding health.

* * * * *

There are other ways to explain each of these phenomena, of course. But taken together, they suggest that we are less interested in "health at any cost," and more interested in treatments that third parties will appreciate.

Like King Charles II, we want the very best medicine for ourselves (especially when others can see that it's the best). Like the woman bringing food to a sick friend, we want to help people in need (and maximize the credit we get for it). And because there are two reasons to consume and provide medicine—health and conspicuous care—we end up overtreated.

Religion

Every fall, monarch butterflies from all over the United States and southern Canada flock south to their wintering sites in Mexico, where they hibernate[1] in trees until their return trip in March. On the Serengeti plain, giant herds of wildebeest undertake the circular "great migration," roving in constant search of greener pastures. On Christmas Island, red crabs spend most of the year in the island's interior forests, but come October, they scramble to the coasts to mate and lay eggs. Their swarms are so thick that the island has to shut down its coastal roads, lest they become littered with flattened crab carcasses.[2]

Animal migrations are among the most spectacular and cinematic natural phenomena on the planet. But there's one epic migration you're unlikely to find in a nature documentary: the Hajj. It's the largest annual gathering of *Homo sapiens* on Earth.[3] For five days every year, millions of Muslims from across the world converge on Mecca, a sacred but otherwise unremarkable city at the edge of the Arabian desert. Here the pilgrims undertake a series of rituals. They walk seven times counterclockwise around the Kaaba—the black, cube-shaped building at the center of the world's largest mosque. (See Figure 5.) They also shave their heads; run back and forth between two hills; stand vigil from noon until sunset; drink water from the Zamzam well; camp overnight on the plain of Muzdalifa; sacrifice a lamb, goat, cow, or camel; and cast stones at three pillars in a symbolic stoning of the devil.[4]

What drives these pilgrims is no ordinary biological motive. Unlike the monarch butterflies, they aren't in search of a more hospitable climate.[5] Unlike the wildebeests, Muslims don't travel to Mecca in search of food.

Figure 5. Muslims surrounding the Kaaba in Mecca. SOURCE: prmustafa / iStock

And unlike the crabs of Christmas Island, they aren't looking for mates; in fact, sexual activity is strictly prohibited during the Hajj.[6]

From the perspective of an animal struggling to survive and reproduce, the Hajj seems like an enormous waste of resources. A pilgrim traveling from San Francisco, for example, will have to take a week off work, buy an expensive plane ticket to Saudi Arabia, and uproot from her breezy, temperate city to camp out in the sweltering desert—and all for *what*, exactly?

Religion. There's perhaps no better illustration of the elephant in the brain. In few domains are we more deluded, especially about our own agendas, than in matters of faith and worship. When Henry VIII sought to have his first marriage annulled under the guise of piety, or when religious leaders launch imperialist crusades, we can be forgiven for questioning their motives.[7] But most of what people do in the name of God isn't so blatantly opportunistic. And yet, as we'll see, there's a self-serving logic to even the most humble and earnest of religious activities.

THE MYSTERY OF RELIGION

The Hajj may be singularly distinctive, but Muslims are hardly alone in undertaking dramatic actions in the name of their religion. Around the world, worshippers wear funny hats, elaborate costumes, special underwear, and tiny logos around their necks. They speak in tongues, dance ecstatically, and dip their babies in baths of holy water. And while all of these practices are peculiar, many of them seem downright counterproductive—a waste of precious energy, resources, and even fertility and health. Around the world, worshippers routinely undermine their narrow self-interest by fasting, sacrificing healthy animals, abstaining from certain sexual practices, and undergoing ritual mutilations like piercing, scarification, self-flagellation, and circumcision. Christian Scientists swear off blood transfusions. Mormon men spend two of their prime years stationed off in remote provinces doing missionary work. Many people earmark 10 percent of their income for the church. Even the most mundane form of religious devotion—weekly attendance at church—is like a miniature Hajj: people from a wide geographic area converge at a single location to kneel, bow, pray, sing, chant, and dance in the name of their faith.

The extremes of religious behavior are even more striking. Tibetan Buddhist monks, for example, spend weeks hunched over a flat surface, meticulously placing millions of grains of colored sand to produce an intricate "sand mandala," only to destroy it almost as soon as they're finished. Even more astonishing (from a Darwinian perspective) is the fact that these monks, along with religious leaders of many other traditions, take vows of poverty and chastity, effectively removing themselves from both the rat race and the gene pool. Yet other religious zealots undertake the ultimate sacrifice by martyring themselves in the name of their religions.

What, on Darwin's green Earth, is going on here?

Actually, religion presents not one but two striking puzzles. In addition to the behaviors, we also have to explain the menagerie of peculiar religious *beliefs*. A quick tour of the these would include gods, angels, ghosts, demons, talking animals, virgin births, prophecies, possessions, exorcisms, afterlives of all sorts, revelation, reincarnation, transubstantiation, and superaquatic perambulation—to name just a few. And that doesn't even include creation myths, a particularly rich vein of exotic beliefs.

Where—again, on Earth—do these supernatural beliefs come from?

DO BELIEFS EXPLAIN BEHAVIORS?

It's tempting to try to collapse these two puzzles into one, by assuming that the strange supernatural beliefs *cause* the strange behaviors. This seems straightforward enough: We believe in God, *therefore* we go to church. We're scared of Hell, *therefore* we pray.[8] All that would be left to explain, then, is where the beliefs come from.[9]

Let's call this the *belief-first model* of religious behavior, as in Figure 6.

Although this turns out not to be the view held by most anthropologists and sociologists, it's nevertheless a popular perspective, in part because it's so intuitive. After all, our beliefs cause our behaviors in many areas of life—like when believing "I'm out of milk" causes us to visit the market. In fact, the belief-first model is something that both believers and nonbelievers often agree on, especially in the West. Debates between prominent theists and atheists, for example, typically focus on the evidence for God or the lack thereof. Implicit in these debates is the assumption that beliefs are the central cause of religious participation.[10]

And yet, as we've seen throughout the book, beliefs aren't always in the driver's seat. Instead, they're often better modeled as *symptoms* of the

Figure 6. Belief-First Model of Religion

underlying incentives, which are frequently social rather than psychological. This is the religious elephant in the brain: We don't worship simply because we believe. Instead, we worship (and believe) because it helps us as social creatures.

Before we discuss how religion is strategic, it might help to put the belief-first model in perspective. For one thing, not all religions put such a premium on doctrine. Most religions are fairly lax on questions of private belief as long as adherents demonstrate *public acceptance* of the religion.[11] In this regard, faith-based religions like Christianity and Islam are the exception rather than the rule.[12] Historical religions, such as those of the ancient Greeks and Romans, were less concerned with doctrinal propositions like, "Zeus rules the gods on Mount Olympus," and more concerned with ritual observance, like coming out to celebrate on public holidays. Other religions, like Hinduism, Judaism, and Shintoism, are as much ethnicities and cultural traditions as they are sets of beliefs about supernatural entities, and people can be wholly accepted as members of the religion without believing in the literal existence of the gods in question. Many Jews, for example, consider themselves atheists, and yet continue practicing Judaism—going to temple, keeping kosher, and celebrating the high holidays.

At the same time, we engage in a wide variety of activities that have a religious or even cult-like feel to them, but which are entirely devoid of supernatural beliefs.[13] When Muslims face Mecca to pray, we call it "religion," but when American schoolchildren face the flag and chant the Pledge of Allegiance, that's just "patriotism." And when they sing, make T-shirts, and put on parades for homecoming, that's "school spirit." Similarly, it's hard to observe what's happening in North Korea without comparing it to a religion; Kim Jong-un may not have supernatural powers, but he's nevertheless worshipped like a god. Other focal points for quasi-religious devotion include brands (like Apple), political ideologies, fraternities and sororities, music subcultures (Deadheads, Juggalos), fitness movements (CrossFit), and of course, sports teams—soccer, notoriously, being a "religion" in parts of Europe and most of Latin America. The fact that these behavioral patterns are so consistent, and thrive even in the absence of supernatural beliefs, strongly suggests that the beliefs are a secondary factor.

Finally, we'd like to make a plea for some charity and humility, especially from our atheist readers. It's easy for nonbelievers to deride supernatural beliefs as "delusions" or "harmful superstitions," with the implication that believers are brainwashed into doing things they wouldn't otherwise do. Now we, your two coauthors, aren't religious ourselves, and we have no special love for religion. And we don't want to deny that people are sometimes harmed by their religions. (Just ask the families of those who died at Jonestown.) Nevertheless, we think people can generally intuit what's good for them, even if they don't have an analytical understanding of *why* it's good for them. In particular, they have a keen sense for their concrete self-interest, for when things are working out in their favor versus when they're getting a raw deal. So whenever adherents feel trapped or oppressed by their religion, as many do, they're probably right.[14] But in most times and places, people feel powerfully attracted to religion. They continue to participate, week after week and year after year—not with reluctance but with tremendous zeal. And we'd like to give them the benefit of the doubt that they know what's good for them.[15]

In fact, the vast majority of weekly churchgoers are socially well-adjusted and successful across a broad range of outcomes. Compared to their secular counterparts, religious people tend to smoke less,[16] donate and volunteer more,[17] have more social connections,[18] get and stay married more,[19] and have more kids.[20] They also live longer,[21] earn more money,[22] experience less depression,[23] and report greater happiness and fulfillment in their lives.[24] These are only correlations, yes, which exist to some extent because healthier, better-adjusted people choose to join religions. Still, it's hard to square the data with the notion that religions are, by and large, harmful to their members.

If religions are delusions, then, they seem to be especially useful ones. And to understand why, we'll have to expand our scope beyond the supernatural beliefs and seemingly maladaptive practices.

RELIGIONS AS SOCIAL SYSTEMS

Given the other chapters in this book, it's clear that we're going to seek to explain religion not by looking *inward*, to our self-deceiving minds, but rather by looking *outward*, to social incentives. We've already seen how social incentives can lead to some pretty strange behaviors, like painting cave walls and using leeches as "medicine." But what kind of social incentives lead us to practice religion?

The answer given by most serious scholars of religion is community. Or to give it the emphasis it deserves:

Community, *community*, **community**!

"Religion," says Jonathan Haidt, "is a team sport."[25] "God," says Émile Durkheim, "is society writ large."[26] In this view, religion isn't a matter of *private* beliefs, but rather of *shared* beliefs and, more importantly, *communal practices*. These interlocking pieces work together, creating strong social incentives for individuals to act (selfishly) in ways that benefit the entire religious community. And the net result is a highly cohesive and cooperative social group. A religion, therefore, isn't just a set of propositional beliefs about God and the afterlife; it's an entire social system.[27]

Figure 7 shows this in the form of a diagram:[28]

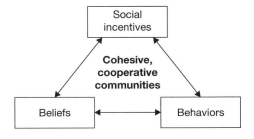

Figure 7. Communal Model of Religion

It's worth taking a moment to reflect on the logic of community. Communities provide benefits to the people living in them; otherwise, everyone would just live on their own.[29] Some of these benefits, like safety in numbers and economic specialization, come more or less for free, simply by virtue of congregation. But many other benefits require individuals to forego their narrow self-interest in the name of cooperation.

Unfortunately, cooperation is hard. Groups that are chock full of peaceful, rule-following cooperators are ripe for exploitation. In a religious context, cheaters can take many forms. Some people might put on a show of great piety, but then mistreat others whenever it's convenient—like a wolf in sheep's clothing, preying on the flock. Others will simply engage in the casual form of cheating known as free-riding. This might entail people taking advantage of church services without giving anything back, or perhaps seeking help from a religious group during their time of need, but then abandoning it as soon as they're back on their feet. Even something as simple as reading email during a sermon could be construed as cheating.

To lock in the benefits of cooperation, then, a community also needs robust mechanisms to keep cheaters at bay. We've seen this before (in Chapters 3 and 4 on norms and cheating, respectively). But in addition to the standard tools for norm enforcement—monitoring, gossip, and punishment—religions have a few extra tricks up their sleeve.

In the next few sections, we'll examine various features of religion, including (but by no means limited to) supernatural beliefs. We'll be approaching them as social technologies designed to discourage cheating and facilitate cooperation within a community. It's in light of these goals that the stranger facets of religion begin to make sense.

SACRIFICE, LOYALTY, AND TRUST

For an individual human living alone in the woods, it never makes sense to take a resource and just throw it away or burn it up. But add a few other humans to the scene, and suddenly it can be perfectly rational—because, as we've seen many times, sacrifice is socially attractive.[30] Who makes a better ally: someone who's only looking out for number one or someone who shows loyalty, a willingness to sacrifice for others' benefit? Clearly it's the latter. And the greater the sacrifice, the more trust it engenders.

Friends and family make sacrifices for each other all the time. But we can't sacrifice for every person we might meet for an ephemeral, one-off interaction. The solution that religions have struck upon is for members to make *ritual sacrifices* in the name of the group. In nominal terms, many sacrifices are made to a god, but following Durkheim, we should note that God often functions as a symbol for society. So whenever people make a sacrifice to *your* god, they're implicitly showing loyalty to you—and to everyone else who worships at the same altar.[31]

Crucially, rituals of sacrifice are honest signals whose cost makes them hard to fake. It's easy to *say*, "I'm a Muslim," but to get full credit, you also have to *act* like a Muslim—by answering the daily calls to prayer, for example, or undertaking the Hajj. Actions speak louder than words, and expensive actions speak the loudest.

Personal sacrifices, then, are a way of "paying one's dues" to a social group. Some groups require a large upfront payment in the form of an initiation ritual, like a fraternity hazing or military boot camp. By setting up barriers to entry and forcing initiates to pay a high cost, groups ensure that only the most devoted and committed are admitted as members.[32] Regular religious rituals work the same way, but rather than (or in addition to) requiring one large upfront cost, these are smaller ongoing costs— a way of paying dues on a weekly or yearly basis.

These rituals of sacrifice take many different forms, depending on which type of resource is being sacrificed. *Food*, for example, is a common offering, whether it's an animal sacrifice, a libation, or fruit left at the temple for the gods. *Money* is sacrificed through alms, tithing, and other acts of charity. *Health* is sacrificed by fasting, and in much more graphic displays by mortification of the flesh (e.g., self-flagellation). During the Mourning of Muharram, for example, some Muslims beat themselves bloody with chains, swords, and knives—an extreme sacrifice showing equally extreme devotion.[33] Some types of *pleasure* are also foregone in the name of religion, as when people abstain from drugs, alcohol, and certain sexual practices, or when a Catholic gives up chocolate for Lent.

Time and *energy* are perhaps the easiest resources to waste, and we offer them in abundance. Examples include weekly church attendance, sitting shiva, and the Tibetan sand mandalas we saw earlier. This helps explain why people don't browse the web during church. Yes, you probably have "better things to do" than listen to a sermon, which is precisely why you get loyalty points for listening patiently. In other words, the boredom of sermons may be a feature rather than a bug.

Status is sacrificed by many acts of worship, especially rituals that involve the body, like kneeling, bowing, and prostrating.[34] Jesus famously washed the feet of his disciples. Even the simple act of wearing a yarmulke is understood as a symbolic way for Jews to humble themselves before God. Less symbolically, many practices also serve to stigmatize practitioners in the eyes of outsiders. By wearing "strange" clothes or refusing to eat from the same plates as secular folk, members of a given sect lose standing in broader society (while gaining it within the sect, of course).[35]

Fertility isn't often wasted, but when it is, it's wasted in a big way, as when religious leaders take vows of celibacy.[36] Note that positions of greater trust and authority require larger sacrifices; if the Pope had children, for example, his loyalty would be split between his family and his faith, and Catholics would have a harder time trusting him to lead the Church.[37]

Some rituals combine many different resources into a single sacrificial act. A pilgrimage like the Hajj is a cornucopic offering of time, energy, money, and sometimes health, all "wasted" for the sake of cementing one's dedication to Islam. In exchange for these acts of devotion, a pilgrim earns greater trust and higher standing among other Muslims, both back home and around the world.

Note, however, that a community's supply of social rewards is limited, so we're often competing to show *more* loyalty than others—to engage in a "holier than thou" arms race. And this leads, predictably, to the kind of extreme displays and exaggerated features we find across the biological world. If the Hajj seems extravagant, remember the peacock's tail or the towering redwoods.

But note, crucially, that sacrifice isn't a zero-sum game; there are big benefits that accrue to the entire community. All these sacrifices work to maintain high levels of commitment and trust among community members, which ultimately reduces the need to monitor everyone's behavior.[38] The net result is the ability to sustain cooperative groups at larger scales and over longer periods of time.[39]

Today, we facilitate trust between strangers using contracts, credit scores, and letters of reference. But before these institutions had been invented, weekly worship and other costly sacrifices were a vital social technology. In 1000 A.D., church attendance was a pretty good (though imperfect) way to gauge whether someone was trustworthy. You'd be understandably wary of your neighbors who *didn't* come to church, for example, because they're not "paying their dues" to the community. Society can't trust you unless you put some skin in the game.

Even in the modern world, religious observance continues to be an important social cue. To give just one example, Americans seem unwilling to support an atheist for president. A 2012 Gallup poll, for instance, found that atheists came in dead last in electability, well behind other marginalized groups like Hispanics and gay people.[40] In fact, Americans would sooner see a Muslim than an atheist in the Oval Office.[41] An atheist kneels before no one, and for many voters, this is a frightening proposition.

PROSOCIAL NORMS

Like all communities, religions are full of norms that constrain individual behavior. These norms can be especially useful, both to the community at large and to individual members,[42] especially when properly calibrated to the economic and ecological conditions the group is facing.

Let's take a look at two common sets of religious norms.

One set concerns how to treat others. All major world religions understandably condemn theft, violence, and dishonesty, but they also celebrate positive virtues like compassion, forgiveness, and generosity. Charity is one of the main pillars of Islam, for example, while Christians are exhorted to "love thy neighbor" and "turn the other cheek" after a perceived wrong. Jains practice an extreme form of nonviolence extending to all animals, even insects. Certainly all this cooperative niceness has its advantages, and groups full of nice people tend to outcompete those full of nasty people. The problem, of course, is how to keep cheaters from ruining the party.

One solution, as we've seen, is costly signaling, which helps keeps less-committed people out of the group. But just as important are the mechanisms for norm enforcement that we saw in Chapter 3: monitoring and punishment. For all the talk of universal love and turning the other cheek, it's important to note that religious communities *do* frequently punish transgressors, whether by censuring, shunning, or stoning them. In fact, these two strategies—traditional norm enforcement, plus paying "dues" through costly rituals—reinforce each other. After you've paid a lot of dues, made a lot of friends, and accumulated a lot of social capital over the years, the threat of being kicked out of a group becomes especially frightening. And this, in turn, reduces the need for expensive monitoring.[43]

The other important set of religious norms governs sex and family life. As Jason Weeden and colleagues have pointed out, religions can be understood, in part, as *community-enforced mating strategies.*[44]

Human mating patterns vary a lot around the world and depend on many factors, like resource availability, sex ratios, inheritance rules, and the economics of childrearing. One particularly interesting pair of strategies represents a divide in many Western countries (the United States in particular). On one side is the mating strategy pursued by members of the traditional, religious right, which involves early marriage, strict monogamy, and larger families. On the other side is the strategy pursued by members of the liberal, secular left, which involves delayed marriage, relaxed monogamy, and smaller families.

Of these two mating strategies, the traditional one functions best in a tight-knit community, since it benefits from strong communal norms. As such, religious communities tend to frown on anything that interferes with monogamy and high fertility, including contraception, abortion, and divorce, along with pre- and extramarital sex.[45] If you're someone who wants to follow this mating strategy, it behooves you to be around like-minded people who will help keep everyone in line. When the whole community is aligned on this, there are a lot of advantages. Babies will be born and raised in two-parent households, fathers will have confidence in their paternity, and everyone can spend less energy monitoring and policing their spouses for fidelity.[46] High fertility also means everyone will help with child-rearing, and more generally will support and encourage family life (vs., say, careerism).

To the secular mentality, many of these norms—like the one against contraception—make little sense, especially on moral grounds. Why shouldn't an individual woman be allowed to use birth control? But in a tight-knit community, each woman's "individual" choices have social externalities. If you're using birth control, you're also more likely to delay marriage, get an advanced degree, and pursue a dynamic, financially rewarding career. This makes it harder on your more traditional, family-oriented neighbors. Your lifestyle interferes with theirs (and vice versa), and avoiding such tensions is largely why we self-segregate into communities in the first place.

RITUALS OF SYNCHRONY

"Religion is a myth you can dance to."—Andrew Brown[47]

Modern armies no longer line up in neat rows and charge each other from opposite sides of a battlefield. Strangely, however, they still train that way, for example, during marching drills. This practice is useful, it turns out, not to prep for actual battle conditions, but to build trust and solidarity among soldiers in a unit.

Our species, for reasons that aren't entirely clear, is wired to form social bonds when we move in lockstep with each other.[48] This can mean marching together, singing or chanting in unison, clapping hands to a beat, or even just wearing the same clothes. In the early decades of the 20th century, IBM used corporate songs to instill a sense of unity among their workers.[49] Some companies in Japan still use these practices today.

In 2009, Stanford psychologists Scott Wiltermuth and Chip Heath demonstrated this synchrony–solidarity effect experimentally. They first asked groups of students to perform synchronized movements (such as marching around campus together), then had them play "public goods" games to measure the degree to which individuals were willing to take risks for the benefit of the group. What they found across three experiments is that "people acting in synchrony with others cooperated more in subsequent group economic exercises, even in situations requiring personal sacrifice."[50]

Religions are understandably keen to take advantage of this effect. Almost every major religious tradition involves some form of synchronized movement. Hare Krishnas, for example, use song and dance in their religious practice and public outreach. Most modern Christians don't dance as part of their worship, but early Christians did (at least until the Middle Ages),[51] and most congregations even today continue to chant and sing in unison. Even shared silence can foster solidarity, like in a Quaker meeting house, or when an otherwise boisterous congregation takes a moment to pray quietly together. When daily life is clamorous, even a few seconds' reprieve, taken in the context of fellowship, can be a powerful experience.

SERMONS

It's easy to see how sermons help promote cooperation within a religious community. Without them, how will people know which values to uphold, which norms to follow, and how to punish cheaters? But a sermon is more than just a lecture, its utility more than mere education. It's also a *ritual*, a means of transforming social reality—one that we participate in simply by attending.

Here's how it works. When you attend a sermon, you're doing more than passively acquiring information. You're also implicitly endorsing the sermon's message as well as the preacher's leadership, the value of the community, and the legitimacy of the entire institution. Simply by attending, you're letting everyone else know that you support the church and agree to be held to its standards. The pews aren't just a place to listen; they're also a place to see and be seen by fellow churchgoers.

Imagine a preacher addressing a congregation about the virtue of compassion. What's the value of attending such a sermon? It's not just that you're getting personal advice, as an individual, about how to behave (perhaps to raise your chance of getting into Heaven). If that were the main point of a sermon, you could just as well listen from home, for example, on a podcast.[52] The real benefit, instead, comes from listening *together* with the entire congregation. Not only are *you* learning that compassion is a good Christian virtue, but *everyone else* is learning it too—and you know that they're learning it, and they know that you're learning it, and so forth. (And if anyone happens to miss this particular sermon, don't worry: the message will be repeated again and again in future sermons.) In other words, sermons generate *common knowledge* of the community's norms. And everyone who attends the sermon is tacitly agreeing to be held to those standards in their future behavior. If an individual congregant later fails to show compassion, ignorance won't be an excuse, and everyone else will hold that person accountable. This mutual accountability is what keeps religious communities so cohesive and cooperative.

For better or worse, this dynamic works even for controversial norms. If a preacher rails against contraception or homosexuality, for example, you might personally disagree with the message. But unless enough people "boo" the message or speak out against it, the norm will lodge itself in the common consciousness.[53] Thus, by attending a sermon, you're learning not just what "God" or the preacher thinks, but also what the rest of your congregation is willing to accept.

BADGES

Given all the benefits to being part of a community, it's useful for members to be able to distinguish insiders from outsiders. How else will they know who's likely to be a good cooperator? This problem becomes especially acute as communities grow in size and complexity. In a small forager band with only a handful of neighboring bands, everyone tends to know everyone else by face or by name, and rarely comes in contact with a complete stranger. But in large agrarian empires or industrial civilizations, full of migrant traders and workers, it's really useful to be able to evaluate strangers on sight.

Thus there's a role for *badges*: visible symbols that convey information about group membership.[54] In a religious context, badges may include special hairstyles, clothing, hats or turbans, jewelry, tattoos, and piercings. Even dietary rules and other mandated behaviors, like midday or pre-meal prayers, can function as badges, since they allow others to see who's a member of which religion.

Religious badges are reinforced at home and church, but they have the most value (as badges) out in public, in the market or town square. The baker who wears a yarmulke at his bakery, for example, is sending two different (but related) messages to two different audiences. To other Jews, he's saying:

FYI, I'm Jewish—so we share many of the same norms and values. You can trust me. Also note that I'm endorsing our tribe conspicuously, in public. I'm fully committed to Judaism; it's an inescapable part of my identity.

Here he's using his badge as a demonstration of loyalty, hoping to earn more trust from fellow Jews. But he's also sending a message to gentiles:

My actions here reflect not only on me as an individual, but on Jews everywhere. If I behave badly, my Jewish peers are liable to punish me for tarnishing our collective reputation. Knowing this, you can more readily trust that I'll behave according to accepted Jewish standards of conduct.

In this way, a badge is similar to a brand. When Nabisco puts its logo on a new product, the consumer is assured of a certain quality, because Nabisco would suffer a loss of reputation if the new product were terrible. And if a truly bad product does happen to land on grocery store shelves, Nabisco will probably issue a recall. Similarly, Christians who swear on the Bible are less likely to perjure themselves, for fear they'll be "recalled" or otherwise punished by their community.

SUPERNATURAL BELIEFS

Finally, we return to supernatural beliefs. And now, instead of seeing them as mere superstitions, we're ready to understand how they might serve useful functions in the context of a community struggling to cooperate.[55]

As we've pointed out in previous chapters (particularly Chapter 5 on self-deception), the value of holding certain beliefs comes not from acting on them, but from convincing others that you believe them. This is especially true of religious beliefs. They aren't particularly useful or practical for individuals in isolation, and yet we experience large social rewards for adopting them and/or punishment for not adopting them. This is what it means for a belief to be an orthodoxy. Whether you accept it can make the difference between the warm embrace of fellowship and the cold shoulder of ostracism. Faced with such powerful incentives to believe, is it any wonder our brains fall in line?

But why do communities care what we believe? Why do our peers reward or punish us?

Consider the belief in an all-powerful moralizing deity—an authoritarian god, perhaps cast as a stern father, who promises to reward us for good behavior and punish us for bad behavior. An analysis of this kind of belief should proceed in three steps. (1) People who believe they risk punishment for disobeying God are more likely to behave well, relative to nonbelievers. (2) It's therefore in everyone's interests to *convince others* that they believe in God and in the dangers of disobedience. (3) Finally, as we saw in Chapter 5, one of the best ways to convince others of one's belief is to *actually* believe it. This is how it ends up being in our best interests to believe in a god that we may not have good evidence for.

For similar reasons, it's also useful to believe that God is always watching—and that He knows everything, even our "private" deeds and innermost thoughts, and will judge us with perfect justice. The more fervently we profess belief in such a god, the more we'll develop a reputation for doing right at all times, even when other *people* aren't watching.[56] This kind of reputation is especially attractive in those we seek as leaders, since they have a lot of room to behave badly behind closed doors.

At the margin, these beliefs cause believers to behave more morally than they would otherwise. And from the point of view of a perfectly selfish organism, this extra "good" behavior is an unfortunate cost. The ideal situation would be for the brain to be able to have its cake (convincing others that it fears God's wrath) and eat it too (go on behaving as if it didn't fear God at all). But human brains aren't powerful enough to pull off such perfect hypocrisy, especially when others are constantly probing our beliefs. So the next best thing is often to internalize the belief, while remaining inconsistent enough to occasionally give in to temptation.

This helps make sense of the belief in moralizing god(s), but leaves us with a great many other supernatural beliefs to explain. Some of these beliefs clearly help reinforce facets of each religion's social system. The belief that Muhammad was the final prophet, for example, conveniently closes the book on disruptive new revelations. In Christianity, the belief that priests are (or aren't) necessary to intermediate between God and the laity helps determine their role in the church body. It's easy to see the virtues of such beliefs: they're politics by way of theology.

Still other beliefs, however, seem entirely arbitrary, and yet they're as hotly debated as any other beliefs. For example, in some Christian denominations, baptism is believed to be necessary for salvation, whereas in others, it's more like an optional bonus. Meanwhile, endless arguments rage over arcane doctrinal minutiae, such as the exact nature of the Trinity or whether a cracker literally turns into the flesh of Jesus during communion.[57] What are we to make of these seemingly inconsequential beliefs?

Perhaps they function as badges—markers of loyalty to one particular religion or branch instead of another.[58] A good badge allows us to answer the central question about loyalty: Are you with us or against us? This is why issues of doctrine are especially pronounced when discussing religion across a divide (atheist vs. theist, Catholic vs. Protestant, etc.). What you believe tells people which tribe you're in, whose side you're on. And thus these beliefs, too, play a political role, rather than a merely philosophical role.

In this way, many orthodox beliefs are like the hat and hairstyle requirements we mentioned earlier. They can be entirely arbitrary, as long as they're consistent and distinctive. It doesn't *really* matter what a sect believes about transubstantiation, for example, or the nature of the Trinity. In particular, it doesn't affect how people behave. But as long as everyone within a sect believes the same thing, it works as an effective badge. And if the belief happens to be a little weird, a little stigmatizing in the eyes of nonbelievers, then it also functions as a sacrifice.

There's an analogy here with spectator sports. Precisely because there are no selfish material reasons to prefer the Giants over the Dodgers, your support of a specific team serves as an excellent signal of loyalty to the local community.[59] It's unlikely that your home team is objectively better or more entertaining than any other team, but it is *your* team, after all, and that makes a world of difference. And the more support you show for it—including rabid, stigmatizing behaviors like wearing face paint to a game—the more support you'll get from fellow fans.

In the same way, the craziness of religious beliefs can function as a barometer for how strong the community is—how tightly it's able to circle around its sacred center, how strongly it rewards members for showing loyalty by suppressing good taste and common sense. The particular strangeness of Mormon beliefs, for example, testifies to the exceptional strength of the Mormon moral community. To maintain such stigmatizing beliefs in the modern era, in the face of science, the news media, and the Internet, is quite the feat of solidarity. And while many people (perhaps even many of our readers) would enjoy being part of such a community, how many are willing to "pay their dues" by adopting a worldview that conflicts with so many of their other beliefs, and which nonbelievers are apt to ridicule?

These high costs are exactly the point. Joining a religious community isn't like signing up for a website; you can't just hop in on a lark. You have to get socialized into it, coaxed in through social ties and slowly acculturated to the belief system. And when this process plays out naturally, it won't even feel like a painful sacrifice because you'll be getting more out of it than you give up.

CELIBACY AND MARTYRDOM

Most of the religious behaviors we've been discussing in this chapter are *adaptive*—or at least, that's what we've been arguing. They help us get along and get ahead within religious communities, and often in the broader context of life and reproduction. But what are we to make of the most extreme religious behaviors, like celibacy and martyrdom? These are in no way biologically adaptive to the individual. So might *these behaviors* be explained by the individual's religious beliefs—for example, a belief in the afterlife and its promise of eternal rewards?

Certainly the beliefs might give individuals a small psychological push toward such self-destructive behaviors, but there's another, much larger force we need to consider: social status. Prestige, glory, and the admiration of one's fellows. We've seen how small sacrifices, like weekly church attendance, can function as a gambit: a sacrifice in one domain (time and energy) in the hope of securing a larger gain in some other domain (trust). Similarly, we might view martyrs and priests as following the same instincts that, under normal circumstances, serve them, and all the rest of us, quite well.[60]

An analogy that's often used by biologists to describe such instincts is *hill-climbing*. Individual brains are built to go "up" in pursuit of higher and higher social status (or any other measure of reward). So we scramble our way toward the top of whatever hill or mountain we happen to find in our local vicinity. Sometimes, we consider going down to find a better route up, or wandering randomly in hope of finding an even higher peak off in the distance. But mostly we just climb skyward as if on autopilot. And in most landscapes, these instincts serve us very well. But if we happen to find ourselves in a nonstandard landscape, one that our brains weren't designed for, the same instincts can lead us to bad outcomes.

To continue the analogy, we might model the landscape of a religious community as a *volcano*—a cone-shaped mountain with a perilous crater at the top. Every day, as a worshipper, you seek to climb higher, which often (counterintuitively) requires you to make sacrifices. Each sacrifice earns you more trust and respect from your peers, taking you further up the slope. It may get steeper and the air more rarefied. With each step, you run the risk of slipping back down or getting clawed down by rivals. But you steel yourself to press onward. You make ever larger sacrifices, which continue to work out in your favor—until one day, without realizing it, you push yourself too far. Your brain, expecting a simple mountain, took a step that felt like "up." But in reality, the mountain was a volcano, and your final step sent you tumbling over the edge and into the crater.

It's important to note that these hill-climbing accidents aren't at all unique to religious landscapes. In dietary landscapes, we seek tasty fats and sugars, which were almost always "up" (in health terms) for our ancestors—until one day we're stricken with diabetes or a heart attack. In military landscapes, we learn to show bravery, earning ever more respect from our comrades—right up until we take a bullet. Drug addicts seek ever-more-pleasurable highs until they overdose. And in literal mountaineering, risk-taking explorers might search for higher and higher peaks to climb, each summit bringing more glory—until one day their reach exceeds their grasp and they plummet to an untimely death.

In all of these cases, instincts that are adaptive in one context can lead us fatefully astray in another. But we shouldn't jump to the conclusion that the instincts are necessarily maladaptive, or that the people acting on them are hopelessly foolish or deluded. They're just chasing their highs, same as the rest of us.

Politics

I n the preceding chapters, we've mainly used the word "politics" to refer to small-scale "coalition politics," like the kind of maneuvering that takes place in a band of hunter-gatherers or a modern workplace. In such situations, rival coalitions compete for control, and individuals seek to ally themselves with powerful coalitions (or at least avoid visibly opposing them). And since this often involves unsavory tactics like bootlicking, backstabbing, and rumor-mongering, we try hard not to appear as if we're "playing politics"—though we're happy, when we can, to accuse our rivals of such behavior.

However, the word "politics" is often used with an entirely different connotation. In some prestigious walks of life, such as art, literature, and philosophy, many people aren't at all embarrassed to be "political"; in fact, they often talk as if it were their highest aspiration. Far from the grubby, low-stakes game of office politics, this is the politics of *citizenship, activism*, and *statecraft*: helping steer a nation in pursuit of the common good. This noble image of politics has been around since at least the time of the ancient Greeks. Aristotle's book *Politics*, for example, was intended (in the words of one scholar) "to bring to our attention the splendor of politics and of the moral virtue that people show in politics."[1]

But does the grand political arena really bring out our moral virtue? Contrast Aristotle's conception of politics with what we see on the TV show *House of Cards*. No doubt its scenarios are exaggerated to make for gripping entertainment, but we all recognize its portrayal of the dark underbelly of national politics: the back-room dealings, bad-faith promises, and bald-faced lies. "Laws," it's often remarked, "are like sausages: it's better not to see them being made."

Rather than focusing on the behavior and motives of career politicians, however, in this chapter we're going to examine how *ordinary citizens* participate in formal democratic politics. This includes voting and registering with political parties, of course, which are some of the activities for which there's especially good data. But we also, in our role as citizens, follow the news, deliberate the issues, and debate with our friends. We put up lawn signs and fix bumper stickers to our cars. Sometimes we attend political protests or get involved in political campaigns.

The question, as always, is why.

THE POLITICAL DO-RIGHT

To help illuminate our political motives, let's consider an archetype for the ideal politically engaged citizen: the conscientious, civic-minded *Do-Right*.

True to their name, Do-Rights are engaged with politics for all the "right" reasons. They're not after their own selfish ends; they simply want to make a difference for others, to improve society for current and future citizens. They're not starry-eyed idealists, but rather hard-nosed pragmatists who are willing to make hard choices and compromise when necessary to achieve the best outcomes. There's nothing at all performative about their actions in the political sphere; they're not angling for credit or personal glory. Instead, they're earnestly, single-mindedly focused on doing what's best for their country.

Now, given that humans are competitive social animals, it would be surprising if we chose this one arena—national politics—to suddenly live up to our altruistic ideals. Nevertheless, some facets of our behavior appear to support the Do-Right picture of our political motives.

For one thing, the literature on voting makes it clear that people mostly *don't* vote for their material self-interest, that is, for the candidates and policies that would make them personally better off.[2] Jonathan Haidt provides some examples in *The Righteous Mind*:

Parents of children in public school are not more supportive of government aid to schools than other citizens; young men subject to the draft are not more opposed to military escalation than men too old to be drafted; and people who lack health insurance are not more likely to support government-issued health insurance than people covered by insurance.[3]

Even if a person wanted to vote "selfishly," however, the bigger problem is that voting doesn't make sense as an economic activity.[4] Voting costs time and effort—not just a trip to the polls, but also the work required to form an opinion beforehand, like reading news and watching debates. And yet the personal benefits are infinitesimal. It's true that your life might improve if Candidate A is elected instead of Candidate B, but the odds that your single vote will tip the scales is miniscule. In the 2008 U.S. presidential election, for example, this figure was estimated at 1 in 60 million.[5] So even if you stood to gain an enormous $500,000 worth of personal value (including subjective benefits) from Candidate A's election, in *expected value*, your vote would still be worth less than a penny. In terms of outcomes and probabilities, you'd be better off buying a lottery ticket.

Similar cost–benefit calculations apply to other, more involved forms of political participation, like attending rallies, donating to interest groups, and working for political campaigns. Compared to voting, these activities plausibly offer a greater chance of influencing national outcomes, but they also require greater investment. Citizens who simply want better political outcomes *for themselves* would be wasting their energies.

It would seem, then, that only an altruistic Do-Right should be motivated enough to invest in the political process. Not surprisingly, however, there are a number of cracks in this flattering picture. It's easy to *say* we're acting like Do-Rights, but our actions often betray other, less visible motives.

In what follows, we'll present a few puzzles that cast doubt on the Do-Right model of political behavior. But before we tarnish the image of voters, it's important to clarify that this isn't an indictment of democracy. We're questioning the motives of individual citizens, not the efficacy of any particular system (democracy or otherwise). Even if voters turn out not to be ideal Do-Rights, democracy could still be a great form of government—or as Winston Churchill put it, "the worst form of government, except for all those other forms that have been tried."[6] In fact, much of the appeal of democracy is that it *doesn't* require citizens to be saints.

With that in mind, let's start picking apart our political motives, shall we?

PUZZLES

Puzzle 1: Disregard for Vote Decisiveness

The 1-in-60-million figure we saw earlier applies to the *average* U.S. voter. Individual voters, however, aren't necessarily average, and their odds of deciding a presidential election depend on which state they live in.[7] During the 2008 race, for example, voters in "battleground" or "swing" states, like Colorado and New Hampshire, had relatively high odds of deciding the election, at 1 in 10 million. But in states like Oklahoma and New York, where one party is all but guaranteed to win, the odds were closer to 1 in 10 *billion*.[8] That's an astonishing 1,000-fold difference.

Faced with these realities, pragmatic Do-Rights should be considerably more eager to vote when they find themselves in a swing state. After all, the costs of voting are the same in each state, whereas the benefits (i.e., a chance to influence national outcomes) are substantially higher in swing states. Do-Rights in these states won't necessarily be 1,000 times more likely to vote, but the effect should be clear and significant.

Real voters, however, show remarkably little concern for whether their votes are likely to make a difference. Swing states see only a modest uptick in turnout, somewhere between one and four percentage points.[9] In other words, decisiveness seems to matter to less than 4 out of every 100 eligible voters.[10] Equally surprising is the fact that so many people bother to vote in *non*–swing states. If these voters were perfectly altruistic Do-Rights, many would consider doing other, more impactful things in lieu of voting, such as volunteering at an after-school program.

None of this is absolutely damning for the Do-Right model, but it highlights that our voting behavior isn't an act of practical, straightforward altruism.

Puzzle 2: Uninformed Voters

As voters, Do-Rights should care deeply about being *informed*. If they don't understand the issues, they might as well flip a coin or abstain from voting altogether.

Real voters, however, show more interest in the status, personalities, and election drama of politicians than in their track records or policy positions. In fact, people often show great interest in "elections" that have almost no policy consequences, such as for student class president or best singer on *The Voice* TV show. Even in meaningful elections, however, voters act more like sports fans rooting for their favored team than like analysts trying to figure out which team *ought* to win.

When it comes to specific political issues, voters are notoriously ignorant. For example, only 29 percent of American adults can name their congressperson, let alone discuss their congressperson's voting record.[11] When asked, "What percentage of the federal budget goes to foreign aid?" voters typically estimated 25 percent, and said they thought 10 percent was an appropriate level. In fact, American "bilateral foreign aid" clocks in at only 0.6 percent.[12]

These examples of voter ignorance abound, and such ignorance plausibly influences our political positions. Relative to better-informed citizens, less-informed citizens consistently prefer different policies.[13] On economic issues, for example, Bryan Caplan identifies a number of areas in which the average voter deviates from expert consensus: an antiforeign bias, an antimarket bias, a make-work bias, and a pessimistic bias (systematically underestimating the value of economic progress).[14]

Now, while an earnest Do-Right might freely admit ignorance about some political issues, real voters rarely do. When people are asked the same policy question a few months apart, they frequently give different answers—not because they've changed their minds, but because they're making up answers on the spot, without remembering what they said last time.[15] It is even easy to trick voters into explaining why they favor a policy, when in fact they recently said they opposed that policy.[16]

If our goal is better outcomes, we should care not just about the overall intentions and spirit of policy; we should also care about how policies will be implemented, such as how outcomes will be measured, or whether a particular task is assigned to local, state, or federal government. Far more important than mere technicalities, these choices often determine whether a well-intended policy will succeed or fail.[17] The devil, as they say, is in the details.

Real voters, however, seem apathetic about practical details, and prefer instead to focus on values and ideals. We'd rather debate hot-button identity issues, like gay marriage or immigration, than issues that hinge on an understanding of facts, like trade agreements or net neutrality. And we see a similar bias when electing our representatives. As long as our politicians talk a good game, we don't seem to care whether they're skilled at crafting bills and shepherding them through the system.[18] Across the board, we seem to prefer high-minded rhetoric over humble pragmatism.

Note that political Do-Rights don't need to devote their entire lives to politics. They just need to spend their "political time" wisely and calibrate their level of involvement accordingly. By this logic, Do-Rights should happily *abstain* from a vote if they judge themselves significantly less informed than the average voter. On such issues, they might even consider it their patriotic duty to stay out of the country's political business and to encourage other uninformed voters to do likewise.[19] Suffice it to say, however, that this attitude is uncommon among real citizens, many of whom shake their heads in disdain at nonvoters (for reasons we'll explore in a moment).

Puzzle 3: Entrenched Opinions and Strong Emotions

An ideal political Do-Right will be the opposite of an ideologue. Because Do-Rights are concerned only with achieving the best outcomes for society, they won't shy away from contrary arguments and evidence. In fact, they'll welcome fresh perspectives (with an appropriately critical attitude, of course). When a smart person disagrees with them, they'll listen with an open mind. And when, on occasion, they actually change one of their political beliefs, they're apt to be grateful rather than resentful. Their pride might take a small hit, but they'll swallow it for the sake of the greater good. Think of an effective business leader, actively seeking out different perspectives in order to make the best decisions—that's how a Do-Right would consume political information.

But of course, that's not at all how real voters behave. Most of us live quite happily in our political echo chambers, returning again and again to news sources that support what we already believe. When contrary opinions occasionally manage to filter through, we're extremely critical of them, although we're often willing to swallow even the most specious evidence that confirms our views. And we're more likely to engage in political shouting matches, full of self-righteous confidence, than to listen with the humility that we may (gasp!) be wrong.[20]

The fact that we attach strong emotions to our political beliefs is another clue that we're being less than fully honest intellectually. When we take a pragmatic, outcome-oriented stance to a given domain, we tend to react more dispassionately to new information. We do this every day in most areas of our lives, like when we buy groceries, pack for a vacation, or plan a birthday party. In these practical domains, we feel much less pride in what we believe, anger when our beliefs are challenged, or shame in changing our minds in response to new information. However, when our beliefs serve *non-pragmatic* functions, emotions tend to be useful to protect them from criticism.

Yes, the stakes may be high in politics, but even that doesn't excuse our *social* emotions. High-stakes situations might reasonably bring out stress and fear, but not pride, shame, and anger.[21] During a national emergency, for example, we hope that our leaders won't be *embarrassed* to change their minds when new information comes to light. People are similarly cool and dispassionate when discussing existential risks like global pandemics and asteroid impacts—at least insofar as those risks are politically neutral. When talk turns to *politicized* risks like global climate change, however, our passions quickly return.

All of this strongly suggests that we hold political beliefs for reasons other than accurately informing our decisions.

✳ ✳ ✳ ✳ ✳

These are just a few of the inconsistencies between our civic ideals and our actual behavior. To explain these and other puzzles, we'll have to make use of another political archetype—one whose motives are, not surprisingly, less noble than those of the altruistic Do-Right.

THE APPARATCHIK

In the Soviet Union during the 1930s, a single party ran the government, which had unprecedented control over ordinary lives. And Joseph Stalin ran that party with an iron fist. *Apparatchiks* were government or party officials, and political loyalty was so central to their lives that the word has now come to mean "a very loyal member of an organization who always obeys orders."[22]

For a Soviet apparatchik, it wasn't enough simply to show great loyalty to Stalin; those who didn't show *more* loyalty than others were suspected of disloyalty and often imprisoned or killed. In *The Gulag Archipelago*, the Russian novelist and historian Aleksandr Solzhenitsyn gives a dramatic example of these extreme incentives:

> At the conclusion of the conference, a tribute to Comrade Stalin was called for. Of course, everyone stood up, and the small hall echoed with stormy applause. For three minutes, four minutes, five minutes, the applause continued. It was becoming insufferably silly even to those who really adored Stalin. However, who would dare be the *first* to stop? So the applause went on—six, seven, eight minutes! They couldn't stop now till they collapsed with heart attacks! Finally, after eleven minutes, the director of the paper factory assumed a businesslike expression and sat down in his seat. And, oh, a miracle took place! To a man, everyone else stopped dead and sat down. They had been saved!

That, however, was how the [secret police] discovered who the independent people were. And that was how they went about eliminating them. That same night the factory director was arrested. They easily pasted ten years [in a labor camp] on him.[23]

The kicker? Stalin himself wasn't even in the room. His cult of personality was strong enough to sustain 11 minutes of applause even in his absence.

At least 600,000 people were killed in these ways during Stalin's purges.[24] And similar dynamics have played out in China under Mao Zedong and in North Korea under the Kim family regime.[25]

Now, most of us don't live in a totalitarian state. But even in modern, pluralistic democracies, we face the same *kind* of incentives as the apparatchik. (Ours are just much weaker.) We, too, are rewarded for professing the "right" beliefs and punished for professing the "wrong" ones—not by any central authority but by our fellow citizens. And yes, our societies aren't dominated by a single political party, but whenever an issue becomes factionalized, framed as Us against Them, we should expect to find ourselves behaving more like an apparatchik competing to show loyalty to our team.

Note that the coalitions that command our loyalty aren't always the kind we typically consider "political." Each of us is a member of many different groups, which can be nested within each other or else partially overlapping, as in a Venn diagram. We live in neighborhoods, cities, states, and nations; we work on teams within companies; and we worship at churches belonging to denominations of overarching religions. We're also tied to a given race, ethnicity, gender, and sexual orientation. All of these groups compete for our loyalties; note, for example, Madeleine Albright's insistence that "there's a special place in hell for women who don't help each other."[26] And how much loyalty we feel to each group depends on many factors, both personal and cultural. As the political scientist Samuel Huntington points out, Westerners typically have a lot of national loyalty, whereas Arab Muslims are less devoted to their nation than to their extended family and tribe (on the one hand), and to their entire religion

and civilization (on the other).[27] These tensions among our various loyalties are, in part, what makes politics so complex and full of drama.

When we suggest that our political behavior is driven largely by coalition loyalty, then, we're not trying to single out *political parties* (Democrat,
Republican) or *political ideologies* (liberal, conservative) as the fundamental focal points. The left–right split happens to be important in modern
liberal democracies, especially the United States in recent, more-polarized
decades, but changing circumstances can shift the focal points. When a
nation goes to war, for example, intra-national political divisions often
take a back seat to patriotism and national unity.

In other words, context matters—a lot. Nevertheless, our hypothesis is that
the political behavior of ordinary, individual citizens is often better explained
as an attempt to signal loyalty to "our side" (whatever side that happens to
be in a particular situation), rather than as a good-faith attempt to improve
outcomes. In addition to the Do-Right's motives, then, we also harbor the
motives of the apparatchik: wanting to appear loyal to the groups around us.

This is the key to making sense of our political behavior. It's not just an
attempt to influence outcomes; it's also, in many ways, a performance.

POLITICAL INCENTIVES IN DAILY LIFE

Crucial to the argument we're making is the fact that politics isn't an isolated arena confined to the voting booth and a handful of explicitly political activities. Rather, the incentives from "politics" spill out into many
other areas of life, forcing our inner apparatchik to be ever vigilant about
our political posture.

Take dating and marriage, for instance. People tend to date and marry
other members of their political party.[28] And they want the same for their
children: a 2010 survey found that 49 percent of Republicans and 33 percent of Democrats said they would be upset if their child married someone from the opposite party.[29]

In another survey, 80 percent of people chose to award a scholarship
to a member of their favored political party, even when another applicant
had better grades. In fact, this political favoritism was stronger than racial

favoritism.[30] Stanford's Shanto Iyengar, who did the survey on scholarships, put it this way:

> Political identity is fair game for hatred, racial identity is not. . . . You cannot express negative sentiments about social groups in this day and age. But political identities are not protected by these constraints. A Republican is someone who chooses to be Republican, so I can say whatever I want about them.[31]

In some professions, political affiliations matter substantially for success on the job. College professors, for example, skew heavily Democrat—not just by the numbers,[32] but also in their hiring practices. Among sociology professors, a quarter admitted that they would favor a Democrat over a Republican for a job in their department.[33] (Presumably, even more of them harbor an unacknowledged or unconscious bias against Republican applicants.) And such biases are reflected in the actual hiring data. Holding constant the quality of their publications, Republican academics (compared to Democrats) have jobs at significantly lower-tier colleges. This effect is larger than the effect for women, who also seem to face discrimination in academic jobs.[34]

Even in our daily lives, we feel pressure to conform to the political opinions of those around us. Among frequent conversation partners, for example, U.S. citizens talk about politics at least as often as they talk about work, sports, or entertainment. But since disagreement can cause interpersonal strife, having different political beliefs from friends and family can take its toll on relationships.[35] As the economist Russ Roberts points out, expressing unpopular political opinions can put a "frost in the air" or cause friends to "edge away from us on the picnic blanket,"[36] hence the common wisdom not to discuss politics in polite company.

All these incentives—romantic, professional, and social—undoubtedly put pressure on us to adopt the political beliefs of our local communities. But insofar as we cave to these pressures, it certainly doesn't happen overnight. We've all been in situations where we've had to admit to an unpopular political opinion, and we don't suddenly change our minds for fear of a few disapproving scowls.[37] But when the same forces play out slowly, over years or even decades, we shouldn't be surprised to find our beliefs slowly falling into line. And in the extreme case—when we're socialized from birth into a politically homogenous community—we might find it all but impossible to notice these social influences on our beliefs. Our political views will simply seem right, natural, and true.

THE LOGIC OF LOYALTY SIGNALING

Let's now take a closer look at some of the predictions made by the loyalty-signaling (apparatchik) model, to see how they're borne out in our political beliefs and behaviors.

Self-Interest versus Group Interest

First, and perhaps most important, the desire to signal loyalty helps explain why we don't always vote our self-interest (i.e., for the candidates and policies that would bring us, as individuals, the greatest benefit). Rather, we tend to vote for our *groups'* interests.[38] Naturally, on many issues, our group and self-interests align. But when they don't, we often choose to side with our groups. In this way, politics (like religion) is a team sport.

When a particular issue is polarized geographically, for example, people who live in the South will tend to vote for whichever position is (commonly perceived to be) in the South's interest. When an issue is racially polarized, blacks will tend to vote for whatever seems to help blacks overall (even if some individual black voters might be hurt by it). And of course, when an issue is polarized across the major political parties, we tend to vote the party line. It's not that we never break rank and vote against our group interests, but when we do, we risk appearing disloyal to our peers and our communities.

Expressive Voting and the Appeal of Badges

Political scientists often distinguish between "instrumental voting" and "expressive voting." Instrumental voters use their votes in order to influence outcomes. They may be entirely altruistic (like a Do-Right) or entirely selfish, but regardless, they want their votes to make a difference. Expressive voters, however, don't care about outcomes, but instead derive "expressive" value from the act of voting.[39] Even if all of their chosen candidates end up losing in the election, expressive voters will still be happy to have cast their ballots.

An apparatchik, then, is an expressive voter, but not just any expressive voter. While political scientists are mostly agnostic about why people like to express themselves at the voting booth, some treat expressive voting as an act of *consumption*—something we do in order to feel good, without concern for external benefits.[40] In this view, voting is seen as providing a psychological reward, like getting to "affirm one's identity" or "feel a sense of belonging." But as we've seen many times in this book, explanations that are strictly psychological often fall prey to self-deception, and at any rate are often trumped by social explanations. Incentives that begin and end within one's own head ultimately lead nowhere, whereas *external* incentives have real consequences, both material and biological. Thus the apparatchik is an expressive voter who is rewarded *socially* for expressing him- or herself at the polls.

Now, voting is protected by the secret ballot (an important institution that prevents the most egregious forms of voter manipulation). But to get credit for our political beliefs, we need to advertise them; people can't reward us for what they can't see. For an apparatchik, then, the real benefits come not from voting per se, but rather from all the activities surrounding the election, like attending rallies, discussing the issues, posting to social media, and watching election coverage with friends and family.[41] It's during these social activities, and not just at the polls, that it's important for us to express our political opinions. Actually casting the ballot is largely a formality—a little "cherry on top" of the political sundae.

The need to advertise our political beliefs also helps to explain the appeal of political "badges"—conspicuous symbols of group membership like the kind we discussed in Chapter 15.[42] In the physical world, for example, we put up lawn signs and bumper stickers, while on social media, we use politically charged hashtags and change our profile pictures to show support for the cause-du-jour. We also embrace slogans like "Black lives matter" or "Guns don't kill people; people kill people." As arguments, these slogans radically oversimplify the issues—but as badges, they work great.

In part, our use of badges can be interpreted as Do-Right activism, an attempt to change other people's minds. But as we saw in previous chapters, we often use badges to affiliate with nonpolitical groups like sports teams, music subcultures, and religious communities. This suggests there's value in advertising our tribal loyalties, apart from trying to "make a difference" in the political realm.

Loyalty Demands Sacrifice

Anyone can act sensibly in their narrow self-interest. In order to demonstrate loyalty, we have to do things that other, less loyal people *wouldn't* do—like cheering 11 minutes for Comrade Stalin.[43]

This logic helps shed light on our voting behavior. Apparatchiks don't mind that voting is less personally rewarding than buying a lottery ticket. In fact, the sacrifice is, in some ways, what actually motivates them to vote. If voting were a straightforward act of self-interest, it would lose much if not all of its value as a loyalty signal.

Beyond showing loyalty to specific political coalitions (e.g., by voting Republican), voting also functions as a display of loyalty to the nation as a whole. This is the popular belief that voting is a civic duty, something we're just supposed to do, personal costs and benefits be damned. Thus we earn patriotism points by hauling ourselves down to the polls (especially in the middle of a busy day) and kneeling at the altar of democracy—as long as we make sure to advertise our sacrifice to others, of course. This helps explain why many U.S. polling stations hand out stickers that say, "I Voted," replete with an American flag (see Box 16).

Another sacrifice we make in the name of politics is limiting our social, professional, and romantic opportunities. The more ideological alignment we require from coworkers, friends, and spouses, the smaller our pool of available options. In this way, a Democrat who refuses to work at a company with conservative values sends a message to her liberal peers: "I care so much about 'our side' in politics that I'm even willing to forego professional opportunities."[44] Naturally, she may not be conscious of such messages, but the counterfactual embarrassment she might feel if she took the "conservative" job suggests that she has an audience somewhere in mind.

Box 16: Kevin's Misadventures in Do-Right Voting

For the 2000 U.S. presidential election, when I was a fresh-faced college student, I tried my hand at a "rational" voting process. I was committed to voting for whichever candidate best matched my own views, so I quantified my positions on a variety of issues, then asked my better-informed friend to do the same for each of the major candidates. According to the spreadsheet we put together, the best match was Al Gore, the Democratic nominee—so that's who I voted for.

Now, many readers could probably design a better system. But all in all, it was pretty sensible. And yet, instead of refining the process for subsequent elections, I abandoned it after just a single use. Why?

Well, psychologically speaking, the method was distinctly unsatisfying. It produced a result, but there was no joy in arriving at it. Moving past the psychological, however, there were very few *social* rewards to this process. It didn't provide opportunities for me to discuss or debate the issues with my friends, nor to advertise my loyalty to one political team over another. Yes, the Democratic candidate was popular among my left-leaning peers—but I wasn't voting for the Democrats per se. The very fact that I was *open* to voting for Bush betrayed my lack of political loyalty. As if to drive home the point, when Bush eventually won the election, I wasn't particularly disappointed. Sure, my preferred candidate had lost, but without an associated team to root for, it was hard to get too worked up over it. If politics is a team sport, "rational" voting is like playing Tetris alone in the corner.

Loyalty Demands (Strategic) Irrationality

As we saw in Chapter 5, contexts that reward loyalty are a breeding ground for self-deception and strategic irrationality. For our beliefs to function as loyalty signals, we can't simply "follow the facts" and "listen to reason." Instead, we have to believe things that are *beyond* reason, things that other, less-loyal people *wouldn't* believe.[45]

This helps explain why voters feel little pressure to be informed. As long as we adopt the "right" beliefs—those of our main coalitions—we get full credit for loyalty. We don't need to be well informed because the truth isn't particularly relevant to our expressive agendas. The main actions we take based on our political beliefs are preaching and voting, neither of which has practical consequences for our lives (only social consequences). And on the rare occasions when our political beliefs *do* suggest concrete actions, we're happy to ignore their suggestions and act as we would even if we believed the opposite. For example, we might think, "Everyone deserves access to the same opportunities" and yet fiercely compete to get our kids into the best schools. This kind of mild hypocrisy might bother us on occasion, but it probably won't keep us up at night.

We have to strike a balance, though, between critical thinking and mindless obedience. If we adopt beliefs that are too far-fetched, we risk looking foolish, thereby offsetting the benefit we get for showing loyalty. Thus the best apparatchiks are highly intelligent and even skeptical, as long as their skepticism stops short of questioning the sacred tenets of their political groups.

The fact that we use political beliefs to express loyalty, rather than to take action, also explains why we're emotionally attached to our beliefs, and why political discussions often generate more heat than light. When our beliefs are anchored not to reasons and evidence, but to social factors we don't share with our conversation partners (like loyalty to different political groups[46]), disagreement is all but inevitable, and our arguments fall on deaf ears. We may try to point out one another's hypocrisy, but that's not exactly a recipe for winning hearts and minds.

Good arguments and evidence may eventually prevail, of course, but it rarely happens during heated conversations with our political enemies. Reasoning is a social process,[47] and we typically have to convince disinterested third parties before there's any chance our opponents will accept defeat. Thus (and with apologies to Martin Luther King Jr.) the arc of politics may bend toward truth, but it's a long and tortuous arc.

Disdain for Compromise

A common symptom of loyalty signaling is an unwillingness to compromise. Now, if you're a Do-Right pragmatist concerned only with outcomes, compromise can be very attractive, since it's often the best way to make progress. But when you're doing politics as a performance, like an apparatchik, you don't care about outcomes as much as you care about the appearance of loyalty. And what better way to signal your loyalty than to say, "I'm not budging. It's my (group's) way or the highway."

This kind of attitude admits to no middle ground: "You're either with us or against us." In such polarized climates, anyone who advocates for compromise risks being accused of insufficient loyalty. More generally, any attempt to deviate from the preexisting consensus will be considered suspect. We see this kind of attitude during elections: voters typically punish politicians who change their positions to match the changing opinions of their constituents,[48] even though it's in the spirit of democracy for a representative to "reflect the will of the people." Plausibly, this is because some voters feel betrayed, and their anger more than offsets the appeal of the politician's new, more popular opinion.

One-Dimensional Politics

Given the vast range of issues and the positions we can take on those issues, it might seem strange that people who support strong border controls also tend to favor lower taxes, school choice, and traditional marriage—and that people who oppose any of these also tend to oppose the others. We find this clustering of positions not just among citizens, but also in our politicians. For example, 80 percent of the votes of U.S. congressional representatives are explained by a single left–right ideological dimension, and a similar focus is found in other nations.[49] Why do we see such a high degree of correlation among political beliefs?

While intellectuals have at times tried to explain the one key moral dimension that underlies most political disputes, in fact, different societies at different times have had quite different main political dimensions.[50] Instead of being caused by a key moral dispute, this phenomenon of low-dimensional politics seems to be a general feature of competing political coalitions. That is, political groups tend to join alliances until there are only a few major coalitions, after which members show loyalty by focusing on issues that most clearly distinguish them from opposing coalitions. (And with only two main coalitions, only one main dimension separates them.) Voters and politicians who instead focus on other, less-distinguishing issues are penalized, as those issues seem to distract from the main fight.

These largest coalitions can break down and re-form during national political "realignments," exposing some of the underlying tensions.[51] For example, prior to the 1850s, politics in America was driven largely by economic issues like tariffs, the national bank, and public lands. Then, in the 1850s and 1860s, it became polarized instead between pro- and antislavery (leading ultimately to the Civil War).[52] What this and other realignments make clear is that the main political parties have not always stood firm behind fixed principles, but instead are a complex patchwork of (sometimes conflicting) agendas—strange bedfellows brought together by common interests and held together, in part, by the bonds of loyalty.

Extreme Activists

So far we've mostly focused on citizens who devote only a small fraction of their energies to politics. But what about our most politically engaged citizens, those who sacrifice the most for political causes? Are they better modeled as Do-Rights or apparatchiks?

Consider the case of soldiers. In some sense, these are our most extreme activists, in that they risk their lives to favor our nation over other nations. And yes, they're motivated by patriotism, but at the same time, it's well known that soldiers fight more out of loyalty to their immediate comrades than to distant organizations or nations.[53]

Likewise, terrorists—including the most extreme version, suicide terrorists—seem more motivated by the desire to bond with and impress their compatriots. Terrorist groups frequently reject compromise, for example, even when it could help their overall cause, and they don't disband when they achieve their stated goals.[54]

Within nations, our most devoted activists are plausibly those who see themselves as political "soldiers" fighting for a cause, but whom opponents see as political "terrorists," since their actions risk hurting both themselves and others. Either way, we should be skeptical that their activism ultimately counts as self-sacrifice, since they stand to gain a lot of credit from their immediate peers. To give just one example, those who devote themselves to a politician's campaign often expect to be given a role in the new administration, if their candidate wins the election.

CONCLUSION

Why should humble citizens (read: selfish primates) care what happens in distant halls of power—especially regarding actions in the political arena, like voting, which are mostly futile? Aren't we better off minding our own business and tending to local issues, like those at home and in the workplace?

The answer we've given in this chapter is that we use far-off national politics as a medium in which to jockey for local advantages. As apparatchiks, we're motivated less by civic virtue than by the desire to appear loyal to our political coalitions. And if politics is a performance, then our audience is mostly our peers—friends and family, coworkers and bosses, churchmates and potential romantic partners, and anyone who might follow us on social media.

Understandably, this picture is incomplete. We certainly have other political motives, both psychological and social. Some of us have strong inner Do-Rights who do, occasionally, take the helm, even if it means losing friends. Others among us may be more interested in appearing smart than loyal. In some rare cases, we may even be rewarded for political *nonconformity*.[55] But by and large, when we stand up and cheer for our political beliefs, we're acting like Soviet apparatchiks.

Conclusion

"Our virtues are most frequently but vices in disguise."

"We cannot look squarely at either death or the sun."

—FRANÇOIS DE LA ROCHEFOUCAULD, 1678

Intelligent observers have long noted that while we profess many noble reasons for our behavior, other less-noble motives usually lurk in the background—and we find it hard to look squarely at them. In this book, we have steeled ourselves to confront some of these hidden motives that drive our behavior, both in our personal lives and some of our largest social institutions. Even so, we have only scratched the surface. Some of our explanations will surely be wrong, not to mention incomplete. (It's hard to look directly at the elephant!) And of course there remain plenty of other behaviors and institutions in need of similar treatment.

What's more important in the space we have left, however, is thinking about what to *do* with all these explanations. How can we use an awareness of the elephant to live better lives, both as individuals and as a society?

Your two coauthors have spent a lot of time thinking about this question, but we certainly don't have all the answers. In fact, we struggle—both personally and intellectually—with many of the issues raised in this book. The facets of human nature we've tried to illuminate here are complex, full of moral gray areas, and open to many interpretations. In what follows, we'll attempt to sketch out some of the implications of our thesis, but we do so with considerable humility. As we've mentioned, we're hardly the first thinkers to grapple with these questions, and if the answers were clear and easy, our species would have already put them into practice.

The biggest lesson from Part I is that we ignore the elephant because doing so is strategic. Self-deception allows us to act selfishly without having to appear quite so selfish in front of others. If we admit to harboring hidden motives, then, we risk looking bad, thereby losing trust in the eyes of others. And even when we simply acknowledge the elephant to ourselves, in private, we burden our brains with self-consciousness and the knowledge of our own hypocrisy. These are real downsides, not to be shrugged off.

That said, there *are* benefits to cultivating an awareness of our species' darker motives. Let's look at some of them now.

PUTTING THE ELEPHANT TO USE

Better Situational Awareness

The first benefit is situational awareness—a better, deeper understanding of the human social world. It's easy to buy into the stories other people would sell us about their motives, but like the patter of a magician, these stories are often misleading. "I'm doing this for your benefit," says every teacher, preacher, politician, boss, and parent. Even friends do it, for example, when they give smug "helpful" advice. The prosocial explanations offered for these behaviors may contain partial truths, but what's left unstated is often just as important (if not more so), and it helps to know what to look for.

When other people's body language makes us uneasy, in some sense, it may be intended to do so, even if they don't realize or acknowledge it.[1] When meetings at work seem like an unnecessary waste of time, such waste may in fact be the point; costly rituals can serve to keep a team cohesive or help anxious leaders cement control over their subordinates. And if we want to waste less time on such activities, we'll need to address the root of the problem, or else find other ways to fulfill the same functions.

The next time we're worried that we can't afford the best medicine, we may find comfort in the idea that it's not necessarily our health that's at stake, but maybe just our self- and social images. The next time we feel manipulated by an advertisement, sermon, or political campaign, we should remember the third-person effect: messages are often targeted at us by way of our peers. We may still choose to go along with the message, but at least we'll know why. The next time someone at a party exhorts us to visit some great museum or exotic travel destination, it helps to consider that such advice may not actually be for our benefit, even if it's presented that way. We shouldn't let other people make us feel inferior—at least, not without our consent.

Physician, Heal Thyself

Yes, it's useful to understand the motives of others. But if that's all readers take away from this book, they're missing the much larger and more important point: we often misunderstand our *own* motives. We have a gaping blind spot at the very center of our introspective vision. If we're going to second-guess our coworkers and friends, we shouldn't give ourselves an easy pass. In fact, knowing about our own blind spots should make us even more careful when pointing fingers at others. After all, many of our perceptions are colored by self-interest, including our perceptions of what other people are up to. So let's set aside the speck in their eyes, and attend to the log in our own.

If you felt any pangs of indignation or self-righteousness while reading about other people's behavior in this book, try hard to un-feel them. That boss who calls "unnecessary" meetings might well be you (though of course you won't see them as unnecessary). That friend offering smug advice? That's you too. This kind of self-knowledge is the small gift that Robert Burns pined for in his poem "To a Louse": to see ourselves as others see us.

The next time you butt heads with a coworker or fight with your spouse, keep in mind that both sides are self-deceived, at least a little bit. What feels, to each of you, overwhelmingly "right" and undeniably "true" is often suspiciously self-serving, and if nothing else, it can be useful to take a step back and reflect on your brain's willingness to distort things for your benefit. There's common ground in almost every conflict, though it may take a little digging to unearth it beneath all the bullshit.

Above all, what the elephant teaches us is humility. It's a call for more thoughtful interactions with our fellow self-deceivers, a spur to step outside our own conniving minds. There's a second side to every story, if only we can quiet our egos enough to hear it (see Box 17).

Box 17: No Direct Accusations

A good rule of thumb for applying "hidden motive" explanations is not to use them in the second person, but only in first and third (and ideally in the plural).[2] In other words, we should avoid accusing the specific person or people across from us of harboring selfish motives. Such an accusation would not only be rude, it would also be tenuous. People are complex, and we can never know all that's going on in another's mind or life. To admit the ubiquity of selfish motives is not to deny the existence of lofty motives; both can (and do) coexist within the same person.

In general, the kind of explanations we've advanced in this book are more compelling at the species level, as distal explanations for overall patterns of human behavior. When applied to individuals, as proximal psychological causes of specific behaviors, the same explanations are often hollow and unpersuasive.

Showing Off

While it may not suit everyone, an ability to talk candidly about common human motives can signal some attractive qualities. People who are able to acknowledge uncomfortable truths and discuss them dispassionately can show a combination of honesty, intellectual ability, and perhaps even courage (or at least a thick skin). And those who can do so tactfully, without seeming to brag, accuse, or complain, may seem especially impressive.

Not every community values these qualities to the same degree; in particular, many communities prioritize a commitment to orthodox views over impartial truth-seeking. Nevertheless, some readers may find themselves rewarded for acknowledging hidden human motives.

Choosing to Behave Better

Another benefit to confronting our hidden motives is that, if we choose, we can take steps to mitigate or counteract them. For example, if we notice that our charitable giving is motivated by the desire to look good and that this leads us to donate to less-helpful (but more-visible) causes, we can deliberately decide to subvert our now-not-so-hidden agenda.

Of course, we should realize that, at any one time, we have a limited budget for self-improvement. Some of us might be tempted to swear off hypocrisy all at once, and vow always to act on the ideals we most admire. But this would usually go badly. In all likelihood, our mind's Press Secretary issued this "zero hypocrisy" edict without sufficient buy-in and support from the rest of our mental organization. Better to start with just one area, like charity, and try to adjust our mixture of motives there in ways that we can sustain. Once that first area is stable, then we can lather, rinse, and repeat for other areas.

Another promising strategy is to put ourselves in situations where our hidden motives better align with our ideal motives. For example, if we want to express sincere yet accurate beliefs, we might get into the habit of betting on our beliefs. Or, for charity, we might join the effective altruism movement, in order to surround ourselves with people who will judge our charitable giving more by its effects than by superficial appearances. Incentives are like the wind: we can choose to row or tack against it, but it's better if we can arrange to have the wind at our backs (see Box 18.).

Please note, however, that other people may care much less about our motives and more about the consequences of our actions. Yes, we might really work hard to become a great scientist or surgeon for personal glory (rather than for the greater good), but if a selfish motive is what it takes to create a great scientist or surgeon, the rest of the world may be OK with that.

Box 18: Kevin's Alignment of Motives

I've been lucky enough in my professional life to experience both circumstances: having the wind at my back and struggling to tack against it.

In my previous role as an engineering manager, I felt remarkably little tension between my selfish and prosocial motives. I can count on one hand the number of times I felt tempted to prioritize personal gain over doing what was best for the team—not because I'm a saint, but because the corporate culture was healthy enough to reward me for doing the right thing. I acknowledge I'm probably a bit self-deceived here and fail to remember many situations where my motives were divergent. But on the whole, the wind was at my back, and I felt highly motivated and fulfilled.

While writing this book, however, I had the opposite experience. As mentioned in Chapter 9, this book is more of a "vanity project" than something I'm doing because I expect it will be useful to others. Certainly some readers will find value in it, but it's unlikely to be valuable enough to justify the opportunity cost of taking on other projects. Partly as a result, I often found myself reluctant to talk about the book, even among friends and family. The tension between my selfish and prosocial motives was acutely painful.

Enlightened Self-Interest

While some readers will take the elephant as a challenge to behave better, others may be tempted to throw up their hands. If it's in our nature to be selfish, why beat ourselves up over it? Why bother striving for higher ideals?

There's some evidence to suggest that our standards and our behavior can indeed degrade in this way, as the economist Robert Frank has argued. In one study, undergrads reported a greater willingness to act dishonestly after taking an economics course that emphasized self-interest as a model for human behavior. (This effect was stronger than for students who took other courses, such as an astronomy course, or even the same economics course when taught by a professor who didn't emphasize self-interest.[3]) More generally, people who are "cynical," that is, who attribute lower motives to others, tend to cooperate less.[4] Are we doing the world a disservice, then, by calling attention to the elephant and by describing it as "normal" and "natural"?

Perhaps. Certainly we admit that teaching students about the elephant may have the direct effect of inducing selfishness. But this won't necessarily be the only effect in a community that takes the ideas in this book seriously. Such a community may learn to enforce better norms against selfishness, for example, by being less willing to accept the shallow appearances of prosocial motives. There's a whole complex game to be worked out here, well beyond the scope of this final chapter.

In any case, we need to be careful to avoid the naturalistic fallacy—the mistaken idea that what's natural (like some amount of human selfishness) is therefore good. So let us be clear: this book is *not* an excuse to behave badly. We can acknowledge our selfish motives without endorsing or glorifying them; we need not make virtues of our vices.

At the same time, however, it would be a mistake to conclude that virtue requires us to somehow "rise above" our biological impulses. Humans are living creatures through and through; we can't transcend our biology any more than we can transcend the laws of physics. So if we define virtue as something that arises from nonbiological causes, we set a literally impossible standard. If we want to improve ourselves, it must somehow be *through* our biological heritage.

By the same token, we can't ignore incentives—for example, by telling people that "good behavior" requires them to abandon their self-interest. The more sacrifice and suffering we demand in the name of virtue, the less rewarding it will be—and taken to an extreme, it means that "bad" people will fare better than "good" ones in our society.

Where does this leave us, then? By what path can we hope to improve our collective welfare?

Enter here the philosophy of "enlightened self-interest." This is the notion that we can do well for ourselves by doing good for others. It's the philosophy described by Alexis de Tocqueville, preached by Adam Smith, and practiced by Benjamin Franklin.[5] In the biological literature, it's known as "indirect reciprocity" or "competitive altruism."[6] Remember the Arabian babblers we met in Chapter 1? Each bird works its tail feathers off to provide food and protection for the group, not from the goodness of its heart but largely out of self-interest. And so too in our species.

In light of this, we absolutely need ideals—not just as personal goals to strive for, but also as yardsticks by which to judge others and to let ourselves be judged in return. There's real value to be had in promising to behave well (and in staking our reputation on that promise), in large part because it makes us more attractive as an ally. Such a pledge can't *guarantee* our good behavior, of course. We may still cut corners here and there, or cheat when no one's looking. But it nevertheless incentivizes us to behave better than if we refused to be held to any standard.

And yes, if we profess high ideals but then fail to live up to them, that may make us hypocrites. But the alternative—having no ideals—seems worse. "Hypocrisy," writes La Rochefoucauld, "is the tribute that vice pays to virtue." In other words, it's *taxing* to be a hypocrite, but that very tax is a key disincentive to bad behavior.[7]

Designing Institutions

Beyond what we can do in our personal lives, however, is what we can do when we're in positions to influence policy or help reform institutions. This is where an understanding of the elephant really starts to pay off. Maybe most laypeople don't need to understand their hidden motives, but those who make policy probably should.

A common problem plagues people who try to design institutions without accounting for hidden motives. First they identify the key goals that the institution "should" achieve. Then they search for a design that best achieves these goals, given all the constraints that the institution must deal with. This task can be challenging enough, but even when the designers apparently succeed, they're frequently puzzled and frustrated when others show little interest in adopting their solution. Often this is because they mistook professed motives for real motives, and thus solved the wrong problems.

Savvy institution designers must therefore identify *both* the surface goals to which people give lip service *and* the hidden goals that people are also trying to achieve. Designers can then search for arrangements that actually achieve the deeper goals while also serving the surface goals—or at least giving the appearance of doing so. Unsurprisingly, this is a much harder design problem. But if we can learn to do it well, our solutions will less often meet the fate of puzzling disinterest.

We should take a similar approach when reforming a preexisting institution by first asking ourselves, "What are this institution's hidden functions, and how important are they?" Take education, for example. We may wish for schools that focus more on teaching than on testing. And yet, some amount of testing is vital to the economy, since employers need to know which workers to hire. So if we tried to cut too much from school's testing function, we could be blindsided by resistance we don't understand—because those who resist may not tell us the real reasons for their opposition. It's only by understanding where the resistance is coming from that we have any hope of overcoming it.

Not all hidden institutional functions are worth facilitating, however. Some involve quite wasteful signaling expenditures, and we might be better off if these institutions performed only their official, stated functions. Take medicine, for example. To the extent that we use medical spending to show how much we care (and are cared for), there are very few positive externalities. The caring function is mostly competitive and zero-sum, and—perhaps surprisingly—we could therefore improve collective welfare by *taxing* extraneous medical spending, or at least refusing to subsidize it. Don't expect any politician to start pushing for healthcare taxes or cutbacks, of course, because for lawmakers, as for laypeople, the caring signals are what makes medicine so attractive. These kinds of hidden incentives, alongside traditional vested interests, are what often make large institutions so hard to reform.

Thus there's an element of hubris in any reform effort, but at least by taking accurate stock of an institution's purposes, both overt and covert, we can hope to avoid common mistakes. "The curious task of economics," wrote Friedrich Hayek, "is to demonstrate to men how little they really know about what they imagine they can design."[8] In this regard, our approach falls squarely in an economic tradition.

One promising approach to institutional reform is to try to acknowledge people's need to show off, but to divert their efforts away from wasteful activities and toward those with bigger benefits and positive externalities. For example, as long as students must show off by learning something at school, we'd rather they learned something useful (like how to handle personal finances) instead of something less useful (like Latin). As long as scholars have a need to impress people with their expertise on some topic, engineering is a more practical domain than the history of poetry. And scholars who show off via intellectual innovation seem more useful than scholars who show off via their command of some static intellectual tradition.

PERSPECTIVE

Moving beyond the pragmatic to the aesthetic, many readers may wonder how to make peace with such a seemingly cynical portrait of our species. The answer, in a word, is perspective. So let's step back for a moment and put all these ideas in context.

First and foremost, humans are who we are, and we'll probably remain this way for a good while, so we might as well take accurate stock of ourselves. If many of our motives are selfish, it doesn't mean we're unlovable; in fact, to many sensibilities, a creature's foibles make it even more endearing. The fact that we're self-deceived—and that we've built elaborate institutional structures to accommodate our hidden motives—makes us far more interesting than textbook *Homo economicus*. This portrait of human nature hints at some of the depth found in the characters of the world's great novels: Moriarty, Caulfield, Ahab, Bovary, Raskolnikov. Straightforward characters aren't nearly as compelling, perhaps because they strike us as less than fully human.

And even when our motives are fundamentally selfish, there's still a huge and meaningful difference between violent criminals and people whose "selfishness" causes them to provide (too much) medical care or donate to (inefficient) charities. Even if a philanthropist's *motives* are selfish, her *behaviors* need not be—and we would be fools to conflate these two ways of measuring virtue.

Whatever we may have said about evolution's tendency to produce selfish creatures, the fact remains that humans get along with each other spectacularly well, and nothing we've seen in this book can take that away from us. It is a wonderful quirk of our species that the incentives of social life don't reward strictly ruthless behavior. Leaders who are too domineering are often penalized. Rampant lying and cheating are often caught and punished. Freeloaders frequently get the boot. At the same time, people are often positively rewarded—with friendship, social status, a better reputation—for their service to others. As if our oversized brains and hairless skin didn't make us an uncanny enough species, our genes long ago decided that, in the relentless competition to survive and reproduce, their best strategy was to *build ethical brains.*

Of course we aren't perfect cooperators—did anyone expect us to be?—but for evolved creatures, we're remarkably good at it. Our charities, schools, and hospitals may never be perfect, but we don't see chimps or dolphins (or flesh-and-blood elephants) giving us a run for our money.

When John F. Kennedy described the space race with his famous speech in 1962, he dressed up the nation's ambition in a suitably prosocial motive. "We set sail on this new sea," he told the crowd, "because there is new knowledge to be gained, and new rights to be won, and they must be won and used for the progress of all people." Everyone, of course, knew the subtext: "We need to beat the Russians!"

In the end, our motives were less important than what we managed to achieve by them. We may be competitive social animals, self-interested and self-deceived, but we cooperated our way to the god-damned moon.

INTRODUCTION

1. Wikiquote, "Karl Popper," last modified March 15, 2017, https://en.wikiquote. org/wiki/Karl_Popper.
2. Emerson 2012.
3. La Rochefoucauld 1982, 89.
4. Cf. Robert Wright's remark that "All told, the Darwinian notion of the unconscious is more radical than the Freudian one. The sources of self-deception are more numerous, diverse, and deeply rooted, and the line between conscious and unconscious is less clear" (2010, 324).
5. Trivers 2011.
6. For a related point, see Heaney and Rojas 2015, 8.
7. Here's another example: When a police chief vehemently denies that race plays any role in street-level police work, in contradiction to the statistics gathered by his or her department (Glass 2015), those of us who understand the psychology of bias roll our eyes. It's not only *possible* for police to harbor unconscious racial biases, but it's been shown that the vast majority of us (both police and civilians) *do*, in fact, harbor such biases (Greenwald, McGhee, and Schwartz 1998). Calling people out on racial, gender, or class biases, however, is relatively easy, because there are political points to be scored by doing so.
8. Trivers 2011.
9. The Wachowskis 1999.

CHAPTER 1

1. Dunbar 2010.
2. Social grooming isn't confined to primates. It's a fixture of social life for many species, including cats, dogs, lions, horses, bats, and macaws.
3. Dunbar and Sharman 1984; Dunbar 1991, 2010.

4. Lehmann, Korstjens, and Dunbar 2007.

5. Dunbar 2010.

6. Ibid.

7. Dunbar 1991.

8. Ibid.; Goosen 1981.

9. Dunbar 2010.

10. Seyfarth 1977.

11. De Waal 1997.

12. Ventura et al. 2006.

13. Schino 2007; Dunbar 1980; Seyfarth and Cheney 1984.

14. Dunbar 1991.

15. This is similar to how animals are programmed to engage in sex, but aren't necessarily programmed to understand how it leads to conception and childbirth.

16. This and subsequent information about the Arabian babbler is taken from Zahavi and Zahavi (1999).

17. Notably, mating, unlike feeding, is *not* an activity that the males compete to give lower-ranked others more opportunities to do. Here the logic of evolution is laid bare.

18. Krebs and Dawkins 1984.

19. This kind of appeal was made perhaps most famously by Konrad Lorenz (2002). It was mostly put to rest by the gene-centered theory of evolution, pioneered by Ronald Fisher in the 1930s and popularized by Richard Dawkins in his 1976 book *The Selfish Gene*.

CHAPTER 2

1. *Wikipedia*, s.v. "*Sequoia sempervirens*," last modified February 18, 2017, https://en.wikipedia.org/wiki/Sequoia_sempervirens. Actually, redwoods have adaptations that allow them to absorb moisture directly from fog, through their needles, so they don't have to transport all of it from the ground. But still, they get most of their water from their roots.

2. Angier 2008.

3. Dunbar 2002, 2003.

4. Ridley 1993.

5. Pinker and Bloom 1990.

6. Trivers 2011.

7. Social competition may be a necessary factor, but it's far from sufficient, especially given that other species exhibit plenty of social competition and yet haven't evolved the same intelligence we have. For more on some of the unique conditions our ancestors faced, see Box 3 in Chapter 3.

8. For good popular overviews, see Geoffrey Miller's *The Mating Mind* (2000) or Matt Ridley's *The Red Queen* (1993).

9. There may still be differences, however, like a male preference for female youth. See Ridley 1993, 272–95.

10. Ibid., 341.

11. Technically, a peacock's tail is called a "train."

12. Henrich and Gil-White 2001.

13. Cheng et al. 2013.

14. *Wikipedia*, s.v. "Great Purge," last modified February 22, 2017, https://en.wikipedia.org/wiki/Great_Purge.

15. Truth be told, what we call "prestige" is often dominance in disguise. We like to *appear* to have and associate with prestige, but to actually have and associate with dominance.

16. Economists call these side effects "externalities."

17. Actually, in ancient Greek, "political" refers to the *polis* or city. Thus humans, for Aristotle, were more precisely "animals of the city." Nevertheless, the word "political" has evolved over the years, such that we now use it to describe behavioral patterns that don't necessarily take place in the *polis*.

18. De Waal 1982. Fun fact—in 1994, the (human) politician Newt Gingrich, then the U.S. Speaker of the House, made *Chimpanzee Politics* required reading for first-year members of Congress.

19. De Waal 2005, 45.

20. Connor, Heithaus, and Barre (1999) on dolphins; Wittemyer, Douglas-Hamilton, and Getz (2005) on elephants.

21. Dessalles 2007, 356.

22. Bucholz 2006.

23. For readers more familiar with modern guides to getting ahead, a similar contrast exists between Robert Greene's *48 Laws of Power* (1998) and Dale Carnegie's *How to Win Friends and Influence People* (1936).

24. Cf. Ayn Rand's statement, "Judge, and be prepared to be judged" (Rand and Branden 1964, 71).

25. Some biologists use a more precise definition of a signal, namely, any trait or behavior that evolved in order to modify the behavior of the receiver in ways that benefit the sender. For more on this, see Box 8 in Chapter 7.

26. "Expense," here, is a broad notion, which may include material resources, energy, time, attention, physical risk, or social risk—or anything else correlated to an organism's reproductive success. See Miller 2009, 115.

27. Számadó 1999; Lachmann, Szamado, and Bergstrom 2001; Pentland and Heibeck 2010, 17.

28. Zahavi 1975.

29. Or as the 18th-century American preacher Jonathan Edwards put it: "Godliness is more easily feigned in words than in actions" (1821, 374).

30. As the philosopher Arthur Schopenhauer wrote about sexual love: "It is the ultimate goal of almost all human effort. . . . It knows how to slip its love-notes and ringlets even into ministerial portfolios and philosophical manuscripts" (1966, 533).

CHAPTER 3

1. Thanks to Mills Baker for this example.

2. Hobbes 2013, ch. 17.

3. Mostly drawn from Youngberg and Hanson 2010, as well as Boehm 1999, and Brown 1991.

4. Trivers 1971.

5. According to Flack, Jeannotte, and de Waal (2004), chimps are capable of a very limited form of proto-norm enforcement, which they use primarily to curtail violence. When two chimps are fighting or fixing to fight, it's not uncommon for a third chimp to intervene to try to make peace. This behavior has been found in other primate species as well.

6. Bingham 2000.

7. Boehm 1999.

8. Ibid.

9. Bingham 2000.

10. Brown 1991.

11. Ibid.

12. Axelrod 1986.

CHAPTER 4

1. ☺

2. Geehr 2012.

3. Actually these adaptations aren't necessarily evolved, i.e., innate. They might be *learned* by individual brains as they navigate the world and interact with other humans. But there's evidence that at least some of them are innate (or the result of innate predispositions).

4. Cosmides and Tooby 1992.

5. von Grünau and Anston 1995.

6. See studies referenced in Bateson et al. (2013). For cartoon eyes experiments, see Haley and Fessler (2005). Some studies have shown that fake eye cues promote generosity, but two recent meta-analyses (Northover et al. 2017) suggest otherwise, casting some doubt on all eye-cue effects.

7. Zhong, Bohns, and Gino 2010.

8. Shariff and Norenzayan 2007.

9. Elias 2000.

10. The word "knowledge" carries a lot of philosophical baggage, e.g., the issue of how to distinguish (true) knowledge from (mere) belief. But none of that baggage need carry over to the phrase "common knowledge." Here, when we use the word "knowledge," we mean belief or awareness, where the degree of certainty is left ambiguous.

11. Chwe 2001.

12. One way to measure the openness of a secret is by the size of the largest group in which it's common knowledge.

13. Kaufman 2014.

14. Lin and Brannigan 2006; see also Zader 2016.

15. This is a slightly simplified story. Pollard (2007), for example, argues that England had other incentives to break from Rome.

16. *Wikipedia*, s.v. "Greenwashing," last modified February 22, 2017, https://en.wikipedia.org/wiki/Greenwashing.

17. Chwe 2001.

18. Mattiello 2005.

19. This may or may not be a norm violation in a given society, but it typically requires at least a modicum of discretion. At the very least, for example, it's considered rude to kiss and tell.

20. Flanagan 2012.

CHAPTER 5

1. Wickler 2007.

2. Goodenough 1991.

3. Trivers 2011.

4. As we'll see, words like "really" and "actually" are problematic when trying to describe our mental states, but we'll let it slide for now.

5. Starek and Keating 1991.

6. You might think we'd be biased in the conservative direction—imagining we're less healthy, in order to take extra precautions. Certainly some people are (e.g., hypochondriacs), but the majority of us are biased in the risky direction. We overestimate how healthy we are.

7. Croyle et al. 2006.

8. Brock and Balloun 1967.

9. Van der Velde, van der Pligt, and Hooykaas 1994.

10. Dawson, Savitsky, and Dunning 2006.

11. Alicke and Govorun 2005.

12. Freud 1992; Baumeister, Dale, and Sommer 1998.
13. Fenichel 1995; Baumeister et al. 1998.
14. Sackeim 2008.
15. Or reinforcement learning.
16. Judith Rich Harris (2006) describes self-esteem as a "sociometer," a kind of thermostat for our social worth. As such, we want to enhance our self-esteem, but only if it correlates with actual social value (as perceived by others). Kurzban (2012) makes a similar point: "Self-esteem just isn't the sort of thing the mind should be designed to bring about (i.e., 'be motivated' to do). The mind's systems might evolve to bring about fitness-relevant states of affairs, such as satiety, popularity, and sex, but not 'self-esteem.'"
17. To be pedantic, it's called the "Nobel Memorial Prize in Economic Sciences," and Schelling shared it with Robert Aumann in 2005.
18. Chicken is a mixed-motive game because even though only one player can win the game, both players have a shared interest in staying alive.
19. Schelling 1980, 43.
20. Kurzban 2012.
21. Trivers 2011.
22. Often attributed to Twain, but probably apocryphal. See O'Conner and Kellerman 2013.
23. Tibbetts and Dale 2004.
24. Kuran 1995, 38.
25. Trivers 2011.
26. Cf. George Orwell: "He wears a mask, and his face grows to fit it" (Orwell 1950, 6).
27. Kuran 1995, 7.
28. Of course, they lie a fair amount, too—but don't we all?
29. Lahaye 2014.
30. Haldeman and DiMona 1978.
31. Adapted from *Wikibooks*, s.v. "Chinese Stories/Calling a Deer a Horse," last modified February 28, 2015, https://en.wikibooks.org/wiki/Chinese_Stories/Calling_a_deer_a_horse.
32. Kurzban 2012, 98.
33. Isaacson 2011, 118.
34. Kurzban 2012.
35. Haidt 2006.
36. McGilchrist 2012.
37. Kenrick and Griskevicius 2013, ch. 2. See also Kenrick 2011.
38. Cosmides and Tooby 1992.
39. Minsky 1988.

40. Weiskrantz 1986: blindsight. See also Dehaene et al. (2006) for a discussion of how different parts of the brain can be aware of information without it becoming fully conscious.

41. Perry 2014.

42. Kenrick and Griskevicius 2013, 144.

43. Closely related to modularity is the notion of *context-dependence*. Information can be readily available to our brains in one context, but almost impossible to retrieve in another. We've all had the experience of leaving a stressful situation only to discover that we're ravenously hungry. It's not that our bodies and brains were perfectly satiated beforehand. They "knew" about the hunger, but it simply wasn't enough of a priority to promote to our full conscious attention, which was too busy focusing on more urgent matters.

44. Cf. George Orwell's memorable description of "crimestop" in *1984*: "CRIMESTOP means the faculty of stopping short, as though by instinct, at the threshold of any dangerous thought. It includes the power of not grasping analogies, of failing to perceive logical errors, of misunderstanding the simplest arguments . . . , and of being bored or repelled by any train of thought which is capable of leading in a heretical direction. CRIMESTOP, in short, means protective stupidity" (Orwell 1983, ch. 9).

CHAPTER 6

1. Hume 1739/1978.

2. Attributed to J. P. Morgan, but probably not original to him. See O'Toole 2014.

3. Gazzaniga and Reuter-Lorenz 2010.

4. Gazzaniga 1998.

5. McGilchrist 2009, 98–99

6. Gazzaniga and LeDoux 2013, 149.

7. Also known as "anosognosia."

8. Ramachandran, Blakeslee, and Sacks 1998, 110.

9. Gazzaniga and Reuter-Lorenz 2010, 34–35; Gazzaniga 1989. "I have called this area of the left hemisphere the interpreter because it seeks explanations for internal and external events and expands on the actual facts we experience to make sense of, or *interpret*, the events of our life" (italics in the original; Gazzaniga 2000).

10. Haidt 2012, 91–92.

11. Blakeslee 2004, 37.

12. Dennett 1991, 227–29.

13. Nisbett and Wilson 1977.

14. T. D. Wilson 2002.

15. This analogy is courtesy of Darcey Riley.
16. Packard 1957, 39–40.
17. Plassmann et al. 2008: wine. Nisbett and Wilson 1977: pantyhose.
18. In some cases it may actually be our *perceptions*, rather than our verbal judgments, that are affected by the experimental subterfuge. In other words, the strategic information distortion happens earlier, and the Press Secretary doesn't have to rationalize anything. See Plassmann et al. 2008; and cf. Trivers's remark that self-deception takes place at "every single stage" of information processing.
19. Johansson et al. 2005; see also Hall et al. (2010) for choice blindness when tasting jam and smelling tea.
20. Nisbett and Wilson 1977.
21. One might see our human capacity to give counterfeit reasons in order to deceive others as a perversion of our basically solid ability to reason privately, i.e., to decide what to believe by collecting reasons for and against such beliefs. But in fact, it has been plausibly argued that our uniquely human tendency to collect reasons is primarily designed for social effect. That is, humans developed an ability to collect reasons mainly for the purpose of persuading others to support predetermined conclusions. This can help explain common human tendencies toward overconfidence, confirmation bias, relying more on reasons for public (vs. private) decisions, and occasionally preferring worse outcomes when it's easier to find supporting reasons (e.g., the sunk cost fallacy). See Mercier and Sperber 2011.

CHAPTER 7

1. See, e.g., Borg: "93 percent of our message is conveyed by the language of the body (including voice)" (2009, 18). The "over 90 percent" myth comes from two papers by Albert Mehrabian (Mehrabian and Wiener 1967; Mehrabian and Ferris 1967), which are perfectly reasonable experiments whose conclusions were stretched (by others) far beyond their proper context.
2. Navarro 2008, 2–4.
3. Spence 1987; see also Mlodinow: "One of the major factors in social success, even at an early age, is a child's sense of nonverbal cues" (2013, 124).
4. Pentland and Heibeck 2010, ch. 1; Mlodinow 2013, 109–10.
5. Mlodinow 2013, 109–10.
6. Darwin 2012, ch. 14.
7. Trivers 2011, 55–56; see also Kahneman 2011, ch. 1.
8. Pentland and Heibeck 2010, 30.
9. Bradbury and Vehrencamp 1998.
10. Dall et al. 2005.

11. Bradbury and Vehrencamp 1998.

12. For more on pacifying behaviors, see Navarro 2008, 35–50.

13. As quoted in Wallace, Carey. "How to Talk to Kids about Art." Time, March 11, 2015. http://time.com/3740746/how-to-talk-to-kids-about-art/.

14. With the exception of deliberate gestures, which *are* often arbitrary and culturally specific. The thumbs-up gesture, for example, signifies approval in most English-speaking countries, but is a profound insult in other countries like Iran, West Africa, and Sardinia—more like our middle-finger gesture (Axtell 1997, 108). Other gestures include winking, nodding, pointing, and saying *shhh* with a finger to the lips.

15. Navarro 2008, 63–65.

16. Ekman and Friesen 1971.

17. No doubt there are minor exceptions to these examples of body language, as when we close our eyes to pay better attention to music or speech. But the general principles should be clear enough.

18. Zahavi 1975.

19. Számadó 1999; Lachmann, Szamado, and Bergstrom 2001; Pentland and Heibeck 2010, 17.

20. Eibl-Eibesfeldt 2009, 246; Brown 1991.

21. On the covert nature of flirting, see Gersick and Kurzban 2014.

22. Eibl-Eibesfeldt 2009, 239–43.

23. Ibid., 240–41.

24. Hall 1966, 113–29. Hall distinguishes four distances: public distance, social distance, personal distance, and intimate distance. The exact distances depend on both culture and context, of course. But whatever the rules for what's appropriate between strangers, soon-to-be-lovers must somehow violate them.

25. Eibl-Eibesfeldt 2009, 243. Rhythmic dancing is also used as a fitness display for mate choice; see, e.g., Hugill, Fink, and Neave 2010.

26. Eibl-Eibesfeldt 2009, 239.

27. Brown 1991.

28. Buss 2002.

29. Fine, Stitt, and Finch 1984.

30. Humans may also use pheromones for non-sexual purposes, e.g., after shaking hands (Frumin et al. 2015).

31. Wedekind et al. 1995.

32. Savic, Berglund, and Lindström 2005.

33. Zhou et al. 2014.

34. For a discussion of literal grooming behavior in humans, see Nelson and Geher 2007.

35. Dunbar 2010.

36. Ibid., citing Sugawara 1984.

37. Navarro 2008, 93.

38. Eibl-Eibesfeldt 2009, 452–55.

39. Lakoff and Johnson 1980.

40. *Online Etymology Dictionary*, s.v. "confrontation," www.etymonline.com/.

41. Johnstone, Keith. 2015. Impro: Improvisation and the Theater. New York: Routledge.

42. *Wikipedia*, s.v. "Hand-kissing," last modified, February 10, 2017, https://en.wikipedia.org/wiki/Hand-kissing.

43. Sometimes we say that a person "has" high status or "is" high in status, as though status were an objective attribute or quantity. But a better approach is to treat status as contextual. You can be the high-status person in one room, but walk down the hall find yourself the low person on the totem pole. This is just something to keep in mind as we talk about "high-status individuals" or "low-status individuals." It's all relative.

44. Jordania 2014.

45. Giles, Coupland, and Coupland 1991, 33.

46. Johnstone 1985, 59; Ardrey 1966, 48; Pentland and Heibeck 2010, 6–7.

47. Gregory and Webster 1996; see also Pentland and Heibeck (2010) for a similar result in the context of salary negotiations.

48. Gregory and Gallagher 2002.

49. Henrich and Gil-White 2001.

50. Ibid.

51. Ibid.; Mazur et al. 1980; Harris 2006, 178.

52. Henrich and Gil-White 2001.

53. Dovidio and Ellyson 1982; Exline, Ellyson, and Long 1975; Ellyson et al. 1980.

54. Mlodinow 2013, 122.

55. Exline et al. 1975.

56. Exline et al. 1980.

57. Dovidio et al. 1988.

58. Sexual jealousy, coalition politics, and status competition are potentially very destructive to groups who don't attempt to regulate them.

59. Knapp 1972, 91–92.

60. No doubt there are other reasons as well. We tend to neglect social skills in formal curricula, even apart from body language. Moreover, teaching nonverbal communication to our children also opens the door to deception. Once you understand the basic principles, you can use body language to

mislead others about your intentions, e.g., by maintaining an open posture even around your bitter enemies.

CHAPTER 8

1. The word "laugh" actually derives from Old English *hliehhan*, which (like "ha ha ha") is an onomatopoeic rendering of the sound of laughter.
2. From Kozintsev: "While it has been traditionally believed that laughter normally appears at the age of one to four months (about a month later than smiling), recent observations demonstrate that certain infants laugh already at the age of seventeen to twenty-six days (Kawakami et al., 2006)" (2011, 98).
3. Black 1984; Provine 2000, 64.
4. Two other involuntary social behaviors are *blushing*, which Darwin called "the most peculiar . . . of all expressions" (2012, ch. 13), and *weeping*. For a great overview of weeping and tears, see Vingerhoets (2013).
5. Of course, we can exert *some* deliberate, conscious influence over our laughter, e.g., when we try to force or stifle a laugh. But the results are often unnatural. Forced and stifled laughter are the exceptions that prove the more general rule, which is that we typically aren't in control of when we laugh.
6. Morreall 1987; although, see Sully (1902) for the first articulation of laughter as a play signal.
7. Even as recently as 1989, Irenäus Eibl-Eibesfeldt, one of the leading scholars of animal behavior, suggested that laughter may be an ancient form of aggression. "The rhythmic sounds," he writes, "are reminiscent of threat and mobbing sounds made by lower primates, and the baring of teeth may be derived from an intention to bite" (Eibl-Eibesfeldt 2009).
8. Kant tried to explain laughter by appealing to the principle—questionable even for its time—that movements in our thoughts are mirrored "harmonically" by movements in our bodily organs. Presumably, then, a joke which jostles our thoughts must simultaneously jostle our diaphragm? But of course this is nonsense. From *The Critique of Judgment*:

    > The jest must have something in it capable of momentarily deceiving us.
    > Hence, when the semblance vanishes into nothing, the mind looks back
    > in order to try it over again, and thus by a rapidly succeeding tension and
    > relaxation it is thrown to and fro and put in oscillation. . . . It is readily
    > intelligible how the sudden act above referred to, of shifting the mind
    > now to one standpoint and now to the other, to enable it to contemplate
    > its object, may involve a corresponding and reciprocal straining and
    > slackening of the elastic parts of our viscera, which communicates itself

to the diaphragm (and resembles that felt by ticklish people). (Kant 2007, 162)

9. Provine 2000, 24.

10. Ibid., 45.

11. Ibid., 137–42. Laugh tracks may not be as popular now, but even during their heyday in the 1960s, they were used primarily in radio and on television, rather than in feature films. This is because a movie is designed to be watched in the theater, among a large audience, so no fake laughter is necessary.

12. Provine 2000, 93; Plooij 1979. We find a similar regulatory function of laughter when a father throws his three-year-old daughter into the air and catches her. If the toddler laughs, dad knows she's enjoying the game and wants it to continue. If instead she gives a yelp or an alarmed cry, dad knows to stop at once.

13. Eastman 1936.

14. Ross, Owren, and Zimmermann 2010.

15. Provine 2000, 76, 92.

16. Ibid., 96.

17. Ibid., 92.

18. Kozintsev 2010, 109.

19. Eastman 1936, 9.

20. Ibid.

21. Ibid., 15.

22. Of course, play is *functional* in the sense that it helps an animal learn about itself and its environment. But play is *nonfunctional* in the sense that it serves no practical purpose in the immediate context in which it's performed.

23. Akst 2010.

24. Bateson 1955.

25. Pellis and Pellis (1996) also highlight the importance of contextual cues.

26. Bekoff 1995.

27. Provine 2000, 77.

28. Flack, Jeannotte, and de Waal 2004.

29. Eibl-Eibesfeldt 2009.

30. Occasionally we laugh in response neither to our own actions nor to those of our playmates, but simply to an impartial event. If we're talking to a friend on an airplane, for example, and the plane takes a momentary dip, we might let out a little chuckle—to let our friend know that, in spite of the small scare, we're still feeling safe and happy.

31. Grice 1975; Dessalles 2007.

32. Children might have evolved to laugh a bit more often than strictly necessary—perhaps to let their parents know that they're OK, even when they're out of

sight. But as we get older, we learn to economize on our communication, announcing the play signal only when it's directly relevant, i.e., only when we're provoked.

33. Some thinkers have argued that we laugh at puns because they violate the linguistic norm that words and sentences should have one clear meaning. This seems plausible, but we might also laugh in order to show the punster that we get the joke: "I see what you did there," our laughter announces.

34. Kozintsev 2010, 92–9. Another analogy is that the relationship between humor and laughter is like the relationship between candy and our taste for sweets. The moment we lick a lollipop, it's the candy that causes our sensation of sweetness. But at the same time, our preference for sweet things evolved long before lollipops (or even the discovery of sugar cane), and lollipops were invented specifically in order to tickle our taste buds in an enjoyable way. Similarly, humor (like candy) is a cultural artifact specifically designed to tickle our minds in a pleasing way.

35. Even if one of the participants is only imagined, i.e., the author of a comic strip.

36. The "safe" metaphor works for orgasms too, but of course they require a different combination to unlock.

37. Eastman 1936 (emphasis removed).

38. And a store of value, and a unit of account. Together, these three properties qualify something as "money."

39. Duhigg 2012.

40. Provine 2000, 3. The full quote is "Because laughter is largely unplanned and uncensored, it is a powerful probe into social relationships."

41. McGraw and Warren (2010): "The benign-violation hypothesis suggests that three conditions are jointly necessary and sufficient for eliciting humor: A situation must be appraised as a violation, a situation must be appraised as benign, and these two appraisals must occur simultaneously."

42. The coda of the joke ("you racist!") provides an additional little tickle. Mary is calling John a racist, but of course they're friends and she's just playing. So John laughs even harder.

43. Branigan 2014.

44. Trope and Liberman 2010.

45. Wikiquote, "Mel Brooks," last modified April 18, 2016, https://en.wikiquote.org/wiki/Mel_Brooks.

46. *South Park*, season 6 episode 1, "Jared Has Aides."

47. Wikiquote, "Comedy," last modified January 7, 2017, https://en.wikiquote.org/wiki/Comedy.

48. Note that the popular girls haven't defined Maggie completely outside their circle of concern; it just takes a more serious episode to jostle them out of a playful mood. If Maggie fell, broke her neck, and was screaming for help, you can be pretty sure those girls wouldn't be laughing or even stifling a laugh. Their mood would turn deadly serious in an instant.
49. Kozintsev 2010, 108.
50. Chwe 2001.
51. Brown 2011, 61.
52. Burr 2014 (edited lightly for clarity).
53. Sullivan 2014.
54. Attribution to Oscar Wilde is disputed; see O'Toole 2016.

CHAPTER 9
1. Corballis 2008; Stam 1976, 255.
2. Dunbar 2004.
3. Miller 2000, ch. 10: courtship; Locke 2011; Dunbar 2004: gossip; Flesch 2007: storytelling.
4. Dunbar: "Language in freely forming natural conversations is principally used for the exchange of social information" (2004).
5. Carpenter, Nagell, and Tomasello 1998.
6. Miller: "When healthy respect for an adaptation tips over into awe, it becomes impossible to make any progress in understanding the selection pressures that shaped the adaptation" (2000, 345).
7. Uomini and Meyer (2013) suggest as early as 1.75 million years ago.
8. Miller: "Very few 'theories of language evolution' identify particular selection pressures that could favor the gradual accumulation of genetic mutations necessary to evolve a complex new mental capacity that has costs as well as benefits" (2000, 345).
9. Costs include time, calories expended as a listener, and the potential distraction (i.e., the fact that it's harder to monitor the environment for threats and opportunities while absorbed as a listener).
10. Eyes, in contrast, have evolved independently in more than 50 animal lineages. See Land and Nilsson 2002.
11. Dessalles 2007, 320; "The human obsession with divulging anything of interest, instead of jealously keeping the information to themselves, requires an explanation" (ibid., 321).
12. Ibid., 320, 325.
13. Kin selection offers another possible benefit, but a minor one in most human talk.
14. Dessalles 2007; listeners (not speakers) detect against cheating.

15. Ibid., 339.
16. Miller 2000, 350.
17. Dessalles 2007, 338.
18. Miller 2000, 350–51.
19. Grice 1975; Dessalles: "As a parameter of conversation, relevance is an omnipresent and necessary condition. If we take an extreme case, anyone whose utterances are consistently non-relevant is soon dismissed as mentally ill" (2007, 282).
20. Dessalles 2007, 337.
21. The main divergence between these theories is that Miller's allows speakers to show off the quality of their *genes*, not just their value as an ally in future interactions.
22. In which case, you're liable to be grateful and consider it a favor that needs to be returned.
23. This is similar to what we'll see in Chapter 11, where there's value in the artifacts themselves, but where there's often more value in what the art (and the ability to produce it) says about the artist.
24. Miller 2000, 351.
25. Ibid., 355–6.
26. Dessalles (2007, 349–55) argues that conversation skill—in particular, the consistent ability to know things first—is an especially useful criterion for choosing leaders of a coalition, since they will be making decisions that affect the whole coalition.
27. Burling 1986.
28. Locke 1999, 2011.
29. Note that, like a listener evaluating a speaker, you don't really care *how* he managed to produce relevant, useful, new tools from his backpack. Maybe, while he was rummaging around in there, he actually assembled the bird feeder from scratch (rather than pulling out a pre-assembled feeder that he had collected sometime in the past). As long as he can do this kind of thing consistently, you'll be very happy to have him around.
30. This random approach, marrying breadth and depth, is similar to the strategy used by the Israeli airport security to sniff out terrorists. If they simply asked visitors a predetermined set of basic questions—like "What's the purpose of your visit?" or "Where are you staying?"—liars could easily prepare canned answers. Instead, security staff members are trained to interrogate their subjects randomly and deeply. "What did you do on Tuesday?" "How long was the line at the museum?" "Did the line snake back and forth, or was it straight?" By probing subjects in this way, it's easier to tell who's lying and who's giving a real story.

31. Dessalles 2007, 348, 352.
32. BrainyQuote, s.v. "Thomas Jefferson," BrainyQuote.com, Xplore Inc, 2017. https://www.brainyquote.com/quotes/quotes/t/thomasjeff106229.html, accessed March 3, 2017.
33. Stephens 2007, 7, 8.
34. Ibid., 10.
35. Ibid.
36. Arrow et al. 2008.
37. Trivers 2002.
38. Macilwain 2010.
39. See Dessalles 2007, 337–8. The main difference between academia and news is that academic prestige is gained largely by earning the respect of the prestigious elites, while news prestige is gained by earning wide respect among large audiences.
40. Miller 2000, 350.
41. Pfeiffer and Hoffmann 2009.
42. Alston et al. 2011. Like most things, research seems to suffer from diminishing returns to effort.
43. The Defense Advanced Research Projects Agency (DARPA) is a U.S. Department of Defense agency at the forefront of tech research that intersects with military use.
44. Hanson 1995, 1998.
45. Bornmann, Mutz, and Daniel 2010. Less than 20 percent of the variation in their evaluations is explained by a tendency to agree.
46. Peters and Ceci 1982.
47. Nyhan 2014.
48. And in case you're wondering, no, it's not about the money; book royalties are unlikely to justify the time and effort we've put into this project.

CHAPTER 10

1. Keynes 1931, 358–73.
2. Of note,

   A Harvard Business School survey of 1,000 professionals found that 94% worked at least 50 hours a week, and almost half worked more than 65 hours. Other research shows that the share of college-educated American men regularly working more than 50 hours a week rose from 24% in 1979 to 28% in 2006. According to a recent survey, 60% of those who use smartphones are connected to work for 13.5 hours or more a day. European labour laws rein in overwork, but in

> Britain four in ten managers, victims of what was once known as 'the American disease,' say they put in more than 60 hours a week. (*The Economist* 2014)

3. Another important way we compete for status is by doing prestigious work—conspicuous *production* alongside conspicuous consumption. See, e.g., Avent 2016. Or as Venkatesh Rao says, "We 'shop around' for careers. We look for prestigious brands to work for. We look for 'fulfillment' at work. Sometimes we even accept pay cuts to be associated with famous names. This is work as fashion accessory and conversation fodder" (Rao 2013). In this chapter, however, we focus only on the consumption side of the equation.

4. In fact, Veblen foresaw exactly this "rebuttal" to Keynes. He writes, "As increased industrial efficiency makes it possible to procure the means of livelihood with less labor, the energies of the industrious members of the community are bent to the compassing of a higher result in conspicuous expenditure, rather than slackened to a more comfortable pace" (Veblen 2013, ch. 5).

5. Our emotions and thinking habits are so well trained, and so finely calibrated to our wealth and social setting, that we're able to make purchasing decisions more or less on autopilot. It's only by getting outside ourselves, then—by taking other perspectives or imagining choices we *wouldn't* make—that we're able to glimpse the big-picture logic behind our decisions.

6. Griskevicius, Tybur, and Van den Bergh 2010; see also Kenrick and Griskevicius 2013, 147–50.

7. To prime with a status-seeking motive, subjects were asked to read a short imaginative scenario about their first day at a new job in which they were eager to impress their boss and move up the corporate ladder.

8. Griskevicius et al. 2010.

9. DeMuro 2013.

10. Sexton and Sexton 2014.

11. Per Miller:

> [T]he key traits that we strive to display are the stable traits that differ most between individuals and that most strongly predict our social abilities and preferences. These include physical traits, such as health, fertility, and beauty; personality traits, such as conscientiousness, agreeableness, and openness to novelty; and cognitive traits, such as general intelligence. These are the biological virtues that people try to broadcast, with the unconscious function of attracting respect, love, and support from friends, mates, and allies. Displaying such traits is the key 'latent motive' that marketers strive to comprehend. (2009, 15)

12. Of course, it's not nearly so simple, and many historical contingencies (like denim's use in the American Wild West) help account for the symbolic value of blue jeans. For more, see Davis 1994, 69–77.

13. Schor 1998, 48, 54.

14. Teenagers are acutely aware of these cultural associations, largely because they're in the process of constructing their lifestyle identities and finding friends who respond positively to them. But established adults are often nestled too snugly in their cultural niches to notice just how carefully they've been chosen.

15. Obviously this thought experiment doesn't cover shared experiences like dining out, going to concerts with friends, travel experiences, etc.

16. Miller 2009, 20; Schor 1998, 45–7; see also, Chwe 2001, 47, 49, for a distinction between "social" and "non-social" goods. Chwe lumps network-effect goods like Xboxes and credit cards in the "social" category.

17. You might argue that we appreciate our own jewelry, but such enjoyment is, in part, the joy of imagining how others will react to it.

18. Cf. Veblen: "The domestic life of most classes is relatively shabby, as compared with the éclat of that overt portion of their life that is carried on before the eyes of observers" (2013, ch. 5).

19. "The infrequency with which people repeat wardrobe choices is another class marker—at a special occasion, to have one's dress remarked on as a repeat is an embarrassment among the better-heeled (note the term, by the way). To wear the same clothes to the office too often is a taboo" (Schor 1998, 37).

20. Schor 1998, 56–60.

21. As of January 1, 2017, a four-pack of black Hanes Men's ComfortSoft T-Shirts was priced at $15.42.

22. "Although these signaling links must be commonly understood by the consumer's socially relevant peer group, they need not involve the actual product at all" (Miller 2009, 97–98).

23. Hollis 2011.

24. Davison 1983.

25. Miller 2009, 98; Chwe 2001, 38.

26. Chan 2009.

27. Marketed as Lynx in the United Kingdom.

28. Schor 1998, 45–48.

29. Nielsen (2016) gives 54.3 million homes for Superbowl 50 on February 7, 2016.

30. There are other differences too, of course.

31. Chwe 2001, 37–60. It's not nearly so simple, of course, as there are confounding factors like the prestige of highly popular TV programs. But Chwe argues convincingly that advertisers pay more-than-linearly based on audience size

(see Chwe 2001, 49–60). Some of this, certainly, is due to network effects other than social signaling. Xbox, for example, needs to create a lot of buy-in from gamers in order to also convince video game studios to make games for their platform. Per Chwe: "Fisher, McGowan, and Evans (1980) find that local television station revenue increases not only in the total number of households viewing but also in the square of the total number of households viewing. Similarly, Ottina (1995, p. 7) finds that the larger the local television market, the more advertising revenue is generated per household. Wirth and Bloch (1985, p. 136) find that the rates charged by local stations for a spot on the program MASH increase more than linearly in the number of viewing households" (2001, 60).

32. "All ads effectively have two audiences: potential product buyers, and potential product viewers who will credit the product owners with various desirable traits" (Miller 2009, 99).

33. Miller 2009, 99.

CHAPTER 11

1. E. O. Wilson 2012, 279; Miller 2000, 260.
2. Aubert et al. 2014.
3. Balter 2009: engravings; Power 1999, 92–12: red ocher body art.
4. Brown 1991, 140.
5. Dissanayake 1980.
6. Ibid.
7. Gallie 1955.
8. Dissanayake 1980; Eibl-Eibesfeldt 2009, 677.
9. Changizi 2010.
10. "We use *function* here in its biological sense. Put simply, a function of a trait is an effect of that trait that causally explains its having evolved and persisted in a population: Thanks to this effect, the trait has been contributing to the fitness of organisms endowed with it" (Mercier and Sperber 2011).
11. Pinker 1997, 534.
12. Brown 1991, 140; Dissanayake 1988; Dissanayake 1992, by way of Miller 2000, 259.
13. From Miller: "In his 1897 book *The Beginnings of Art*, Ernst Grosse commented on art's wastefulness, claiming that natural selection would 'long ago have rejected the peoples which wasted their force in so purposeless a way, in favor of other peoples of practical talents; and art could not possibly have been developed so highly and richly as it has been'" (2000, 260).
14. Dissanayake 1988, 1992.

15. Cochran and Harpending 2009.
16. Rowland 2008, 1. All but three species are polygamous and bower-building. Miller 2000, 268.
17. Miller 2000, 268.
18. Rowland 2008, 1.
19. Miller 2000, 269.
20. Borgia 1985.
21. Zahavi 2003.
22. Male bowerbirds also need to develop their taste for a good-looking bower, both in order to construct one themselves and to know which of their rivals' bowers to bother sabotaging. And like the females, they do this by visiting the bowers of other males. In fact, before they mature, male bowerbirds are almost indistinguishable from the females, and often pose as suitors to inspect the bowers of their future rivals.
23. Uy, Patricelli, and Borgia 2000.
24. Although cf. Miller's observation that "sexually mature males have produced almost all of the publicly displayed art throughout human history" (2000, 275).
25. Sometimes called "fitness indicators." See, e.g., Miller 2009, 12–13, 90–92.
26. Miller 2009, 100–104. Other fitness-display functions include soliciting support from family members, deterring predators and parasites, and intimidating rival groups.
27. Miller: "A burning sensation does not carry an intellectual message saying 'By the way, this spinal reaction evolved to maximize the speed of withdrawing your extremities from local heat sources likely to cause permanent tissue damage injurious to your survival prospects.' It just hurts, and the hand withdraws from the flame" (2000, 275–76).
28. We might even include the painting's frame, the lighting used to illuminate it, and the wall it's displayed on, since they're also part of the overall perceptual experience of a painting.
29. Smith and Newman 2014.
30. Newman and Bloom 2012 provide experimental data showing that laypeople place significantly less value on replicas compared to originals.
31. Prinz 2013.
32. Miller 2000, 281.
33. Ibid., 282.
34. Wallace 2004.
35. Lewis 2002, 317.
36. Miller 2000, 286.
37. Ibid., 286–87; Benjamin 1936.

38. Veblen 2013, ch. 6.
39. Miller 2000, 287.
40. For more on synthetic gemstones, see Miller 2009, 95.
41. Trufelman 2015.
42. Lurie 1981, 138–39.
43. Ibid., 115–53.

CHAPTER 12

1. Singer 1999.
2. Singer 1972.
3. Using the estimated cost of $200,000 for four years' worth of college, divided by GiveWell's estimate that you can save a child's life in Malawi or the Democratic Republic of Congo for around $3,500 per child (GiveWell 2016).
4. Singer 2009, 81–4.
5. Ibid.
6. Ibid.
7. "We estimate the cost per child life saved . . . at about $3,500" (GiveWell 2016). Note that these estimates from GiveWell fluctuate periodically as they update their models.
8. Singer 2015.
9. White 1989, 65–71; see also Sullivan 2002 (as cited in Peloza and Steel 2005).
10. Giving USA 2015.
11. Americans donated $358 billion to charity in 2014 (Giving USA 2015). In 2013, $39 billion of that went to help developing countries. These figures are for *private* donations. In 2011, the federal government provided an additional $31 billion in foreign aid (not all of which is directed toward humanitarian causes; Center for Global Prosperity 2013).
12. Hope Consulting 2010.
13. Desvousges et al. 1992.
14. Kahneman and Frederick 2002.
15. Baron and Szymanska 2011; Fox, Ratner, and Lieb 2005.
16. Miller 2000, 323.
17. Ibid.
18. Or in the economic parlance, "to provision public goods."
19. Andreoni 1989, 1990.
20. From Baron and Szymanska (2011): "The magnitude of the glow may be roughly constant for each act of contributing (Margolis, 1982)."
21. Technically, Andreoni's model is agnostic about the "why" behind the warm glow. This isn't a criticism of Andreoni's model per se, but an attempt to spur us to ask the questions that the warm glow theory ignores. See Niehaus

2013 for another example of a "warm glow"–type shallow psychological explanation.

22. Jackson and Latané 1981.
23. Bull and Gibson-Robinson 1981.
24. Hoffman, McCabe, and Smith 1996.
25. Haley and Fessler 2005; Rigdon et al. 2009. Note that Nettle et al. (2013) found that eyespots increased the probability that someone will donate, but not the average amount that people donate.
26. Grace and Griffin 2006; Miller 2000, 323.
27. Glazer and Konrad 1996.
28. Andreoni and Petrie 2004.
29. Miller 2000, 323.
30. Glazer and Konrad 1996; Harbaugh 1998.
31. Polonsky, Shelley, and Voola 2002.
32. Bekkers 2005; see also Bryant et al. 2003.
33. Bekkers 2005.
34. Carman 2003.
35. Ibid.
36. Meer 2011.
37. Baron and Szymanska 2011 (emphasis in the original was rendered in capital letters rather than italics).
38. Giving USA 2015.
39. Charness and Gneezy 2008. Giving names makes people more generous in the Dictator Game, but not the Ultimatum Game.
40. Schelling, Bailey, and Fromm 1968. Even without identifying information, people are more generous when the recipients of their generosity are already determined, versus when the recipients will be determined in the future. See Small and Loewenstein 2003.
41. O'Toole 2010b.
42. United Way 2016.
43. Barrett 2015.
44. Kiva 2017.
45. "Using $5.31 as the average cost per net in the countries that AMF is considering future distributions in, we estimate the cost per child life saved through an AMF-funded LLIN [long-lasting insecticide-treated net] distribution at about $2,838" (Givewell 2016).
46. West and Brown 1975; Landry et al. 2005.
47. Iredale, Van Vugt, and Dunbar 2008.
48. Griskevicius, Tybur, and Sundie 2007.

49. A recent meta-analysis (Shanks et al. 2015) has cast doubt on experiments that find behavioral effects from "romantic priming." So we should take Griskevicius's experiment with a grain of salt. Nevertheless, the finding is consistent with other results, such as the fact that men donate more to attractive female solicitors.

50. Subjects weren't asked about donating money, but rather about volunteer work (like helping at a homeless shelter) and acts of heroism (like saving someone from drowning). Men and women showed different patterns in the kinds of altruism they displayed: Men were more likely to act heroically, while women were more likely to be generous with their time. Subjects were also asked about show-offy purchases, and men's attitudes toward these purchases (relative to women's attitudes) were more affected by the mating motive.

51. West 2004.

52. "[W]hen a millionaire does not really care whether his money does good or not, provided he finds his conscience eased and his social status improved by giving it away, it is useless for me to argue with him. I mention him only as a warning to the better sort of donors that the mere disbursement of large sums of money must be counted as a distinctly suspicious circumstance in estimating personal character. Money is worth nothing to the man who has more than enough, and the wisdom with which it is spent is the sole social justification for leaving him in possession of it" (Shaw, quoted in Finch 2010, 298).

53. Emerson 1995, 298.

54. As early as the 12th century, the Jewish philosopher Maimonides distinguished various "levels of charity" in part based on how anonymous the donor was. Acts of charity in which the donor is known to the recipient were considered less noble than anonymous acts.

55. You'll have to forgive evolutionary psychology for being heteronormative. The field doesn't really understand homosexuality (yet).

56. This view finds additional support from surveys and lab studies. See Bekkers and Wiepking 2011, sec. 5.

57. However questionable Mother Teresa's actual track record may be.

58. Boehm 1999, 70–2.

59. Glazer and Konrad 1996.

60. IGN is the Iodine Global Network, which, as it happens, is one of GiveWell's most recommended charities. Iodine deficiency can lead to cognitive impairment, especially in children, and it's one of the most easily preventable health problems. IGN adds iodine to salt for something like a dime per person per year.

61. Of course, this doesn't imply that people who donate strategically lack compassion—not by a long shot. It's simply that planned donations don't allow

us to demonstrate *involuntary* compassion, so to the extent that we do plan our donations, we don't earn as many social rewards for it.

62. Kornhaber 2015.

63. The quote can be reasonably attributed to him, but not the exact phrasing. See O'Toole 2013.

64. Collins 2011. After the first 100 years, some of the funds were to be left compounding for another 100 years.

65. Hanson 2012.

CHAPTER 13

1. In the literature, this is call the "human capital model." In other words, school is a place where students go to develop their human capital, i.e., skills, knowledge, habits, etc.

2. Gioia 2016: admission statistics; Belkin and Korn 2015: tuition facts.

3. We take these values from Caplan 2017, who in turn drew them from supplementary data for Carnevale, Rose, and Cheah 2011 (supplied by Stephen Rose).

4. The raw data comes from Snyder and Dillow 2011, 228–30, 642. Caplan 2017 (preprint): judgment of (non)utility. Of course, some of these subjects may be personally rewarding to students, but they're of very little use in explaining why employers value a high school education.

5. Snyder and Dillow 2011, 412: raw data; Caplan 2017 (preprint): judgment of (non)utility.

6. Caplan 2017 (preprint) (quote is elided between "psychologists" and "have measured"). "For overviews, see Detterman and Sternberg 1993 and Haskell 2000. Barnett and Ceci 2002 is an excellent critical review of this massive literature" (ibid.).

7. Pfeffer and Sutton 2006, 38; Hayek et al. 2015.

8. Eren and Henderson 2011.

9. Brown, Roediger, and McDaniel 2014.

10. See Gwern 2016.

11. Edwards 2012; see also Carrell, Maghakian, and West 2011, which found that a 50-minute delay in start times was as effective (in improving student performance) as a one standard deviation increase in teacher quality.

12. Clearly there are many factors at play here (busing schedules, after-school programs, etc.), but there's rarely any acknowledgment that trade-offs *against* learning are being made.

13. These figures on the marginal returns to education (both personal and national) are estimated in Caplan (2017, preprint), drawn from a range of

estimates in Pritchett (2001); Islam (1995); Benhabib and Spiegel (1994); Krueger and Lindahl (2001, 1125); Lange and Topel (2006, 462–70); de la Fuente and Doménech (2006). Further complicating the matter is the prospect that there may be some "reverse causation," where increases in national income trigger more schooling rather than the other way around. See, e.g., Bils and Klenow (2000).

14. Spence 1973. Once again, it's not technically a "Nobel Prize," but the "Nobel Memorial Prize in Economic Sciences."

15. Actually it's not just that employers want to directly evaluate each worker's productivity for themselves. Employers also want show off their employees to outsiders such as customers, suppliers, and investors. When we, Robin and Kevin, visit firms, we often hear them brag (discreetly) about the prestigious degrees of their employees.

16. Also note that you'll probably be agnostic about *how*, exactly, she managed to get these good grades. She might not be particularly intelligent, for example, but if she's able to compensate by staying organized and working extra hard, she's going to bring those same qualities to the job. Or maybe she's lazy, but brilliant enough that it doesn't matter. Either way, her grades have proven that she can get things done.

17. Or perhaps it was said by Grant Allen. See O'Toole 2010a.

18. Thiel 2014.

19. On the psychic costs, consider:

    Carolyn Walworth, a junior at [high-achieving] Palo Alto High School, recently wrote: "As I sit in my room staring at the list of colleges I've resolved to try to get into, trying to determine my odds of getting into each, I can't help but feel desolate."

    She confessed to panic attacks in class, to menstrual periods missed as a result of exhaustion. "We are not teenagers," she added. "We are lifeless bodies in a system that breeds competition, hatred, and discourages teamwork and genuine learning." (Bruni 2015)

20. See Carey 2015 for more on online courses; The Thiel Fellowship, "About," http://thielfellowship.org/about/.

21. Macskássy 2013. The analogous figure was 15 percent for high school graduates.

22. One recent study (Bruze 2015) suggests that, in Denmark, people are earning "on the order of half of their returns to schooling through improved marital outcomes."

23. *Online Etymology Dictionary*, s.v. "academy," http://www.etymonline.com/index.php?allowed_in_frame=0&search=academy.

24. *Wikipedia*, s.v. "Prussian education system," last modified February 16, 2017, https://en.wikipedia.org/wiki/Prussian_education_system.

25. Kirkpatrick 2010; *Wikipedia*, s.v. "Pledge of Allegiance," last modified March 3, 2017, https://en.wikipedia.org/wiki/Pledge_of_Allegiance.

26. Aghion, Persson, and Rouzet 2012.

27. Lott 1999.

28. Diamond 1997.

29. Bowles and Gintis 1976, 40–1.

30. Spring 1973; Braverman 1974; Weber 1976; Brint 2011.

31. The effect of school on culture might be just as important as its effect on individual students. It may be, for example, that the high prestige of schools from ancient times helped us all (students, parents, broader society) come to tolerate, and even celebrate, its domesticating influence. That is, if it had been easy to get parents to accept sending their kids off for domestication training, it would have been cheaper and more effective just to send them off to do child labor. But if that was a hard sell, the cover story of "learning from prestigious teachers" might have made school an easier sell. For more on the link between learning and prestige, see Henrich and Gil-White (2001) and Henrich (2015).

32. Clark 1987.

33. Ibid.

34. Almås et al. 2010.

35. Weber 1976, 330.

36. Ibid., 329.

37. In his acceptance speech for New York City's Teacher of the Year award in 1989, John Gatto said what many teachers surely recognize, but few are willing to state so baldly. "Schools and schooling," he said, "are increasingly irrelevant to the great enterprises of the planet. No one believes anymore that scientists are trained in science classes or politicians in civics classes or poets in English classes. The truth is that schools don't really teach anything except how to obey orders" (1990).

38. Gaither and Cavazos-Gaither 2008, 313.

CHAPTER 14

1. World Bank Open Data, http://data.worldbank.org/.

2. The quotation has been edited for clarity. This is the full quote:

    In our area of the country, when somebody gets sick that we know or has passed, we take over food. Have you noticed it? We take over food. You can *buy* that food, you can go to the deli and the grocery store, get something great, hire somebody to bake it. But put it down in the big list of important things for life: *you get a lot more credit if you make it yourself.* You can put it on your grandmother's platter, but the women in the kitchen will say, "*I know where she got that chicken.*" I'm telling you, it works out that way. (Robertson 2017)

3. According to de Waal (1996), these helping behaviors extend deep into the prehistoric and even prehuman past. Neanderthals, for example, cared for their injured group members in this way. We know this because adult skeletons have been found with leg bones that were broken during childhood. Even non-primate species have been observed caring for sick and injured group members. These include dolphins, whales, and elephants.

4. From Hanson 2008: "Shamans and doctors have long been in demand, even though the common wisdom among medical historians today is that such doctors did very little useful on average until this century (Fuchs 1998)."

5. Belofsky 2013, (trepanation) 8, (toothworms) 74–75, (lead shields) 60.

6. Ibid., 101–102: "Wielding a scalpel-like *seton*, doctors would cut into their patients with a 'sawing motion.' Foreign objects, usually dried peas or beans, would then be inserted into the gash to promote proper infection and oozing. A doctor would reopen the wound, often every day, for weeks or months afterward, to make sure it didn't heal."

7. Ibid., 47.

8. Szabo 2013.

9. Margolick 1990.

10. Waldfogel 1993.

11. And we will look mainly at the U.S. because that is where we have the best data.

12. Skinner and Wennberg 2000.

13. Mullan 2004; Cutler et al. 2013.

14. Auster, Leveson, and Sarachek 1969.

15. Age- and sex-adjusted death rates.

16. Fisher et al. 2003. See also Fisher et al. (2000): "Residence in areas of greater hospital capacity is associated with substantially increased use of the hospital, even after controlling for socioeconomic characteristics and illness burden. This increased use provides no detectable mortality benefit."

17. Byrne et al. 2006.

18. Skinner and Wennberg 2000. This estimate was not significantly different from zero. The size of this dataset allowed researchers to control for many factors, including patient age, gender, and race; zip code urbanity, education, poverty, income, disability, and marital and employment status; and hospital-area illness rates.

19. At the 95 percent confidence interval. Here we're using a "50 days lost per 1 percent added mortality" rule of thumb.
20. Skinner and Wennberg 2000.
21. Hadley 1982.
22. Brook et al. 2006; Newhouse and Insurance Experiment Group 1993.
23. The partially subsidized groups also included a "maximum dollar expenditure." Once a patient paid the maximum amount in a given year, the rest of his or her care was free.
24. Manning et al. 1987.
25. Measured in total dollar value of all services covered under the insurance plans. See ibid.
26. Unfortunately the RAND study wasn't large enough to detect effects on death rates, so it tracked only intermediate measures of health.
27. Actually there were 23 physiological measures, but we're omitting one measure (long-distance vision) because the treatment for it—corrective lenses—seems to us more a matter of physics than medicine.
28. Newhouse and Insurance Experiment Group 1993. In fact, the researchers found an "almost significant" result (at the 6 percent significance level) that free medicine actually *hurt* the subset of patients who started out both poor and healthy.
29. Brook et al. 1984. Again we're omitting the statistically significant (but entirely predictable) improvement in long-distance vision that accompanies a subsidy for eyeglasses.
30. Siu et al. 1986; Pauly 1992; Newhouse and Insurance Experiment Group 1993.
31. Not every lottery winner ended up enrolling in Medicaid, and not every lottery loser ended up without insurance. There was, however, a meaningful difference between the two groups: in the year following the lottery, winners were 25 percentage points more likely to have insurance than losers.
32. Finkelstein et al. 2012.
33. Baicker et al. 2013.
34. Finkelstein et al. 2012.
35. Baicker et al. 2013.
36. Such a cutback might be done by raising the price of medicine across the board or by banning the treatments that have the weakest empirical support.
37. Tuljapurkar, Li, and Boe 2000; McKinlay and McKinlay 1977; Bunker (2001) estimates. (More at Lewis 2012.) Note, however, than many scientists mistakenly pronounce medicine as responsible for most of our health gains. From Bunker (2001):

The Nobel Laureate and President of Rockefeller University, Joshua Lederberg, wrote that "by the 1960s we could celebrate the conquest of polio and the transformation of formerly lethal infections to easy targets for penicillin and other miracle drugs . . . greater life expectancy—from 47 years in 1900 to 70 in 1960—can be attributed almost entirely to this mastery of infection. . . ." The Nobel Laureate and former research director of Burroughs Wellcome, the pharmaceutical company, George Hitchings, claimed that "the increase in life expectancy over the last 50 years has been attributed to new medicines."

38. Ioannidis 2005a, 2005b. From Lewis (2012): "The impact of a treatment in a clinical trial is known to be much higher than its effect in everyday clinical practice."

39. Ioannidis 2005a, 2005b.

40. Aizenman 2010.

41. Getzen 2000.

42. Waber et al. 2008.

43. Emanuel 2013.

44. Periyakoil et al. 2014. Doctors, having witnessed the futility of heroic end-of-life care, are famously keen on avoiding it for themselves, when they become terminally ill.

45. Mundinger et al. 2000.

46. Schneider and Epstein 1998.

47. Mennemeyer, Morrisey, and Howard 1997. In New York City, where patients have their choice among many different hospitals, poor-performing hospitals actually saw an *increase* in admissions relative to high-performing hospitals. See also Vladeck et al. 1988.

48. Mennemeyer et al. 1997.

49. Institute of Medicine et al. 1999; Leape 2000.

50. Institute of Medicine et al. 1999; National Academy of Sciences 2015.

51. Gawande 2007; Jain 2009.

52. Lundberg 1998; see also Nichols, Aronica, and Babe 1998, which found that approximately two-thirds of the undiagnosed conditions revealed by autopsy would have been treatable had they been caught earlier.

53. Shojania et al. 2002.

54. O'Connor 2011.

55. Westra, Kronz, and Eisele 2002.

56. Staradub et al. 2002 (second opinions caused 8 percent of breast-cancer screenings to result in a different surgical treatment plan).

57. Mandatory second-opinion programs: Gertman et al. 1980 (8 percent of elective surgery recommendations were overturned); McCarthy, Finkel, and Ruchlin 1981 (between 12 and 19 percent of elective surgery recommendations were overturned); Althabe et al. 2004 (25 percent of recommended C-sections in Latin America were overturned).
58. Lantz et al. 1998.

CHAPTER 15
1. Technically, they enter "diapause," an insect analog of hibernation.
2. Pocklington 2013.
3. Katz 2013.
4. *Wikipedia*, s.v. "Hajj," last modified March 6, 2017, https://en.wikipedia.org/wiki/Hajj.
5. In fact, Mecca is unbearably hot, reaching *average* daily highs of 110°F (43°C) from June through September. (The Hajj takes place annually by the lunar calendar, and therefore falls on different dates on the solar calendar every year.)
6. *Wikipedia*, s.v. "Ihram," last modified January 8, 2017, https://en.wikipedia.org/wiki/Ihram.
7. As the 16th-century diplomat Ogier Ghiselin de Busbecq said of the Spanish conquistadors, "Religion is the pretext, gold the real object" (Forster 2005, 40).
8. Cf. Pascal's wager.
9. This is the approach taken by the New Atheists, for example. And while there's a lot of insight to be gleaned from it (notably, the idea that religious beliefs are designed to take advantage of our cognitive quirks), it's largely a distraction from our focus in this book.
10. Haidt 2012, 249–50.
11. Rappaport 1999.
12. Sosis and Kiper 2014.
13. Anderson 2006.
14. There's a lot more to be said about the downsides of religion, as the New Atheists (Dennett, Dawkins, Harris, Hitchens) have argued in great detail, but it's mostly not our goal to tally up the pros and cons and pass judgment on the whole enterprise. Note, importantly, that religion can be *useful for adherents* without necessarily being *good for the entire species*. It's perfectly consistent to believe that religious participation is a selfish individual strategy and that, on net, it's bad for the world. In this way, religion would be like any other form of clannishness: when everyone else is organizing into clans around you, it may be necessary for you to join one, while at the same time wishing that clans didn't exist and everyone could just get along.

15. In other words, we're going to provide a *functionalist* account of religion (Swatos and Kivisto 1998, 193–96). Cf. Haidt: "To resolve [the puzzle of religious participation], either you have to grant that religiosity is (or at least, used to be) beneficial or you have to construct a complicated, multi-step explanation of how humans in all known cultures came to swim against the tide of adaptation and do so much self-destructive religious stuff" (2012, 252).

16. Strawbridge et al. 1997.

17. Schlegelmilch, Diamantopoulos, and Love 1997: donations. Becker and Dhingra 2001: volunteering. See also Putnam and Campbell: "By many different measures religiously observant Americans are better neighbors and better citizens than secular Americans—they are more generous with their time and money, especially in helping the needy, and they are more active in community life" (2010, 461; as quoted in Haidt 2012, 267).

18. Strawbridge et al. 1997.

19. Mahoney et al. 2002, 63; Strawbridge et al. 1997; Kenrick 2011, 151.

20. Frejka and Westoff 2008; Kenrick 2011, 151.

21. McCullough et al. 2000; Hummer et al. 1999; Strawbridge et al. 1997.

22. Steen 1996.

23. Wink, Dillon, and Larsen 2005.

24. Lelkes 2006.

25. Haidt 2012, ch. 11.

26. This is frequently attributed to Durkheim (who wrote in French), though it may be apocryphal. Nevertheless, it's a great capsule summary of his views, especially those articulated in Durkheim 1995.

27. Few scholars attempt to define religion precisely and unambiguously; there are simply too many boundary cases (like Confucianism) to draw a bright line between religion and non-religion. Most scholars, instead, attempt to associate religion with a cluster of interrelated features, and the more features something has, the more we're willing to call it a "religion." Here, for example, are a few "definitions" of religion. Atran and Henrich (2010): "an interwoven complex of rituals, beliefs, and norms." Rue (2005): "a natural social system comprising a narrative core buttressed by intellectual, aesthetic, experiential, ritual, and institutional strategies." Sosis and Kiper (2014): "a fuzzy set that comprises (but is not limited to) commitments to supernatural agents, emotionally imbued symbols, altered states of consciousness, ritual performance, myth, and taboo."

28. Cf. Haidt 2012, 251.

29. D. S. Wilson: "Religions exist primarily for people to achieve together what they cannot achieve on their own" (2002, 159).

30. Roberts and Iannaccone: "It never makes sense in an economic context for me, a perfectly rational person, to take a resource and just burn it up. But in a group context, strange as it may seem, this can be efficient" (2006).

31. Sosis and Alcorta: "Religions often maintain intragroup solidarity by requiring costly behavioral patterns of group members. The performance of these costly behaviors signals commitment and loyalty to the group and the beliefs of its members. Thus, trust is enhanced among group members, which enables them to minimize costly monitoring mechanisms that are otherwise necessary to overcome the free-rider problems that typically plague collective pursuits" (2003).

32. Iannaccone: "It can be shown, both formally and empirically, that apparently gratuitous sacrifices can function to mitigate a religion's free-rider problems by screening out halfhearted members and inducing higher levels of participation among those who remain" (1998).

33. *Wikipedia*, s.v. "Mourning of Muharram," last modified February 5, 2017, https://en.wikipedia.org/wiki/Mourning_of_Muharram.

34. Johnstone 1985.

35. Iannaccone 1992, 1998.

36. For a smaller sacrifice of fertility, some Christian teenagers wear purity rings as a public commitment to delay sex until marriage.

37. This also helps explain why eunuchs have historically held privileged positions.

38. On raising commitment as a way to reduce costly monitoring, see Sosis and Alcorta 2003; Iannaccone 1992, 1998. For more general evidence of religious cooperativeness (not necessarily caused by sacrifices), see Tan and Vogel 2008; Ruffle and Sosis 2006; Atran and Henrich 2010. For an overview, see Haidt 2012, 256–57, 265–67.

39. On group size in relation to costly rituals, see Roes and Raymond 2003; Johnson 2005 (both via Atran and Henrich 2010). On longevity as a function of costly rituals, see Sosis and Bressler 2003. More broadly, on the longevity of religious vs. secular communities, see Sosis 2000. Sosis and Alcorta 2003.

40. Jones 2012.

41. Ibid.

42. Some group members may be worse off, e.g., alpha males who might otherwise be able to dominate the group. And everyone will be incentivized to selfishly cheat and evade the norms. But for most people, if it's a decision about whether (a) to join the group and abide by the norms, or (b) to join a different group without any norms, they'll be better off joining the stricter group.

43. Sosis and Alcorta 2003.

44. Kenrick 2011, ch. 10; Weeden, Cohen, and Kenrick 2008; Durant and Durant 1968.

45. Even the prohibition on masturbation can be understood as a way to make early marriage more attractive.
46. Kenrick 2011, 151–53.
47. Brown 2012.
48. Perhaps it's a rehearsal for war. See McNeill 1997; Jordania 2011.
49. Hutchinson 2014.
50. Wiltermuth and Heath 2009.
51. Ehrenreich 2007.
52. Of course, many people do enjoy listening to sermons by podcast, but they're the exception rather than the rule.
53. This is similar to the third-person effect we saw in Chapter 10, which is responsible for the efficacy of advertising and other forms of propaganda. As the editor for the website Upworthy put it, "You're not preaching to the choir. You're preaching to the choir's friends" (Abebe 2014).
54. On badges in a religious context, see Iannaccone 1992, 1998; Atran and Henrich 2010. More generally, badges can convey information about any underlying feature, not just group membership. For an overview, see Miller 2009, 116–19.
55. This isn't to deny that the specific form they take is, in part, determined by our cognitive quirks. But this section helps explain why religious beliefs, unlike other supernatural beliefs, aren't weeded out by critical reflection, but are instead sticky, central features of religious systems.
56. Of course, if we're caught cheating, the outrage will be all the stronger.
57. *Transubstantiation* is the belief that the crackers and wine literally become the flesh and blood of Christ, while *consubstantiation* is the belief that they become flesh and blood only spiritually, while retaining all the physical properties of crackers and wine.
58. Note that our word "faith," which is often used in reference to religious belief, originally meant loyalty or trustworthiness (*Online Etymology Dictionary*, s.v. "faith," http://www.etymonline.com/index.php?term=faith).
59. If there *were* substantive reasons to prefer one team over another—if the Dodgers were more entertaining, say, or gave $100 rewards to anyone caught wearing their apparel—then being a fan would reflect only your narrow individual interests, rather than your loyalty to a particular community.
60. Evolutionary psychologists are quick to point out that humans aren't "biological fitness maximizers." If we were, we'd do a *lot* of things differently. No one would smoke, gamble, or watch pornography. We'd use a lot less birth control. Men would donate sperm at every opportunity, and women would donate their eggs. No one would ever adopt a child, no matter how much happiness it might bring, nor would we ever stop to smell the roses. Clearly, this doesn't describe

our species. Instead of explicitly trying to maximize reproductive success, we are "adaptation executors." Our brains were built with various instincts that, in the ancestral environment, tended to help our ancestors leave more descendants.

CHAPTER 16

1. Mansfield as quoted in Wehner 2014.
2. Haidt: "Many political scientists used to assume that people vote selfishly, choosing the candidate or policy that will benefit them the most. But decades of research on public opinion have led to the conclusion that self-interest is a weak predictor of policy preferences" (2012, 85). See also Caplan 2007.
3. Haidt: "See review in Kinder 1998. The exception to this rule is that when the material benefits of a policy are 'substantial, imminent, and well-publicized,' those who would benefit from it are more likely to support it than those who would be harmed. See also D. T. Miller 1999 on the 'norm of self-interest'" (2012, 85–6, footnote).
4. At least, not in any straightforward way. See Caplan 2007.
5. Gelman, Silver, and Edlin 2012.
6. Churchill seemed to be quoting an unsourced aphorism. See Langworth 2011, 573.
7. For those unfamiliar with the U.S. Electoral College system, here's how it works. First, within each state, the candidate with the most votes is usually awarded *all* of that state's "electoral votes." These electoral votes are then tallied up (from all the states), and the candidate with the most electoral votes is elected president.
8. Gelman et al. 2012.
9. Gerber et al. 2009.
10. In contrast, presidential elections (compared to midterm elections) draw out an extra 16 out of every 100 eligible voters (Gerber et al. 2009).
11. Delli-Carpini and Keeter 1997. For what it's worth, neither Kevin nor Robin can name their congressperson.
12. "American Public Vastly Overestimates Amount of U.S. Foreign Aid," WorldPublicOpinion.org, November 29, 2010, accessed April 26, 2017, http://worldpublicopinion.net/american-public-vastly-overestimates-amount-of-u-s-foreign-aid/.
13. Althaus 2003; Kraus, Malmfors, and Slovic 1992.
14. Caplan 2007.
15. Converse 1964.
16. Hall, Johansson, and Strandberg 2012.

17. Bruce Yandle, for example, describes the crucial difference between regulating facets of production (bad) vs. regulating final outcomes directly (good). He also describes the costs and benefits of regulating at the federal vs. state levels. See Yandle 1983; Yandle 1999.

18. Volden and Wiseman 2014.

19. Note that there are ways to vote well that don't require a voter to be informed about national issues. In "retrospective voting," for example, you vote to re-elect the incumbent if your life improved (more than you expected) during the incumbent's term, and otherwise you vote to replace the incumbent with someone else. If most voters did this, incumbents would have strong incentives to make people's lives go well. But most voters are reluctant to put much weight on this voting strategy.

20. Also suggestive is the fact of many consistent, smooth long-term trends in public opinion on policy. If opinion changes resulted mainly from new information, they would follow a random walk, wherein future changes are hard to predict from past changes.

21. Technically, anger isn't a "social emotion," at least not by the strictest definition: "an emotion that requires the representation of the mental states of other people" (*Wikipedia*, s.v. "Social emotions," last modified January 29, 2017, https://en.wikipedia.org/wiki/Social_emotions).

22. *Merriam-Webster*, s.v. "apparatchik," accessed March 8, 2017, https://www.merriam-webster.com/dictionary/apparatchik.

23. Solzhenitsyn 1973, 69–70. Note that the quotation has been edited for length and clarity.

24. *Wikipedia*, s.v. "Great Purge," last modified February 22, 2017, https://en.wikipedia.org/wiki/Great_Purge.

25. Dikötter 2010: China. Tudor and Pearson 2015: North Korea.

26. Albright 2016.

27. Huntington 1997, 174–5.

28. Klofstad, McDermott, and Hatemi 2013.

29. A 2010 survey analyzed in Iyengar, Sood, and Lelkes (2012). In 1960, the figures were much lower: 5 percent for Republicans and 4 percent for Democrats. A Pew study in 2014 found the numbers to be 30 percent for conservatives and 23 percent for liberals (Pew Research Center 2014).

30. Iyengar and Westwood 2015. See also Klein and Chang 2015; Smith, Williams, and Willis 1967.

31. Klein and Chang 2015.

32. Klein and Stern 2009. Across the United States, the ratio of Democrats to Republicans is about 1. But among college professors the ratio is 5, and in

the humanities and social sciences, it's closer to 8. These latter ratios have doubled over the last 40 years. Economists are often distrusted by other academics in part because their ratio is a "conservative" 3. See also Cardiff and Klein 2005.

33. Gross 2013.
34. Rothman, Lichter, and Nevitte 2005.
35. Gerber et al. 2012
36. Roberts and Caplan 2007 (not verbatim quotes).
37. Note, however, that when people hold opinions they claim are "unpopular," and yet express *pride* in their nonconformity, we should take their claims with a grain of salt. What looks "unpopular" to one audience is often an act of pandering to another, less visible constituency. To give just one example, Griskevicius et al. (2006) suggests that men might profess "unpopular" political opinions because nonconformity makes them more attractive to women. See also Kuran 1995, 31.
38. Haidt 2012, 86.
39. See, e.g., Brennan and Hamlin 1998; Schuessler 2000.
40. Jones and Hudson 2000.
41. This also explains why even people who don't vote take the trouble to form— and more importantly, to discuss—their political opinions.
42. Haidt 2012, 86.
43. This is the old honest or costly signaling principle at work.
44. A more colorful example is the website votergasm.org, where visitors can pledge to withhold sex from nonvoters for a week to four years following an election. See Sohn 2004.
45. Cf. Steven Pinker's remark: "People are embraced or condemned according to their beliefs, so one function of the mind may be to hold beliefs that bring the belief-holder the greatest number of allies, protectors, or disciples, rather than beliefs that are most likely to be true" (2013, 286).
46. Another factor that can lead to disagreement is having different goals. For example, one person might prioritize blue-collar jobs, while another person prioritizes economic efficiency. But political discourse often requires us to have the shared overarching goal of "the common good," i.e., what's best for all of us together. Or at least, we have to pretend that's our goal.
47. Mercier and Sperber 2011.
48. Tavits: "Voters rewarded political parties for changing economic positions, but punished parties for changing other social positions . . . even those parties that make [social] policy adjustments that correspond to the preference shifts of voters lose votes" (2007).

49. Poole and Rosenthal 1987; Voeten 2001.
50. Poole and Rosenthal 2007; Voeten 2001.
51. *Wikipedia*, s.v. "Party realignment in the United States," last modified December 12, 2016, https://simple.wikipedia.org/wiki/Party_realignment_in_the_United_States.
52. Poole and Rosenthal 2000.
53. Costa and Kahn 2009.
54. Abrahms 2008, 2011.
55. This plausibly accounts for the attitude of many libertarians, for example. See also Griskevicius et al. (2006), who explain some kinds of nonconformity by an appeal to mating motives.

CHAPTER 17

1. Of course, we also need to be careful about jumping to conclusions. Kevin once interviewed a college student whose body language seemed arrogant and dismissive, only to learn later, after rejecting the student for the job, that his impressions were entirely mistaken. He feels terrible about it to this day.
2. Credit to Paul Crowley for this point.
3. Frank, Gilovich, and Regan 1993. Cf. Goethe's remark: "If you treat an individual as he is, he will remain how he is. But if you treat him as if he were what he ought to be and could be, he will become what he ought to be and could be." See also Stafford 2013.
4. Stavrova and Ehlebracht 2016.
5. Tocqueville 2013, sect. II, ch. 8; Smith 2013; McClure 2014.
6. See Nowak and Highfield 2011.
7. Farrell and Finnemore 2013.
8. Hayek 1988.

Abebe, Nitsuh. 2014. "Watching Team Upworthy Work Is Enough to Make You a Cynic. or Lose Your Cynicism. Or Both. Or Neither." *Daily Intelligencer*, March 23.

Abrahms, Max. 2008. "What Terrorists Really Want: Terrorist Motives and Counterterrorism Strategy." *International Security* 32 (4), Spring: 8–105.

Abrahms, Max. 2011. "Does Terrorism Really Work? Evolution in the Conventional Wisdom since 9/11." *Defence and Peace Economics* 22 (6): 583–94.

Aghion, Philippe, Torsten Persson, and Dorothee Rouzet. 2012. "Education and Military Rivalry." NBER Working Paper No. 18049, National Bureau for Economic Research, Cambridge, MA.

Aizenman, N. C. 2010. "Hospital Infection Deaths Caused by Ignorance and Neglect, Survey Finds." *Washington Post*, July 13.

Akst, Jef. 2010. "Recess." *The Scientist*, October 1.

Albright, Madeleine. 2016. "Madeleine Albright: My Undiplomatic Moment." *New York Times*, February 12. https://www.nytimes.com/2016/02/13/opinion/madeleine-albright-my-undiplomatic-moment.html.

Alicke, Mark D., and Olesya Govorun. 2005. "The Better-Than-Average Effect." *The Self in Social Judgment* 1: 85–106.

Almås, Ingvild, Alexander W. Cappelen, Erik Ø. Sørensen, and Bertil Tungodden. 2010. "Fairness and the Development of Inequality Acceptance." *Science* 328 (5982): 1176–78.

Alston, Julian, Matthew Andersen, Jennifer James, and Philip Pardey. 2011. "The Economic Returns to U.S. Public Agricultural Research." *American Journal of Agricultural Economics* 93 (5): 1257–77.

Althabe, Fernando, José Belizán, José Villar, Sophie Alexander, Eduardo Bergel, Silvina Ramos, Mariana Romero, Allan Donner, Gunilla Lindmark, Ana Langer, Ubaldo Farnot, José G. Cecatti, Guillermo Carroli, and Edgar Kestler. 2004. "Mandatory Second Opinion to Reduce Rates of Unnecessary Caesarean Sections in Latin America: A Cluster Randomised Controlled Trial." *The Lancet* 363 (9425): 1934–40.

Althaus, Scott. 2003. *Collective Preferences in Democratic Politics*. Cambridge, UK: Cambridge University Press.

Anderson, Benedict. 2006. *Imagined Communities: Reflections on the Origin and Spread of Nationalism.* London: Verso.

Andreoni, James. 1989. "Giving with Impure Altruism: Applications to Charity and Ricardian Equivalence." *The Journal of Political Economy* 97 (6): 1447–58.

Andreoni, James. 1990. "Impure Altruism and Donations to Public Goods: A Theory of Warm-Glow Giving." *The Economic Journal* 100 (401): 464–77.

Andreoni, James, and Ragan Petrie. 2004. "Public Goods Experiments without Confidentiality: A Glimpse Into Fund-Raising." *Journal of Public Economics* 88 (7): 1605–23.

Angier, Natalie. 2008. "Political Animals (Yes, Animals)." *New York Times,* January 22.

Ardrey, Robert. 1966. *The Territorial Imperative.* New York: Atheneum.

Arrow, Kenneth, Robert Forsythe, Michael Gorham, Robert Hahn, Robin Hanson, John O. Ledyard, Saul Levmore, Robert Litan, Paul Milgrom, Forrest D. Nelson, George R. Neumann, Marco Ottaviani, Thomas C. Schelling, Robert J. Shiller, Vernon L. Smith, Erik Snowberg, Cass R. Sunstein, Paul C. Tetlock, Philip E. Tetlock, Hal R. Varian, Justin Wolfers, and Eric Zitzewitz. 2008. "The Promise of Prediction Markets." *Science* 320 (5878), May 16: 877–8878.

Atran, Scott, and Joseph Henrich. 2010. "The Evolution of Religion: How Cognitive By-Products, Adaptive Learning Heuristics, Ritual Displays, and Group Competition Generate Deep Commitments to Prosocial Religions." *Biological Theory* 5 (1): 18–30.

Aubert, Maxime, A. Brumm, M. Ramli, T. Sutikna, E. W. Saptomo, B. Hakim, M. J. Morwood, G. D. van den Bergh, L. Kinsley, and A. Dosseto. 2014. "Pleistocene Cave Art from Sulawesi, Indonesia." *Nature* 514 (7521): 223–27.

Auster, Richard, Irving Leveson, and Deborah Sarachek. 1969. "The Production of Health, an Exploratory Study." *Journal of Human Resources* 4 (4): 411–36.

Avent, Ryan. 2016. "Why Do We Work So Hard?" *The Economist 1843,* April. https://www.1843magazine.com/features/why-do-we-work-so-hard.

Axelrod, Robert. 1986. "An Evolutionary Approach to Norms." *American Political Science Review* 80 (4): 1095–1111.

Axtell, Roger. 1997. *Gestures: The Do's and Taboos of Body Language Around the World.* Hoboken, NJ: Wiley.

Baicker, Katherine, Sarah L. Taubman, Heidi L. Allen, Mira Bernstein, Jonathan H. Gruber, Joseph P. Newhouse, Eric C. Schneider, Bill J. Wright, Alan M. Zaslavsky, and Amy N. Finkelstein. 2013. "The Oregon Experiment—Effects of Medicaid on Clinical Outcomes." *New England Journal of Medicine* 368 (18): 1713–22.

Balter, Michael. 2009. "Early Start for Human Art? Ochre May Revise Timeline." *Science* 323 (5914): 569.

Barnett, Susan M., and Stephen J. Ceci. 2002. "When and Where Do We Apply What We Learn?: A Taxonomy for Far Transfer." *Psychological Bulletin* 128 (4): 612.

Baron, Jonathan, and Ewa Szymanska. 2011. "Heuristics and Biases in Charity." In *The Science of Giving: Experimental Approaches to the Study of Charity*, edited by Daniel M. Oppenheimer and Christopher Y. Olivia, 215–35. New York: Psychology Press.

Barrett, William. 2015. "The Largest U.S. Charities for 2015." Forbes, December 9. http://www.forbes.com/sites/williampbarrett/2015/12/09/the-largest-u-s-charities-for-2015/.

Bateson, Gregory. 1955. "A Theory of Play and Fantasy." *Psychiatric Research Reports* 2: 39–51.

Bateson, Melissa, Luke Callow, Jessica Holmes, Maximilian Roche, and Daniel Nettle. 2013. "Do Images of 'Watching Eyes' Induce Behaviour That Is More Pro-Social or More Normative? A Field Experiment on Littering." *PLoS One* 8 (12): e82055.

Baumeister, Roy F., Karen Dale, and Kristin L. Sommer. 1998. "Freudian Defense Mechanisms and Empirical Findings in Modern Social Psychology: Reaction Formation, Projection, Displacement, Undoing, Isolation, Sublimation, and Denial." *Journal of Personality* 66 (6): 1081–1124.

Becker, Penny Edgell, and Pawan H. Dhingra. 2001. "Religious Involvement and Volunteering: Implications for Civil Society." *Sociology of Religion* 62 (3): 315–35.

Bekkers, René. 2005. "It's Not All in the Ask. Effects and Effectiveness of Recruitment Strategies Used by Nonprofits in the Netherlands." 34th Arnova Annual Conference, Washington, DC.

Bekkers, René, and Pamala Wiepking. 2011. "A Literature Review of Empirical Studies of Philanthropy: Eight Mechanisms That Drive Charitable Giving." *Nonprofit and Voluntary Sector Quarterly* 40 (5): 924–73.

Bekoff, Marc. 1995. "Play Signals as Punctuation: The Structure of Social Play in Canids." *Behaviour* 132 (5): 419–29.

Belkin, Douglas, and Melissa Korn. 2015. "Stanford Extends Free Tuition to More Middle-Class Students." *Wall Street Journal*, April 3.

Belofsky, Nathan. 2013. *Strange Medicine: A Shocking History of Real Medical Practices Through the Ages*. New York: TarcherPerigee.

Benhabib, Jess, and Mark M. Spiegel. 1994. "The Role of Human Capital in Economic Development Evidence from Aggregate Cross-Country Data." *Journal of Monetary Economics* 34 (2): 143–73.

Benjamin, Walter. 1936. *The Work of Art in the Age of Mechanical Reproduction.* Translated by Harry Zohn. https://www.marxists.org/reference/subject/ philosophy/works/ge/benjamin.htm.

Bils, Mark, and Peter J. Klenow. 2000. "Does Schooling Cause Growth?" *American Economic Review* 90 (5): 1160–83.

Bingham, Paul. 2000. "Human Evolution and Human History: A Complete History." *Evolutionary Anthropology: Issues, News, and Reviews* 9 (6): 248–57.

Black, Donald W. 1984. "Laughter." *JAMA: The Journal of the American Medical Association* 252 (21): 2995–98.

Blakeslee, Thomas. 2004. *Beyond the Conscious Mind: Unlocking the Secrets of the Self.* Bloomington, IL: iUniverse.

Boehm, Christopher. 1999. *Hierarchy in the Forest: Egalitarianism and the Evolution of Human Altruism.* Cambridge, MA: Harvard University Press.

Borg, James. 2009. *Body Language: 7 Easy Lessons to Master the Silent Language.* Upper Saddle River, NJ: FT Press.

Borgia, Gerald. 1985. "Bower Quality, Number of Decorations and Mating Success of Male Satin Bowerbirds (*Ptilonorhynchus violaceus*): An Experimental Analysis." *Animal Behaviour* 33 (1): 266–71.

Bornmann, Lutz, Rüdiger Mutz, and Hans-Dieter Daniel. 2010. "A Reliability-Generalization Study of Journal Peer Reviews: A Multilevel Meta-Analysis of Inter-Rater Reliability and Its Determinants." *PLoS One* 14331 (December 14).

Bowles, Samuel, and Herbert Gintis. 1976. *Schooling in Capitalist America.* New York: Basic Books.

Bradbury, Jack W., and Sandra L. Vehrencamp. 1998. *Principles of Animal Communication.* Sunderland, MA: Sinauer Associates.

Branigan, Tania. 2014. "China Bans Wordplay in Attempt at Pun Control." *The Guardian*, November 28.

Branwen, Gwern. 2009. "Education Is Not about Learning." Gwern. net, July 25. Last modified March 8, 2017. http://www.gwern.net/ education-is-not-about-learning#school-hours.

Braverman, Harry. 1974. *Labor and Monopoly Capital: The Degradation of Work in the Twentieth Century.* New York: NYU Press.

Brennan, Geoffrey, and Alan Hamlin. 1998. "Expressive Voting and Electoral Equilibrium." *Public Choice* 95 (1-2): 149–75.

Brint, Steven. 2011. "The Educational Lottery." *Los Angeles Review of Books*, November 15.

Brock, Timothy C., and Joe L. Balloun. 1967. "Behavioral Receptivity to Dissonant Information." *Journal of Personality and Social Psychology* 6 (4 pt 1): 413.

Brook, Robert H., Emmett B. Keeler, Kathleen N. Lohr, Joseph P. Newhouse, John
    E. Ware, William H. Rogers, Allyson Ross Davies, Cathy D. Sherbourne, George
    A. Goldberg, Patricia Camp, Caren Kamberg, Arleen Leibowitz, Joan Keesey, and
    David Reboussin. 2006. "The Health Insurance Experiment: A Classic RAND
    Study Speaks to the Current Health Care Reform Debate." RAND Research Brief
    RB-9174-HHS. Santa Monica, CA: RAND Corporation. http://www.rand.org/
    pubs/research_briefs/RB9174.html.

Brook, Robert H., John E. Ware, William H. Rogers, Emmett B. Keeler, Allyson Ross
    Davies, Cathy D. Sherbourne, George A. Goldberg, Kathleen N. Lohr, Patricia
    Camp, and Joseph P. Newhouse. 1984. "The Effect of Coinsurance on the Health
    of Adults: Results from the RAND Health Insurance Experiment." RAND Report
    R-3055-HHS. Santa Monica, CA: RAND Corporation. http://www.rand.org/
    pubs/reports/R3055.html.

Brown, Andrew. 2012. "You Can't Dance to Atheism." *The Guardian* (blog),
    September 6.

Brown, Donald E. 1991. *Human Universals*. New York: McGraw-Hill.

Brown, Peter C., Henry L. Roediger, and Mark A. McDaniel. 2014. *Make It Stick*.
    Cambridge, MA: Harvard University Press.

Brown, Richard. 2011. *A Companion to James Joyce*. West Sussex, UK: Wiley-Blackwell.

Bruni, Frank. 2015. "Best, Brightest—and Saddest?" *New York Times,* April 11.

Bruze, Gustaf. 2015. "Male and Female Marriage Returns to Schooling."
    International Economic Review 56 (1): 207–34.

Bryant, W. Keith, Haekyung Jeon-Slaughter, Hyojin Kang, and Aaron Tax. 2003.
    "Participation in Philanthropic Activities: Donating Money and Time." *Journal of
    Consumer Policy* 26 (1): 43–73.

Bucholz, Robert. 2006. "Foundations of Western Civilization II: A History of the
    Modern Western World." *Great Courses* No. 8700.

Bull, Ray, and Elizabeth Gibson-Robinson. 1981. "The Influences of Eye-Gaze, Style
    of Dress, and Locality on the Amounts of Money Donated to a Charity." *Human
    Relations* 34 (10): 895–905.

Bunker, John P. 2001. "The Role of Medical Care in Contributing to Health
    Improvements within Societies." *International Journal of Epidemiology* 30
    (6): 1260–63.

Burling, Robbins. 1986. "The Selective Advantage of Complex Language." *Ethology
    and Sociobiology* 7 (1): 1–16.

Burr, Bill. 2014. "Smoking Past the Band." *Comedians in Cars Getting Coffee,*
    season 5, episode 3, November 17. http://comediansincarsgettingcoffee.com/
    bill-burr-smoking-past-the-band.

Buss, David M. 2002. "Human Mate Guarding." *Neuroendocrinology Letters* 23 (Suppl. 4): 23–29.

Byrne, Margaret M., Kenneth Pietz, LeChauncy Woodard, and Laura A. Petersen. 2006. "Health Care Funding Levels and Patient Outcomes: A National Study." *Health Economics* 16 (4): 385–93.

Caplan, Bryan. 2007. *The Myth of the Rational Voter: Why Democracies Choose Bad Policies.* Princeton, NJ: Princeton University Press.

Caplan, Bryan. 2017. *The Case Against Education.* Princeton, NJ: Princeton University Press.

Carey, Kevin. 2015. "Here's What Will Truly Change Higher Education: Online Degrees That Are Seen as Official." *New York Times*, March 5.

Cardiff, Christopher F., and Daniel B. Klein. 2005. "Faculty Partisan Affiliations in All Disciplines: A Voter-Registration Study." *Critical Review* 17 (3-4): 237–55.

Carman, Katherine Grace. 2003. "Social Influences and the Private Provision of Public Goods: Evidence from Charitable Contributions in the Workplace." Unpublished manuscript. Palo Alto, CA: Stanford University.

Carnegie, Dale. 1936. *How to Win Friends and Influence People.* New York: Simon & Schuster.

Carnevale, Anthony, Stephen Rose, and Ban Cheah. 2011. *The College Payoff: Education, Occupations, Lifetime Earnings.* Washington, DC: Georgetown University Center on Education and the Workforce.

Carpenter, Malinda, Katherine Nagell, and Michael Tomasello. 1998. "Social Cognition, Joint Attention, and Communicative Competence from 9 to 15 Months of Age." *Monographs of the Society for Research in Child Development* 63 (4): i–174.

Carrell, Scott E., Teny Maghakian, and James E. West. 2011. "A's from Zzzz's? The Causal Effect of School Start Time on the Academic Achievement of Adolescents." *American Economic Journal: Economic Policy* 3 (3): 62–81.

Center for Global Prosperity. 2013. "The Index of Global Philanthropy and Remittances 2013: With a Special Report on Emerging Economics." Hudson Institute, Washington, DC. http://www.hudson.org/content/researchattachments/attachment/1229/2013_indexof_global_philanthropyand_remittances.pdf.

Chan, Sewell. 2009. "New Targets in the Fat Fight: Soda and Juice." *New York Times*, August 31.

Changizi, Mark. 2010. *The Vision Revolution: How the Latest Research Overturns Everything We Thought We Knew about Human Vision.* Dallas, TX: Benbella Books.

Charness, Gary, and Uri Gneezy. 2008. "What's in a Name? Anonymity and Social Distance in Dictator and Ultimatum Games." *Journal of Economic Behavior & Organization* 68 (1): 29–35.

Cheng, Joey T., Jessica L Tracy, Tom Foulsham, Alan Kingstone, and Joseph Henrich. 2013. "Two Ways to the Top: Evidence That Dominance and Prestige Are Distinct Yet Viable Avenues to Social Rank And Influence." *Journal of Personality and Social Psychology* 104 (1): 103.

Chwe, Michael Suk-Young. 2001. *Rational Ritual: Culture, Coordination, and Common Knowledge*. Princeton, NJ: Princeton University Press.

Clark, Gregory. 1987. "Why Isn't the Whole World Developed? Lessons from the Cotton Mills." *The Journal of Economic History* 47 (1): 141–73.

Cochran, Gregory, and Henry Harpending. 2009. *The 10,000 Year Explosion: How Civilization Accelerated Human Evolution*. New York: Basic Books.

Collins, Paul. 2011. "Trust Issues." *Lapham's Quarterly* 4 (4, Fall). http://laphamsquarterly.org/future/trust-issues.

Connor, Richard C., Michael R. Heithaus, and Lynne M. Barre. 1999. "Superalliance of Bottlenose Dolphins." *Nature* 397 (6720): 571–72.

Converse, Philip. 1964. "The Nature of Belief Systems in Mass Publics." In *Ideology and Discontent*, edited by David Apter, 206–61. New York: Free Press.

Corballis, Michael. 2008. "Not the Last Word." Review of *The First Word: The Search for the Origins of Language*, by Christine Kenneally. *American Scientist* 96 (1, January-February): 68.

Cosmides, Leda, and John Tooby. 1992. "Cognitive Adaptations for Social Exchange." In *The Adapted Mind: Evolutionary Psychology and the Generation of Culture*, edited by J. Barkow, L. Cosmides, and J. Tooby, 163–228. New York: Oxford University Press.

Costa, Dora L. & Matthew E. Kahn. 2009. *Heroes and Cowards: The Social Face of War*. Princeton, NJ: Princeton University Press.

Croyle, Robert T., Elizabeth F. Loftus, Steven D. Barger, Yi-Chun Sun, Marybeth Hart, and JoAnn Gettig. 2006. "How Well Do People Recall Risk Factor Test Results? Accuracy and Bias among Cholesterol Screening Participants." *Health Psychology* 25 (3): 425.

Cutler, David, Jonathan Skinner, Ariel Dora Stern, and David Wennberg. 2013. "Physician Beliefs and Patient Preferences: A New Look at Regional Variation in Health Care Spending." NBER Working Paper No. 19320, National Bureau for Economic Research, Cambridge, MA.

Dall, Sasha RX, Luc-Alain Giraldeau, Ola Olsson, John M. McNamara, and David W. Stephens. 2005. "Information and Its Use By Animals in Evolutionary Ecology." *Trends in Ecology & Evolution* 20 (4): 187–93.

Darwin, Charles. 2012. *The Expression of the Emotions in Man and Animals*. Project Gutenberg, released 1998. www.gutenberg.org/ebooks/1227.

Davis, Fred. 1994. *Fashion, Culture, and Identity*. Chicago: University of Chicago Press.

Davison, W. Phillips. 1983. "The Third-Person Effect in Communication." *Public Opinion Quarterly* 47 (1): 1–15.

Dawkins, Richard. 1976. *The Selfish Gene.* New York: Oxford University Press.

Dawson, Erica, Kenneth Savitsky, and David Dunning. 2006. " 'Don't Tell Me, I Don't Want to Know': Understanding People's Reluctance to Obtain Medical Diagnostic Information." *Journal of Applied Social Psychology* 36 (3): 751–68.

Dehaene, Stanislas, Jean-Pierre Changeux, Lionel Naccache, Jérôme Sackur, and Claire Sergent. 2006. "Conscious, Preconscious, and Subliminal Processing: A Testable Taxonomy." *Trends in Cognitive Sciences* 10 (5): 204–11.

de la Fuente, Angel, and Rafael Doménech. 2006. "Human Capital in Growth Regressions: How Much Difference Does Data Quality Make?" *Journal of the European Economic Association* 4 (1): 1–36.

Delli-Carpini, M. X., and S. Keeter. 1997. *What Americans Know about Politics and Why It Matters.* New Haven CT: Yale University Press.

de Miguel, C., and Maciej Henneberg. 2001. "Variation in Hominid Brain Size: How Much Is Due to Method?" *Homo* 52 (1): 3–58.

DeMuro, Doug. 2013. "Hatchback vs Sedan: Why You Might Want to Consider a Hatchback." *AutoTrader,* June. http://www.autotrader.com/car-news/hatchback-vs-sedan-why-you-might-want-to-consider-a-hatchback-209345.

Dennett, Daniel C. 1991. *Consciousness Explained.* New York: Little, Brown.

Dessalles, Jean-Louis. 2007. *Why We Talk: The Evolutionary Origins of Language.* New York: Oxford University Press.

Desvousges, William, Reed Johnson, Richard Dunford, Kevin Boyle, Sara Hudson, and Nicole Wilson. 1992. *Measuring Nonuse Damages Using Contingent Valuation: An Experimental Evaluation of Accuracy.* Monograph 92-1, No. BM. Research Triangle Park, NC: Research Triangle Institute.

Detterman, Douglas K., and Robert J. Sternberg. 1993. *Transfer on Trial: Intelligence, Cognition, and Instruction.* New York: Ablex.

de Waal, Frans. 1982. *Chimpanzee Politics: Power and Sex among Apes.* Baltimore: Johns Hopkins University Press.

de Waal, Frans. 1996. *Good Natured: The Origins of Right and Wrong in Humans and Other Animals.* Cambridge, MA: Harvard University Press.

de Waal, Frans. 1997. "The Chimpanzee's Service Economy: Food for Grooming." *Evolution and Human Behavior* 18 (6): 375–86.

de Waal, Frans. 2005. *Our Inner Ape.* New York: Penguin.

Diamond, Jared. 1997. *Guns, Germs, and Steel: The Fates of Human Societies.* New York: W. W. Norton.

Dikötter, Frank. 2010. *Mao's Great Famine: The History of China's Most Devastating Catastrophe, 1958–1962.* New York: Bloomsbury.

Dissanayake, Ellen. 1980. "Art as a Human Behavior: Toward an Ethological View of Art." *Journal of Aesthetics and Art Criticism* 38 (4): 397–406.

Dissanayake, Ellen. 1988. *What Is Art For?* Seattle: University of Washington Press.

Dissanayake, Ellen. 1992. *Homo Aestheticus: Where Art Comes from and Why.* New York: Free Press.

Dovidio, John, and Steve Ellyson. 1982. "Decoding Visual Dominance: Attributions of Power Based on Relative Percentages of Looking While Speaking and Looking While Listening." *Social Psychology Quarterly* 45 (2): 106–13.

Dovidio, John, Steve Ellyson, Caroline Keating, Karen Heltman, and Clifford Brown. 1988. "The Relationship of Social Power to Visual Displays of Dominance Between Men and Women." *Journal of Personality and Social Psychology* 54 (2): 233–42.

Duhigg, Charles. 2012. "How Companies Learn Your Secrets." *New York Times Magazine*, February 16.

Dunbar, Robin I. M. 1980. "Determinants and Evolutionary Consequences of Dominance among Female Gelada Baboons." *Behavioral Ecology and Sociobiology* 7 (4): 253–65.

Dunbar, Robin I. M., and M. Sharman. 1984. "Is social grooming altruistic?" *Zeitschrift für Tierpsychologie* 64 (2): 163–73.

Dunbar, Robin I. M. 1991. "Functional Significance of Social Grooming In Primates." *Folia Primatologica* 57 (3): 121–31.

Dunbar, Robin I. M. 2002. "The Social Brain Hypothesis." *Foundations in Social Neuroscience* 5 (71): 69.

Dunbar, Robin I. M. 2003. "The Social Brain: Mind, Language, and Society in Evolutionary Perspective." *Annual Review of Anthropology* 32: 163–81.

Dunbar, Robin I. M. 2004. "Gossip in Evolutionary Perspective." *Review of General Psychology* 8 (2): 100.

Dunbar, Robin I. M. 2010. "The Social Role of Touch in Humans and Primates: Behavioural Function and Neurobiological Mechanisms." *Neuroscience & Biobehavioral Reviews* 34 (2): 260–68.

Durant, Will, and Ariel Durant. 1968. *The Lessons of History*. New York: Simon & Schuster.

Durkheim, Émile. 1995. *The Elementary Forms of Religious Life*. Translated by Karen E. Fields. New York: Free Press.

Eastman, Max. 1936. *Enjoyment of Laughter*. New York: Simon & Schuster.

The Economist. 2014. "Why Is Everyone So Busy?" December 20. http://www.economist.com/news/christmas-specials/21636612-time-poverty-problem-partly-perception-and-partly-distribution-why.

Edwards, Finley. 2012. "Early to Rise? The Effect of Daily Start Times on Academic Performance." *Economics of Education Review* 31 (6): 970–83.

Edwards, Jonathan. 1821. *A Treatise Concerning Religious Affectations, in Three Parts*. Philadelphia, PA: James Crissy.

Ehrenreich, Barbara. 2007. *Dancing in the Streets: A History of Collective Joy*. New York: Holt.

Eibl-Eibesfeldt, Irenäus. 2009. *Human Ethology*. Piscataway, NJ: Transaction.

Ekman, Paul, and Wallace V. Friesen. 1971. "Constants across Cultures in the Face and Emotion." *Journal of Personality and Social Psychology* 17 (2): 124.

Elias, Norbert. 2000. *The Civilizing Process: Sociogenetic and Psychogenetic Investigations*. Translated by Edmund Jephcott. Oxford, UK: Blackwell.

Ellyson, Steve L., John F. Dovidio, Randi L. Corson, and Debbie L. Vinicur. 1980. "Visual Dominance Behavior in Female Dyads: Situational and Personality Factors." *Social Psychology Quarterly* 43 (3): 328–36.

Emanuel, Ezekiel. 2013. "Better, If Not Cheaper, Care." *New York Times*, January 3.

Emerson, Ralph Waldo. 1995. *The Heart of Emerson's Journals*, edited by Bliss Perry. New York: Dover.

Emerson, Ralph Waldo. 2012. *Essays*. Project Gutenberg, released 2005. www. gutenberg.org/ebooks/16643.

Eren, Ozkan, and Daniel J. Henderson. 2011. "Are We Wasting Our Children's Time by Giving Them More Homework?" *Economics of Education Review* 30 (5): 950–61.

Exline, Ralph, Steve Ellyson, and Barbara Long. 1975. "Visual Behavior as an Aspect of Power Role Relationships." In *Nonverbal Communication of Aggression*, Vol. 2 of *Advances in the Study of Communication and Affect*, edited Patricia Pliner, Lester Krames, Thomas Alloway, 21–52. New York: Springer.

Exline, Ralph, John F. Dovidio, Randi L. Corson, and Debbie L. Vinicur. 1980. "Visual Dominance Behavior in Female Dyads: Situational and Personality Factors." *Social Psychology Quarterly* 43 (3): 328–36.

Farrell, Henry, and Martha Finnemore. 2013. "The End of Hypocrisy: American Foreign Policy in the Age of Leaks." *Foreign Affairs*, November/December.

Fenichel, Otto. 1995. *The Psychoanalytic Theory of Neurosis*. New York: W. W. Norton.

Finch, Robert P. 2010. A Shaw Anthology. United States: Laplace Publications and Art Bank.

Fine, Gary Alan, Jeffrey L. Stitt, and Michael Finch. 1984. "Couple Tie-Signs and Interpersonal Threat: A Field Experiment." *Social Psychology Quarterly* 47 (3): 282–86.

Finkelstein, Amy, Sarah Taubman, Bill Wright, Mira Bernstein, Jonathan Gruber, Joseph P. Newhouse, Heidi Allen, Katherine Baicker, and Oregon Health Study Group. 2102. "The Oregon Health Insurance Experiment: Evidence from the First Year" *Quarterly Journal of Economics* 127 (3): 1057–106.

Fisher, Franklin M., John J. McGowan, and David S. Evans. 1980. "The Audience-Revenue Relationship for Local Television Stations." *Bell Journal of Economics* 11 (2): 694–708.

Fisher, Elliott S., John E. Wennberg, Therese A. Stukel, Jonathan S. Skinner, Sandra M. Sharp, Jean L. Freeman, and Alan M. Gittelsohn. 2000. "Associations among Hospital Capacity, Utilization, and Mortality of U.S. Medicare Beneficiaries, Controlling for Sociodemographic Factors." *Health Services Research* 34 (6): 1351.

Fisher, Elliott S., David E. Wennberg, Thrse A. Stukel, Daniel J. Gottlieb, F. Lee Lucas, and Etoile L. Pinder. 2003. "The Implications of Regional Variations in Medicare Spending. Part 1: The Content, Quality, and Accessibility of Care." *Annals of Internal Medicine* 138 (4): 273–87.

Flack, Jessica C., Lisa A. Jeannotte, and Frans de Waal. 2004. "Play Signaling and the Perception of Social Rules by Juvenile Chimpanzees (*Pan troglodytes*)."*Journal of Comparative Psychology* 118 (2): 149.

Flanagan, Caitlin. 2012. "Jackie and the Girls: Mrs. Kennedy's JFK problem—and Ours." *The Atlantic*, July/August. http://www.theatlantic.com/magazine/archive/2012/07/jackie-and-the-girls/309000/.

Flesch, William. 2007. *Comeuppance: Costly Signaling, Altruistic Punishment, and Other Biological Components of Fiction*. Cambridge, MA: Harvard University Press.

Forster, Edward S. 2005. *The Turkish Letters of Ogier Ghiselin de Busbecq*. Baton Rouge: Louisiana State University Press.

Fox, Craig R., Rebecca K. Ratner, and Daniel S. Lieb. 2005. "How Subjective Grouping of Options Influences Choice and Allocation: Diversification Bias and the Phenomenon of Partition Dependence." *Journal of Experimental Psychology: General* 134 (4): 538.

Frank, Robert H., Thomas Gilovich, and Dennis T. Regan. 1993. "Does Studying Economics Inhibit Cooperation?" *The Journal of Economic Perspectives* 7 (2): 159–71.

Frejka, Tomas, and Charles F. Westoff. 2008. "Religion, Religiousness and Fertility in the U.S. and in Europe." *European Journal of Population/Revue européenne de Démographie* 24 (1): 5–31.

Freud, Anna. 1992. *The Ego and the Mechanisms of Defence*. London: Karnac Books.

Frumin, Idan, Ofer Perl, Yaara Endevelt-Shapira, Ami Eisen, Neetai Eshel, Iris Heller, Maya Shemesh, Aharon Ravia, Lee Sela, Anat Arzi, and Noam Sobel. 2015. "A Social Chemosignaling Function for Human Handshaking." *Elife* 4 (March 3): e05154.

Fuchs, Victor R. 1998. "Health, Government, and Irving Fisher." Technical Report 6710, National Bureau for Economic Research, Cambridge, MA.

Gaither, Carl C., and Alma E. Cavazos-Gaither. 2008. *Gaither's Dictionary of Scientific Quotations*. Berlin/Heidelberg: Springer Science + Business Media.

Gallie, Walter Bryce. 1995. "Essentially Contested Concepts." *Proceedings of the Aristotelian Society* 56: 167–98.

Gatto, John. 1990. "Why Schools Don't Educate." *The Sun* 175, June. http://thesunmagazine.org/archives/937.

Gawande, Atul. 2007. "The Checklist." *New Yorker*, December 10.

Gazzaniga, Michael S. 1989. "Organization of the Human Brain." *Science* 245 (4921): 947–52.

Gazzaniga, Michael S. 1998. "The Split Brain Revisited." *Scientific American* 279 (1): 50–55.

Gazzaniga, Michael S. 2000. "Cerebral Specialization and Interhemispheric Communication." *Brain* 123 (7): 1293–326.

Gazzaniga, Michael S., and Joseph E. LeDoux. 2013. *The Integrated Mind*. Berlin/Heidelberg: Springer Science + Business Media.

Gazzaniga, Michael S., and Patricia Ann Reuter-Lorenz. 2010. *The Cognitive Neuroscience of Mind: A Tribute to Michael S. Gazzaniga*. Cambridge, MA: MIT Press.

Geehr, Carly. 2012. "Do Olympic or Competitive Swimmers Ever Pee in the Pool?" Quora, July 30. https://www.quora.com/Do-Olympic-or-competitive-swimmers-ever-pee-in-the-pool/answer/Carly-Geehr.

Gelman, Andrew, Nate Silver, and Aaron Edlin. 2012. "What Is the Probability Your Vote Will Make a Difference?" *Economic Inquiry* 50 (2): 321–26.

Gerber, Alan S., Gregory A. Huber, David Doherty, and Conor M. Dowling. 2012. "Disagreement and the Avoidance of Political Discussion: Aggregate Relationships and Differences across Personality Traits." *American Journal of Political Science* 56 (4): 849–74.

Gerber, Alan, Gregory Huber, Conor Dowling, David Doherty, and Nicole Schwartzberg. 2009. "Using Battleground States as a Natural Experiment to Test Theories of Voting." Paper presented at the American Political Science Association, Toronto, September 3–6.

Gersick, Andrew, and Robert Kurzban. 2014. "Covert Sexual Signaling: Human Flirtation and Implications for Other Social Species." *Evolutionary Psychology* 12 (3): 549–69.

Gertman, Paul M., Debra A. Stackpole, Dana Kern Levenson, Barry M. Manuel, Robert J. Brennan, and Gary M. Janko. 1980. "Second Opinions for Elective Surgery: The Mandatory Medicaid Program in Massachusetts." *New England Journal of Medicine* 302 (21): 1169–74.

Getzen, Thomas E. 2000. "Health Care Is an Individual Necessity and a National Luxury: Applying Multilevel Decision Models to the Analysis of Health Care Expenditures." *Journal of Health Economics* 19 (2): 259–70.

Giles, Howard, Nikolas Coupland, and Justine Coupland, eds. 1991. "Accommodation Theory: Communication, Context, and Consequence." In *Contexts of Accommodation: Developments in Applied Sociolinguistics*, edited by Howard Giles, Justine Coupland, and Nikolas Coupland, 1–68. Cambridge, UK: Cambridge University Press.

Gioia, Michael. 2016. "Stanford's Admission Rate Drops to 4.69 Percent." *Stanford Daily*, March 25.

GiveWell. 2016. "Against Malaria Foundation." Top Charities, November. Accessed January 7, 2017. http://www.givewell.org/charities/against-malaria-foundation.

Giving USA. 2015. "Americans Donated an Estimated $358.38 Billion to Charity in 2014; Highest Total in Report's 60-year History." The Giving Institute, June 16. https://givingusa.org/giving-usa-2015-press-release-giving-usa-americans-donated-an-estimated-358-38-billion-to-charity-in-2014-highest-total-in-reports-60-year-history/.

Glass, Ira. 2015. "Copes See It Differently." *This American Life*, No. 547. Radio broadcast, February 6.

Glazer, Amihai, and Kai A. Konrad. 1996. "A Signaling Explanation for Charity." *The American Economic Review* 86 (4): 1019–28.

Goodenough, Ursula W. 1991. "Deception by Pathogens." *American Scientist* 79 (4): 344–55.

Goosen, C. 1981. "On the Function of Allogrooming in Old-World Monkeys." In *Primate Behavior and Sociobiology*, edited by A. B. Chiarelli and R. S. Corruccini, 110–120. Proceedings in Life Sciences. Berlin/Heidelberg/Springer.

Grace, Debra, and Deborah Griffin. 2006. "Exploring Conspicuousness in the Context of Donation Behaviour." *International Journal of Nonprofit and Voluntary Sector Marketing* 11 (2): 147–54.

Greene, Robert. 1998. *The 48 Laws of Power*. New York: Viking.

Greenwald, Anthony G., Debbie E. McGhee, and Jordan L. K. Schwartz. 1998. "Measuring Individual Differences in Implicit Cognition: The Implicit Association Test." *Journal of Personality and Social Psychology* 74 (6): 1464.

Gregory Jr., Stanford W., and Timothy J. Gallagher. 2002. "Spectral Analysis of Candidates' Nonverbal Vocal Communication: Predicting U.S. Presidential Election Outcomes." *Social Psychology Quarterly* 65 (3): 298–308.

Gregory Jr., Stanford W., and Stephen Webster. 1996. "A Nonverbal Signal in Voices of Interview Partners Effectively Predicts Communication Accommodation and Social Status Perceptions." *Journal of Personality and Social Psychology* 70 (6): 1231.

Grice, H. Paul. 1975. "Logic and Conversation." In *Syntax and Semantics 3: Speech Acts*, edited by Peter Cole and Jerry L. Morgan, 41–58. New York: Academic Press.

Griskevicius, Vladas, Noah Goldstein, Chad Mortensen, Robert Cialdini, and Douglas Kenrick. 2006. "Going Along versus Going Alone: When Fundamental Motives Facilitate Strategic (Non) Conformity." *Journal of Personality and Social Psychology* 91 (2): 281.

Griskevicius, Vladas, Joshua M. Tybur, and Bram Van den Bergh. 2010. "Going Green to Be Seen: Status, Reputation, and Conspicuous Conservation." *Journal of Personality and Social Psychology* 98 (3): 392.

Griskevicius, Vladas, Joshua M. Tybur, and Jill M. Sundie. 2007. "Blatant Benevolence and Conspicuous Consumption: When Romantic Motives Elicit Strategic Costly Signals." *Journal of Personality and Social Psychology* 93 (1): 85.

Gross, Neil. 2013. *Why Are Professors Liberal and Why Do Conservatives Care?* Cambridge, MA: Harvard University Press.

Hadley, Jack. 1982. *More Medical Care Better Health?* Washington, DC: Urban Institute Press.

Haidt, Jonathan. 2006. *The Happiness Hypothesis: Finding Modern Truth in Ancient Wisdom*. New York: Basic Books.

Haidt, Jonathan. 2102. *The Righteous Mind: Why Good People Are Divided by Politics and Religion*. New York: Vintage.

Haldeman, Harry R., and Joseph DiMona. 1978. *The Ends of Power*. New York: Dell.

Haley, Kevin J., and Daniel M. T. Fessler. 2005. "Nobody's Watching?: Subtle Cues Affect Generosity in an Anonymous Economic Game." *Evolution and Human Behavior* 26 (3): 245–56.

Hall, Edward Twitchell. 1966. *The Hidden Dimension*. New York: Doubleday.

Hall, Lars, Petter Johansson, and Thomas Strandberg. 2012 . "Lifting the Veil of Morality: Choice Blindness and Attitude Reversals on a Self-Transforming Survey." *PLoS One* 7 (9): e45457.

Hall, Lars, Petter Johansson, Betty Tärning, and Thérèse Deutgen. 2010. "Magic at the Marketplace: Choice Blindness for the Taste of Jam and the Smell of Tea." *Cognition* 117 (1): 54–61.

Hanson, Robin. 1995. "Comparing Peer Review to Information Prizes." *Social Epistemology* 9 (1): 49–55.

Hanson, Robin. 1998. "Patterns of Patronage: Why Grants Won Over Prizes in Science." Working Paper, University of California, Berkeley, July 28. http://hanson.gmu.edu/whygrant.pdf.

Hanson, Robin. 2008. "Showing That You Care; The Evolution of Health Altruism," *Medical Hypotheses* 70 (4): 724–42.

Hanson, Robin. 2012. "Marginal Charity." *Overcoming Bias* (blog), November 24. http://www.overcomingbias.com/2012/11/marginal-charity.html.

Harbaugh, William T. 1998. "What Do Donations Buy?: A Model of Philanthropy Based on Prestige and Warm Glow." *Journal of Public Economics* 67 (2): 269–84.

Harris, Judith Rich. 2006. *No Two Alike: Human Nature and Human Individuality.* New York: W. W. Norton.

Haskell, Robert E. 2000. *Transfer of Learning: Cognition and Instruction.* Cambridge, MA: Academic Press.

Hayek, Anne-Sophie, Anne-Sophie, Claudia Toma, Dominique Oberlé, and Fabrizio Butera. 2015. "Grading hampers cooperative information sharing in group problem solving." *Social Psychology* 46 (3): 121–31.

Hayek, Friedrich. 1988. *The Fatal Conceit: The Errors of Socialism.* Chicago: University of Chicago Press.

Heaney, Michael, and Fabio Rojas. 2015. *Party in the Street: The Antiwar Movement and the Democratic Party after 9/11.* New York: Cambridge University Press.

Henrich, Joseph. 2015. *The Secret of Our Success: How Culture Is Driving Human Evolution, Domesticating Our Species, and Making Us Smarter.* Princeton, NJ: Princeton University Press.

Henrich, Joseph, and Francisco J. Gil-White. 2001. "The Evolution of Prestige: Freely Conferred Deference as a Mechanism for Enhancing the Benefits of Cultural Transmission." *Evolution and Human Behavior* 22 (3): 165–96.

Hobbes, Thomas. 2013. *Leviathan.* Project Gutenberg, released 2009. http://www.gutenberg.org/ebooks/3207.

Hoffman, Elizabeth, Kevin McCabe, and Vernon L. Smith. 1996. "Social Distance and Other-Regarding Behavior in Dictator Games." *American Economic Review* 86 (3): 653–60.

Hollis, Nigel. 2011. "Why Good Advertising Works (Even When You Think It Doesn't)." *The Atlantic*, August 31. http://www.theatlantic.com/business/archive/2011/08/why-good-advertising-works-even-when-you-think-it-doesnt/244252/.

Hope Consulting. 2010. "Money for Good: The U.S. Market for Impact Investments and Charitable Gifts from Individuals Summary Findings." Aspen Institute, San Francisco, CA, August. http://www.aspeninstitute.org/sites/default/files/content/docs/ande/ANDE_MFGSummaryNote_15AUG10.pdf.

Hugill, Nadine, Bernhard Fink, and Nick Neave. 2010. "The Role of Human Body Movements in Mate Selection." *Evolutionary Psychology* 8 (1): 66–89.

Hume, David. (1739) 1978. *A Treatise of Human Nature.* London: John Noon.

Hummer, Robert, Richard G. Rogers, Charles B. Nam, and Christopher G. Ellison. 1999. "Religious Involvement and U.S. Adult Mortality." *Demography* 36 (2): 273–85.

Huntington, Samuel P. 1997. *The Clash of Civilizations and the Remaking of World Order.* New York: Touchstone.

Hutchinson, Lee. 2014. "Tripping through IBM's Astonishingly Insane 1937 Corporate Songbook." *Ars Technica*, August 29.

Iannaccone, Laurence R. 1992. "Sacrifice and Stigma: Reducing Free-Riding in Cults, Communes, and Other Collectives." *Journal of Political Economy* 100 (2): 271–91.

Iannaccone, Laurence R. 1998. "Introduction to the Economics of Religion." *Journal of Economic Literature* 36 (3): 1465–95.

Ioannidis, John P. A. 2005a. "Contradicted and Initially Stronger Effects in Highly Cited Clinical Research." *Journal of the American Medical Association* 294 (2): 218–28.

Ioannidis, John P. A. 2005b. "Why Most Published Research Findings Are False." *PLoS Med* 2 (8): e124.

Iredale, Wendy, Mark Van Vugt, and Robin Dunbar. 2008. "Showing Off in Humans: Male Generosity as a Mating Signal." *Evolutionary Psychology* 6 (3): 386–92.

Institute of Medicine, Committee on Quality of Health Care in America, Molla S. Donaldson, Janet M. Corrigan, and Linda T. Kohn. 1999. *To Err Is Human: Building a Safer Health System.* Washington, DC: National Academy Press.

Islam, Nazrul. 1995. "Growth Empirics: A Panel Data Approach." *Quarterly Journal of Economics* 110 (4): 1127–70.

Iyengar, Shanto, Gaurav Sood, and Yphtach Lelkes. 2012. "Affect, Not Ideology a Social Identity Perspective on Polarization." *Public Opinion Quarterly* 76 (3): 405–31.

Iyengar, Shanto, and Sean J. Westwood. 2015. "Fear and Loathing across Party Lines: New Evidence on Group Polarization." *American Journal of Political Science* 59 (3): 690–707.

Isaacson, Walter. 2011. *Steve Jobs.* New York: Simon & Schuster.

Jackson, Jeffrey M., and Bibb Latané. 1981. "Strength and Number of Solicitors and the Urge toward Altruism." *Personality and Social Psychology Bulletin* 7 (3): 415–22.

Jain, Manoj. 2009. "A Skeptic Becomes a True Believer." *Washington Post*, February 10.

Johansson, Petter, Lars Hall, Sverker Sikström, and Andreas Olsson. 2005. "Failure to Detect Mismatches between Intention and Outcome in a Simple Decision Task." *Science* 310 (5745): 116–19.

Johnson, Dominic D. P. 2005. "God's Punishment and Public Goods." *Human Nature* 16 (4): 410–46.

Johnstone, Keith. 1985. *Impro: Improvisation and the Theatre*. New York: Theatre Arts Books.

Jones, Jeffrey M. 2012. "Atheists, Muslims See Most Bias as Presidential Candidates." Gallup, June 21. http://www.gallup.com/poll/155285/atheists-muslims-bias-presidential-candidates.aspx

Jones, Philip, and John Hudson. 2000. "Civic Duty and Expressive Voting: Is Virtue Its Own Reward?" *Kyklos* 53 (1): 3–16.

Jordania, Joseph. 2011. *Why Do People Sing?: Music in Human Evolution*. Tbilisi, Georgia: Logos.

Jordania, Joseph. 2014. *Tigers, Lions, and Humans: History of Rivalry, Conflict, Reverence and Love*. Tbilisi, Georgia: Logos.

Kahneman, Daniel. 2011. *Thinking, Fast and Slow*. New York: Farrar, Straus and Giroux.

Kahneman, Daniel, and Shane Frederick. 2002. "Representativeness Revisited: Attribute Substitution in Intuitive Judgment." In *Heuristics and Biases: The Psychology of Intuitive Judgment*, edited by Thomas Gilovich, Dale Griffin, and Daniel Kahneman, 49. Cambridge, UK: Cambridge University Press.

Kant, Immanuel. 2007. *The Critique of Judgment*. Translated by James Creed Meredith. Revised and edited by Nicholas Walker. Oxford, UK: Oxford University Press.

Kaufman, Myles. 2014. "The Curious Case of U.S. Ticket Resale Laws." Seatgeek.com, September 28. Last modified February 22, 2017. https://seatgeek.com/tba/articles/ticket-resale-laws/.

Katz, Andrew. 2013. "As the Hajj Unfolds in Saudi Arabia, A Deep Look Inside the Battle against MERS." *Time*, October 16.

Kawakami, Kiyobumi, Kiyoko Takai-Kawakami, Masaki Tomonaga, Juri Suzuki, Tomiyo Kusaka, and Takashi Okai. 2006. "Origins of Smile and Laughter: A Preliminary Study." *Early Human Development* 82 (1): 61–66.

Kenrick, Douglas T. 2011. *Sex, Murder, and the Meaning of Life: A Psychologist Investigates How Evolution, Cognition, and Complexity Are Revolutionizing Our View of Human Nature*. New York: Basic Books.

Kenrick, Douglas T., and Vladas Griskevicius. 2013. *The Rational Animal: How Evolution Made Us Smarter Than We Think*. New York: Basic Books.

Keynes, John Maynard. 1931. *Essays in Persuasion*. London: Macmillan.

Kinder, Donald. 1998. "Attitude and Action in the Realm of Politics." In *Handbook of Social Psychology*, 4th ed., edited by D. Gilbert, S. Fiske, and G. Lindzey, pp. 778–867. New York: Oxford University Press.

Kirkpatrick, Melanie. 2010. "One Nation, Indivisible." *Wall Street Journal*, October 11.

Kiva. 2017. "Maria's story." Kiva.org, accessed January 7. https://www.kiva.org/lend/
    1020392.

Klein, Daniel B., and Charlotta Stern. 2009. "By the Numbers: The Ideological
    Profile of Professors." In *The Politically Correct University: Problems, Scope, and
    Reforms*, edited by Robert Maranto, Richard E. Redding, and Fredrick M. Hess,
    15–36. Washington, DC: National Research Initiative, American Enterprise
    Institute.

Klein, Ezra, and Alvin Chang. 2015. "Political Identity Is Fair Game for
    Hatred": How Republicans and Democrats Discriminate." *Vox News*, December
    7. http://www.vox.com/2015/12/7/9790764/partisan-discrimination

Klofstad, Casey A., Rose McDermott, and Peter K. Hatemi. 2013. "The Dating
    Preferences of Liberals and Conservatives." *Political Behavior* 35 (3): 519–38.

Knapp, Mark. 1972. *Nonverbal Communication in Human Interaction*.
    New York: Holt, Rinehart and Winston.

Kornhaber, Spencer. 2015. "Empathy: Overrated?" *The Atlantic*, July 3. http://www.
    theatlantic.com/health/archive/2015/07/against-empathy-aspen-paul-bloom-
    richard-j-davidson/397694/.

Kozintsev, Alexander. 2010. *The Mirror of Laughter*. Translated by Richard Martin.
    New Brunswick, NJ: Transaction.

Kraus, Nancy, Torbjörn Malmfors, and Paul Slovic. 1992. "Intuitive
    Toxicology: Expert and Lay Judgments of Chemical Risks." *Risk Analysis* 12
    (2): 215–32.

Krebs, John R., and Richard Dawkins. 1984. "Animal Signals: Mind-Reading and
    Manipulation." In *Behavioural Ecology: An Evolutionary Approach*, 2nd ed., edited
    by J. R. Krebs and N. B. Davies, 380–402. Oxford, UK: Blackwell Scientific.

Krueger, Alan B., and Mikael Lindahl. 2001. "Education for Growth: Why and for
    Whom?" Journal of Economic Literature 39 (4): 1101–36.

Kuran, Timur. 1995. *Private Truths, Public Lies: The Social Consequences of
    Preference Falsification*. Cambridge, MA: Harvard University Press.

Kurzban, Robert. 2012. *Why Everyone (Else) Is a Hypocrite: Evolution and the
    Modular Mind*. Princeton, NJ: Princeton University Press.

Lachmann, Michael, Szabolcs Szamado, and Carl T. Bergstrom. 2001. "Cost and
    Conflict in Animal Signals and Human Language." *Proceedings of the National
    Academy of Sciences* 98 (23): 13189–94.

Lahaye, Rick. 2014. "Looking for Help: What's the Distinction between Self-
    Deception and Self-Concealment?" Research Gate, September 1. https://www.
    researchgate.net/post/Looking_for_help_Whats_the_distinction_between_self-
    deception_and_self-concealment.

Lakoff, George, and Mark Johnson. 1980. *Metaphors We Live By*. Chicago: University of Chicago Press.

Land, Michael F., and Dan-Eric Nilsson. 2002. *Animal Eyes*. New York: Oxford University Press.

Landry, Craig, Andreas Lange, John A. List, Michael K. Price, and Nicholas G. Rupp. 2005. "Toward an Understanding of the Economics of Charity: Evidence from a Field Experiment." Working Paper, National Bureau for Economic Research (NBER), Cambridge, MA, and Resources for the Future (RFF), Washington, DC. http://ices.gmu.edu/wp-content/uploads/2010/07/Fall_09_Price.pdf.

Lange, Fabian, and Robert Topel. 2006. "The Social Value of Education and Human Capital." In *Handbook of the Economics of Education*, Vol. 1, edited by Eric A. Hanushek and Finis Welch, 459–509. Amsterdam: North-Holland.

Lantz, Paula, James House, James Lepkowski, David Williams, Richard Mero, and Jieming Chen. 1998. "Socioeconomic Factors, Health Behaviors, and Mortality: Results from a Nationally Representative Prospective Study of U.S. Adults." *Journal of the American Medical Association* 279 (21): 1703–708.

Langworth, Richard. 2011. *Churchill by Himself: The Definitive Collection of Quotations*. New York: Public Affairs.

La Rochefoucauld, François. 1982. *Maxims*. Translated by Leonard Tancock. London, UK: Penguin.

Leape, Lucian L. 2000. "Institute of Medicine Medical Error Figures Are Not Exaggerated." *Journal of the American Medical Association* 284 (1): 95–97.

Lehmann, Julia, A. H. Korstjens, and R. I. M. Dunbar. 2007. "Group Size, Grooming and Social Cohesion in Primates." *Animal Behaviour* 74 (6): 1617–29.

Lelkes, Orsolya. 2006. "Tasting Freedom: Happiness, Religion and Economic Transition." *Journal of Economic Behavior & Organization* 59 (2): 173–94.

Lewis, Gregory. 2012. "How Many Lives Does a Doctor Save?" 80,000 Hours (blog), August 19. https://80000hours.org/2012/08/how-many-lives-does-a-doctor-save/.

Lewis, Jeff. 2002. *Cultural Studies—The Basics*. London: SAGE.

Lin, Zhiqiu, and Augustine Brannigan. 2006. "The Implications of a Provincial Force in Alberta and Saskatchewan." In *Laws and Societies in the Canadian Prairie West*, 1670–1940, edited by Louis A. Knafla and Jonathan Swainger, 240. Vancouver, Canada: UBC Press.

Locke, John. 1999. *Why We Don't Talk to Each Other Anymore: The De-Voicing of Society*. New York: Simon & Schuster.

Locke, John. 2011. *Duels and Duets: Why Men and Women Talk So Differently*. New York: Cambridge University Press.

Lorenz, Konrad. 2002. *On Aggression*. Hove, UK: Psychology Press.

Lott, Jr., John R. 1999. "Public Schooling, Indoctrination, and Totalitarianism." *Journal of Political Economy* 107 (S6): S127–57.

Lundberg, George D. 1998. "Low-Tech Autopsies in the Era of High-Tech Medicine: Continued Value for Quality Assurance and Patient Safety." *Journal of the American Medical Association* 280 (14): 1273–74.

Lurie, Alison. 1981. *The Language of Clothes*. New York: Random House.

Macilwain, Colin. 2010. "Science Economics: What Science Is Really Worth." *Nature* 465: 682–84.

Macskássy, Sofus Attila. 2013. "From Classmates to Soulmates." *Facebook Data Science*, October 7. https://www.facebook.com/notes/facebook-data-science/from-classmates-to-soulmates/10151779448773859.

Mahoney, Annette, Kenneth Pargament, Nalini Tarakeshwar, and Aaron Swank. 2002. "Religion in the Home in the 1980s and 1990s: A Meta-Analytic Review and Conceptual Analysis of Links between Religion, Marriage, and Parenting." *Journal of Family Psychology* 15 (4):559–96.

Manning, Willard G., Joseph P. Newhouse, Naihua Duan, Emmett B. Keeler, and Arleen Leibowitz. 1987. "Health Insurance and the Demand for Medical Care: Evidence from a Randomized Experiment." *American Economic Review* 77 (3): 251–77.

Margolick, David. 1990. "In Child Deaths, a Test for Christian Science." *New York Times*, August 6.

Margolis, Howard. 1982. *Selfishness, Altruism, and Rationality: A Theory of Social Choice*. Chicago: University of Chicago Press.

Mattiello, Elisa. 2005. "The Pervasiveness of Slang in Standard and Non-Standard English." *Mots Palabras Words* 6: 7–41.

Mazur, Allan, Eugene Rosa, Mark Faupel, Joshua Heller, Russell Leen, and Blake Thurman. 1980. "Physiological Aspects of Communication via Mutual Gaze." *American Journal of Sociology* 86 (1): 50–74.

McCarthy, Eugene G., Madelon Lubin Finkel, and Hirsch S. Ruchlin. 1981. "Second Opinions on Elective Surgery: The Cornell/New York Hospital Study." *The Lancet* 317 (8234): 1352–54.

McClure, Christopher S. 2014. "Learning from Franklin's Mistakes: Self-Interest Rightly Understood in the Autobiography." *The Review of Politics* 76 (1): 69–92.

McCullough, Michael, William Hoyt, David Larson, and Carl Thoresen. 2000. "Religious Involvement and Mortality: A Meta-Analytic Review." *Health Psychology* 19 (3): 211.

McGilchrist, Iain. 2012. *The Master and His Emissary: The Divided Brain and the Making of the Western World*. New Haven, CT: Yale University Press.

McGraw, A. Peter, and Caleb Warren. 2010. "Benign Violations Making Immoral Behavior Funny." *Psychological Science* 21 (8): 1141–49.

McKinlay, John B., and Sonja M. McKinlay. 1977. "The Questionable Contribution of Medical Measures to the Decline of Mortality in the United States in the Twentieth Century." *Milbank Quarterly* 55 (3): 405–28.

McNeill, William H. 1997. *Keeping Together in Time*. Cambridge, MA: Harvard University Press.

Meer, Jonathan. 2011. "Brother, Can You Spare a Dime? Peer Pressure in Charitable Solicitation." *Journal of Public Economics* 95 (7): 926–41.

Mehrabian, A., and Ferris, S. R. 1967. "Inference of Attitudes from Nonverbal Communication in Two Channels." *Journal of Consulting Psychology* 31 (3): 48–258

Mehrabian, A., and Wiener, M. 1967. "Decoding of Inconsistent Communications." *Journal of Personality and Social Psychology* 6: 109–14

Mennemeyer, Stephen T., Michael A. Morrisey, and Leslie Z. Howard. 1997. "Death and Reputation: How Consumers Acted upon HCFA Mortality Information." *Inquiry* 34 (2): 117–28.

Mercier, Hugo, and Dan Sperber. 2011. "Why Do Humans Reason? Arguments for an Argumentative Theory." *Behavioral and Brain Sciences* 34 (2): 57–111.

Miller, Dale T. 1999. "The Norm of Self-Interest." *American Psychologist* 54 (12): 1053.

Miller, Geoffrey. 2000. *The Mating Mind: How Sexual Choice Shaped the Evolution of Human Nature*. Norwell, MA: Anchor Books.

Miller, Geoffrey. 2009. *Spent: Sex, Evolution, and Consumer Behavior*. New York: Penguin.

Minsky, Marvin. 1988. *The Society of Mind*. New York: Touchstone.

Mlodinow, Leonard. 2013. *Subliminal: How Your Unconscious Mind Rules Your Behavior*. New York: Vintage.

Morreall, John, ed. 1987. *The Philosophy of Laughter and Humor*. Albany, NY: SUNY Press.

Mullan, Fitzhugh. 2004. "Wrestling with Variation: An Interview with Jack Wennberg." *Health Affairs* 23: 73–80.

Mundinger, Mary, Rick Kane, Elizabeth Lenz, and Michael Shelanski. 2000. "Primary Care Outcomes in Patients Treated by Nurse Practitioners or Physicians: A Randomized Trial." *Journal of the American Medical Association* 283 (1): 59–68.

National Academy of Sciences. 2015. "Improving Diagnosis in Health Care." Quality Chasm Series. Washington, DC: National Academy Press, September 22.

Navarro, Joe, and Marvin Karlins. 2008. *What Every Body Is Saying: An Ex-FBI Agent's Guide to Speed-Reading People.* New York: Harper Collins.

Nelson, Holly, and Glenn Geher. 2007. "Mutual Grooming in Human Dyadic Relationships: An Ethological Perspective." *Current Psychology* 26 (2): 121–40.

Nettle, Daniel, Zoe Harper, Adam Kidson, and Melissa Bateson. 2013. "The Watching Eyes Effect in the Dictator Game: It's Not How Much You Give, It's Being Seen to Give Something." *Evolution and Human Behavior* 34 (1): 35–40.

Newhouse, Joseph P., and Insurance Experiment Group. 1993. *Free for All? Lessons from the RAND Health Insurance Experiment.* Cambridge, MA: Harvard University Press.

Newman, George E., and Paul Bloom. 2012. "Art and Authenticity: The Importance of Originals in Judgments of Value." *Journal of Experimental Psychology: General* 141 (3): 558.

Nichols, L., P. Aronica, and C. Babe. 1998. "Are Autopsies Obsolete?" *American Journal of Clinical Pathology* 110 (2): 210–18.

Niehaus, Paul. 2013. "A Theory of Good Intentions." Working Paper, University of California, San Diego, November 15. http://cgeg.sipa.columbia.edu/sites/default/files/cgeg/S13_Niehaus_0.pdf.

Nielsen. 2016. "Super Bowl 50 Draws 111.9 Million TV Viewers, 16.9 Million Tweets." Nielsen Company, February 8. http://www.nielsen.com/us/en/insights/news/2016/super-bowl-50-draws-111-9-million-tv-viewers-and-16-9-million-tweets.html.

Nisbett, Richard, and Timothy Wilson. 1977. "Telling More Than We Can Know: Verbal Reports on Mental Processes." *Psychological Review* 84 (3): 231–59.

Northover, Stefanie, William Pedersen, Adam Cohen, and Paul Andrews. 2017. "Artificial Surveillance Cues Do Not Increase Generosity: Two Meta-Analyses." *Evolution and Human Behavior* 38 (1):144–53.

Nowak, Martin, and Roger Highfield. 2011. *SuperCooperators: Altruism, Evolution, and Why We Need Each Other to Succeed.* New York: Free Press.

Nyhan, Brendan. 2014. "Increasing the Credibility of Political Science Research: A Proposal for Journal Reforms." Working Paper, Dartmouth College, Hanover, NH, September 11. http://www.dartmouth.edu/~nyhan/journal-reforms.pdf.

O'Connor, Anahad. 2011. "Getting Doctors to Wash Their Hands." *New York Times* (blog), September 1.

O'Conner, Patricia, and Stewart Kellerman. 2013. "Quote Magnets." *Grammarphobia* (blog), January 14. http://www.grammarphobia.com/blog/2013/01/quote-magnets.html.

Orwell, George. 1950. *Shooting an Elephant and Other Stories*. London: Secker and Warburg.

Orwell, George. 1983. *Nineteen Eighty-Four*. New York: Houghton Mifflin Harcourt.

O'Toole, Garson. 2010a. "Never Let Schooling Interfere with Your Education." *Quote Investigator*, September 25. http://quoteinvestigator.com/2010/09/25/schooling-vs-education/.

O'Toole, Garson. 2010b. "A Single Death Is a Tragedy; a Million Deaths Is a Statistic." *Quote Investigator*, May 21. http://quoteinvestigator.com/2010/05/21/death-statistic/.

O'Toole, Garson. 2013. "It Is the Mark of a Truly Intelligent Person to be Moved by Statistics." *Quote Investigator*, February 20. http://quoteinvestigator.com/2013/02/20/moved-by-stats/.

O'Toole, Garson. 2014. "A Person Has Two Reasons for Doing Anything: A Good Reason and the Real Reason." *Quote Investigator*, May 22. http://quoteinvestigator.com/2014/03/26/two-reasons/.

O'Toole, Garson. 2016. "If You Want to Tell People the Truth, You'd Better Make Them Laugh or They'll Kill You." *Quote Investigator*, March 17. http://quoteinvestigator.com/2016/03/17/truth-laugh/.

Ottina, Theresa J. 1995. *Advertising Revenues per Television Household: A Market by Market Analysis*. Washington, DC: National Association of Broadcasters.

Packard, Vance. 1957. *The Hidden Persuaders*. New York: David McKay.

Pauly, Mark V. 1992. "Effectiveness Research and the Impact of Financial Incentives on Outcomes." In *Improving Health Policy and Management: Nine Critical Research Issues for the 1990s*, edited by Stephen M. Shortell and Uwe E. Reinhardt, 151–94. Ann Arbor, MI: Health Administration Press.

Pellis, Sergio M., and Vivien C. Pellis. 1996. "On Knowing It's Only Play: The Role of Play Signals in Play Fighting." *Aggression and Violent Behavior* 1 (3): 249–68.

Peloza, John, and Piers Steel. 2005. "The Price Elasticities of Charitable Contributions: A Meta-Analysis." *Journal of Public Policy & Marketing* 24 (2): 260–72.

Pentland, Alex, and Tracy Heibeck. 2010. *Honest Signals: How They Shape Our World*. Cambridge, MA: MIT Press.

Periyakoil, Vyjeyanthi S., Eric Neri, Ann Fong, and Helena Kraemer. 2014. "Do Unto Others: Doctors' Personal End-Of-Life Resuscitation Preferences and Their Attitudes toward Advance Directives." *PloS One* 9 (5): e98246.

Perry, Sarah. 2014. *Every Cradle Is a Grave: Rethinking the Ethics of Birth and Suicide*. Charleston, WV: Nine-Banded.

Peters, Douglas P., and Stephen J. Ceci. 1982. "Peer-Review Practices of Psychological Journals: The Fate of Published Articles, Submitted Again." *Behavioral and Brain Sciences* 5 (2):187–95, June.

Pew Research Center. 2014. "Political Polarization in the American Public: Section 3: Political Polarization and Personal Life." U.S. Politics & Policies, June 12. http://www.people-press.org/2014/06/12/section-3-political-polarization-and-personal-life/.

Pfeffer, Jeffrey, and Robert I. Sutton. 2006. *Hard Facts, Dangerous Half-Truths, and Total Nonsense: Profiting from Evidence-Based Management*. Brighton, MA: Harvard Business Press.

Pfeiffer, Thomas, and Robert Hoffmann. 2009. "Large-Scale Assessment of the Effect of Popularity on the Reliability of Research." *PLoS One* 4 (6): e5996.

Pinker, Steven. 1997. *How the Mind Works*. New York: W. W. Norton.

Pinker, Steven. 2013. *Language, Cognition, and Human Nature: Selected Articles*. New York: Oxford University Press.

Pinker, Steven, and Paul Bloom. 1990. "Natural Language and Natural Selection." *Behavioral and Brain Sciences* 13 (4): 707–27.

Plassmann, Hilke, John O'Doherty, Baba Shiv, and Antonio Rangel. 2008. "Marketing Actions Can Modulate Neural Representations of Experienced Pleasantness." *Proceedings of the National Academy of Sciences* 105 (3): 1050–54.

Plooij, Frans. 1979. "How Wild Chimpanzee Babies Trigger the Onset of Mother-Infant Play—And What the Mother Makes of It." In *Before Speech: The Beginning of Interpersonal Communication*, edited by Margaret Bullowa, 223. Cambridge, UK: Cambridge University Press.

Pocklington, Rebecca. 2013. "Pictured: Millions of Migrating Crabs Force Roads to Close on Christmas Island." *Mirror*, December 30.

Pollard, Albert Frederick. 2007. *Henry VIII*. Project Gutenberg. www.gutenberg.org/ebooks/20300.

Polonsky, Michael Jay, Laura Shelley, and Ranjit Voola. 2002. "An Examination of Helping Behavior—Some Evidence from Australia." *Journal of Nonprofit & Public Sector Marketing* 10 (2): 67–82.

Poole, Keith T., and Howard Rosenthal. 1987. "Analysis of Congressional Coalition Patterns: A Unidimensional Spatial Model." *Legislative Studies Quarterly* 12 (1):55–75.

Poole, Keith T., and Howard Rosenthal. 2000. *Congress: A Political-Economic History of Roll Call Voting*. New York: Oxford University Press.

Poole, Keith T., and Howard Rosenthal. 2007. *Ideology and Congress*. New Brunswick, NJ: Transaction.

Power, Camilla. 1999. "Beauty Magic: The Origins of Art." In *The Evolution of Culture* edited by Robin Dunbar, Chris Knight, and Camilla Power, 92–112. New Brunswick, NJ: Rutgers University Press.

Prinz, Jesse. 2013. "How Wonder Works." Aeon, June 21. https://aeon.co/essays/why-wonder-is-the-most-human-of-all-emotions.

Pritchett, Lant. 2001. "Where Has All the Education Gone?" *World Bank Economic Review* 15 (3): 367–91.

Provine, Robert R. 2000. *Laughter: A Scientific Investigation.* New York: Penguin.

Ramachandran, Vilayanur S., Sandra Blakeslee, and Oliver W. Sacks. 1998. *Phantoms in the Brain: Probing the Mysteries of the Human Mind.* New York: William Morrow.

Rand, Ayn, and Nathaniel Branden. 1964. *The Virtue of Selfishness: A New Concept of Egoism.* New York: Signet.

Rao, Venkatesh. 2013. "You Are Not an Artisan." *Ribbonfarm*, July 10. http://www.ribbonfarm.com/2013/07/10/you-are-not-an-artisan/.

Rappaport, Roy A. 1999. *Ritual and Religion in the Making of Humanity.* Vol. 110. Cambridge, UK: Cambridge University Press.

Ridley, Matt. 1993. *The Red Queen: Sex and the Evolution of Human Nature.* New York: Viking Press.

Rigdon, Mary, Keiko Ishii, Motoki Watabe, and Shinobu Kitayama. 2009. "Minimal Social Cues in the Dictator Game." *Journal of Economic Psychology* 30 (3): 358–67.

Roberts, Russ, and Bryan Caplan. 2007. "Caplan on the Myth of the Rational Voter." *EconTalk*, June 25. http://www.econtalk.org/archives/2007/06/caplan_on_the_m.html.

Roberts, Russ, and Iannaccone, Larry. 2006. "The Economics of Religion." *EconTalk*, October 9. http://www.econtalk.org/archives/2006/10/the_economics_o_7.html.

Robertson, Jeanne. 2017. "Don't Send a Man to the Grocery Store." Video, accessed January 8. http://jeannerobertson.com/VideoGroceryStore.htm.

Roes, Frans L., and Michel Raymond. 2003. "Belief in Moralizing Gods." *Evolution and Human Behavior* 24 (2): 126–35.

Ross, Marina Davila, Michael J. Owren, and Elke Zimmermann. 2010. "The Evolution of Laughter in Great Apes and Humans." *Communicative & Integrative Biology* 3 (2): 191–94.

Rothman, Stanley, S. Robert Lichter, and Neil Nevitte. 2005. "Politics and Professional Advancement among College Faculty." *The Forum* 3 (1): 1–16.

Rowland, Peter, ed. 2008. *Bowerbirds.* Clayton, Victoria, Australia: CSIRO.

Rue, Loyal D. 2005. *Religion Is Not about God: How Spiritual Traditions Nurture Our Biological Nature and What to Expect When They Fail.* New Brunswick, NJ: Rutgers University Press.

Ruffle, Bradley J., and Richard Sosis. 2006. "Cooperation and the In-Group-Out-Group Bias: A Field Test on Israeli Kibbutz Members and City Residents." *Journal of Economic Behavior & Organization* 60 (2): 147–63.

Sackeim, Harold. 2015. "Deception." Interview by Robert Krulwich. *Radiolab*, podcast audio. Original NPR broadcast 2008.

Savic, Ivanka, Hans Berglund, and Per Lindström. 2005. "Brain Response to Putative Pheromones in Homosexual Men." *Proceedings of the National Academy of Sciences of the United States of America* 102 (20): 7356–61.

Schelling, Thomas. 1980. *The Strategy of Conflict*. Cambridge, MA: Harvard University Press.

Schelling, Thomas, Martin Bailey, and Gary Fromm. 1968. "The Life You Save May Be Your Own." In *Problems in Public Expenditure Analysis:* Papers Presented at a Conference of Experts Held Sept. 15–16, 1966. Vol. 2: Brookings Conference on Government Expenditures, edited by Samuel B. Chase, 127–62. Washington, DC: Brookings Institution.

Schino, Gabriele. 2007. "Grooming and Agonistic Support: A Meta-Analysis of Primate Reciprocal Altruism." *Behavioral Ecology* 18 (1): 115–20.

Schlegelmilch, Bodo B., Adamantios Diamantopoulos, and Alix Love. 1997. "Characteristics Affecting Charitable Donations: Empirical Evidence from Britain." *Journal of Marketing Practice: Applied Marketing Science* 3 (1): 14–28.

Schneider, Eric C., and Arnold M. Epstein. 1998. "Use of Public Performance Reports: A Survey of Patients Undergoing Cardiac Surgery." *Journal of American Medical Association* 279 (20): 1638–42.

Schopenhauer, Arthur. 1966. *The World as Will and Representation*. Vol. 2. Translated by E. F. J. Payne. New York: Dover.

Schor, Juliet B. 1998. *The Overspent American: Why We Want What We Don't Need*. New York: Basic Books.

Schuessler, Alexander A. 2000. "Expressive Voting." *Rationality and Society* 12 (1): 87–119.

Sexton, Steven E., and Alison L. Sexton. 2014. "Conspicuous Conservation: The Prius Halo and Willingness to Pay for Environmental Bona Fides." *Journal of Environmental Economics and Management* 67 (3): 303–17.

Seyfarth, Robert M. 1977. "A Model of Social Grooming among Adult Female Monkeys." *Journal of Theoretical Biology* 65 (4): 671–98.

Seyfarth, Robert M., and Dorothy L. Cheney. 1984. "Grooming, Alliances and Reciprocal Altruism in Vervet Monkeys." *Nature* 308: 541–43.

Shanks, David R., Miguel A. Vadillo, Benjamin Riedel, and Lara M. C. Puhlmann. 2015. "Romance, Risk, and Replication: Can Consumer Choices and Risk-Taking Be Primed by Mating Motives?" *Journal of Experimental Psychology: General* 144 (6): e142.

Shariff, Azim F., and Ara Norenzayan. 2007. "God Is Watching You: Priming God Concepts Increases Prosocial Behavior in an Anonymous Economic Game." *Psychological Science* 18 (9): 803–809.

Shojania, Kaveh, Elizabeth Burton, Kathryn McDonald, and Lee Goldman. 2002. "The Autopsy as an Outcome and Performance Measure." Agency for Healthcare Research and Quality, Evidence Report/Technology Assessment No. 58, October.

Singer, Peter. 1972. "Famine, Affluence, and Morality." *Philosophy and Public Affairs* 1 (1): 229–43.

Singer, Peter. 1999. "The Singer Solution to World Poverty." *New York Times Magazine*, September 5.

Singer, Peter. 2009. *The Life You Can Save: How to Do Your Part to End World Poverty*. New York: Random House.

Singer, Peter. 2015. "The Logic of Effective Altruism." *Boston Review*, July 6. http://bostonreview.net/forum/peter-singer-logic-effective-altruism.

Siu, Albert L., Frank A. Sonnenberg, Willard G. Manning, George A. Goldberg, Ellyn S. Bloomfield, Joseph P. Newhouse, and Robert H. Brook. 1986. "Inappropriate Use of Hospitals in a Randomized Trial of Health Insurance Plans." *New England Journal of Medicine* 315 (20): 1259–66.

Skinner, Jonathan S., John Wennberg. 2000. "How Much Is Enough? Efficiency and Medicare Spending in the Last Six Months of Life." In *The Changing Hospital Industry: Comparing For-Profit and Not-for-Profit Institutions*, edited by David Cutler. Chicago: University of Chicago Press.

Small, Deborah A., and George Loewenstein. 2003. "Helping a Victim or Helping the Victim: Altruism and Identifiability." *Journal of Risk and Uncertainty* 26 (1): 5–16.

Smith, Adam. 2013. *An Inquiry into the Nature and Causes of the Wealth of Nations*. Project Gutenberg, released 2009. http://www.gutenberg.org/ebooks/3300.

Smith, Carole, Lev Williams, and Richard Willis. 1967. "Race, Sex, and Belief as Determinants of Friendship Acceptance." *Journal of Personality and Social Psychology* 5 (2):127–37.

Smith, Rosanna K., and George E. Newman. 2014. "When Multiple Creators Are Worse Than One: The Bias toward Single Authors in the Evaluation of Art." *Psychology of Aesthetics, Creativity, and the Arts* 8 (3): 303.

Snyder, Thomas D., and Sally A. Dillow. 2011. "Digest of education statistics, 2010 (NCES 2011–2015)." National Center for Education Statistics, U.S. Department of Education.

Sohn, Amy. 2004. "Crossing the Party Line." *New York*, November 8. http://nymag. com/nymetro/nightlife/sex/columns/mating/10260/.

Solzhenitsyn, Aleksandr. 1973. *The Gulag Archipelago Volume 1: An Experiment in Literary Investigation*. Translated by Thomas P. Whitney. New York: Harper and Row.

Sosis, Richard, and Candace Alcorta. 2003. "Signaling, Solidarity, and the Sacred: The Evolution of Religious Behavior." *Evolutionary Anthropology: Issues, News, and Reviews* 12 (6): 264–74.

Sosis, Richard, and Eric R. Bressler. 2003. "Cooperation and Commune Longevity: A Test of the Costly Signaling Theory of Religion." *Cross-Cultural Research* 37 (2): 211–39.

Sosis, Richard, and Jordan Kiper. 2014. "Religion Is More Than Belief: What Evolutionary Theories of Religion Tell Us about Religious Commitment." In *Challenges to Religion and Morality: Disagreements and Evolution,* edited by Michael Bergmann and Patrick Kain, 256–76. New York: Oxford University Press.

Spence, Michael. 1973. "Job Market Signaling." *The Quarterly Journal of Economics* 87 (3): 355–74.

Spence, Susan H. 1987. "The Relationship between Social—Cognitive Skills and Peer Sociometric Status." *British Journal of Developmental Psychology* 5 (4): 347–56.

Spring, Joel H. 1973. *Education and the Rise of the Corporate State.* Boston: Beacon Press.

Stafford, Tom. 2013. "Does Studying Economics Make You More Selfish?" BBC Future, October 22.

Stam, J. H. 1976. *Inquiries into the Origins of Language.* New York: Harper and Row.

Staradub, Valerie L., Kathleen A. Messenger, Nanjiang Hao, Elizabeth L. Wiely, and Monica Morrow. 2002. "Changes in Breast Cancer Therapy Because of Pathology Second Opinions." *Annals of Surgical Oncology* 9 (10): 982–87.

Starek, Joanna E., and Caroline F. Keating. 1991. "Self-Deception and Its Relationship to Success in Competition." *Basic and Applied Social Psychology* 12 (2): 145–55.

Stavrova, Olga, and Daniel Ehlebracht. 2016. "Cynical Beliefs about Human Nature and Income: Longitudinal and Cross-Cultural Analyses." *Journal of Personality and Social Psychology* 110 (1):116–32.

Steen, Todd P. 1996. "Religion and Earnings: Evidence from the NLS Youth Cohort." *International Journal of Social Economics* 23 (1): 47–58.

Stephens. Mitchell. 2007. *A History of the News*, 3rd ed. New York: Oxford University Press.

Strawbridge, William J., Richard D. Cohen, Sarah J. Shema, and George A. Kaplan. 1997. "Frequent Attendance at Religious Services and Mortality over 28 Years." *American Journal of Public Health* 87 (6): 957–61.

Sugawara, Kazuyoshi. 1984. "Spatial Proximity and Bodily Contact among the Central Kalahari San." *African Study Monographs*, supplementary issue 3: 1–43. Kyoto University, Research Committee for African Area Studies.

Sullivan, Aline. 2002. "Affair of the Heart." *Barron's* 82 (49): 28.

Sullivan, James. 2014. "Bill Burr Gets into a Groove, Just Like His Comedy Heroes." *Boston Globe*, September 30.

Sully, James. 1902. *An Essay on Laughter: Its Forms, Its Causes, Its Development and Its Value*. New York: Longmans, Green.

Swatos, William H., and Peter Kivisto. 1998. *Encyclopedia of Religion and Society*. Walnut Creek, CA: AltaMira.

Szabo, Liz. 2013. "Book Raises Alarms about Alternative Medicine." *USA Today*, July 2.

Számadó, Szabolcs. 1999. "The Validity of the Handicap Principle in Discrete Action–Response Games." *Journal of Theoretical Biology* 198 (4): 593–602.

Tan, Jonathan H. W., and Claudia Vogel. 2008. "Religion and Trust: An Experimental Study." *Journal of Economic Psychology* 29 (6): 832–48.

Tavits, Margit. 2007. "Principle vs. Pragmatism: Policy Shifts and Political Competition." *American Journal of Political Science* 51 (1):151–65.

Thiel, Peter. 2014. "Thinking Too Highly of Higher Ed." *Washington Post*, November 21.

Tibbetts, Elizabeth A., and James Dale. 2004. "A Socially Enforced Signal of Quality in a Paper Wasp." *Nature* 432 (7014): 218–22.

Tocqueville, Alexis. 2013. *Democracy in America*. Vol. 2 (of 2). Translated by Henry Reeve. Project Gutenberg, released 2009. https://www.gutenberg.org/files/816/816-h/816-h.htm#link2HCH0029.

Trivers, Robert. 1971. "The Evolution of Reciprocal Altruism." *Quarterly Review of Biology* 46 (1): 35–57.

Trivers, Robert. 2002. *Natural Selection and Social Theory: Selected Papers of Robert Trivers*. New York: Oxford University Press.

Trivers, Robert. 2011. *The Folly of Fools: The Logic of Deceit and Self-Deception in Human Life*. New York: Basic Books.

Trope, Yaacov, and Nira Liberman. 2010. "Construal-Level Theory of Psychological Distance." *Psychological Review* 117 (2): 440.

Trufelman, Avery. 2015. "Hard to Love a Brute." *99% Invisible*, podcast episode 176, August 11. http://99percentinvisible.org/episode/hard-to-love-a-brute/.

Tudor, Daniel, and James Pearson. 2015. *North Korea Confidential: Private Markets, Fashion Trends, Prison Camps, Dissenters and Defectors*. North Clarendon, VT: Tuttle.

Tuljapurkar, Shripad, Nan Li, and Carl Boe. 2000. "A Universal Pattern of Mortality Decline in the G7 Countries." *Nature* 405 (6788): 789–92.

United Way. n.d. "Paying It Forward." Accessed February 4, 2016. https://www.unitedway.org/our-impact/stories/paying-it-forward.

Uomini, Natalie Thaïs, and Georg Friedrich Meyer. 2013. "Shared Brain Lateralization Patterns in Language and Acheulean Stone Tool Production: A Functional Transcranial Doppler Ultrasound Study." *PloS One* 8 (8): e72693.

Uy, J. Albert C., Gail L. Patricelli, and Gerald Borgia. 2000. "Dynamic Mate-Searching Tactic Allows Female Satin Bowerbirds Ptilonorhynchus Violaceus to Reduce Searching." *Proceedings of the Royal Society of London B: Biological Sciences* 267 (1440): 251–56.

van der Velde, Frank W., Joop van der Pligt, and Christa Hooykaas. 1994. "Perceiving AIDS-Related Risk: Accuracy as a Function of Differences in Actual Risk." *Health Psychology* 13 (1): 25.

Veblen, Thorstein. 2013. *The Theory of the Leisure Class*. Project Gutenberg, released 2008. http://www.gutenberg.org/ebooks/833.

Ventura, Raffaella, Bonaventura Majolo, Nicola F. Koyama, Scott Hardie, and Gabriele Schino. 2006. "Reciprocation and Interchange in Wild Japanese Macaques: Grooming, Cofeeding, and Agonistic Support." *American Journal of Primatology* 68 (12): 1138–49.

Vingerhoets, Ad. 2013. *Why Only Humans Weep: Unravelling the Mysteries of Tears*. New York: Oxford University Press.

Vladeck, Bruce, Emily Goodwin, Lois Myers, and Madeline Sinisi. 1988. "Consumers and Hospital Use: The HCFA 'Death List.'" *Health Affairs* 7 (1): 122–25.

Voeten, Erik. 2001. "Outside Options and the Logic of Security Council Action." *American Political Science Review* 95: 845–58.

Volden, Craig, and Alan E. Wiseman. 2014. *Legislative Effectiveness in the United States Congress: The Lawmakers*. New York: Cambridge University Press.

Von Grünau, Michael, and Christina Anston. 1995. "The Detection of Gaze Direction: A Stare-in-the-Crowd Effect." *Perception* 24 (11): 1297–313.

Waber, Rebecca, Baba Shiv, Ziv Carmon, and Dan Ariely. 2008. "Commercial Features of Placebo and Therapeutic Efficacy." *Journal of the American Medical Association* 299 (9):1016–17.

The Wachowskis. 1999. *The Matrix*. Burbank, CA: Warner Bros.

Waldfogel, Joel. 1993. "The Deadweight Loss of Christmas." *The American Economic Review* 83 (5): 1328–36.

Wallace, David Foster. 2004. "Consider the Lobster." *Gourmet Magazine*, August, 50–64.

Weber, Eugen. 1976. *Peasants into Frenchmen: The Modernization of Rural France, 1870–1914*. Palo Alto, CA: Stanford University Press.

Wedekind, Claus, Thomas Seebeck, Florence Bettens, and Alexander J. Paepke. 1995. "MHC-Dependent Mate Preferences in Humans." *Proceedings of the Royal Society of London B: Biological Sciences* 260 (1359): 245–49.

Weeden, Jason, Adam B. Cohen, and Douglas T. Kenrick. 2008. "Religious Attendance as Reproductive Support." *Evolution and Human Behavior* 29 (5): 327–34.

Wehner, Peter. 2014. "The Nobility of Politics." *Commentary Magazine*, July 16.

Weiskrantz, Lawrence. 1986. *Blindsight: A Case Study and Implications*. New York: Oxford University Press.

West, Patrick. 2004. *Conspicuous Compassion: Why Sometimes It Really Is Cruel to Be Kind*. London: Coronet Books.

West, Stephen G., and T. Jan Brown. 1975. "Physical Attractiveness, the Severity of the Emergency and Helping: A Field Experiment and Interpersonal Simulation." *Journal of Experimental Social Psychology* 11 (6): 531–38.

Westra, William H., Joseph D. Kronz, and David W. Eisele. 2002. "The Impact of Second Opinion Surgical Pathology on the Practice of Head and Neck Surgery: A Decade Experience at a Large Referral Hospital." *Head & Neck* 24 (7): 684–93.

White, Arthur H. 1989. "Patterns of Giving." In *Philanthropic Giving: Studies in Varieties and Goals*, edited by Richard Magat, 65–71. Yale Studies on Nonprofit Organizations. New York: Oxford University Press.

Wickler, Wolfgang. 1998. "Mimicry." *Encyclopedia Britannica*. Last modified December 1, 2000. https://www.britannica.com/science/mimicry.

Wilson, David Sloan. 2002. *Darwin's Cathedral: Evolution, Religion, and the Nature of Society*. Chicago: University of Chicago Press.

Wilson, Edward O. 2012. *The Social Conquest of Earth*. New York: Liveright.

Wilson, Timothy D. 2002. *Strangers to Ourselves: Discovering the Adaptive Unconscious*. Cambridge, MA: Belknap.

Wiltermuth, Scott S., and Chip Heath. 2009. "Synchrony and Cooperation." *Psychological Science* 20 (1): 1–5.

Wink, Paul, Michele Dillon, and Britta Larsen. 2005. "Religion as Moderator of the Depression-Health Connection Findings from a Longitudinal Study." *Research on Aging* 27 (2): 197–220.

Wirth, Michael O., and Harry Bloch. 1985. "The Broadcasters: The Future Role of Local Stations and the Three Networks." In *Video Media Competition: Regulation, Economics, and Technology*, edited by Eli M. Noam, 121–37. New York: Columbia University Press.

Wittemyer, George, Iain Douglas-Hamilton, and Wayne Marcus Getz. 2005. "The Socioecology of Elephants: Analysis of the Processes Creating Multitiered Social Structures." *Animal Behaviour* 69 (6): 1357–71.

Wright, Robert. 2010. *The Moral Animal: Why We Are, the Way We Are: The New Science of Evolutionary Psychology*. Reprint, New York: Vintage.

Yandle, Bruce. 1983. "Bootleggers and Baptists—the Education of a Regulatory Economist." *Regulation* 7: 12.

Yandle, Bruce. 1999. "Bootleggers and Baptists in Retrospect." *Regulation* 22: 5.

Youngberg, David, and Robin Hanson. 2010. "Forager Facts." Working Paper, May. http://hanson.gmu.edu/forager.pdf.

Zader, Rachel. 2016. "What Are Some Things That Cops Know, but Most People Don't?" *Quora*, February 7. https://www.quora.com/What-are-some-things-that-cops-know-but-most-people-dont/answer/Rachel-Zader.

Zahavi, Amotz. 1975. "Mate Selection—A Selection for a Handicap." *Journal of Theoretical Biology* 53 (1): 205–14.

Zahavi, Amotz. 2003. "Indirect Selection and Individual Selection in Sociobiology: My Personal Views on Theories of Social Behaviour." *Animal Behaviour* 65 (5): 859–63.

Zahavi, Amotz, and Avishag Zahavi. 1999. *The Handicap Principle: A Missing Piece of Darwin's Puzzle*. New York: Oxford University Press.

Zhong, Chen-Bo, Vanessa K. Bohns, and Francesca Gino. 2010. "Good Lamps Are the Best Police Darkness Increases Dishonesty and Self-Interested Behavior." *Psychological Science* 21 (3): 311–14.

Zhou, Wen, Xiaoying Yang, Kepu Chen, Peng Cai, Sheng He, and Yi Jiang. 2014. "Chemosensory Communication of Gender through Two Human Steroids in a Sexually Dimorphic Manner." *Current Biology* 24 (10): 1091–95.

References to figures, tables and boxes use italicized *f, t* and *b.*